MW00453029

Legal Studies: Terminology and Transcription

5E

Wanda Roderick-Bolton

R & W Associates
Naples, Florida

SOUTH-WESTERN
CENGAGE Learning

Australia • Brazil • Japan • Korea • Mexico • Singapore • Spain • United Kingdom • United States

Legal Studies: Terminology & Transcription

By Wanda Roderick-Bolton

VP/Editorial Director:
Jack W. Calhoun

VP/Editor-in-Chief:
Dave Shaut

Senior Publisher:
Karen Schmohe

Acquisitions Editor:
Joseph Vocca

Project Manager:
Dr. Inell Bolls

Production Editor:
Carol Spencer

Production Manager:
Tricia Boies

Director Educational Marketing:
Carol Volz

Marketing Manager:
Lori Pegg

Channel Manager:
Brian Joyner

Marketing Coordinator:
Wright, Georgianna

Manufacturing Coordinator:
Charlene Taylor

Design Project Manager:
Stacy Jenkins Shirley

Cover and Internal Design:
Lisa Albonetti

Copyeditor:
Gary Morris

Production House:
Electro-Publishing

Rights and Permissions Manager:
Linda Ellis

Printer:
Edwards Brothers/Ann Arbor, MI

Expect More from South-Western. And Get It!

Legal Office Projects
by Gilmore
0-538-72123-5
These task-based projects allow for a hands on approach to legal document preparation, layout formatting, and the transcribing of these documents.

Legal Office: Document Processing
by Gilmore
0-538-71918-4
This text-workbook familiarizes the legal office assistant with various fields of law and the proper preparation of the legal documents utilized in each field.

Legal Office: Concepts and Procedures
by Cummins
0-538-71917-6
This introductory text presents an understanding of the basic concepts of the law.

Technology & Procedures for Administrative Professionals
by Fulton-Calkins
0-538-72590-7
The 12th edition of this market-leading text provides the knowledge and skills necessary for today's administrative professional to compete in a technologically advanced, global workplace.

Online Training for the Administrative Professional
by Jennings, Rigby & Stulz
0-538-72491-9
This completely online program consists of blocks of content covering office skills requested by today's employers and skills needed by all office professionals.

Preface

Understanding legal terminology is an essential requirement for employees in a legal office. You must understand the tools with which you are working in order to be able to key legal documents, transcribe, and follow legal procedures. In the legal field, these tools are the legal words that are used. Many misunderstandings and frustrations on the job can be eliminated with a basic understanding of these terms. The study of legal terminology is only a part of the skills and knowledge necessary for the legal employee, but it is a very vital and necessary skill in order to succeed in the legal field. With a basic understanding of legal vocabulary, the job will be much easier, and you, the legal employee, will be a more effective participant and contributor in the legal profession.

During my many years of teaching in the area of court reporting, the frequency of errors in student transcripts resulting from lack of knowledge of legal terms pointed out the need for a systematic approach for the learning of basic legal terminology. Errors such as "leaps and bounds" instead of "metes and bounds," "quickclaim deed" instead of "quitclaim deed," and a "causal relationship" transcribed as a "casual relationship" may appear humorous on the surface but are not so funny when the fortunes or lives of people are at stake.

OBJECTIVES OF TEXT

This text–workbook is intended to give you knowledge and understanding of over 900 terms commonly used in the legal profession. You will learn to define the terms and to use them in legal context. Pronunciation guides are provided for each word, and the correct pronunciation is reinforced by prerecorded dictation. Keyboarding practice from printed copy will assist you in learning the correct spelling of each term, and all objectives are reinforced as you learn to transcribe the terms from prerecorded dictation. Therefore, upon successful completion of this course, you should be able to:

1. Correctly spell, pronounce, and define the legal terms presented;

2. Transcribe the legal terms on a computer, either directly from the prerecorded dictation or from machine shorthand notes.

INSTRUCTIONAL LEVEL

This course may be taught in a traditional classroom setting, and it is also very adaptable to an individualized instructional system. It will provide a good background for you, should you desire to work in a legal office as a receptionist/typist, administrative assistant, stenographer, paralegal, or research assistant. Should you choose to become a court reporter, captionist, real-time reporter, note-reader/transcriber, or transcriptionist, you can benefit from this course. Should you choose work in a legal office or in the court reporting field, you must, of course, have a much broader knowledge of legal vocabulary than this course provides. However, this course will give you an excellent background for legal keyboarding, legal shorthand, legal office procedures, and business law courses.

In order to succeed in legal/terminology transcription, you should be able to keyboard—a prerequisite for any of the named jobs in the legal field. The course is also designed so that if you use a shorthand system (either pen or machine), you can integrate that skill into the study of this course.

The tear-out feature of the text-workbook allows pages that are to be copied on a computer to be torn out first and put to the side of the keyboard. If the machine shorthand procedure is used, tear out the appropriate page and put it on the desk when writing on your shorthand machine. In both instances, you will find it easier to work with individual pages than with an open book.

LENGTH OF COURSE

The course consists of 32 lessons, each containing 25-30 terms. If you plan to follow the keyboarding/transcription procedure, the course will take approximately 40 clock hours to complete. It will take approximately 50 clock hours to follow the machine shorthand/transcription procedure.

SELF-EVALUATIONS

At the end of each section, there is a short quiz that you will use as a self-evaluation. This enables you to check on your understanding and comprehension of the subject matter presented in each lesson. These self-evaluations should not be used for grading purposes. Answers to the self-evaluations begin on page 494 in the Appendix.

TESTS

Your instructor will give you an evaluation after every two text-workbook lessons. These evaluations will be used as a measurement of your understanding and comprehension of the material and should be graded by your instructor. The evaluations consist of prerecorded dictation material to be transcribed and objective questions that you will complete.

DICTATION

Practice Dictation. The practice dictation for each of the 32 lessons is available on CD. The dictation rate is approximately 80 words a minute. Each term presented in a given lesson is included in the dictation material for that lesson.

Evaluations CDs. In addition to the lesson practice dictation material, eight evaluations on CD-ROM are also available. After every two lessons, there is dictated material on a CD similar to what you will hear on the practice CDs. An evaluation is to be given at the completion of every two text-workbook lessons. Evaluations will be administered by your instructor or a specially designated person. Each evaluation consists of three sections—A, B, and C. Be sure that you complete all three sections before going to the next lesson.

AREAS OF LAW COVERED

The various areas of law are listed and arranged in a logical sequence to provide some continuity as you progress through the course. The general areas are introduced first, followed by the most common specific areas, such as criminal and civil. Progression is then made into other specific areas that will give you an understanding of the terminology used in most law firms, whether the lawyer happens to be in general law practice or in a specialized area. Two lessons are used to cover the terminology in most of the areas. However, for areas such as bankruptcy and partnerships where the number of specific terms is limited, there is only one lesson. After Lesson 10, the lessons may be rearranged or a specific selection may be made to meet your individual needs.

SELECTION OF TERMINOLOGY

The terminology was selected from books on legal secretarial training, law books, legal dictionaries, legal documents, and court transcripts. Also, attorneys and other legal personnel were consulted regarding specific terms.

The most commonly used terms, as well as those with special legal meanings in each area, were selected. Terms that are used very infrequently were avoided, as one of the main objectives was to develop a general basic background in legal terms. The use of certain terms will vary from state to state, and those are identified throughout the course. Some of the most commonly used Latin terms are also included. Even though you will learn some legal procedures from the study of the terminology, this is not intended to be a course in law.

PRONUNCIATIONS

The pronunciations for most of the terms in this course are based on the pronunciation guide of *Merriam-Webster's Collegiate Dictionary*.

ILLUSTRATIONS

Legal forms and documents illustrating the use of many terms are included in this edition. These forms and documents are provided only for the purpose of assisting you in learning the definitions of the terms and how they are used in the legal field. You should be aware that the forms and documents shown in the illustrations will vary from state to state except for those used in federal courts, such as the bankruptcy forms. A list of illustrations is included on page viii.

LESSONS AND EVALUATIONS

At the beginning of each lesson, there is a general introduction that explains the content of the lesson and gives the objectives that you are to complete for the lesson.

Part A—Terminology and Definitions

The first list of legal terms presented in each lesson consists of 12 to 15 terms. The pronunciation and definition for each term is given. llustrations are also provided for many of the legal terms. The illustrations will assist you in further understanding the definition and usage of the terms. Study the words carefully, and be sure that you understand the definition and can spell and pronounce the term correctly.

Self-Evaluation A—Terminology and Definition Recall

The self-evaluation will require you to recall the terms that were presented in Part A. The format will be blanks, multiple choice, or matching. The answers are provided in the key on page 494 so that you can check the answers as soon as you have completed the self-evaluation. This provides reinforcement for learning, and you should restudy any incorrect answers. These evaluations were designed as a self-help tool.

Part A—Keying Legal Terms

Further reinforcement of the terms and definitions is provided in this part. In the first part, you will key the legal terms presented in the lesson. This will assist you in learning the correct spelling for each of the terms. The sentences in the second part reemphasize the terms and the definitions. The terms are presented in legal context or usage whenever possible. If you are following the machine shorthand procedure, key the material on your shorthand machine. Then transcribe from your shorthand notes on your computer, or, if you are using computer-aided transcription (CAT), proofread and edit your transcript.

Part A—Transcribing from Dictation

Since the dictated material on the CD-ROM is the same as the practiced material keyed from printed copy, your main adaptation in this part will be to transcribe from sound or from your machine shorthand notes. By practicing the material beforehand, your frustrations will be minimized as you move into this section. Also, the prerecorded dictation will help you learn the correct pronunciation of the legal terms.

This part of the lesson provides you with the opportunity to transcribe from dictation, make mistakes, and relearn before an evaluation. After you have transcribed the dictation, check your transcript with the printed copy and restudy any part that gave you difficulty.

Part B is a repeat of the above learning situations using 12-15 more new legal terms.

Evaluations

Section A. This part of the evaluation is prerecorded for you to transcribe either directly on your computer or from your machine shorthand notes. It consists of the same legal terms, but the dictation varies in content from that given in the lessons. A form with directions is provided at proper intervals in your text-workbook. You will turn in this evaluation to your instructor for checking and grading. Each dictated evaluation is dictated at approximately 80 words per minute.

Sections B and C. These parts provide a written evaluation of your knowledge of the legal terms and definitions. They are to be turned in to your instructor for checking along with Section A. Both parts recap the lesson and are an indication, along with the dictation section, of whether or not you have fully comprehended the lesson and are ready to continue. Sections B and C of the evaluation consist of multiple choice and matching questions.

REFERENCE SECTION

The Reference Section on pages 488–493 consists of four parts:

Latin Words and Phrases: Approximately 30 additional Latin words and phrases with pronunciations and definitions are in this section. This will provide you with a further understanding of Latin terms that are used in the legal field.

Proofreading Guidelines: Information to help improve your proofreading skills is presented in this section along with a list of proofreader's marks.

Words Often Confused: Words that are often confused because they sound alike or have similar spellings are listed along with the definition for each word.

Legal Transcription Basics: This section covers some general and basic rules for preparing legal instruments.

INDEX

An Index is included at the end of the text-workbook on pages 501–504. It is an alphabetized listing of the terms, including the page number where the term is presented.

INSTRUCTOR'S RESOURCE CD

An Instructor's e-manual is available on CD-ROM for instructors using this new edition of the text-workbook. The e-manual contains additional information on teaching methods, grading procedures, and grading scales. Also, the 16 evaluations for testing purposes are included on this CD.

ACKNOWLEDGMENTS

Many students, instructors, administrative assistants, court reporters, businesspeople, legal personnel, and lawyers assisted with the content and organization of this text-workbook throughout each of the five editions.

The author expresses thanks to all who have contributed time and suggestions and special thanks to the reviewers, Diane Gilmore, Springfield, Tennessee and Barbara Tietsort, Raymond Walters College, Cincinnati, Ohio for their helpful comments during the development process of this fifth edition.

Table of Contents

List of Illustrations

Lesson

1

Courts and Legal Systems

A knowledge of the federal and state court systems, of the sources of our laws, and of the classifications of law is an essential basis for the understanding of legal terminology. The names and types of courts may vary from state to state, but the ones most commonly used are defined. Our law is an outgrowth of the legal systems of other countries. Therefore, the most common types of law upon which our system is based are also included. When you complete this lesson, you will have an understanding of the general terms used in reference to our courts and legal systems, which will help you learn the terminology taught in the following lessons.

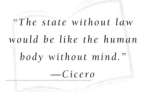

"The state without law would be like the human body without mind."
—*Cicero*

Part A | TERMINOLOGY AND DEFINITIONS

Directions: Study the terms, pronunciations, and definitions until you are thoroughly familiar with them. In order to complete this lesson successfully, you must understand the meaning and usage of all the legal terms presented. If you are using a shorthand system, write each legal term one time on your shorthand machine.

Legal Term	Pronunciation	Definition
		Federal Court System: (See Figure 1-1, page 3.)
1. U.S. Supreme Court	ū s sə–ˊprēm kōrt	The highest court in the federal judicial system. Composed of a chief justice and eight associate justices. This court has final jurisdiction in matters tried in the lower federal courts and can also hear certain cases on appeal from the highest courts in the state systems if a constitutional question of federal law is involved.
2. U.S. Court of Appeals	ū s kōrt əv ə -ˊpēls	An appellate court. Reviews cases from lower federal courts. There are currently 13 judicial circuits, each of which has a U.S. Court of Appeals.
3. U.S. District court	ū s ˊdis-trikt kōrt	A federal trial court or a federal court of original jurisdiction. The court in which a case is first tried in the federal court system.
4. special courts	ˊspesh- əl kōrts	There are several special U.S. courts that have limited jurisdiction, including the Court of Claims, the Court of Customs and Patent Appeals, and the Tax Court.
		State Court System: (See Figure 1-2, page 3.)
5. supreme court	sə -ˊprēm kōrt	The highest court in most state court systems. Certain cases decided in a state supreme court may be appealed to the U.S. Supreme Court if a constitutional question of federal law is involved.

6. court of appeal	kōrt əv ə-ˈpēl	A court that reviews cases from the trial courts or lower courts. The highest court in states not having a supreme court.
7. appellate court	ə-ˈpel-ət kōrt	Same as court of appeal. A court that reviews cases that are appealed from a lower court.
8. trial court	trīl kōrt	A court of original jurisdiction. Hears a case the first time it is tried in court.
9. court of original jurisdiction	kōrt əv ə-ˈrij-ən-l jür-əs-ˈdik- shən	A court that hears a case the first time it is tried in court. A trial court is a court of original jurisdiction.
10. court of record	kōrt əv ˈrek-ərd	A court in which all proceedings are recorded for future reference. Trial courts, appellate courts, and supreme courts are usually courts of record.
11. probate court	ˈprō-bāt kōrt	A court that deals with the probate of wills and the settlement of estates. May also be called orphan's court or surrogate court. In some states the probate court has jurisdiction over the estates of minors and the appointment of guardians.
12. lower or inferior court	lōr ər in-ˈfir-ē-ər kōrt	A court that has a very limited jurisdiction and whose cases may be appealed to a higher court. In some states a written record is not required for the proceedings.
13. court not of record	kōrt nät əv ˈrek-ərd	A court in which the proceedings are not required to be recorded. Usually the lower or inferior courts are courts not of record. However, many states now require all courts to be courts of record. A court not of record, such as a small claims court, cannot impose fines or imprisonment.
14. small claims court	smȯl klāms kōrt	A court established in some states to settle minor disputes between individuals in which the parties represent themselves without the assistance of attorneys. Usually the judge's decision is final, and the case cannot be appealed to a higher court.

FIGURE 1-1 Federal Court System

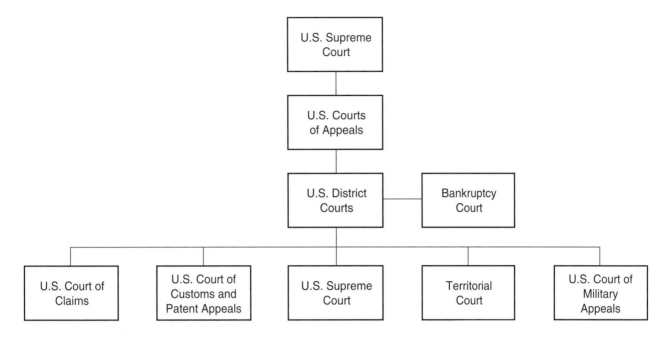

FIGURE 1-2 State Court Systems (The courts in each state vary, so this chart is intended to give only a general overview of the structure of the state court systems.)

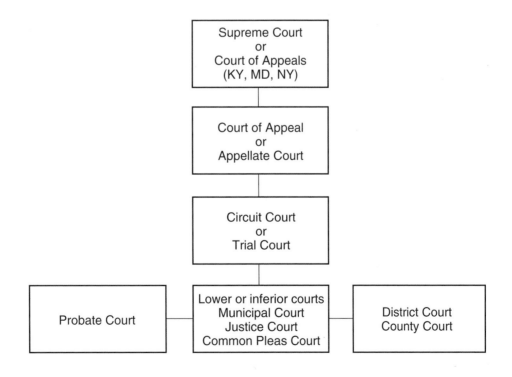

Self-Evaluation A | Terminology and Definition Recall

Directions: In the Answers column at the right of each statement, write the letter that represents the word or group of words that correctly completes the statement. After you have completed this self-evaluation, check your answers with the key on page 494. If you have any incorrect answers, review the definitions for those terms before going on with this lesson. Then unless otherwise directed, submit this self-evaluation to your instructor.

ANSWERS

1. A court having jurisdiction over wills, the settlement of estates, the estates of minors, and the appointment of guardians is known as a/an (a) appellate court, (b) special court, (c) probate court.

   1. _____

2. A court in which all proceedings are recorded for future reference is a (a) court of record, (b) court not of record, (c) small claims court.

   2. _____

3. A court that has very limited jurisdiction and whose cases may be appealed to a higher court is a (a) court of original jurisdiction, (b) probate court, (c) lower or inferior court.

   3. _____

4. A state court that reviews cases from the trial courts is referred to as a (a) court of original jurisdiction, (b) court of appeal, (c) supreme court.

   4. _____

5. The federal appellate court is called the (a) U.S. Court of Appeals, (b) U.S. District Court, (c) U.S. Special Court.

   5. _____

6. A court in which the proceedings are not required to be recorded is referred to as a (a) court not of record, (b) court of record, (c) trial court.

   6. _____

7. A court that hears a case the first time it is tried in court is called a (a) lower or inferior court, (b) court of original jurisdiction, (c) court of appeal.

   7. _____

8. The highest court in the federal judicial system is composed of a chief justice and (a) seven associate justices, (b) eight associate justices, (c) nine associate justices.

   8. _____

9. The highest court in the federal judicial system is called the (a) U.S. Supreme Court, (b) special court, (c) supreme court.

   9. _____

10. The highest court in most states is called the (a) U.S. Supreme Court, (b) special court, (c) supreme court.

    10. _____

11. A federal trial court or a federal court of original jurisdiction is a (a) U.S. Supreme Court, (b) U.S. Court of Appeals, (c) U.S. District Court.

    11. _____

12. In the federal court system, the Court of Claims, the Court of Customs and Patents, and the Tax Court are (a) U.S. District Courts, (b) special courts, (c) U.S. Courts of Appeals.

    12. _____

13. If there is a dispute between states or residents of two different states, the case would be filed in the (a) U.S. Court of Appeals, (b) U.S. District Court, (c) supreme court.

    13. _____

14. If someone damages your personal property and a large sum of money is not involved, you would probably file the case in a/an (a) small claims court, (b) appellate court, (c) special court.

    14. _____

15. If you lost the decision in a case in a court of original jurisdiction or a trial court, you could file for the case to be reviewed in a/an (a) supreme court, (b) probate court, (c) appellate court.

    15. _____

KEYING LEGAL TERMS

Directions: Unless otherwise instructed, use 1-inch margins and double spacing. Correct all errors. Follow one of the procedures below.

WORDS

Keyboarding Procedure
On your computer, key the following words at least two times, concentrating on the correct spelling and pronunciation.

Machine Shorthand Procedure
On your computer, key the following words once, concentrating on the correct spelling and pronunciation. Then write each word one time on your shorthand machine. Transcribe from your shorthand notes one time on your computer, or, if you are using computer-aided transcription (CAT), proofread and edit your transcript.

special courts	U.S. Supreme Court	U.S. District Court
court of original jurisdiction	U.S. Court of Appeals	supreme court
trial court	court of record	appellate court
court of appeal	lower or inferior court	court not of record
probate court	small claims court	

SENTENCES

Keyboarding Procedure
Key each of the following sentences one time on your computer. Concentrate on the correct spelling and pronunciation of each underlined legal term.

Machine Shorthand Procedure
Write the following sentences one time on your shorthand machine. Transcribe from your shorthand notes one time on your computer, or, if you are using computer-aided transcription (CAT), proofread and edit your transcript.

These sentences will be used for practice dictation on the Transcription CD.

The American judicial system has a dual court system, consisting of one federal court system and fifty state court systems. The federal court system deals with cases involving the federal government, suits between states, suits between citizens of two different states, and specific matters in the various <u>special courts</u> established for that purpose.

The <u>U.S. Supreme Court</u> is the highest court in the federal judicial system and is composed of a chief justice and eight associate justices. The <u>U.S. District Court</u> is a federal trial court or <u>court of original jurisdiction</u>. If the state of Illinois were suing the state of Missouri, the case would be filed in a U.S. District Court. A case tried in the U.S. District Court may be appealed to the <u>U.S. Court of Appeals</u>. The U.S. Supreme Court may then be petitioned to hear the case. There are several special courts in the federal court system, such as the Court of Claims, the Court of Customs and Patent Appeals, and the Tax Court.

The highest court in most states is called the <u>supreme court</u>. A <u>trial court</u> or court of original jurisdiction hears a case the first time it is tried in court. If you were going to sue another resident or business located in your state, you would file the case in a trial court. A trial court is usually a <u>court of record</u>, meaning that all the proceedings are recorded verbatim, or word for word. A case tried in a trial court may be appealed to an <u>appellate court</u> or a <u>court of appeal</u> and then to the supreme court. Certain cases heard by the state supreme court, or the highest court in a state system, may be appealed to the U.S. Supreme Court.

A court of small or restricted jurisdiction, such as a municipal court, is known generally as a <u>lower or inferior court</u> and, in most cases, is a <u>court not of record</u>. However, the trend in many states is to require all courts to be courts of record. A case tried in a lower or inferior court may be reviewed in a trial court and could then follow the appellate procedure, the same as a case originally tried in a trial court.

A <u>probate court</u> has jurisdiction over the probate of wills, the settlement of estates, and, in some states, the estates of minors and the appointment of guardians.

<u>Small claims courts</u> have been established in some states to handle minor disputes between individuals. For example, if the dry cleaners ruin your slacks, you could file the case to be settled in a small claims court without the assistance of an attorney.

TRANSCRIBING FROM DICTATION

Directions: This dictation emphasizes and reinforces the legal terms and definitions you have studied. Listen carefully to the pronunciation of each of the legal terms. Unless otherwise directed, use 1-inch margins and double spacing. Correct all errors. Follow one of the procedures below.

Keyboarding Procedure
Using the Transcription CD, Lesson 1, Part A, transcribe the dictation directly at your computer.

Machine Shorthand Procedure
Using the Transcription CD, Lesson 1, Part A, take the dictation on your shorthand machine and then transcribe from your notes on your computer, or, if you are using computer-aided transcription (CAT), proofread and edit your transcript.

When you have finished transcribing or proofreading and editing Part A of the practice dictation, check your transcript with the printed copy. If you made any mistakes in the transcription, you should review and practice those words several times before going on to Part B.

Part B | Terminology and Definitions

Directions: Study the terms, pronunciations, and definitions until you are thoroughly familiar with them. In order to complete this lesson successfully, you must understand the meaning and usage of all the legal terms presented. If you are using a shorthand system, write each legal term one time on your shorthand machine.

Legal Term	Pronunciation	Definition
		Sources of Law:
1. constitutional law	kän-stə -tü-shən-l lȯ	A branch of public law that deals with the interpretation and validity of federal and state constitutions. Constitutional law may be amended by the U.S. Supreme Court or by the highest state courts.
2. statutory law	′stach-ə-tōr-ē lȯ	Law that has been created by statute or legislation passed by the U.S. Congress or the state legislatures. Sometimes called written law.

3. common law	ˈkäm- n lȯ	A body of law that originated in England and has been adopted as the major source of law in the United States. Common law operates through the rule of precedent (like cases in the future to be decided in a like manner). Under common law, the rights of the individual are emphasized over the rights of the government.
4. case law	kās lȯ	Same as common law or unwritten law. Based on cases used as precedents rather than on statutes or other sources of law.
5. Napoleonic Code	nə-ˈpō-lē-ən-ik kōd	Law that originated in France and was adopted by the state of Louisiana as the basis for its state law. It is also referred to as Code Civil, Civil law, or Code Napoleon. Emphasis is on the rights of the state over the rights of the individual.

Classifications of Law:

6. public law	ˈpəb-lik lȯ	A body of law to which the general public is subject, including constitutional, administrative, and criminal law.
7. private law	ˈprī-vət lȯ	A body of law that deals with relationships between private individuals, such as contracts, civil injuries, domestic relations, and partnerships.
8. substantive law	ˈsəb-stən-tiv lȯ	The body of law that creates and defines our rights and duties.
9. procedural law	prə-ˈsēj-rəl lȯ	The body of law that establishes the procedures to be followed for remedial action in court when one's rights have been violated. Also called adjective law.
10. administrative law	əd-ˈmin-ə-strāt-iv lȯ	A branch of public law that deals with the various administrative agencies created by the government and defines the scope of power of those administrative agencies.
11. federal law	ˈfed-rəl lȯ	Law that is created by the federal government and is unaffected by state laws.
12. state law	stāt lȯ	Laws that are created by a state and are effective only in that state.
13. local and municipal ordinances	ˈlō-kəl ən myù-ˈnis-pəl ˈȯrd-nəns-əs	Laws or rules that are created by a local or municipal government and are effective only in that particular governmental unit.

Self-Evaluation B | Terminology and Definition Recall

Directions: In the Answers column, write the letter from Column 1 that represents the word or phrase that best matches each item in Column 2. After you have completed this self-evaluation, check your answers with the key on page 494. If you have any incorrect answers, review the definitions for those terms before going on with this lesson. Then unless otherwise directed, submit this self-evaluation to your instructor.

COLUMN 1	COLUMN 2	ANSWERS
a. administrative law	1. The branch of public law that deals with the various administrative agencies created by the government and defines the scope of their power.	1. *a*
b. case law	2. Law that originated in England and is the basis for the laws in most of our states.	2. *d*
c. civil law	3. Law that is created by statute (ruling) in the legislatures and is sometimes called written law.	3. *m*
d. common law	4. Law that creates and defines our rights and duties.	4. *n*
e. constitutional law	5. Law that establishes the steps to be followed when one's rights have been violated.	5. *j*
f. federal law	6. A law, a rule, or an ordinance enacted or adopted by a county, city, or township; it is effective only in the governmental unit that created it.	6. *g*
g. local and municipal ordinances	7. The part of law that deals with relationships between private individuals.	7. *i*
h. Napoleonic Code	8. A branch of public law that deals with the interpretation and validity of federal and state constitutions.	8. *e*
i. private law	9. Law that is created by a state and is effective only in that state.	9. *l*
j. procedural law	10. Law that is based on cases used as precedents rather than on statutes or other sources of law.	10. *b*
k. public law	11. Law that is created by the federal government and is unaffected by state laws.	11. *f*
l. state law	12. The body of law that includes constitutional, administrative, and criminal law to which the general public is subject.	12. *k*
m. statutory law	13. The form of law that originated in France and was adopted by the state of Louisiana.	13. *h*
n. substantive law		

Lesson

2

General Legal Terminology

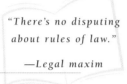

"There's no disputing about rules of law."

—*Legal maxim*

There are many legal terms that apply to the entire field of law. Several of these are presented in this lesson so that you will be familiar with them as you get into the study of the more specific areas of law. Legal terms are mostly everyday English words, but many times they have a totally different meaning when used in the legal field. For example, you will find that the words suit, party, bench, and bar have different legal meanings than they have in common usage. When you complete this lesson, you will have a knowledge of some of the general terminology used in its legal context.

Part A | TERMINOLOGY AND DEFINITIONS

Directions: Study the terms, pronunciations, and definitions until you are thoroughly familiar with them. In order to complete this lesson successfully, you must understand the meaning and usage of all the legal terms presented. If you are using a shorthand system, write each legal term one time on your shorthand machine.

Legal Term	Pronunciation	Definition
1. lex	leks	Latin term for law. A system of written or unwritten law for a given jurisdiction.
2. lexicon	′lek-sə-kän	Latin. A dictionary of legal terms.
3. code books	kōd bůks	Books containing the laws that have been created by state and federal legislatures.
4. Corpus Juris Secundum	′kȯr-pəs ′jür-əs si-′kənd-əm	An encyclopedia of laws commonly used as a reference by lawyers.
5. jurisprudence	jür-ə-′sprüd-ns	The philosophy or science of law.
6. statute	′stach-üt	A law created by a state or federal legislature.
7. bar	bär	The legal profession. Lawyers are members of the bar. An attorney guilty of misconduct may be censored by the bar association.
8. judge	jəj	The presiding officer of a court of law.
9. bench	bench	A court of law. Also, the judge's seat in a court of law.
10. jurist	′jür-əst	One who has a thorough knowledge of law and has written extensively on legal subjects. Do not confuse with a juror.

11. prosecuting attorney	′präs-i-kyüt-iŋ ə-′tər-nē	An appointed or elected official who represents the people or the state in criminal cases. For example, whenever a public law has been violated, such as the commission of murder, the prosecuting attorney, who may also be called a district attorney in some jurisdictions, represents the "People," or the public, and attempts to prosecute the defendant.
12. defense attorney	di-′fens ə-′tər-nē	One who represents the defendant in court cases or legal matters.
13. in propria persona	in prō-′prē-ə pər-′sō-nə	Latin. In one's own proper person. One who acts without the assistance of an attorney. Sometimes shortened to in pro per. For example, if a defendant chooses not to be represented by an attorney, he or she is said to appear in propria persona, or in pro per.
14. esquire	′es-kwīr	A title written after the surname of an attorney. Usually abbreviated to Esq., and no personal or professional title is prefixed to the name.

Self-Evaluation A | Terminology and Definition Recall

Directions: In the Answers column, write the legal term that is most representative of the corresponding statement. After you have completed this self-evaluation, check your answers with the key on page 494. If you have any incorrect answers, review the definitions for those terms before going on with this lesson. Then unless otherwise directed, submit this self-evaluation to your instructor.

ANSWERS

1. The philosophy or science of law is referred to as _____.

    1. *jurisprudence*

2. If you did not know the meaning of a legal term, you would probably look it up in a dictionary of legal terms called a/an _____.

    2. *lexicon*

    nomenclature

3. An appointed or elected official who represents the people, or the public, in a criminal case is the _____.

    3. *attorney*

4. The Latin term for law is _____.

    4. *lex*

5. All members of the legal profession are collectively referred to as the _____.

    5. *bar*

6. The presiding officer in a court of law is known as the _____.

    6. *judge*

7. One who has a thorough knowledge of law and has written extensively on legal subjects is a/an _____.

    7. *jurist*

    propria

    persona

8. If you chose to represent yourself in a lawsuit without the assistance of an attorney, you would be referred to as appearing (a) _____, or (b). _____

    8a. *persona*

    8b. *proper*

9. A law created by a state or federal legislature is a/an _____.

    9. *statute*

    corpus juris

10. An encyclopedia of laws commonly used as a reference by lawyers is known as a/an _____.

    10. *secundum*

11. A title that is written after the surname of an attorney is (a) _____, sometimes abbreviated as (b) _____.

    11a. *esquire*

    11b. *esq.*

12. One who represents the defendant in court cases or other legal matters is the _____.

    12. *defense attorney*

13. Books containing laws that have been created by state and federal legislatures are _____.

    13. *code books*

14. A court of law and, also, the judge's seat in a court of law are called the _____.

    14. *bench*

KEYING LEGAL TERMS

Directions: Unless otherwise instructed, use 1-inch margins and double spacing. Correct all errors. Follow one of the procedures below.

WORDS

Keyboarding Procedure
On your computer, key the following words at least two times, concentrating on the correct spelling and pronunciation.

Machine Shorthand Procedure
On your computer, key the following words once, concentrating on the correct spelling and pronunciation. Then write each word one time on your shorthand machine. Transcribe from your shorthand notes one time on your computer, or, if you are using computer-aided transcription (CAT), proofread and edit your transcript.

lex	lexicon	code books
Corpus Juris Secundum	jurisprudence	statute
bar	judge	bench
jurist	prosecuting attorney	defense attorney
in propria persona	esquire	

SENTENCES

Keyboarding Procedure
Key each of the following sentences one time on your computer. Concentrate on the correct spelling and pronunciation of each underlined legal term.

Machine Shorthand Procedure
Write the following sentences one time on your shorthand machine. Transcribe from your shorthand notes one time on your computer, or, if you are using computer-aided transcription (CAT), proofread and edit your transcript.

These sentences will be used for practice dictation on the Transcription CD.

The Latin term for law is <u>lex</u>. Lex is a system of written or unwritten law for a given jurisdiction. A <u>lexicon</u> is a dictionary of legal terms. If you do not know the meaning of a legal term, you can look up the term in a lexicon. The <u>code books</u> contain the laws that have been created by state and federal legislatures. The <u>Corpus Juris Secundum</u> is an encyclopedia of laws. The Corpus Juris Secundum is commonly used as a legal reference by lawyers.

The philosophy or science of law is known as <u>jurisprudence</u>. Jurisprudence deals with the principles of law and legal relations. A <u>statute</u> is a law created by a state or federal legislature. The violation of a statute will usually result in a legal proceeding in a court of law.

All members of the legal profession are collectively referred to as the <u>bar</u>. Attorneys follow a code of ethics established by the American Bar Association and may be censored by the bar association if they are found guilty of misconduct in their profession. A <u>judge</u> presides over and administers the law in a court of justice. A court of law may also be referred to as the <u>bench</u>. Also, the bench can mean the seat occupied by the judge in court. A <u>jurist</u> is a person who has a thorough knowledge of the law and who has written extensively on legal subjects. Do not confuse a jurist with a juror.

When a statute has been violated, the judge will hear the case as presented by the prosecuting and defense attorneys. The <u>prosecuting attorney</u> conducts criminal prosecutions on behalf of the state or the people, whereas the <u>defense attorney</u> tries a case in court on behalf of the one who is charged with the crime in the case. If you were charged with a criminal act and you did not want the assistance of a defense attorney, you could appear in court <u>in propria persona</u>, or in pro per. Someone who is in propria persona, or in pro per, is acting in his or her own behalf and does not have the assistance of an attorney.

The title <u>"Esquire"</u> is sometimes written after an attorney's surname. The word esquire is usually abbreviated to Esq., and a personal or professional title is not prefixed to the name. An example is William D. Flannagan, Esq.

TRANSCRIBING FROM DICTATION

Directions: This dictation emphasizes and reinforces the legal terms and definitions you have studied. Listen carefully to the pronunciation of each of the legal terms. Unless otherwise directed, use 1-inch margins and double spacing. Correct all errors. Follow one of the procedures below.

Keyboarding Procedure
Using the Transcription CD, Lesson 2, Part A, transcribe the dictation directly at your computer.

Machine Shorthand Procedure
Using the Transcription CD, Lesson 2, Part A, take the dictation on your shorthand machine and then transcribe from your notes on your computer, or, if you are using computer-aided transcription (CAT), proofread and edit your transcript.

When you have finished transcribing or proofreading and editing Part A of the practice dictation, check your transcript with the printed copy. If you made any mistakes in the transcription, you should review and practice those words several times before going on to Part B.

Part B | TERMINOLOGY AND DEFINITIONS

Directions: Study the terms, pronunciations, and definitions until you are thoroughly familiar with them. In order to complete this lesson successfully, you must understand the meaning and usage of all the legal terms presented. If you are using a shorthand system, write each legal term one time on your shorthand machine.

Legal Term	Pronunciation	Definition
1. legal procedure	´lē-gəl prə-´sē-jər	The method or steps to be followed in any action in a court of law.
2. proceeding	prō-´sēd-iŋ	Any action in a court of law.
3. suit	süt	Any action or proceeding in a court of law whereby one seeks relief or recovery from another who has caused injury to or violated the rights of that person.
4. litigation	lit-ə-´gā-shən	A legal action or suit in a court of law whereby one seeks relief or recovery from another.
5. action	´ak-shən	A legal proceeding or suit in a court of law whereby one seeks relief from another for an injury or a violated right.

6. due process	dü ′präs-es	The legal procedures established which provide that every person has the benefit and protection of the law.
7. justice	′jəs-təs	A just and fair application of the law for every person. Also, a judge is referred to as a justice.
8. client	′klī-ənt	One who employs an attorney to represent or advise him or her in court cases or legal matters.
9. party	′pärt-ē	Any person involved in or affected by a legal proceeding. The plaintiff and the defendant are both parties to a suit.
10. litigant	′lit-i-gənt	A party to an action, a suit, a litigation, or a legal proceeding.
11. plaintiff	′plānt-əf	One who starts an action, a suit, or a proceeding in a court of law. If you file the suit, you are the plaintiff.
12. defendant	di-′fen-dənt	The one against whom an action, a suit, a litigation, or a proceeding is started in a court of law. If you file a suit, the one against whom you file is the defendant.
13. et alius	et ′āl-ē-us	Latin. And another. Abbreviated et al. When et al. is used in a legal document with more than one plaintiff or defendant named, it means all persons previously named are included. For example, if the case title includes the names of Kozak, Wayland, Morris, and Jones as plaintiffs, they may be referred to in the legal document as Kozak, et al.
14. versus	′vər-səs	Latin. Against. When used in a case title, the plaintiff's name is first, followed by "versus," then the defendant's name; for example, Durand versus Selmar. May be abbreviated as vs. or v. (i.e., Durand vs. Selmar or Durand v. Selmar).

Self-Evaluation B | TERMINOLOGY AND DEFINITION RECALL

Directions: In the Answers column, write the letter from Column 1 that represents the word or phrase that best matches each item in Column 2. After you have completed this self-evaluation, check your answers with the key on page 494. If you have any incorrect answers, review the definitions for those terms before going on with this lesson. Then unless otherwise directed, submit this self-evaluation to your instructor.

COLUMN 1	COLUMN 2	ANSWERS
a. action	1. The legal procedure established which provides that every person has the benefit and protection of the law.	1. *d*
b. client	2. One who starts an action, a suit, or a proceeding in a court of law.	2. *l*
c. defendant	3. The legal term meaning "and others."	3. *e*
d. due process	4. The word in the title of a case that means "against."	4. *o*
e. et alius	5. Another name for a litigation, a suit, or an action whereby one seeks recovery from another who has caused injury to or violated the rights of that person.	5. *m*
f. jurisprudence		
g. justice	6. One who employs an attorney to represent or advise him or her in court cases or legal matters.	6. *b*
h. legal procedure	7. Another name for a legal proceeding, suit, or litigation in a court of law by which one person seeks recovery from another for an injury or a violated right.	7. *a*
i. litigant		
j. litigation	8. The one against whom an action, a suit, or a proceeding is started in a court of law.	8. *c*
k. party	9. A just and fair application of law for every person.	9. *g*
l. plaintiff	10. Another name for a proceeding, a litigation, or an action whereby one seeks recovery from another who has caused injury to or violated the rights of that person.	10. *h*
m. proceeding		
n. suit	11. Another name for a proceeding, an action, or a suit in a court of law whereby one seeks recovery from another who has caused injury to or violated the rights of that person.	11. *j*
o. versus		
	12. Another name for a litigant involved in or affected by a legal proceeding.	12. *k*
	13. A party to an action, a suit, or a legal proceeding.	13. *i*
	14. The method to be followed in any action in a court of law.	14. *h*

KEYING LEGAL TERMS

Directions: Unless otherwise instructed, use 1-inch margins and double spacing. Correct all errors. Follow one of the procedures below.

WORDS

Keyboarding Procedure
On your computer, key the following words at least two times, concentrating on the correct spelling and pronunciation.

Machine Shorthand Procedure
On your computer, key the following words once, concentrating on the correct spelling and pronunciation. Then write each word one time on your shorthand machine. Transcribe from your shorthand notes one time on your computer, or, if you are using computer-aided transcription (CAT), proofread and edit your transcript.

legal procedure	proceeding	suit
litigation	action	justice
due process	client	party
litigant	plaintiff	defendant
et alius	versus	

SENTENCES

Keyboarding Procedure
Key each of the following sentences one time on your computer. Concentrate on the correct spelling and pronunciation of each underlined legal term.

Machine Shorthand Procedure
Write the following sentences one time on your shorthand machine. Transcribe from your shorthand notes one time on your computer, or, if you are using computer-aided transcription (CAT), proofread and edit your transcript.

These sentences will be used for practice dictation on the Transcription CD.

When a person starts a legal case, there is a certain <u>legal procedure</u> that must be followed throughout the legal <u>proceeding</u>. A <u>suit</u>, a <u>litigation</u>, a proceeding, and an <u>action</u> all refer to a dispute in a court of law whereby one seeks relief or recovery from another who has caused injury to or violated the rights of that person. If someone owes you money and will not pay, you can start a legal action against that person to recover the money that is owed to you.

Our system of <u>justice</u> strives to apply the law fairly and justly to every person involved in a litigation. The parties to a proceeding are seeking justice by following a course of legal procedures usually referred to as <u>due process</u>. Every person is entitled to due process in our system of justice.

A <u>client</u> is one who employs an attorney to represent or advise him or her in legal proceedings or other legal matters. Any person involved in or affected by a lawsuit is known as a <u>party</u> or <u>litigant</u>. A client who hires an attorney to start a legal proceeding becomes known as the <u>plaintiff</u> in the suit. When a plaintiff starts an action, the person charged with a wrongdoing is called the <u>defendant</u>. Thus, the two most common parties in a lawsuit are the plaintiff and the defendant.

Sometimes there may be more than one plaintiff or defendant in a suit. A group of plaintiffs or defendants may be referred to by using the name of the first one listed followed by <u>et alius</u>, which may be abbreviated to et al. If the case title includes the names of Kozak, Wayland, Morris, and Jones as plaintiffs, they may be referred to in the legal document as Kozak, et al. This means that all the others are also included.

The word <u>versus</u> means against. In the title of a suit, an action, a litigation, or a proceeding, the plaintiff's name is first, followed by versus, then the defendant's name. Versus may be abbreviated vs. or v. If Mr. Cook were suing Mr. Walters, the title of the suit would be Cook versus Walters.

TRANSCRIBING FROM DICTATION

Directions: This dictation emphasizes and reinforces the legal terms and definitions you have studied. Listen carefully to the pronunciation of each of the legal terms. Unless otherwise directed, use 1-inch margins and double spacing. Correct all errors. Follow one of the procedures below.

Keyboarding Procedure
Using the Transcription CD, Lesson 2, Part B, transcribe the dictation directly at your computer.

Machine Shorthand Procedure
Using the Transcription CD, Lesson 2, Part B, take the dictation on your shorthand machine and then transcribe from your notes on your computer, or, if you are using computer-aided transcription (CAT), proofread and edit your transcript.

When you have finished transcribing or proofreading and editing Part B of the practice dictation, check your transcript with the printed copy. If you made any mistakes in the transcription, you should review and practice those words several times before going on to Evaluation 1.

CHECKLIST
I have completed the following for Lesson 2:

	Part A, Date	Part B, Date	Submitted to Instructor Yes	No
Terminology and Definitions	_____	_____	_____	_____
Self-Evaluation	_____	_____	_____	_____
* Keying Legal Terms	_____	_____	_____	_____
Words	_____	_____	_____	_____
Sentences	_____	_____	_____	_____
* Transcribing from Dictation	_____	_____	_____	_____

When you have successfully completed all the exercises in this lesson and submitted to your instructor those requested, you are ready to proceed with Evaluation 1.

* If you are using machine shorthand, submit to your instructor your notes along with your transcript.

Evaluation No. 1 | SECTION A

Directions: This dictation/transcription evaluation will test your spelling and transcription abilities on the legal terms that you studied in the two preceding lessons. Tab once for a paragraph indention, and use 1-inch margins and double spacing unless otherwise instructed. Correct all errors. Follow one of the procedures below.

Keyboarding Procedure

Using the Transcription CD for Evaluation 1, transcribe the dictation directly at your computer.

Machine Shorthand Procedure

Using the Transcription CD for Evaluation 1, take the dictation on your shorthand machine and then transcribe your notes on your computer, or, if you are using computer-aided transcription (CAT), proofread and edit your transcript. **Sections B and C are available from your instructor.**

Lesson 3

General Legal Terms

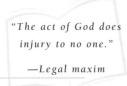

"The act of God does injury to no one."

—*Legal maxim*

Terms that describe the various types of claims and defenses of the parties to a lawsuit are presented in the following exercises. Also included are some related and general legal terms. When you complete this lesson, you should have a knowledge and understanding of terminology involving pleadings and other general legal activities.

Part A | TERMINOLOGY AND DEFINITIONS

Directions: Study the terms, pronunciations, and definitions until you are thoroughly familiar with them. In order to complete this lesson successfully, you must understand the meaning and usage of all the legal terms presented. If you are using a shorthand system, write each legal term one time on your shorthand machine.

Legal Term	Pronunciation	Definition
1. retainer	ri-ʹtā-ner	The fee a client pays to an attorney for representation or assistance in a legal matter.
2. tribunal	trī-ʹbyün-l	A court of justice. Also, all the judges in a particular jurisdiction.
3. adjudicate	ə-ʹjüd-i-kāt	To decide a case by law.
4. complaint	kəm-ʹplānt	The first pleading filed in a civil action whereby the plaintiff states the facts on which the suit is based. (See Figure 3-1, page 31.)
5. declaration	dek-lə-ʹrā-shən	Another name for a first pleading filed in a civil action whereby the plaintiff states the facts on which the suit is based.
6. narratio	na-ʹrā-shē-ō	The Latin word for the first pleading filed in a civil action by the plaintiff in which the facts for the basis of the suit are stated.
7. plea	plē	The first pleading filed by a defendant in an action that states the defendant's answer, based on fact, to the plaintiff's claims.
8. pleadings	ʹplēd-iŋs	The written allegations of what the plaintiff claims and what the defendant denies in a lawsuit. (See Figure 3-1, page 31.)

9. gravamen	grə-ˈvā-mən	The grievance or injury specifically complained of in a pleading. The substantial cause of the action.
10. count	kau̇nt	The various charges in a complaint or declaration made by the plaintiff against a defendant. (See Figure 3-2, page 32.)
11. contest	kən-ˈtest	To dispute the plaintiff's claim in a court of law. If you contest a lawsuit, you are denying the charge.
12. petition	pə-ˈtish-ən	A written application to the court for action upon a legal matter. There are many different kinds of petitions that may be filed with the court. For example, a party to an action may petition the court to set a trial date, to issue a bench warrant, or to probate a will. (See Figure 3-3, page 32.)
13. writ	rit	A written command issued by a court that requires some specified action. The person receiving the writ may be required to do or not to do a specific act. Some of the various types of writs are a writ of habeas corpus, a writ of garnishment, or a writ of restitution. (See Figure 3-4, page 33.)
14. champerty	ˈcham-pərt-ē	An illegal procedure whereby one not involved in the lawsuit makes a deal with a party to the suit to pay the costs of the litigation in exchange for a share of the proceeds from the suit.

FIGURE 3-1 A Complaint

STATE OF MICHIGAN

IN THE CIRCUIT COURT FOR THE COUNTY OF INGHAM

SARAH ANN STONE,

        Plaintiff,

v.   File No. 83-52179

IMAGE GRAPHICS, INC.,

        Defendant.

_____

JASON C. O'MALLEY (P 23345)
PATRICK B. STILWELL (P 36588)
Attorneys for Plaintiff
- -

<u>COMPLAINT</u>

    NOW COMES Sarah Ann Stone, by and through her attorneys, O'Malley & Stilwell, P.C., and for her complaint against defendant states the following:

<u>COMMON ALLEGATIONS</u>

    1. Plaintiff, Sarah Ann Stone ("Stone"), is a resident and citizen of the State of Michigan and resides at 6447 Whitmore Avenue, Lansing, Michigan 48810.

Pleadings

    2. Defendant, Image Graphics, Inc. ("Image"), is a corporation chartered under the laws of the State of Michigan, whose principal administrative offices and place of business is located at 7850 South Washington Avenue, Lansing, Michigan 48933.

    3. Stone was employed by Image as a commercial artist from 1998 until September 2003.

    4. In 2001, Stone, working in conjunction with other staff members at Image, undertook development of certain audiovisual materials ("AV materials") designed to be used by various businesses for in-service training programs.

FIGURE 3-2 A Count

~~~~~~

<div style="text-align:center">

COUNT 1

BREACH OF CONTRACT
</div>

Count

11. Stone restates and realleges and hereby incorporates by reference as though fully set forth herein, the allegations contained in paragraphs 1 through 10 of the Common Allegations of this complaint.

12. Stone and Image entered into a valid and binding contract dated July 17, 2001 ("Contract"), a copy of which is annexed to this complaint and Designated Exhibit "A."

13. Paragraph 2 of the contract provides that where the only time devoted by Stone to the project was the time allocated by Image to Stone for

~~~~~~

FIGURE 3-3 A Petition

Approved, SCAO

Original - Police
Copy - Court

STATE OF MICHIGAN XXXXXXXXXXXX 30th JUDICIAL CIRCUIT	PETITION AND BENCH WARRANT	CASE NO. 83-52179

ORI MI- Court address 2nd Floor, City Hall, Lansing, Michigan 48933   Court telephone no. (517) 555-0650

THE PEOPLE OF ☒ The State of Michigan
☐ _____

V.

Defendant name, address, and telephone no.

Allen J. Polasek
7850 South Washington Avenue
Lansing, Michigan 48933

CTN	SID	DOB

PETITION   A petition is not required if the bench warrant is issued on the court's own motion.

Petitioner requests that a bench warrant be issued and be arrested and held in comtempt of court for:

Allen J. Polasek
Name

☐ failure to appear.
☒ the following reason(s):

Failure to appear for the taking of a deposition under Order Compelling Discovery issued by the Court on October 22, 2003.

I declare that the statements above are true to the best of my information, knowledge, and belief.

October 23, 2003
Date

Jason C. O'Malley
Petitioner's signature

~~~~~~

FIGURE 3-4 A Writ

Approved BY THE MSCA

ORIGINAL - OFFICER RETURN
1st COPY - COURT
2nd COPY - DEFENDANT

STATE OF MICHIGAN 54A **JUDICIAL CIRCUIT**	**WRIT OF RESTITUTION** LANDLORD/TENANT - LAND CONTRACT	**CASE NO.** 885599-LT

6th Floor, City Hall, Lansing, Michigan   (517) 555-3445
Court address   Court telephone no.

Plantiff name and address	Defendant name(s) and address(es)
Capitol Management, Inc. 7720 Wildwood Drive Lansing, Michigan 48912	Justin H. Story 6453 Fairlane Drive, Apt. 201 Lansing, Michigan 48906

Plantiff's attorney, bar no., and telephone no.
Margo B. Griffin (P 55220)
7885 South Cedar Street
Lansing, Michigan 48910   555-7781

APPLICATION

The undersigned makes application for a writ of restitutions and states:

1. On <u>November 24, 2003</u> judgment was entered against Defendant(s), and Plaintiff was awarded
   Date
   possession of the following described property. <u>Apartment 201, 6453 Fairlane Drive, Lansing,</u>

   <u>Michigan 48906</u>

   _____

2. No payment has been made on the judgment and/or no rent has been received since the date of

   judgment, except the sum of $ _____ received under the following conditions: _____

   _____

   _____

3. The party awarded judgment has complied with it terms.

4. The time stated in the judgment to precede the issuance of a writ of restitution has elapsed.

I declare, under the penalty of contempt of court, that to the best of my knowledge, information and belief, there is good ground to support the contents of this pleading.

<u>December 4, 2003</u>   *Margo B. Griffin* (P 55220)
Date   Signature of Attorney Bar. no
                                                      7885 South Cedar Street
                                                      Address
                                                      Lansing, Michigan 48912   555-7781
                                                      City, state, zip   Telephone no.

WRIT

IN THE NAME OF THE PEOPLE OF THE STATE OF MICHIGAN:
To the Court Officer: Based upon the facts set forth in the above application, you are commanded to remove the above named Defendant(s) and other occupants from the premises described, and to restore Plaintiff to peaceful possession.

SEAL   <u>12/4/03</u>   *Hunter G. Mitchell*
            Date issued   District Judge

NOTE: This writ must be served within 60 days of the issuance date.

OFFICER RETURN
WRIT OF RESTITUTION, LANDLORD TENANT, LAND CONTRACT, Form no. DCH107, (3 part, pink) Revised 4/80

Self-Evaluation A | Terminology and Definition Recall

Directions: In the Answers column, write the legal term that is most representative of the corresponding statement. After you have completed this self-evaluation, check your answers with the key on page 494. If you have any incorrect answers, review the definitions for those terms before going on with this lesson. Then unless otherwise directed, submit this self-evaluation to your instructor.

ANSWERS

1. A written command issued by a court that requires a person to do or not to do a specific act is a/an_____.

1. _____

2. The first pleading filed by a defendant in a lawsuit that states the defendant's answer, based on fact, to the plaintiff's claims is a/an _____.

2. _____

3. A court of justice is also referred to as a/an _____.

3. _____

4. A written application to the court for action upon a legal matter, such as the setting of a court date, is a/an _____.

4. _____

5. A Latin term for the first pleading filed by the plaintiff in an action is _____.

5. _____

6. The first pleading filed in an action whereby the plaintiff states the facts on which the suit is based is a/an _____.

6. _____

7. The written allegations of what the plaintiff claims and what the defendant denies in a lawsuit are referred to as _____.

7. _____

8. The grievance or injury specifically complained of in a pleading is _____.

8. _____

9. The fee that a client pays to an attorney for representation or assistance in a legal matter is a/an _____.

9. _____

10. To dispute the plaintiff's claim in a court of law is to _____ the claim.

10. _____

11. The first pleading filed in an action by the plaintiff is a/an _____.

11. _____

12. An illegal procedure whereby one not involved in the lawsuit makes a deal with a party to the suit to pay the costs of the litigation in exchange for a share of the proceeds is called _____.

12. _____

13. To decide a case by law is to _____the case.

13. _____

14. A charge in a complaint or declaration made by the plaintiff against a defendant is called a/an _____.

14. _____

KEYING LEGAL TERMS

Directions: Unless otherwise instructed, use 1-inch margins and double spacing. Correct all errors. Follow one of the procedures below.

WORDS

Keyboarding Procedure
On your computer, key the following words at least two times, concentrating on the correct spelling and pronunciation.

Machine Shorthand Procedure
On your computer, key the following words once, concentrating on the correct spelling and pronunciation. Then write each word one time on your shorthand machine. Transcribe from your shorthand notes one time on your computer, or, if you are using computer-aided transcription (CAT), proofread and edit your transcript.

retainer	tribunal	adjudicate
complaint	declaration	narratio
plea	pleadings	gravamen
count	contest	petition
writ	champerty	

SENTENCES

Keyboarding Procedure
Key each of the following sentences one time on your computer. Concentrate on the correct spelling and pronunciation of each underlined legal term.

Machine Shorthand Procedure
Write the following sentences one time on your shorthand machine. Transcribe from your shorthand notes one time on your computer, or, if you are using computer-aided transcription (CAT), proofread and edit your transcript.

These sentences will be used for practice dictation on the Transcription CD.

If you hire an attorney to represent or assist you in a legal matter, the fee you pay the attorney is called a retainer. To decide or settle a case in a court of law, or a tribunal, is to adjudicate the case. A tribunal may also be used when referring to all the judges in a particular jurisdiction.

Depending upon the state, court, and type of proceeding, an initial pleading whereby the plaintiff states the facts on which the suit is based may be referred to as a complaint or a declaration or by the Latin term narratio. Once a client has retained an attorney for representation in a legal matter, the attorney will prepare a complaint, declaration, or narratio, which will state the facts on which the suit is based. When the defendant in a suit receives the plaintiff's complaint, the defendant will file a plea, which states the defendant's answer, based on fact, to the plaintiff's claim. The plaintiff's written claims and the defendant's written denials make up the pleadings in a lawsuit. The grievance or injury specifically complained of in a pleading is referred to as gravamen.

A count is one of the various charges in a complaint or declaration made by the plaintiff against a defendant. The defendant's plea will answer each count or charge listed in the plaintiff's declaration or complaint. When the defendant disputes the plaintiff's claim, the defendant is said to contest the claim made by the

plaintiff. Of course, a complaint that is contested will be adjudicated in a **tribunal**, or a court of law.

The attorney for either party may <u>petition</u> the court for various matters, such as the setting of a trial date.

The judge may issue a <u>writ</u>, which requires one of the parties to a lawsuit to do or not to do a specific thing.

If someone who is not involved in the lawsuit makes a deal with a party in the lawsuit whereby the uninvolved party will pay all the legal fees in exchange for a share of any money awarded in the suit, this procedure is referred to as <u>champerty</u>. Champerty constitutes an illegal act and is not permitted under law.

TRANSCRIBING FROM DICTATION

Directions: This dictation emphasizes and reinforces the legal terms and definitions you have studied. Listen carefully to the pronunciation of each of the legal terms. Unless otherwise directed, use 1-inch margins and double spacing. Correct all errors. Follow one of the procedures below.

Keyboarding Procedure

Using the Transcription CD, Lesson 3, Part A, transcribe the dictation directly at your computer.

Machine Shorthand Procedure

Using the Transcription CD, Lesson 3, Part A, take the dictation on your shorthand machine and then transcribe from your notes on your computer, or, if you are using computer-aided transcription, proofread and edit your transcript.

When you have finished transcribing or proofreading and editing Part A of the practice dictation, check your transcript with the printed copy. If you made any mistakes in the transcription, you should review and practice those words several times before going on to Part B.

Part B | TERMINOLOGY AND DEFINITIONS

Directions: Study the terms, pronunciations, and definitions until you are thoroughly familiar with them. In order to complete this lesson successfully, you must understand the meaning and usage of all the legal terms presented. If you are using a shorthand system, write each legal term one time on your shorthand machine.

Legal Term	Pronunciation	Definition
1. allege	ə-ˈlej	To make an allegation or a charge.
2. malicious prosecution	mə-ˈlish-əs präs-i-ˈkyü-shən	An action started by a plaintiff without justification and with the intention of damaging the defendant.
3. double jeopardy	ˈdəb-əl ˈjep-ərd-e	A second prosecution for the same offense. Our laws prohibit double jeopardy. If one is found innocent of a crime, he or she cannot be tried again for the same crime.
4. act of God	akt əv gäd	A disaster that occurs as a result of natural causes unaided by any human action. One cannot sue for damages caused by an act of God.
5. jointly and severally	ˈjȯint-lē ən ˈsev-rəl-ē	When a liability involves more than one party, they may all be sued together or they may be sued separately. If you and a friend rent an apartment together and your friend refuses to pay the rent, you may be held liable for all the rent if the lease contains a jointly and severally clause.

6. feasance	´fēz-ns	The proper performance of a legal act.
7. malfeasance	mal-´fēz-ns	The performance of an illegal act. Misconduct.
8. statute of limitations	´stach-üt əv lim-ə-´tā-shəns	A law that requires an action to be started within a certain length of time after the alleged cause occurred. If a case is not filed within the statute of limitations, then it cannot be filed.
9. statute of frauds	´stach-üt əv fròdz	An act which requires that certain kinds of contracts must be in writing and signed before an action based on the contracts can be instituted.
10. per se	pər ´sā	Latin. In itself or by itself.
11. alias	´ā-lē-əs	Latin. Otherwise. An assumed name by which one is also known. If Jane Rosewell also uses the name Jean Rosswell, she is said to have an alias. The abbreviation AKA or a/k/a, which stands for "also known as," is sometimes used to denote an alias. The abbreviation may also be written as A/K/A or aka.
12. minor	´mī-nər	One who is too young to be considered as legally competent. That person is also referred to as an infant.
13. sui juris	´sü-ī ´jùr-əs	Latin. One who is legally capable of managing his or her own actions or affairs.

Self-Evaluation B | Terminology and Definition Recall

Directions: In the Answers column at the right of each statement, write the letter that represents the word or group of words that correctly completes the statement. After you have completed this self-evaluation, check your answers with the key on page 494. If you have any incorrect answers, review the definitions for those terms before going on with this lesson. Then unless otherwise directed, submit this self-evaluation to your instructor.

ANSWERS

1. A liability involving more than one party who may be sued together or sued separately is expressed as (a) double jeopardy, (b) jointly and severally, (c) malicious prosecution.

    1. _____

2. A Latin term meaning in itself or by itself is (a) alias, (b) sui juris, (c) per se.

    2. _____

3. A Latin term meaning that one is legally capable of managing his or her own affairs or actions is (a) alias, (b) sui juris, (c) per se.

    3. _____

4. To make a charge or an allegation that someone committed a wrongful act is to (a) allege, (b) feasance, (c) malfeasance.

    4. _____

5. One who is too young to be considered as legally competent is a/an (a) sui juris, (b) alias, (c) minor.

    5. _____

6. If a plaintiff starts an action without justification and with the intention of damaging the defendant, it is called a (a) double jeopardy, (b) malicious prosecution, (c) feasance.

    6. _____

7. An act which requires that certain kinds of contracts must be in writing and signed before an action based on the contracts can be commenced is the (a) act of God, (b) statute of limitations, (c) statute of frauds.

    7. _____

8. If a person performs an illegal act or is guilty of misconduct, that person is guilty of (a) double jeopardy, (b) feasance, (c) malfeasance.

    8. _____

9. If someone is prosecuted twice for the same offense, it is called (a) double jeopardy, (b) per se, (c) jointly and severally.

    9. _____

10. If a legal act is properly performed, it is called (a) feasance, (b) malfeasance, (c) jointly and severally.

    10. _____

11. A disaster that occurs as a result of natural causes unaided by any human action is a/an (a) act of God, (b) statute of limitations, (c) double jeopardy.

    11. _____

12. A law that requires an action to be started within a certain length of time after the alleged cause occurred is the (a) statute of limitations, (b) statute of frauds, (c) act of God.

    12. _____

13. The Latin term for an assumed name or a second name by which one is also known is a/an (a) sui juris, (b) per se, (c) alias.

    13. _____

KEYING LEGAL TERMS

Directions: Unless otherwise instructed, use 1-inch margins and double spacing. Correct all errors. Follow one of the procedures below.

WORDS

Keyboarding Procedure
On your computer, key the following words at least two times, concentrating on the correct spelling and pronunciation.

Machine Shorthand Procedure
On your computer, key the following words once, concentrating on the correct spelling and pronunciation. Then write each word one time on your shorthand machine. Transcribe from your shorthand one time on your computer, or, if you are using computer-aided transcription (CAT), proofread and edit your transcript.

allege	malicious prosecution	double jeopardy
act of God	jointly and severally	feasance
malfeasance	statute of limitations	statute of frauds
per se	alias	minor
sui juris		

SENTENCES

Keyboarding Procedure
Key each of the following sentences one time on your computer. Concentrate on the correct spelling and pronunciation of each underlined legal term.

Machine Shorthand Procedure
Write the following sentences one time on your shorthand machine. Transcribe from your shorthand notes one time on your computer, or, if you are using computer-aided transcription (CAT), proofread and edit your transcript.

These sentences will be used for practice dictation on the Transcription CD.

<u>Allege</u> means to make a charge or an allegation. If the plaintiff starts a legal action without justification and with the intention of damaging the defendant, it is called <u>malicious prosecution</u>. Malicious prosecution cases terminate in favor of the defendant, and the plaintiff cannot recover in such cases. A second prosecution for the same offense is referred to as <u>double jeopardy</u>. Under our laws, a person cannot be tried for the same crime twice. So, if a person has been found innocent of a crime in a court of law, that person can never be tried for the same crime again.

When a disaster occurs as a result of natural causes unaided by any human action, it is called an <u>act of God</u>. No person can be held responsible for an act of God, and, therefore, no legal action can be taken for any loss from such an occurrence.

<u>Jointly and severally</u> refers to a situation where there is more than one party responsible for a liability, and they may all be sued together or they may be sued separately. If, for example, you and a friend rent an apartment together and the lease contains a jointly and severally clause, then either one of you may be held totally responsible for the full amount of the rent.

The proper performance of a legal act is feasance, but the performance of an illegal act or misconduct is called <u>malfeasance</u>. The <u>statute of limitations</u> is a law that requires an action to be started within a certain length of time after the alleged cause occurred. The <u>statute of frauds</u> is an act that requires that certain kinds of contracts must be in writing before an action based on the contracts can be instituted.

<u>Per se</u> is a Latin term meaning by itself or in itself. If a person is called by an assumed name, he or she is said to have an <u>alias</u>. A <u>minor</u> is one who is too young to be considered legally competent, but <u>sui juris</u> refers to one that is legally capable of managing his or her own actions.

TRANSCRIBING FROM DICTATION

Directions: This dictation emphasizes and reinforces the legal terms and definitions you have studied. Listen carefully to the pronunciation of each of the legal terms. Unless otherwise directed, use 1-inch margins and double spacing. Correct all errors. Follow one of the procedures below.

Keyboarding Procedure

Using the Transcription CD, Lesson 3, Part B, transcribe the dictation directly at your computer.

Machine Shorthand Procedure

Using the Transcription CD, Lesson 3, Part B, take the dictation on your shorthand machine and then transcribe from your notes on your computer, or, if you are using computer-aided transcription (CAT), proofread and edit your transcript.

When you have finished transcribing Part B of the practice dictation, check your transcript with the printed copy. If you made any mistakes in the transcription, you should review and practice those words several times before going on to Lesson 4.

CHECKLIST

I have completed the following for Lesson 3:

	Part A, Date	Part B, Date	Submitted to Instructor Yes	No
Terminology and Definitions				
Self-Evaluation				
* Keying Legal Terms				
Words				
Sentences				
* Transcribing from Dictation				

When you have successfully completed all the exercises in this lesson and submitted to your instructor those requested, you are ready to proceed with Lesson 4.

* If you are using machine shorthand, submit to your instructor your notes along with your transcript.

Lesson
4

General Legal Terms

"Ignorance of the law is no excuse."

—*Legal maxim*

This lesson continues the study of some of the general legal terms that are applicable to all areas of law. When you have completed these exercises, you will have a knowledge and an understanding of the most common general legal terminology. This information will give you a good background for studying the terms dealing with specific legal procedures and the various areas of law.

Part A | TERMINOLOGY AND DEFINITIONS

Directions: Study the terms, pronunciations, and definitions until you are thoroughly familiar with them. In order to complete this lesson successfully, you must understand the meaning and usage of all the legal terms presented. If you are using a shorthand system, write each legal term one time on your shorthand machine.

Legal Term	Pronunciation	Definition
1. ancillary	′an-sə-ler-ē	A secondary proceeding that is based upon another proceeding. An example of an ancillary proceeding would be a situation where a person who dies owns property in a state other than the one where he or she lived. The will would be probated in the state in which that person had lived, and an ancillary proceeding would be filed in the other state in which property was owned.
2. cause of action	′kȯz əv ′ak-shən	The facts that are the basis for a lawsuit. This is a general term that varies from state to state and from one case to another.
3. interpolate	in-′tər-pə-lāt	To alter a document by adding an additional word or words.
4. ipso facto	′ip-sō ′fak-tō	Latin. By the fact itself.
5. sui generis	′sü-ī ′jen-ə-rəs	Latin. Of its own kind. Unique.
6. to wit	tü wit	Namely or scilicet. When used in legal documents, it is preceded by a general term and followed by a term that specifically identifies the general term (for example, assault with a deadly weapon, to wit: a gun).
7. scilicet	′si-lə-set	Latin. To wit. Namely. May be abbreviated as ss. or SS.

8. testimonium clause	tes-tə-ˈmō-nē-əm klȯz	A clause at the end of a document stating that the parties have signed under oath as to the document's contents. Usually begins with "In Witness Whereof" or "In Testimony Whereof" and includes the signatures of the parties. (See Figure 4-1, page 47.)
9. acknowledgment	ik-ˈnäl-ij-mənt	A formal statement made before an authorized person, usually a notary public, whereby one states that the instrument was signed willfully and freely. (See Figure 4-2, page 47.)
10. notary public	ˈnōt-ə-rē ˈpəb-lik	A public officer who is authorized to administer oaths and to certify that documents or instruments are genuine and that the documents were signed in the notary public's presence.
11. seal	sēl	A sign or an impression used to certify that a document or an instrument is genuine.
12. locus sigilli	ˈlō-kəs si-ˈjil-ī	Latin. The place of the seal. Abbreviation L.S. is often used.
13. legal back	ˈlē-gəl bak	A cover prepared for legal documents on which the endorsement is usually printed. It usually includes the names of the parties, the document title, the date executed, and the attorney's name or law firm that prepared it. (See Figure 4-3, page 48.)
14. endorsement	in-ˈdȯr-smənt	Information written on the back of a legal document. (See Figure 4-3, page 48.)

FIGURE 4-1   A Testimonium Clause

~~~~~~

On this _16th_ day of _____June_____ , A.D., 2003,

JAMES NELSON COLE, the above-named Testator, signed the foregoing

instrument in our presence and at the same time declared it to be

his Last Will and Testament, and we do now at his request and in

his presence and in the presence of each other, subscribe our names

as witnesses hereof.

_Brenda S. Reynolds_____   residing at _411 Saunders Road_____
BRENDA S. REYNOLDS   _Lansing_____ , Michigan

_Scott W. Morrison_____   residing at _809 Vanderbilt Drive_____
SCOTT W. MORRISON   _Okemos_____ , Michigan

_Candace N. Ivy_____   residing at _8943 University Drive_____
CANDACE N. IVY   _East Lansing_ , Michigan

-Page Eight and Last-

~~~~~~

FIGURE 4-2   An Acknowledgment

~~~~~~

IN WITNESS WHEREOF, The said party of the first part

has hereunto set her hand the day and year first above written.

_Andrea M. Sanson___   **Seal**
ANDREA M. SANSON

STATE OF MICHIGAN)
) ss.
COUNTY OF INGHAM)

On _____June 11_____ , 2003, before me, a Notary

Public, in and for said County, personally appeared ANDREA M.

SANSON to me known to be the same person described in and who

executed the within instrument, who acknowledged the same to be

her free act and deed.

_Robert T. Gates_____   **Notary Public**
                Notary Public

Ingham County, Michigan

My commission expires: ___July 2___ ,2005.

~~~~~~

FIGURE 4-3   A Legal Back

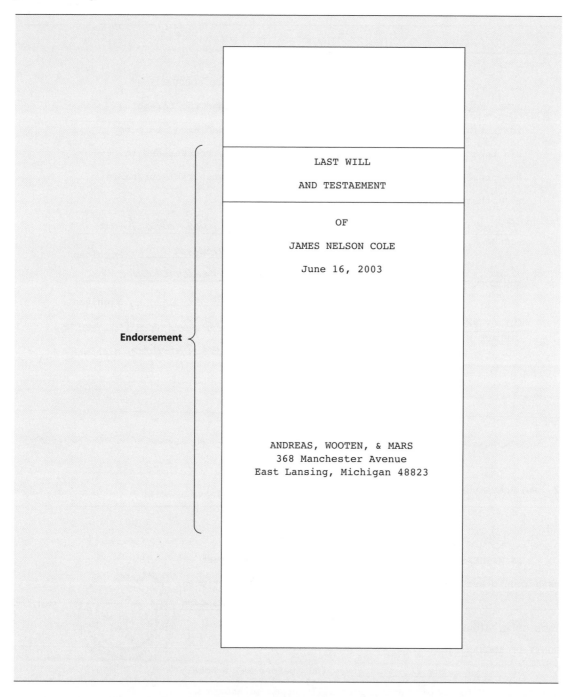

Endorsement

LAST WILL

AND TESTAEMENT

OF

JAMES NELSON COLE

June 16, 2003

ANDREAS, WOOTEN, & MARS
368 Manchester Avenue
East Lansing, Michigan 48823

Self-Evaluation A | Terminology and Definition Recall

Directions: In the Answers column, write the legal term that is most representative of the corresponding statement. After you have completed this self-evaluation, check your answers with the key on page 494. If you have any incorrect answers, review the definitions for those terms before going on with this lesson. Then unless otherwise directed, submit this self-evaluation to your instructor.

ANSWERS

1. A Latin term meaning by the fact itself is _____.

    1. _____

2. A formal statement made before an authorized person, usually a notary public, whereby one states that the instrument was signed willfully and freely, is referred to as a/an _____.

    2. _____

3. A clause at the end of a document stating that the parties have signed under oath as to the document's contents is a/an _____.

    3. _____

4. A Latin term for to wit is _____.

    4. _____

5. A Latin term meaning of its own kind or unique is _____.

    5. _____

6. The facts that are the basis for a lawsuit are referred to as the _____.

    6. _____

7. The Latin term for the place of the seal is _____.

    7. _____

8. A cover prepared for legal documents on which the endorsement is printed is called a/an _____.

    8. _____

9. A public officer who is authorized to administer oaths and to certify that documents or instruments are genuine is a/an _____.

    9. _____

10. Information written on the back of a legal document is called a/an _____.

    10. _____

11. A sign or an impression used to certify that a document or an instrument is genuine is a/an _____.

    11. _____

12. A term meaning namely or scilicet, which when used in legal documents, is preceded by a general term and followed by a term that specifically identifies the general term, is _____.

    12. _____

13. To alter a document by adding an additional word or words is to _____.

    13. _____

14. A secondary proceeding that is based upon another proceeding is a/an _____ proceeding.

    14. _____

KEYING LEGAL TERMS

Directions: Unless otherwise instructed, use 1-inch margins and double spacing. Correct all errors. Follow one of the procedures below.

WORDS

Keyboarding Procedure
On your computer, key the following words at least two times, concentrating on the correct spelling and pronunciation.

Machine Shorthand Procedure
On your computer, key the following words once, concentrating on the correct spelling and pronunciation. Then write each word one time on your shorthand machine. Transcribe from your shorthand notes one time on your computer, or, if you are using computer-aided transcription (CAT), proofread and edit your transcript.

ancillary	cause of action	interpolate
ipso facto	sui generis	to wit
scilicet	testimonium clause	acknowledgment
notary public	seal	locus sigilli
legal back	endorsement	

SENTENCES

Keyboarding Procedure
Key each of the following sentences one time on your computer. Concentrate on the correct spelling and pronunciation of each underlined legal term.

Machine Shorthand Procedure
Write the following sentences one time on your shorthand machine. Transcribe from your shorthand notes one time on your computer, or, if you are using computer-aided transcription (CAT), proofread and edit your transcript.

These sentences will be used for practice dictation on the Transcription CD.

An <u>ancillary</u> proceeding is a secondary proceeding that is based upon another proceeding. For example, if you were living in the state of Kansas and owned property in the state of New Mexico, your will would be probated in Kansas, and an ancillary proceeding would be filed in New Mexico.

A <u>cause of action</u> refers to the facts that are the basis for a lawsuit. To <u>interpolate</u> is to alter a document by adding an additional word or words. <u>Ipso facto</u> is a Latin term meaning by the fact itself. The Latin term <u>sui generis</u> means of its own kind or unique. <u>To wit</u> and <u>scilicet</u> are synonymous terms. Scilicet is the Latin word for to wit. Scilicet and to wit mean that is to say or namely. When used in legal documents, they are preceded by a general term and followed by a term that specifically identifies the general term.

The <u>testimonium clause</u> is a clause at the end of a document stating that the parties have signed under oath as to the document's contents. An <u>acknowledgment</u>, made before an authorized person, usually states that the party willfully and freely signed the instrument.

Documents or instruments are certified as genuine by a <u>notary public</u>. A notary public may also administer oaths. The notary public <u>seal</u> is a sign or an impression used to certify that a document or an instrument is genuine. <u>Locus sigilli</u> is a Latin term meaning the place of the seal. The place where the seal is on a legal document is usually indicated by L.S., the abbreviation for locus sigilli.

A <u>legal back</u> is a cover prepared for a legal document that provides a place for the <u>endorsement</u>. An endorsement is information written on the back of a legal document. The endorsement on the back of a legal document usually includes the names of the parties, the title of the document, the date executed, and the attorney's name.

TRANSCRIBING FROM DICTATION

Directions: This dictation emphasizes and reinforces the legal terms and definitions you have studied. Listen carefully to the pronunciation of each of the legal terms. Unless otherwise directed, use 1-inch margins and double spacing. Correct all errors. Follow one of the procedures below.

Keyboarding Procedure
Using the Transcription CD, Lesson 4, Part A, transcribe the dictation directly at your computer.

Machine Shorthand Procedure
Using the Transcription CD, Lesson 4, Part A, take the dictation on your shorthand machine and then transcribe from your notes on your computer, or, if you are using computer-aided transcription (CAT), proofread and edit your transcript.

When you have finished transcribing Part A of the practice dictation, check your transcript with the printed copy. If you made any mistakes in the transcription, you should review and practice those words several times before going on to Part B.

Part B | TERMINOLOGY AND DEFINITIONS

Directions: Study the terms, pronunciations, and definitions until you are thoroughly familiar with them. In order to complete this lesson successfully, you must understand the meaning and usage of all the legal terms presented. If you are using a shorthand system, write each legal term one time on your shorthand machine.

Legal Term	Pronunciation	Definition
1. incriminate	in-ˈkrim-ə-nāt	To accuse one of a crime. Also, to put oneself or another in danger of being charged with a crime.
2. quasi	ˈkwā-zĭ	Latin. Almost, but not actually, the same as. This term is usually used with another term (for example, quasi ex contractu, which means as if from a contract).
3. chose in action	ˈshōz in ˈak-shən	Personal property that one has a right to but is in the possession of another. Such property may be recovered through a lawsuit.
4. irrevocable	ir-ˈev-ə-kə-bəl	Something that is final and cannot be undone or taken back.
5. recidivist	ri-ˈsid-ə-vəst	One who repeatedly commits criminal acts and cannot be reformed.
6. penal	ˈpēn-l	Having to do with punishment or a penalty.
7. ensue	in-ˈsü	To follow or to come after.

8. collusion	kə-'lü-zhən	When two or more persons secretly agree to participate in a fraudulent act.
9. fraud	frȯd	A misrepresentation of the facts done intentionally to deceive or mislead another. If you buy a ring that you are told is a diamond and it is really cut glass, the person who sold it to you is guilty of fraud.
10. duress	du̇-'res	The use of force to get someone to do something unwillingly. If you do something because another person threatens you, then you did the act under duress.
11. malice	'mal-əs	Purposely doing something that will harm another. An evil intent.
12. turpitude	'tər-pə-tüd	Something that is corrupt, shameful, wicked, or immoral.
13. mens rea	menz 'rē-ə	Latin. A guilty mind or a criminal intent.

Self-Evaluation B | Terminology and Definition Recall

Directions: In the Answers column, write the letter from Column 1 that represents the word or phrase that best matches each item in Column 2. After you have completed this self-evaluation, check your answers with the key on page 494. If you have any incorrect answers, review the definitions for those terms before going on with this lesson. Then unless otherwise directed, submit this self-evaluation to your instructor.

COLUMN 1	COLUMN 2	ANSWERS
a. chose in action	1. To accuse one of a crime or to put oneself or another in danger of being charged with a crime.	1. _____
b. collusion	2. Intentionally deceiving or misleading another by misrepresenting the facts.	2. _____
c. duress	3. Intangible personal property that one has a right to but is in the possession of another and may be recovered through a lawsuit.	3. _____
d. ensue	4. Something that is final and cannot be undone or taken back.	4. _____
e. fraud	5. One who repeats criminal acts and cannot be reformed.	5. _____
f. incriminate	6. A legal term that refers to punishment or a penalty.	6. _____
g. irrevocable	7. A Latin term meaning almost, but not actually, the same as.	7. _____
h. malice	8. To follow or to come after.	8. _____
i. malfeasance	9. Purposely doing something that will harm another or an evil intent.	9. _____
j. mens rea	10. A Latin term meaning a guilty mind or a criminal intent.	10. _____
k. penal	11. Two or more persons secretly agreeing to participate in a fraudulent act.	11. _____
l. quasi	12. Something that is corrupt, shameful, wicked, or immoral.	12. _____
m. recidivist	13. The use of force or threats to get someone to do something against his or her will.	13. _____
n. turpitude		

KEYING LEGAL TERMS

Directions: Unless otherwise instructed, use 1-inch margins and double spacing. Correct all errors. Follow one of the procedures below.

WORDS

Keyboarding Procedure
On your computer, key the following words at least two times, concentrating on the correct spelling and pronunciation.

Machine Shorthand Procedure
On your computer, key the following words once, concentrating on the correct spelling and pronunciation. Then write each word one time on your shorthand machine. Transcribe from your shorthand notes one time on your computer, or, if you are using computer-aided transcription (CAT), proofread and edit your transcript.

incriminate	quasi	chose in action
irrevocable	recidivist	penal
ensue	collusion	fraud
duress	malice	turpitude
mens rea		

SENTENCES

Keyboarding Procedure
Key each of the following sentences one time on your computer. Concentrate on the correct spelling and pronunciation of each underlined legal term.

Machine Shorthand Procedure
Write the following sentences one time on your shorthand machine. Transcribe from your shorthand notes one time on your computer, or, if you are using computer-aided transcription (CAT), proofread and edit your transcript.

These sentences will be used for practice dictation on the Transcription CD.

<u>Incriminate</u> is a term that means to accuse one of a crime or to put oneself or another in danger of being charged with a crime. One cannot be forced to testify in a case to anything that a person feels might incriminate himself or herself in a crime. <u>Quasi</u> is used to indicate that something is almost, but not actually, the same as. A quasi-legal matter would refer to one that is almost, but not entirely, a legal matter.

A <u>chose in action</u> is a right to personal property that is in the possession of another. A chose in action may be recovered through a lawsuit. If an act or deed is final and cannot be undone or changed, it is said to be <u>irrevocable</u>.

A <u>recidivist</u>, one who repeats criminal acts and cannot be reformed, would probably spend many years in a <u>penal</u> institution. Penal refers to something having to do with punishment or a penalty. To <u>ensue</u> is a term meaning to follow or to come after.

<u>Collusion</u>, <u>fraud</u>, <u>duress</u>, <u>malice</u>, <u>turpitude</u>, and <u>mens rea</u> are all terms that refer to some kind of illegal act. If you make an agreement with another person to defraud someone of their rights or to obtain an object forbidden by law, it is collusion. If a person intentionally lies for the purpose of deceiving or misleading

another, that person is guilty of fraud. Therefore, if only one person is involved in committing the illegal act, it is fraud. If two or more persons are involved, it is collusion. Duress is the use of force to get someone to do something unwillingly. Duress, fraud, and collusion all involve malice and mens rea because the intent is evil and wrongful. Turpitude also applies to something that is corrupt, shameful, wicked, or immoral.

TRANSCRIBING FROM DICTATION

Directions: This dictation emphasizes and reinforces the legal terms and definitions you have studied. Listen carefully to the pronunciation of each of the legal terms. Unless otherwise directed, use 1-inch margins and double spacing. Correct all errors. Follow one of the procedures below.

Keyboarding Procedure

Using the Transcription CD, Lesson 4, Part B, transcribe the dictation directly at your computer.

Machine Shorthand Procedure

Using the Transcription CD, Lesson 4, Part B, take the dictation on your shorthand machine and then transcribe from your notes on your computer, or, if you are using computer-aided transcription (CAT), proofread and edit your transcript.

When you have finished transcribing Part B of the practice dictation, check your transcript with the printed copy. If you made any mistakes in the transcription, you should review and practice those words several times before going on to Evaluation 2.

CHECKLIST

I have completed the following for Lesson 4:

	Part A, Date	Part B, Date	Submitted to Instructor Yes	No
Terminology and Definitions	_____	_____	_____	_____
Self-Evaluation	_____	_____	_____	_____
* Keying Legal Terms	_____	_____	_____	_____
Words	_____	_____	_____	_____
Sentences	_____	_____	_____	_____
* Transcribing from Dictation	_____	_____	_____	_____

When you have successfully completed all the exercises in this lesson and submitted to your instructor those requested, you are ready to proceed with Evaluation 2.

* If you are using machine shorthand, submit to your instructor your notes along with your transcript.

Evaluation No. 2 | SECTION A

Directions: This dictation/transcription evaluation will test your spelling and transcription abilities on the legal terms that you studied in the two preceding lessons. Tab once for a paragraph indention, and use 1-inch margins, and double spacing unless otherwise instructed. Correct all errors. Follow one of the procedures below.

Keyboarding Procedure

Using the Transcription CD, Evaluation 2, transcribe the dictation directly at your computer.

Machine Shorthand Procedure

Using the Transcription CD, Evaluation 2, take the dictation on your shorthand machine and then transcribe your notes on your computer, or, if you are using computer-aided transcription (CAT), proofread and edit your computerized transcript. **Sections B and C are available from your instructor.**

Lesson

5

Litigation—Pretrial

Before a case goes to trial, there are many pretrial activities that must take place. Many of these activities involve law office and court personnel; therefore, you should have knowledge and a good understanding of these terms. The terms to be studied in the following exercises will acquaint you with the terminology involved with several of the pretrial activities. To complete this lesson successfully, you should be able to spell, define, pronounce, and transcribe correctly from dictation each of the terms presented.

Part A | TERMINOLOGY AND DEFINITIONS

Directions: Study the terms, pronunciations, and definitions until you are thoroughly familiar with them. In order to complete this lesson successfully, you must understand the meaning and usage of all the legal terms presented. If you are using a shorthand system, write each legal term one time on your shorthand machine.

Legal Term	Pronunciation	Definition
1. caption	′kap-shən	The title page of a court document which includes the case title, the jurisdiction, the venue, the court or docket number, and the document title. Also called style of case. (See Figure 5-1, page 63.)
2. venue	′ven-yü	The geographical location where a case is tried. A change of venue for a case means that the case is tried at a location different from where the case originated. (See Figure 5-1, page 63.)
3. jurisdiction	jür-əs-′dik- shən	The right or authority of a court to hear and adjudge cases. (See Figure 5-1, page 63.)
4. case title	kās ′tit-l	The part of a legal document that contains the names of the parties to the suit. (See Figure 5-1, page 63.)
5. Doe clause	dō klȯz	Fictitious names in a case title. When the name or names of all defendants involved are not known, the unknown defendants are usually referred to as John and Mary Doe. (See Figure 5-1, page 63.)
6. ad damnum clause	ad ′dam-nəm klȯz	Latin. A clause in a complaint that states the plaintiff's damage. (See Figure 5-2, page 63.)
7. prayer for relief	prar fər ri-′lēf	The summary at the end of a complaint that requests the court to grant the plaintiff's demands. (See Figure 5-2, page 63.)

8. filed	fīld	Papers that are placed with the clerk of a court. When papers are placed with the clerk of a court, the papers have been filed.
9. summons	´səm-ənz	A writ that notifies a defendant that a lawsuit has been filed and an appearance must be made before the court at a specified time to answer the charges. (See Figure 5-3, page 64.)
10. service	´sər-vəs	The delivery of a summons to the person named therein. When a person receives a summons, that person has been served. Depending on the state and the type of case, service may be made by a process server (in person or by attachment—posting on the door of the address listed in the summons), by mail, or by publication.
11. appearance	ə-´pir-əns	To be present in court as a party to a lawsuit.
12. answer	´an-sər	A pleading that states the defendant's defense against plaintiff's claims. Also referred to as a response and is sometimes called a responsive pleading.
13. demurrer to complaint	di-´mər-ər tü kəm-´plānt	Disputes the sufficiency in law of the pleading of the other side. The defendant states in a demurrer to complaint that even if the facts in the case are true, there is no legal basis for the complaint; therefore, the defendant should not have to answer the charges.
14. bill of particulars	bil əv pə-´tik-ə-lərs	The detailed facts upon which a complaint is based. Usually supplied by the plaintiff upon the request of the defendant.

FIGURE 5-1 A Caption

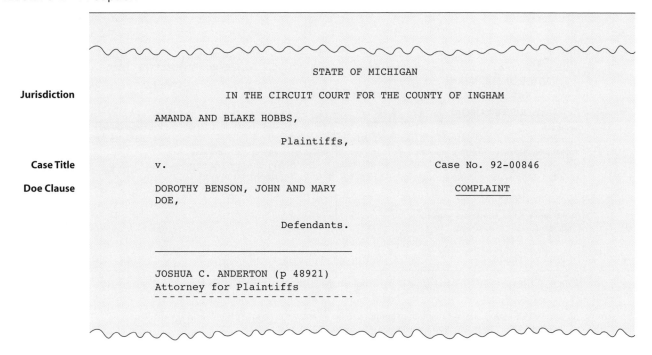

Jurisdiction

Case Title

Doe Clause

STATE OF MICHIGAN

IN THE CIRCUIT COURT FOR THE COUNTY OF INGHAM

AMANDA AND BLAKE HOBBS,

               Plaintiffs,

v.   Case No. 92-00846

DOROTHY BENSON, JOHN AND MARY   COMPLAINT
DOE,

               Defendants.

JOSHUA C. ANDERTON (p 48921)
Attorney for Plaintiffs

FIGURE 5-2 An Ad Damnum Clause and A Prayer for Relief

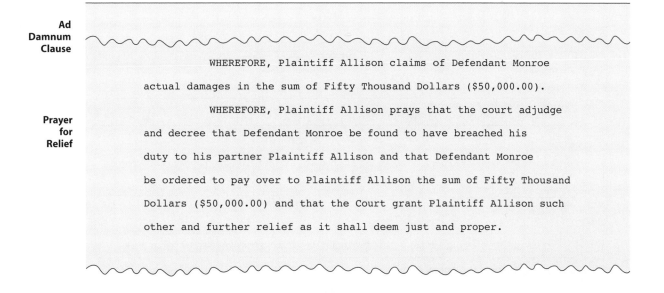

**Ad
Damnum
Clause**

**Prayer
for
Relief**

WHEREFORE, Plaintiff Allison claims of Defendant Monroe
actual damages in the sum of Fifty Thousand Dollars ($50,000.00).

WHEREFORE, Plaintiff Allison prays that the court adjudge
and decree that Defendant Monroe be found to have breached his
duty to his partner Plaintiff Allison and that Defendant Monroe
be ordered to pay over to Plaintiff Allison the sum of Fifty Thousand
Dollars ($50,000.00) and that the Court grant Plaintiff Allison such
other and further relief as it shall deem just and proper.

FIGURE 5-3 A Summons

		ORIGINAL - Court 2nd copy - Plaintiff 1st copy - Defendant 3rd copy - Return
STATE OF MICHIGAN XXXXXXXXXXXX 30th **JUDICIAL CIRCUIT**	**SUMMONS AND COMPLAINT**	**CASE NO.** 92-00846

Court address	Court telephone no.
2nd Floor, City Hall, Lansing, Michigan 48933	(517) 555-0650

Plaintiff name(s) and address(es) and telephone no(s).		Defendant name(s), address(es) and telephone no(s).
Amanda and Blake Hobbs 2421 Seaview River Road Lansing, Michigan 48906 (517) 555-9788	v.	Dorothy Benson, John and Mary Doe 55 Sandlewood Avenue Okemos, Michigan 48864

Plaintiff attorney, bar no., address and telephone no.

Joshua C. Anderton (P 48921)
688 S. Capitol Avenue, Suite 11
Lansing, Michigan 48933
(517) 555-1664

NOTICE TO THE DEFENDANT: In the name of the people of the State of Michigan you are notified:

1. You are being sued.

2. YOU HAVE 21 DAYS after receiving this summons to file an answer or to take other lawful action (28 days if you were served by mail or you were served outside this state).

3. If you do not answer or take other action within the time allowed, judgment may be entered against you for the relief demanded in the complaint.

Issued	This summons expires	Court clerk
6/11/03	12/10/03	*Lois McMahon*

*This summons is invalid unless served on or before its expiration date.

☒ There is no other civil action between these parties arising out of the same transaction or occurrence as alleged in this complaint pending in this court, nor has any such action been previously filed and dismissed or transferred after having been assigned to a judge.

☐ There is now on file in this court a civil action between these parties arising out of the same transaction or occurrence as alleged in the complaint. The action ☐ is pending ☐ was dismissed was transferred. The case number and assigned judge are;

Case no.	Judge	Bar no.

VENUE	
Plaintiff(s) residence	Defendant(s) residence
Lansing, Ingham Co., Michigan	Okemos, Ingham Co., Michigan
Place where action arose or business conducted	
Lansing, Ingham Co., Michigan	

I declare that the complaint information above and attached is true to the best of my information, knowledge, and belief.

June 11, 2003	*Joshua C. Anderton*
Date	Signature of attorney XXXX

COMPLAINT IS STATED ON ATTACHED PAGES. EXHIBITS ARE ATTACHED IF REQUIRED BY COURT RULE.

MC 01 (10/85) **SUMMONS AND COMPLAINT**   MCR 2.102(B) (11), MCR 2.104, MCR 2.107, MCR 2-113(C)(2)(a) and (b)

COURT

Self-Evaluation A | Terminology and Definition Recall

Directions: In the Answers column at the right of each statement, write the letter that represents the word or group of words that correctly completes the statement. After you have completed this self-evaluation, check your answers with the key on page 494. If you have any incorrect answers, review the definitions for those terms before going on with this lesson. Then unless otherwise directed, submit this self-evaluation to your instructor.

ANSWERS

1. If a defendant answers the claims of the plaintiff by stating that even if the facts as presented are true, the claims are not sufficient for a legal action, the answer is called a/an (a) ad damnum clause, (b) Doe clause, (c) demurrer to complaint.

1. _____

2. A clause in a complaint that states the plaintiff's damages is the (a) Doe clause, (b) prayer for relief, (c) ad damnum clause.

2. _____

3. When the names of one or more defendants in a suit are not known, they are identified in the case title by a (a) Doe clause, (b) venue, (c) service.

3. _____

4. The summary at the end of a complaint that requests the court to grant the plaintiff's demands is the (a) prayer for relief, (b) demurrer to complaint, (c) ad damnum clause.

4. _____

5. The right or authority of a court to hear and adjudge cases is referred to as (a) service, (b) venue, (c) jurisdiction.

5. _____

6. The pleading that states the defendant's defense against the plaintiff's claims is the (a) prayer for relief, (b) answer, (c) bill of particulars.

6. _____

7. A writ notifying a defendant that a lawsuit has been filed and an appearance must be made before the court at a specified time to answer the charges is a/an (a) demurrer to complaint, (b) summons, (c) appearance.

7. _____

8. The title page of a court document is the (a) caption, (b) bill of particulars, (c) case title.

8. _____

9. The detailed facts upon which a complaint is based that are usually supplied by the plaintiff upon request of the defendant are contained in a document called a/an (a) summons, (b) answer, (c) bill of particulars.

9. _____

10. The part of a legal document that contains the names of the parties to the suit is called the (a) case title, (b) caption, (c) jurisdiction.

10. _____

11. The delivery of a summons to the person named therein is called (a) service, (b) filed, (c) venue.

11. _____

12. The geographical location where a case is tried is the (a) jurisdiction, (b) appearance, (c) venue.

12. _____

13. Papers that are placed with the clerk of a court are said to be (a) served, (b) filed, (c) answered.

13. _____

14. To be present in a court as a party to a lawsuit is to make a/an (a) caption, (b) service, (c) appearance.

14. _____

KEYING LEGAL TERMS

Directions: Unless otherwise instructed, use 1-inch margins and double spacing. Correct all errors. Follow one of the procedures below.

WORDS

Keyboarding Procedure
On your computer, key the following words at least two times, concentrating on the correct spelling and pronunciation.

Machine Shorthand Procedure
On your computer, key the following words once, concentrating on the correct spelling and pronunciation. Then write each word one time on your shorthand machine. Transcribe from your shorthand notes one time on your computer, or, if you are using computer-aided transcription (CAT), proofread and edit your transcript.

caption	venue	jurisdiction
case title	Doe clause	ad damnum clause
prayer for relief	filed	summons
appearance	service	answer
demurrer to complaint	bill of particulars	

SENTENCES

Keyboarding Procedure
Key each of the following sentences one time on your computer. Concentrate on the correct spelling and pronunciation of each underlined legal term.

Machine Shorthand Procedure
Write the following sentences one time on your shorthand machine. Transcribe from your shorthand notes one time on your computer, or, if you are using computer-aided transcription, proofread and edit your transcript.

These sentences will be used for practice dictation on the Transcription CD.

The **caption** is the title page of a court document and includes the **venue**, the **jurisdiction**, the **case title**, the court case number, and the document title. The venue is the geographical location where a case is tried. A request for change of venue would be a request to have the case tried in another court in a different geographical area. This might occur when the court feels that a defendant could not get a fair trial in the area where the case originated because of too much publicity before the trial. The jurisdiction is the right or authority of a court to hear and adjudge cases. Courts can only hear and decide cases that fall within their jurisdiction. The case title, which is also located in the caption, names the parties to the lawsuit. If the names of one or more of the defendants to a suit are not known, a **Doe clause** is used in the case title. The unknown defendants are then referred to as John and Mary Doe.

The statement of the plaintiff's damages in the complaint is called the **ad damnum** clause. The summary at the end of a complaint that requests the court to grant the plaintiff's demands is the **prayer for relief**. Court documents are **filed** with the clerk of a court. All documents involving a court must be filed with the clerk.

If a person is served with a **summons**, that person is a defendant in a lawsuit and must make an appearance before the court at a specified time to answer the charges. The delivery of a summons to the person named therein is known as the <u>service</u>. When the defendant has received the summons, the defendant is said to have been served.

An appearance is to be present in court as a party to a lawsuit. If one makes an appearance, the person comes into court as a party to a suit. The pleading by which the defendant states the defense against the plaintiff's claims is an <u>answer</u>. A <u>demurrer to complaint</u> is a formal method of saying that the claims of the other side are not sufficient in law for a legal action. In a demurrer to complaint, the defendant states that even though the facts in the plaintiff's charges may be true, there is no legal basis for the suit. Therefore the defendant should not have to answer the charges. The <u>bill of particulars</u> supplies the defendant with the detailed facts upon which a complaint is based.

TRANSCRIBING FROM DICTATION

Directions: This dictation emphasizes and reinforces the legal terms you have studied. Listen carefully to the pronunciation of each of the legal terms. Unless otherwise directed, use 1-inch margins and double spacing. Correct all errors. Follow one of the procedures below.

Keyboarding Procedure
Using the Transcription CD, Lesson 5, Part A, transcribe the dictation directly at your computer.

Machine Shorthand Procedure
Using the Transcription CD, Lesson 5, Part A, take the dictation on your shorthand machine and then transcribe from your notes on your computer, or, if you are using computer-aided transcription (CAT), proofread and edit your transcript.

When you have finished transcribing or proofreading and editing Part A of the practice dictation, check your transcript with the printed copy. If you made any mistakes in the transcription, you should review and practice those words several times before going on to Part B.

Part B | Terminology and Definitions

Directions: Study the terms, pronunciations, and definitions until you are thoroughly familiar with them. In order to complete this lesson successfully, you must understand the meaning and usage of all the legal terms presented. If you are using a shorthand system, write each legal term one time on your shorthand machine.

Legal Term	Pronunciation	Definition
1. omnibus clause	′äm-ni-bəs klóz	A clause at the end of the prayer for relief in a complaint that makes it possible for the court to award relief other than that specifically requested by the plaintiff. (See Figure 5-4, page 70.)
2. motion	′mō-shən	A written or an oral application made to a court or judge for a rule or an order. (See Figure 5-5, page 71.)
3. court docket	kōrt ′däk-ət	A record of the dates and times that cases are to be tried in court.
4. counterclaim	′kaůnt-ər-klām	A claim made by the defendant as a result of the plaintiff's charges in the lawsuit.

5.	cross plaintiff	kròs ′plānt-əf	A defendant who brings a cross-claim against a plaintiff in the same action. Also referred to as cross complainant.
6.	cross defendant	′kròs di-′fen-dənt	The plaintiff who is named as defendant in a cross-claim.
7.	cross-claim	′kròs-klām	A claim brought by a defendant against a plaintiff and/or a codefendant to seek relief against either in the event that there is recovery.
8.	reply	ri-′plī	The plaintiff's answer to the defendant's answer or counterclaim.
9.	recrimination	ri-krim-ə-′nā-shən	A countercharge or counterclaim.
10.	intervenor	int-ər-′vē-nər	A person not originally a party to a suit who voluntarily enters into the action to protect some interest that he or she claims to have in the case.
11.	affidavit	af-ə-′dā-vət	A voluntary written statement made under oath before a notary public or other qualified official. (See Figure 5-6, page 72.)
12.	affiant	ə-′fī-ənt	A person who makes an affidavit. (See Figure 5-6, page 72.)
13.	jurat	′jùr-at	A clause at the end of an affidavit that verifies the time, place, and person before whom the affidavit was made. A jurat begins with the words "SWORN TO AND SUB-SCRIBED." (See Figure 5-6, page 72.)
14.	verification	ver-ə-fə-′kā-shən	Confirmation of the truth of a document made under oath before a notary public.

FIGURE 5-4 An Omnibus Clause

Omnibus Clause

> WHEREFORE, Plaintiff Allison prays that the court adjudge and decree that Defendant Monroe be found to have breached his duty to his partner Plaintiff Allison and that Defendant Monroe be ordered to pay over to Plaintiff Allison a sum in excess of Ten Thousand Dollars ($10,000.00) and that the Court grant Plaintiff Allison such other and further relief as it shall deem just and proper.

FIGURE 5-5 A Motion

STATE OF MICHIGAN

IN THE CIRCUIT COURT FOR THE COUNTY OF INGHAM

AMANDA AND BLAKE HOBBS,

                Plaintiffs,   Case No. 92-00846

v.   MOTION TO QUASH

DOROTHY BENSON, JOHN AND MARY   SUBPOENA DUCES TECUM
DOE,

                Defendants.

_____

JOSHUA C. ANDERTON (P 48921)
Attorney for Plaintiffs
688 S. Capitol Avenue, Suite 11
Lansing, MI 48933
(517) 555-1664

MARIE S. STANLEY (P 55901)
Attorney for Defendants
- -

        NOW COMES Plaintiff Amanda and Blake Hobbs, by and through their attorney, Joshua C. Anderton, and moves this Court under MCR 2.302(c) for an order to quash the subpoena served upon plaintiffs, and in support thereof states as follows:

        1. The attached subpoena (Exhibit A) was served upon Plaintiffs Amanda and Blake Hobbs, seeking production of plaintiffs' income tax returns for the years 2001 through 2002.

        2. The subopoena requests documentation which is totally irrelevant to the instant case in which plaintiffs seek recovery under a contract between the parties. MCR 2.302 (B) (1) limits discovery of nonprivileged materials to those which are relevant.

        3. The subpoena served upon plaintiffs is incapable of being complied with without undue burden, annoyance, embarrassment, expense, and oppression.

        4. The time in the subpoena in which plaintiff is given to produce the required documents is unreasonably short.

        WHEREFORE, plaintiffs respectfully request this Court to quash the subpoena. Further, plaintiffs respectfully request this Court to award them their attorney fees and costs necessitated and incurred in obtaining this order.

                       Respectfully submitted,

Dated: _July 28, 2003_   _Joshua C. Anderton_
                           Joshua C. Anderton (P.48921)
                           Attorney for Plaintiffs

FIGURE 5-6 An Affidavit

AFFIDAVIT

STATE OF MICHIGAN)
) ss.
COUNTY OF INGHAM)

Affiant

DARREL L. KELLY being first duly sworn, says and deposes as follows:

1. That he resides at 4330 Spartan Boulevard, Mason, Michigan 48854.

2. On or about January 17, 2003, he was the purchaser in the closing of a transaction for real property commonly known as 516 Linden Street, East Lansing, Michigan, legally described as Lots 20 and 21, Assessor's Plat of Lot 51, of Angell's Subdivision, being Lot 80 and parts of Lots 78 and 79 of Collage Grove, City of East Lansing, Ingham County, Michigan.

3. The Warranty Deed delivered at said closing inadvertenty listed Daryl L. Kelly as the purchaser.

4. The undersigned is one and the same as Daryl L. Kelly.

Further, Deponent saith not.

Darrel L. Kelly
DARREL L. KELLY

ROBERT T. GATES NOTARY PUBLIC INGHAM COUNTY, MICH

Jurat

SWORN TO AND SUBSCRIBED before me this 23rd day of October 2003, by DARREL L. KELLY.

Robert T. Gates
Notary Public,
Ingham County, Michigan

My commission expires: July 2, 2005

Self-Evaluation B | Terminology and Definition Recall

Directions: In the Answers column, write the letter from Column 1 that represents the word or phrase that best matches each item in Column 2. After you have completed this self-evaluation, check your answers with the key on page 495. If you have any incorrect answers, review the definitions for those terms before going on with this lesson. Then unless otherwise directed, submit this self-evaluation to your instructor.

COLUMN 1	COLUMN 2	ANSWERS
a. affiant	1. The plaintiff's title when the plaintiff is named as defendant in a cross-claim.	1. _____
b. affidavit	2. A voluntary written statement made under oath before a notary public.	2. _____
c. counterclaim	3. A countercharge or a counterclaim.	3. _____
d. court calendar	4. The person who makes an affidavit.	4. _____
e. court docket	5. A clause at the end of a prayer for relief in a complaint that makes it possible for the court to award relief other than that specifically requested by the plaintiff.	5. _____
f. cross defendant		
g. cross plaintiff	6. A claim brought by a defendant against a plaintiff and/or a codefendant to seek relief against either in the event there is recovery in the suit.	6. _____
h. cross-claim		
i. intervenor	7. A person not originally a party to a suit who voluntarily enters into the action to protect some interest that he or she claims to have in the case.	7. _____
j. jurat		
k. motion	8. The plaintiff's response to the defendant's answer or counterclaim.	8. _____
l. omnibus clause		
m. recrimination	9. A record of the dates and times that cases are to be tried in court.	9. _____
n. reply		
o. verification	10. The defendant's title when the defendant brings a cross-claim against the plaintiff in the same proceeding.	10. _____
	11. A claim made by the defendant as a result of the plaintiff's charges in a lawsuit.	11. _____
	12. A clause at the end of an affidavit that verifies the time, place, and person before whom the affidavit was made.	12. _____
	13. An attachment to a document that confirms the truthfulness of the contents of the document.	13. _____
	14. A written or oral application made to a court or judge for a rule or an order.	14. _____

KEYING LEGAL TERMS

Directions: Unless otherwise instructed, use 1-inch margins and double spacing. Correct all errors. Follow one of the procedures below.

WORDS

Keyboarding Procedure
On your computer, key the following words at least two times, concentrating on the correct spelling and pronunciation.

Machine Shorthand Procedure
On your computer, key the following words once, concentrating on the correct spelling and pronunciation. Then write each word one time on your shorthand machine. Transcribe from your shorthand outlines one time on your computer, or, if you are using computer-aided transcription (CAT), proofread and edit your transcript.

omnibus clause	motion	court docket
counterclaim	cross plaintiff	cross defendant
cross-claim	reply	recrimination
intervenor	affidavit	jurat
affiant	verification	

SENTENCES

Keyboarding Procedure
Key each of the following sentences one time on your computer. Concentrate on the correct spelling and pronunciation of each underlined legal term.

Machine Shorthand Procedure
Write the following sentences one time on your shorthand machine. Transcribe from your shorthand notes one time on your computer, or, if you are using computer-aided transcription (CAT), proofread and edit your transcript.

These sentences will be used for practice dictation on the Transcription CD.

An <u>omnibus clause</u> makes it possible for the court to award relief other than that specifically requested by the plaintiff. For example, a plaintiff may request damages in excess of $10,000, whereby the court can then award more than $10,000 if the court so decides.

A written or an oral <u>motion</u> may be made to the court to have the trial date set. If the motion is honored, the trial date will be set and will be entered on the <u>court docket</u>. The defendant may file a <u>counterclaim</u> against the plaintiff in the same proceeding, the defendant becomes the <u>cross plaintiff</u>, or cross complainant, and the plaintiff then becomes the <u>cross defendant</u>. A defendant may bring a <u>cross-claim</u> against a codefendant or the plaintiff or both seeking relief from either in the event there is a recovery in the suit. The plaintiff files a <u>reply</u>, which is to answer to the defendant's counterclaim. A countercharge, or a counterclaim, is also called <u>recrimination</u>. Recrimination would be a countercharge against the person who made the original charge.

An <u>intervenor</u> is a person not originally a party to a suit who voluntarily enters into the action to protect some interest that he or she claims to have in the case.

An <u>affidavit</u>, which is a voluntary written statement made under oath before a notary public or other qualified official, has a <u>jurat</u> clause at the end that verifies the time, place, and person before whom the affidavit was made. The person who makes an affidavit is an <u>affiant</u>. A <u>verification</u> may be attached to a document to confirm the truthfulness of the contents of the document.

TRANSCRIBING FROM DICTATION

Directions: This dictation emphasizes and reinforces the legal terms and definitions you have studied. Listen carefully to the pronunciation of each of the legal terms. Unless otherwise directed, use 1-inch margins and double spacing. Correct all errors. Follow one of the procedures below.

Keyboarding Procedure

Using the Transcription CD, Lesson 5, Part B, transcribe the dictation directly at your computer.

Machine Shorthand Procedure

Using the Transcription CD, Lesson 5, Part B, take the dictation on your shorthand machine and then transcribe from your notes on your computer, or, if you are using computer-aided transcription, proofread and edit your transcript.

When you have finished transcribing Part B of the practice dictation, check your transcript with the printed copy. If you made any mistakes in the transcription, you should review and practice those words several times before going on to Lesson 6.

CHECKLIST

I have completed the following for Lesson 5:

	Part A, Date	Part B, Date	Submitted to Instructor Yes	No
Terminology and Definitions				
Self-Evaluation				
* Keying Legal Terms				
Words				
Sentences				
* Transcribing from Dictation				

When you have successfully completed all the exercises in this lesson and submitted to your instructor those requested, you are ready to proceed with Lesson 6.

* If you are using machine shorthand, submit to your instructor your notes along with your transcript.

Lesson

6

Litigation—Pretrial

"The law helps the vigilant, before those who sleep on their rights."
—*Legal maxim*

This lesson continues the study of the terminology involved in pretrial litigation activities. Several of the terms in this lesson deal with the discovery process; i.e., before a case goes to trial, all parties have an opportunity to learn what evidence and facts anyone connected with the case might have. Upon successful completion of these exercises, you should be able to spell, define, pronounce, and transcribe correctly from dictation each of the terms presented.

Part A | TERMINOLOGY AND DEFINITIONS

Directions: Study the terms, pronunciations, and definitions until you are thoroughly familiar with them. In order to complete this lesson successfully, you must understand the meaning and usage of all the legal terms presented. If you are using a shorthand system, write each legal term one time on your shorthand machine.

Legal Term	Pronunciation	Definition
1. contempt of court	kən-´temt əv kōrt	Intentionally doing something that is against the court rules or that interferes with the administration of justice.
2. bench warrant	bench ´wȯr-ənt	A warrant issued by a judge or the court for the arrest of a person charged with contempt of court or of a person who has been indicted for a crime. (See Figure 6-1, page 79.)
3. subpoena	sə-´pē-nə	A document compelling a witness to appear in court and give testimony at a specified time for the party named therein. A bench warrant may be issued for the arrest of a person who does not obey a subpoena. (See Figure 6-2, page 80.)
4. subpoena duces tecum	sə-´pē-nə ´dü-səs ´tē-kəm	Latin. A writ commanding the person named to produce in court certain designated documents relating to the case.
5. interrogatories	int-ə-´räg-ə-tōr-ēs	Written questions that a witness or a party to the action must answer under oath as a part of the discovery process.
6. disclosure	dis-´klō-zhər	Making known all the facts that one has about a case.
7. concealment	kən-´sēl-mənt	Failure to disclose or reveal the facts a person has about a case that the law requires him or her to make known.

8. court reporter	kort ri-ˈport-ər	One who records verbatim the deposition of a witness or the proceedings in court and produces a written transcript thereof.
9. verbatim	vər-ˈbāt-əm	Something that is stated in exactly the same words. Word for word.
10. deposition	dep-ə-ˈzish-ən	Part of the discovery process whereby the witness answers questions under oath outside of court and a verbatim transcript is prepared of the questions asked and the answers given. The witness testifying in a deposition is called a deponent.
11. transcript	ˈtrans-kript	A printed verbatim copy of a deposition or a court proceeding usually prepared by a court reporter.
12. pretrial stipulations	prē-ˈtrīl stip-yə-ˈlā-shəns	Agreements made between the attorneys as to the conditions or procedures that will be followed in the taking of a deposition.
13. fishing expedition	ˈfish-iŋ ek-spə-ˈdish-ən	A tactic used by some attorneys in the discovery process to try to obtain information from a witness that is not based upon or supported by the allegations.

FIGURE 6-1 A Bench Warrant

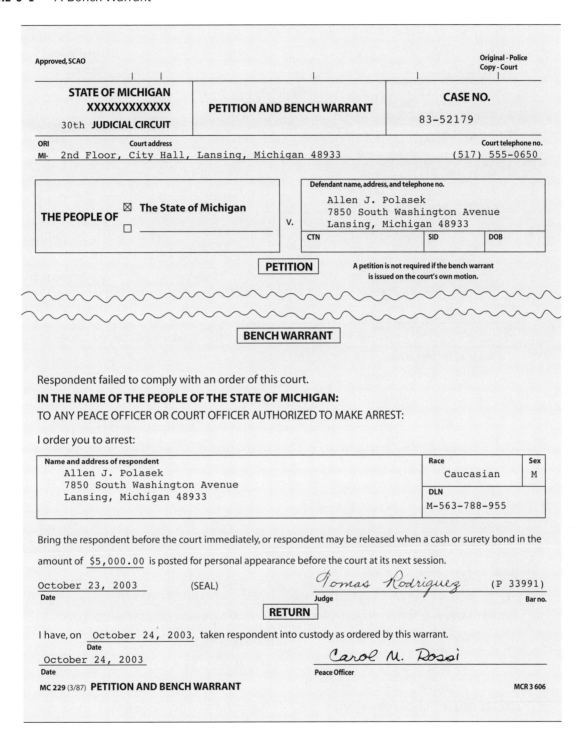

FIGURE 6-2   A Subpoena

Approved, SCAO				Original - Return 1st copy - Witness 2nd copy - File

STATE OF MICHIGAN XXXXXXXXXX 30th **JUDICIAL CIRCUIT** XXXXXXXXXXXXXX	**SUBPOENA** **ORDER TO APPEAR**	**CASE NO.** 92 - 00846

Court address 2nd Floor, City Hall, Lansing, Michigan 48933	Court telephone no. (517) 555-0650

Plaintiff(s) ☐ People of the State of Michigan ☒ Amanda and Blake Hobbs	v.	Defendant name(s) Dorothy Benson, John and Mary Doe
☒ CIVIL ☐ CRIMINAL		Charge
☐ PROBATE In the matter of		

In the Name of the People of the State of Michigan. TO: Dorothy Benson
55 Sandlewood Avenue
Okemos, Michigan 48864

YOU ARE ORDERED to appear personally at the time and place stated:	You may be required to appear from time to time and day to day until you are excused.

Appear at:
1. ☒ The court address above   ☐ Other:

Day 2. Friday	Date August 15, 2003	Time 9:30 a.m.

YOU ARE ALSO ORDERED to:

3. ☒ testify at trial/examination/hearing.

4. ☐ Produce the following items: _____

_____

_____ ☐ Injunction attached

5. ☐ *Testify as to your assets, and bring with you the items listed in line 4 above.
   *Affidavit on reverse side must be completed for judgment debtor examination.

6. ☐ Testify at deposition.

7. ☐ Other: _____

Person requesting subpoena 8. Joshua C. Anderton (P 48921)	Telephone (517) 555-1664
Address City State 688 S. Capitol Avenue, Suite 11, Lansing, Michigan	Zip 48933

FAILURE TO APPEAR AT STATED TIME AND PLACE MAY SUBJECT YOU TO PENALTY FOR CONTEMPT OF COURT.

July 25, 2003
Date
Joshua C. Anderton (P 48921)
XXXXXXXXXXXX/Attorney   Bar no.

JUDGMENT DEBTOR JUDICIAL ENDORSEMENT _____ _____ Date Judge	Court use only ☐ Served ☐ Not served

MC 11 (10/85) **SUBPOENA, Order To Appear**   MCLA 600.1455, 600.1701, 600.6110; MSA 27A.1455, 27A.1701, 27A.6110, MCR 2.506

RETURN

Self-Evaluation A | Terminology and Definition Recall

Directions: In the Answers column, write the legal term that is most representative of the corresponding statement. After you have completed this self-evaluation, check your answers with the key on page 495. If you have any incorrect answers, review the definitions for those terms before going on with this lesson. Then unless otherwise directed, submit this self-evaluation to your instructor.

ANSWERS

1. Something that is stated in exactly the same words, or word for word, is _____.

   1. _____

2. Failure to disclose or reveal the facts a person has about a case that the law requires him or her to make known is referred to as _____.

   2. _____

3. A writ commanding the person named therein to produce in court certain designated documents is a/an _____.

   3. _____

4. A printed verbatim copy of a deposition or a court proceeding usually prepared by a court reporter is a/an _____.

   4. _____

5. A document compelling a witness to appear in court and give testimony at a specified time for the party named therein is a/an _____.

   5. _____

6. The making known of all the facts that one has about a case is _____.

   6. _____

7. Written questions that a witness must answer under oath as a part of the discovery process are _____.

   7. _____

8. The part of the discovery process whereby the witness answers questions under oath outside of court and a verbatim transcript is prepared of the questions asked and the answers given is a/an _____.

   8. _____

9. A warrant issued by a judge or the court for the arrest of a person charged with contempt of court or of a person who has been indicted for a crime is a/an _____.

   9. _____

10. A tactic used by some attorneys in the discovery process to try to obtain information from a witness that is not based upon or supported by the allegations is called a/an _____.

   10. _____

11. Intentionally doing something that is against the court rules or that interferes with the administration of justice is _____.

   11. _____

12. One who records verbatim the deposition of a witness or the proceedings in court and produces a written transcript thereof is a/an _____.

   12. _____

13. Agreements made between the attorneys as to the conditions or procedures that will be followed in the taking of a deposition are _____.

   13. _____

KEYING LEGAL TERMS

Directions: Unless otherwise instructed, use 1-inch margins and double spacing. Correct all errors. Follow one of the procedures below.

WORDS

Keyboarding Procedure
On your computer, key the following words at least two times, concentrating on the correct spelling and pronunciation.

Machine Shorthand Procedure
On your computer, key the following words once, concentrating on the correct spelling and pronunciation. Then write each word one time on your shorthand machine. Transcribe from your shorthand notes one time on your computer.

contempt of court	subpoena	bench warrant
subpoena duces tecum	interrogatories	disclosure
concealment	court reporter	transcript
verbatim	deposition	pretrial stipulations
fishing expedition		

SENTENCES

Keyboarding Procedure
Key each of the following sentences one time on your computer. Concentrate on the correct spelling and pronunciation of each underlined legal term.

Machine Shorthand Procedure
Write the following sentences one time on your shorthand machine. Transcribe from your shorthand notes one time on your computer, or, if you are using computer-aided transcription (CAT), proofread and edit your transcript.

These sentences will be used for practice dictation on the Transcription CD.

If a party intentionally does something that interferes with the administration of justice, a <u>contempt of court</u> charge could be made against the party. In cases of contempt of court or if a witness does not obey a <u>subpoena</u>, the judge may issue a <u>bench warrant</u>. A subpoena is a document that compels a witness to appear in court and give testimony at a specified time for the party named therein. If a party has certain designated documents that are required in court, a <u>subpoena duces tecum</u> is issued commanding the person to bring those documents into court. If the party falls to do so, he or she may be charged with contempt of court, and a bench warrant may be issued for the party's arrest.

A witness may be required to answer <u>interrogatories</u> prior to a trial. Interrogatories are written questions about a case, and they must be answered under oath. A party is required under law to make a <u>disclosure</u> of all facts known about a case. If a party does not disclose the known facts about a case and withholds information that the law requires one to make known, the party is guilty of <u>concealment</u>.

A <u>court reporter</u> is a person who records the proceedings in the discovery process or in court and produces a written <u>transcript</u> of what transpired. The transcript must be <u>verbatim</u>, or word for word. A <u>deposition</u> is the part of the discovery process whereby the attorneys ask a witness questions that the witness must answer orally and under oath prior to the trial. The court reporter prepares a verbatim transcript of the deposition. Prior to the taking of a deposition, the attorneys for each party may agree to certain <u>pretrial stipulations</u> that affect certain procedures in the taking of the deposition. In a deposition, attorneys may ask a wide range of questions regarding the case, but they may not go on a <u>fishing expedition</u>. A fishing expedition refers to a tactic used by some attorneys in the discovery process to try to obtain information from a witness that is not based upon or supported by the allegations.

TRANSCRIBING FROM DICTATION

Directions: This dictation emphasizes and reinforces the legal terms and definitions you have studied. Listen carefully to the pronunciation of each of the legal terms. Unless otherwise directed, use 1-inch margins and double spacing. Correct all errors. Follow one of the procedures below.

Keyboarding Procedure
Using the Transcription CD, Lesson 6, Part A, transcribe the dictation directly at your computer.

Machine Shorthand Procedure
Using the Transcription CD, Lesson 6, Part A, take the dictation on your shorthand machine and then transcribe from your notes on your computer, or, if you are using computer-aided transcription (CAT), proofread and edit your transcript.

When you have finished transcribing Part A of the practice dictation, check your transcript with the printed copy. If you made any mistakes in the transcription, you should review and practice those words several times before going on to Part B.

Part B | TERMINOLOGY AND DEFINITIONS

Directions: Study the terms, pronunciations, and definitions until you are thoroughly familiar with them. In order to complete this lesson successfully, you must understand the meaning and usage of all the legal terms presented. If you are using a shorthand system, write each legal term one time on your shorthand machine.

	Legal Term	Pronunciation	Definition
1.	precedent	′pres-əd-ənt	A judicial decision serving as a guide for future cases that are similar in nature.
2.	notice of lis pendens	′nōt-əs əv lis ′pen-dəns	Latin. A notice issued to inform persons that there is a litigation pending in regard to certain property. (See Figure 6-3, page 86.)
3.	chambers	′cham-bərs	The private office of the judge where business outside of the courtroom is conducted.
4.	pretrial conference	prē-′trīl ′kän-frəns	An informal conference between judge and counsel to discuss a case before it is tried in court in an effort to clarify and expedite its disposition. It is also used to determine if there is adequate evidence to justify proceeding to trial.
5.	examination before trial	ig-zam-ə-′nā-shən bi-′fōr trīl	Inquiry into the facts prior to the trial of a case in order to obtain the information needed to prosecute or defend the action. Sometimes abbreviated as EBT.

6. moot	müt	Something that can be debated, argued, or discussed. A moot point is one that can be argued and is not settled by a court decision.
7. recusation	rē-kyü-ˊzā- shən	An exception or a plea that a particular judge should be disqualified or removed from hearing a case because he or she is prejudiced or has a personal interest in the case. The judge may also recuse or remove himself or herself if he or she deems there is a personal conflict of interest.
8. bond	bänd	A document certifying that one will pay a certain amount of money if certain acts are not performed. A bond may be posted to assure the appearance of a defendant in court. (See Figure 6-4, page 87.)
9. recognizance	ri-ˊkäg-nə-zəns	A commitment made and recorded before a court that a certain act will be done. Serves as a bond in some states and is referred to as released on personal recognizance. A person released on personal recognizance does not have to post a bond.
10. surety bond	ˊshu̇r-ət-ē bänd	A bond insuring that a debt or an obligation will be paid.
11. attachment	ə-ˊtach-mənt	A document issued so that persons or property may be legally taken and held in the custody of the law.
12. garnishment	ˊgär-nish-mənt	A legal notice to a person holding property belonging to a defendant that states the property is the subject of a garnishment, or the act of withholding a defendant's property by the order of the court. Under a garnishment, one's employer may be required to withhold a portion of one's wages to pay a debt which that person owes to another party. (See Figure 6-5, page 88.)
13. garnishee	gär-nə-ˊshē	The one who is in possession of the defendant's property that is the subject of a garnishment.

FIGURE 6-3 A Notice of Lis Pendens

NOTICE LIS PENDENS.   6380

State of Michigan,

Circuit Court for the County of _Ingham_

DARREL L. KELLY
                                                                PLAINTIFF
                                                                                    NOTICE LIS PENDENS
vs.

SACHICO P. LIN   File No. _45-3175_
                                                                DEFENDANT

Notice is Hereby Given, That an action has been commenced and is pending in said Court, upon a

Complaint filed by the above named Plaintiff _____ against the above named Defendant _____ for

a defect in title

and that the premises affected by the said action were, at the time of commencement of said action, and at the

time of filing this notice, situated in the _City_ of _East Lansing_

County of _Ingham_ State of Michigan, and are described in said _Warranty_

Deed as follows, to-wit: _Lots 20 and 21, Assessor's Plat of_

Lot 51, Angell's Subdivision, being Lot 80 and parts of Lots 78

and 79 of College Grove, City of East Lansing, Ingham County,

Michigan.

Dated _November 14,_ 20_03_

BUSINESS ADDRESS: Attorney, JANET ATWELL (P 45502)

4598 Westcott Drive

East Lansing, MI 48823

FIGURE 6-4 A Bond

	Original - Court 1st copy - Sheriff or court officer	2nd copy - Defendant 3rd copy - Plaintiff

STATE OF MICHIGAN XXXXXXXXXXX 30th **JUDICIAL CIRCUIT**	**BOND** **Claim and Delivery**	**CASE NO.** 83-52179

Court address
2nd Floor, City Hall, Lansing, Michigan 48933

Court telephone no.
(517) 555-0650

Plaintiff name(s) and address(es)

SARAH ANN STONE
6447 Whitmore Avenue
Lansing, MI 48810

Defendant name(s) and address(es)

IMAGE GRAPHICS, INC.
7850 South Washington Avenue
Lansing, MI 48933

Plaintiff's attorney, bar no., address and telephone no.

Jason C. O'Malley (P 23345)
Patrick B. Stilwell (P 36588)
5219 West Parkway
Holt, MI 48842

v.

Amount of bond $ 5,000.00	Type of bond ☒ Cash ☐ Surety	Principal Allan J. Polasek	☐ Plaintiff ☒ Defendant

Type or print name(s), address(es), and telephone number(s) of sureties

The principal, and surety if applicable, is/are bound jointly and severally to the   ☒ sheriff or court officer   or their
☐ plaintiff
☐ defendant
successors, assigns or legal representatives in the sum stated if the principal fails to perform any of the following obligations:

1. Surrender the property to the person judged entitled to possession;
2. Pay any money that may be recovered against him/her in the action;
3. Diligently prosecute/defend this suit to final judgment; and
4. Perform all other acts required by the court.

October 27, 2003
Date

Allan J. Polasek
Principal signature

Surety signature

Surety signature

The surety(ies) in this bond acknowledge(s) personal worth in the amount of twice the penalties in the bond, over and above all debts and legal exemptions.

Date

Surety

Surety

Subscribed and sworn to before me on _____ County, Michigan.
                Date

My commission expires: _____ Signature _____
         Date   Court Clerk/Notary Public

this bond is approved and filed.

October 27, 2003
Date

Tomas Rodriquez (P 33991)
Judge   Bar no.

MC 38 (6/86) **BOND, CLAIM AND DELIVERY**   MCLA 600.2920; MSA 27A.2920, MCR 3.105, MCR 3.604

COURT

FIGURE 6-5 A Garnishment

Approved, SCAO	Original - Court 1st copy - Garnishes Defendant	2nd copy - Garnishes Defendant for Principal Defendant	3rd copy - Return 4th copy - Plaintiff/Attorney

STATE OF MICHIGAN 54A **JUDICIAL DISTRICT** XXXXXXXXXX	**AFFIDAVIT AND WRIT OF GARNISHMENT** After Judgment	CASE NO. 885599-LT

Court address
6th Floor, City Hall, Lansing, Michigan 48833   **Court telephone no.** (517) 555-3445

Plaintiff name and address Capitol Management, Inc. 7720 Wildwood Drive Lansing, Michigan 48912	v.	**Principal defendant name, address, soc. security no. or employee ID no.** Justin H. Story 6453 Fairlane Drive, Apt. 201 Lansing, Michigan 48906
Plaintiff attorney, bar no., address and telephone no. Margo B. Griffin (P 55220) 7885 South Cedar Street Lansing, Michigan 48910 (517) 555-7781		**Garnishee defendant name and address** Astro Products, Inc. 678 North Turner Lansing, Michigan 48906

AFFIDAVIT   Plaintiff, or <u>Margo B. Griffin</u>, on behalf of plaintiff, being duly sworn says:

1. Plaintiff received judgment against principal defendant in the amount of $<u>560.00</u> on <u>November 24, 2003</u> and the judgment remains unsatisfied.
2. There is now due over and above all legal set-offs, $<u>560.00</u> plus $ <u>22.00</u> costs of this garnishment.
3. Plaintiff knows or with good reason believes that garnishee defendant has possession or control of property belonging to the principal defendant, and/or is indebted to principal defendant, and such indebtedness ☐ is ☐ is not on account of labor performed by principal defendant.

Margo B. Griffin
XXXXXXX/Attorney signature

Subscribed and sworn to before me on <u>December 1, 1997</u>, Ingham   County, Michigan

My commission expires: *July 2, 2005*   Signature   *Robert T. Gates*
XXXXXXXX/Notary Public

WRIT OF GARNISHMENT   **IN THE NAME OF THE PEOPLE OF THE STATE OF MICHIGAN:**

TO THE OFFICER OR PROCESS SERVER: You are ordered to immediately serve the following on the garnishee defendant: this document, a disclosure form, a copy of this document for each principal defendant, and a disclosure fee. After service you must make prompt return to this court.

TO THE GARNISHEE DEFENDANT:
1. **DEFAULT JUDGMENT MAY BE ENTERED AGAINST YOU** unless you file with this court and serve on the plaintiff and principal defendant within **7 DAYS** after service of this writ, your sworn disclosure and calculation sheet, stating your liability to the principal defendant at time of service of this writ.
2. Deliver no property and pay no obligations to the principal defendant, unless allowed by statute or court rule.
3. Do not withhold, pursuant to this writ, any earnings of the principal defendant except to the extent indicated on line 9 of the calculation sheet.
4. Promptly provide the principal defendant with a copy of this affidavit and writ (by personal service or first class mail directed to the principal defendant's last known address).

TO THE PRINCIPAL DEFENDANT:
1. Unless and until the judgment (including the cost of this garnishment) is paid in full, do not dispose of any negotiable instrument representing a debt of the garnishee or of any negotiable instrument of title representing property, in which you claim an interest, held in possession and control of the garnishee defendant, other than earnings not ordered withheld pursuant to this writ.
2. You have 14 days after a disclosure is filed to file a motion to set aside the writ, to answer, or otherwise defend. If you do not take this action within the specified time, an order may be entered without further notice, directing that the property or debt held pursuant to the garnishment be applied to the satisfaction of the plaintiff's judgment.

December 1, 2003
Date

Lisa G. Walker
Deputy Court Clerk   MCL 600.4011; et seq.; MSA 27A.4011 et seq.

MC 12 (6/86)   **AFFIDAVIT AND WRIT OF GARNISHMENT AFTER JUDGMENT**   MCR 3.101, 3.102

COURT

Self-Evaluation B | Terminology and Definition Recall

Directions: In the Answers column at the right of each statement, write the letter that represents the word or group of words that correctly completes the statement. After you have completed this self-evaluation, check your answers with the key on page 495. If you have any incorrect answers, review the definitions for those terms before going on with this lesson. Then unless otherwise directed, submit this self-evaluation to your instructor.

ANSWERS

1. A notice to inform persons that there is a litigation pending in regard to a certain property is a/an (a) attachment, (b) surety bond, (c) notice of lis pendens.

1. _____

2. A commitment made and recorded before a court that a certain act will be done and that serves in some states as a bond is a (a) recognizance, (b) surety bond, (c) garnishment.

2. _____

3. The private office of the judge where business outside of the courtroom is conducted is the (a) pretrial conference, (b) chambers, (c) moot.

3. _____

4. A document that certifies that one will pay a certain amount of money if certain acts are not performed, such as the appearance of a defendant in court, is a/an (a) attachment, (b) bond, (c) notice of lis pendens.

4. _____

5. A judicial decision that serves as a guide for future cases that are similar in nature is a/an (a) attachment, (b) recusation, (c) precedent.

5. _____

6. Something that can be debated, argued, or discussed and has not been settled by court decisions is (a) moot, (b) precedent, (c) chambers.

6. _____

7. A legal notice to a person holding property belonging to a defendant that said property is to be held for the payment of a debt to the plaintiff is a/an (a) attachment, (b) garnishment, (c) garnishee.

7. _____

8. An informal meeting between judge and counsel to discuss a case before it is tried in court in an effort to clarify and expedite its disposition or to determine if there is adequate evidence to justify proceeding to trial is a/an (a) examination before trial, (b) pretrial conference, (c) chambers.

8. _____

9. The one who is in possession of the defendant's property that is the subject of a garnishment, or the act of withholding a defendant's property by the order of the court, is called a (a) precedent, (b) garnishment, (c) garnishee.

9. _____

10. Inquiry into the facts prior to the trial of a case in order to obtain the information needed to prosecute or defend the action is a/an (a) recusation, (b) chambers, (c) examination before trial.

10. _____

11. An exception or a plea that a judge should be disqualified from hearing a case because of prejudice or a personal interest in the case is (a) recognizance, (b) subpoena, (c) recusation.

11. _____

12. A document issued so that persons or property may be legally taken and held in the custody of the law is a/an (a) attachment, (b) garnishee, (c) surety bond.

12. _____

13. A bond that insures that a debt or obligation will be paid is a (a) surety bond, (b) garnishment, (c) subpoena.

13. _____

KEYING LEGAL TERMS

Directions: Unless otherwise instructed, use 1-inch margins and double spacing. Correct all errors. Follow one of the procedures below.

WORDS

Keyboarding Procedure
On your computer, key the following words at least two times, concentrating on the correct spelling and pronunciation.

Machine Shorthand Procedure
On your computer, key the following words once, concentrating on the correct spelling and pronunciation. Then write each word one time on your shorthand machine. Transcribe from your shorthand notes one time on your computer.

precedent	notice of lis pendens	chambers
pretrial conference	examination before trial	moot
recusation	bond	recognizance
surety bond	attachment	garnishment
garnishee		

SENTENCES

Keyboarding Procedure
Key each of the following sentences one time on your computer. Concentrate on the correct spelling and pronunciation of each underlined legal term.

Machine Shorthand Procedure
Write the following sentences one time on your shorthand machine. Transcribe from your shorthand notes one time on your computer, or, if you are using computer-aided transcription (CAT), proofread and edit your transcript.

These sentences will be used for practice dictation on the Transcription CD.

A <u>precedent</u> is a judicial decision that serves as a guide for future cases that are similar in nature. If a title to property is involved in litigation, a <u>notice of lis pendens</u> is filed to inform persons that there is a litigation pending in regard to certain property. The private office of the judge is called <u>chambers</u>. The judge may hold the <u>pretrial conference</u> in chambers rather than in the courtroom. A pretrial conference may be held before a case is tried in court in an effort to determine if there is adequate evidence to justify proceeding to trial.

An <u>examination before trial</u>, commonly referred to as an EBT, is an inquiry into the facts prior to the trial of a case so as to obtain the information needed to prosecute or defend the action. A <u>moot</u> point is one that can be debated, argued, or discussed. A moot point or issue is one that has not been settled by court decisions.

<u>Recusation</u> is an exception or a plea that a particular judge should be disqualified from hearing a case because he or she is prejudiced or has a personal interest in the matter. For example, the judge's ability to hear a case fairly may be challenged if the judge has a personal or business involvement with a party in the case.

A <u>bond</u> is a document that certifies that one will pay a certain amount of money if certain acts are not performed. A bond may be posted to assure the appearance of the defendant in court, or the court may release a person on personal <u>recognizance</u>. A person released on personal recognizance does not have to post a bond. In some cases, a plaintiff must post a <u>surety bond</u> before attaching property owned by a defendant. A surety bond insures that a debt or an obligation will be paid. An <u>attachment</u> is issued so that persons or property may be legally taken and held in the custody of the law.

If the defendant's property is being held by another party, the plaintiff may acquire the property by filing a <u>garnishment</u>. To <u>garnishee</u> a defendant's property, a legal notice is issued to the person holding said property stating that the property is to be held for the payment of a debt to the plaintiff.

TRANSCRIBING FROM DICTATION

Directions: This dictation emphasizes and reinforces the legal terms and definitions you have studied. Listen carefully to the pronunciation of each of the legal terms. Unless otherwise directed, use 1-inch margins and double spacing. Correct all errors. Follow one of the procedures below.

Keyboarding Procedure
Using the Transcription CD, Lesson 6, Part B, transcribe the dictation directly at your computer.

Machine Shorthand Procedure
Using the Transcription CD, Lesson 6, Part B, take the dictation on your shorthand machine and then transcribe from your notes on your computer, or, if you are using computer-aided transcription (CAT), proofread and edit your transcript.

When you have finished transcribing Part B of the practice dictation, check your transcript with the printed copy. If you made any mistakes in the transcription, you should review and practice those words several times before going on to Evaluation 3.

CHECKLIST
I have completed the following for Lesson 6:

	Part A, Date	Part B, Date	Submitted to Instructor Yes	No
Terminology and Definitions	_____	_____	_____	_____
Self-Evaluation	_____	_____	_____	_____
* Keying Legal Terms	_____	_____	_____	_____
Words	_____	_____	_____	_____
Sentences	_____	_____	_____	_____
* Transcribing from Dictation	_____	_____	_____	_____

When you have successfully completed all the exercises in this lesson and submitted to your instructor those requested, you are ready to proceed with Lesson 6.

* If you are using machine shorthand, submit to your instructor your notes along with your transcript.

Evaluation No. 3 | SECTION A

Directions: This dictation/transcription evaluation will test your spelling and transcription abilities on the legal terms that you studied in the two preceding lessons. Tab once for a paragraph indention, and use 1-inch margins and double spacing unless otherwise instructed. Correct all errors. Follow one of the procedures below.

Keyboarding Procedure

Using the Transcription CD, Evaluation 3, transcribe the dictation directly at your computer.

Machine Shorthand Procedure

Using the Transcription CD, Evaluation 3, take the dictation on your shorthand machine and then transcribe from your notes on computer, or, if you are using computer-aided transcription (CAT), proofread and edit your transcript.

Sections B and C are available from your instructor.

Lesson

7

Litigation—Trial and Proceedings

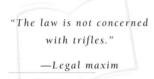

"The law is not concerned with trifles."

—*Legal maxim*

Many nonlawyer personnel do not have an opportunity to observe the proceedings that take place in a courtroom. However, regardless of your legal position, having a knowledge of what transpires once a case goes to trial will help you to understand the importance of the various aspects of your particular involvement in a case. This lesson introduces legal terms that are used in the courtroom during a trial or legal proceeding. Upon successful completion of this lesson, you should have a better understanding of the terms used in litigation.

Part A | TERMINOLOGY AND DEFINITIONS

Directions: Study the terms, pronunciations, and definitions until you are thoroughly familiar with them. In order to complete this lesson successfully, you must understand the meaning and usage of all the legal terms presented. If you are using a shorthand system, write each legal term one time on your shorthand machine.

Legal Term	Pronunciation	Definition
1. trial	trīl	The examination of a civil or criminal case in a court of law with the purpose of deciding an issue.
2. counsel	′kaůn-səl	An attorney who represents or assists a client in a court case.
3. jury	′jůr-ē	A group of persons selected to hear a case in a court of law and sworn to render a verdict based upon the evidence presented in the case. Sometimes referred to as petit jury.
4. juror	′jůr-ər	One who is a member of a jury.
5. veniremen	və-′nī-rē-mən	Jurors.
6. impanel	im-′pan-l	The process of selecting a jury.
7. voir dire	vwä-′dir	French. A preliminary examination by the court of a prospective juror to determine if the person is competent to serve as a juror.
8. challenge	′chal-ənj	To object to a certain person serving as a juror. The challenge may be made by the attorney representing either party in the case.
9. challenge to the array	′chal-ənj tü thē ə-′rā	An objection made to the entire panel of jurors.

10.	challenge for cause	′chal-ənj fər kȯz	An objection made to a juror based on a specified reason, such as a previous criminal record.
11.	peremptory challenge	pə-′rem-trē ′chal-ənj	An objection made to a juror for which no cause is given. There is a limited number of peremptory challenges allowed to each party in a case.
12.	oath	ōth	A swearing or an affirming that one will act faithfully and truthfully.
13.	foreman or forewoman	′fōr-mən ȯr fōr-wu̇m-ən	A juror selected by the other members of the jury to preside over the deliberations and to speak for the jury. Also referred to as the foreperson.

Self-Evaluation A | Terminology and Definition Recall

Directions: In the Answers column, write the letter from Column 1 that represents the word or phrase that best matches each item in Column 2. After you have completed this self-evaluation, check your answers with the key on page 495. If you have any incorrect answers, review the definitions for those terms before going on with this lesson. Then unless otherwise directed, submit this self-evaluation to your instructor.

COLUMN 1	COLUMN 2	ANSWERS
a. challenge	1. Another name for jurors.	1. _____
b. challenge for cause	2. To object to a certain person serving as a juror.	2. _____
c. challenge to the array	3. One who is a member of a jury.	3. _____
d. counsel	4. The examination of a civil or criminal case in a court of law with the purpose of deciding an issue.	4. _____
e. foreman or forewoman	5. A juror selected by the other members of the jury to preside over the deliberations and to speak for the jury.	5. _____
f. impanel	6. A group of persons selected to hear a case in a court of law and sworn to render a verdict based upon the evidence presented in the case.	6. _____
g. jurist		
h. juror	7. A swearing or an affirming that one will act faithfully and truthfully.	7. _____
i. jury	8. An objection made to a juror for which no cause is given.	8. _____
j. oath	9. An attorney who represents or assists a client in a court case.	9. _____
k. peremptory challenge	10. An objection made to the entire panel of jurors.	10. _____
l. trial	11. To go through the process of steps of selecting a jury.	11. _____
m. veniremen	12. An objection made to a juror based on a specified reason, such as a previous criminal record.	12. _____
n. voir dire	13. A preliminary examination by the court of a prospective juror to determine if the person is competent to serve as a juror.	13. _____

KEYING LEGAL TERMS

Directions: Unless otherwise instructed, use 1-inch margins and double spacing. Correct all errors. Follow one of the procedures below.

WORDS

Keyboarding Procedure
On your computer, key the following words at least two times, concentrating on the correct spelling and pronunciation.

Machine Shorthand Procedure
On your computer, key the following words once, concentrating on the correct spelling and pronunciation. Then write each word one time on your shorthand machine. Transcribe from your shorthand notes one time on your computer, or, if you are using computer-aided transcription (CAT), proofread and edit your transcript.

trial	counsel	jury
juror	impanel	voir dire
challenge	challenge to the array	challenge for cause
peremptory challenge	oath	veniremen
foreman or forewoman		

SENTENCES

Keyboarding Procedure
Key each of the following sentences one time on your computer. Concentrate on the correct spelling and pronunciation of each underlined legal term.

Machine Shorthand Procedure
Write the following sentences one time on your shorthand machine. Transcribe from your shorthand notes one time on your computer, or, if you are using computer-aided transcription (CAT), proofread and correct your transcript.

These sentences will be used for practice dictation on the Transcription CD.

A <u>trial</u> is the examination of a civil or criminal case in a court of law with the purpose of deciding an issue. <u>Counsel</u> is an attorney who represents or assists a client in a court case. Cases tried in courts of original jurisdiction or trial courts may be decided by a <u>jury</u>, which is sometimes referred to as petit jury. A jury is a group of persons who are selected to hear a case in a court of law and who have sworn to render a verdict based upon the evidence presented in the case. A <u>juror</u> is one who is a member of a jury.

To <u>impanel</u> a jury is to select the jurors who will decide the issue. Part of the impaneling process is the <u>voir dire</u>, which is the preliminary examination by the court of a prospective juror to determine if the person is competent to serve as a juror.

During the voir dire, counsel for either party may <u>challenge</u> the capability of a juror or jurors. There are three common types of challenges that counsel may exercise. They are <u>challenge to the array</u>, <u>challenge for cause</u>, and <u>peremptory challenge</u>. A challenge to the array is a challenge to the entire panel of jurors. A challenge to a juror based on a specific reason is a challenge for cause. The specific reason for the challenge must be stated to the judge, who will then decide whether or not the prospective juror may sit as a member of the jury. A peremptory challenge is one for which no cause is given. Each party has a certain number of peremptory challenges that they may exercise without giving the judge a reason for the challenge.

Each juror must take an <u>oath</u> to act truthfully and faithfully. Once the jury has been impaneled, the jurors, or the <u>veniremen</u>, will select a <u>foreman or forewoman</u> to preside over the deliberations and to speak for the jury. Veniremen is another name for jurors.

TRANSCRIBING FROM DICTATION

Directions: This dictation emphasizes and reinforces the legal terms and definitions you have studied. Listen carefully to the pronunciation of each of the legal terms. Unless otherwise directed, use 1-inch margins and double spacing. Correct all errors. Follow one of the procedures below.

Keyboarding Procedure

Using the Transcription CD, Lesson 7, Part A, transcribe the dictation directly at your computer.

Machine Shorthand Procedure

Using the Transcription CD, Lesson 7, Part A, take the dictation on your shorthand machine and then transcribe from your notes on your computer, or, if you are using computer-aided transcription (CAT), proofread and edit your transcript.

When you have finished transcribing Part A of the practice dictation, check your transcript with the printed copy. If you made any mistakes in the transcription, you should review and practice those words several times before going on to Part B.

Part B | TERMINOLOGY AND DEFINITIONS

Directions: Study the terms, pronunciations, and definitions until you are thoroughly familiar with them. In order to complete this lesson successfully, you must understand the meaning and usage of all the legal terms presented. If you are using a shorthand system, write each legal term one time on your shorthand machine.

Legal Term	Pronunciation	Definition
1. opening statement	'ōp-niŋ 'stāt-mənt	The first step in a jury trial after the jury has been selected whereby the attorneys make a statement to the jury as to what they plan to prove in the trial.
2. testimony	'tes-tə-mō-nē	Evidence presented by a witness under oath in a court of law. (See Figure 7-1, page 102.)
3. witness	'wit-nəs	One who is called to give testimony under oath in court as to any facts that pertain to the case.
4. direct examination	də-'rekt ig-zam-ə-'nā-shən	The first questioning of a witness in court by the attorney for the party who called the witness to testify. (See Figure 7-1, page 102.)
5. cross-examination	kròs ig-zam-ə-'nā-shən	The questioning of a witness by counsel for the party who is in opposition to the party who called the witness to testify.
6. admissible	əd-'mis-ə-bəl	Evidence that is relevant to a case and may, therefore, be presented in court.

7.	colloquy	´käl-ə-kwē	A talking together, conference, or conversation between the judge and counsel or the judge and witness. Could be in the form of an objection. Deviates from the normal question and answer that takes place between counsel and witness. (See Figure 7-2, page 103.)
8.	objection	əb-´jek-shən	A protest made by counsel to the judge pertaining to certain evidence or a procedure in the trial. (See Figure 7-1, page 102.)
9.	irrelevant	ir-´el-ə-vənt	Evidence presented that is not applicable or related to the issues in the case. An attorney may make an objection to irrelevant evidence.
10.	motion to strike	´mō-shən tü strīk	A request made by counsel to eliminate improper evidence from consideration in deciding an issue. Evidence that is ordered stricken cannot be considered but remains as a part of the record in the event the case is appealed.
11.	physically expunge	´fiz-i-klē ´ik-spənj	To actually remove certain evidence from the record. Only the judge can order evidence to be physically expunged from the record.
12.	sustained	sə-´stānd	The answer of the court when supporting an objection made by counsel.
13.	overruled	ō-və-´rüld	The answer of the court when refusing to support an objection made by counsel.
14.	mistrial	mis-´trīl	A trial that is declared invalid because of an error in the proceedings or the failure of a jury to reach a verdict. When a mistrial occurs, a new jury must be impaneled, and the trial must start over from the beginning.

FIGURE 7-1 Testimony

<u>DIRECT EXAMINATION</u>

BY MRS. SHAPIRO

Q. Mr. Baker, I believe your name was mentioned in yesterday's
   testimony from the witness stand relative to this particular
   incident that occurred on December 28, 2002. Do you remember
   that day, sir?

A. I remember the incident.

Q. Where were you employed at that time?

A. I was employed part time for Midtown Mall as a security
   guard.

Q. Do you recall being in the security office on that particular
   day?

A. On that day, yes, ma'am.

~~~~~~

Q. The type of staple that can be removed by a thumbnail or
   penknife? You can lift them off if you wish to?

A. I would assume so. Yes, ma'am.

                    MR. DANIELS: I object, your Honor. It's
obvious the staples are removable.

                    THE COURT: I sustain the objection.
Ask the direct question, not what is possible.

Q. Was the staple of a nature that with a simple ordinary penknife
   you could easily open the bag and remove the staples from it?

A. In this particular case I never tried, but I assume you could.
   Yes, ma'am.

~~~~~~

FIGURE 7-2 Colloquy

Q. The only people that have access to it then are the five

security guards?

A. The people in the security department have a key. Yes.

                    MRS. SHAPIRO: I have no further

questions of this witness, your Honor.

                    THE COURT: Anything further, Mr.

Daniels?

                    MR. DANIELS: No questions of this

witness, your Honor.

                    THE COURT: You may step down, please.

                    MRS. SHAPIRO: Your Honor, I ask the

Court's permission to have Mr. Baker excused.

                    THE COURT: Any objections, Mr. Daniels?

                    MR. DANIELS: No objections, your Honor.

                    THE COURT: The witness is excused.

Self-Evaluation B | Terminology and Definition Recall

Directions: In the Answers column, write the legal term that is most representative of the corresponding statement. After you have completed this self-evaluation, check your answers with the key on page 495. If you have any incorrect answers, review the definitions for those terms before going on with this lesson. Then unless otherwise directed, submit this self-evaluation to your instructor.

ANSWERS

1. A protest made by counsel to the judge pertaining to certain evidence or a procedure in the trial is a/an _____.

    1. _____

2. Evidence that is relevant to a case and therefore may be presented in court is _____ evidence.

    2. _____

3. Evidence presented by a witness under oath in a court of law is _____.

    3. _____

4. The answer of the court when supporting an objection made by counsel is _____.

    4. _____

5. One who is called to give testimony under oath in court as to any facts that pertain to the case is a/an _____.

    5. _____

6. The first questioning of a witness in court by the attorney for the party who called the witness to testify is _____.

    6. _____

7. The answer of the court in refusing to support an objection made by counsel is _____.

    7. _____

8. A request made by counsel to eliminate improper evidence from consideration in deciding an issue is a/an _____.

    8. _____

9. The questioning of a witness by counsel for the party who is in opposition to the party who called the witness to testify is _____.

    9. _____

10. A trial that is declared invalid because of an error in the proceedings or the failure of a jury to reach a verdict is a/an _____.

    10. _____

11. Evidence presented that is not applicable or related to the issues in the case is _____.

    11. _____

12. A talking together, conference, or conversation between the judge and counsel or the judge and witness is _____.

    12. _____

13. To actually remove certain evidence from the record is to _____ it.

    13. _____

14. The first step in a jury trial after the jury has been selected in which the attorneys state` to the jury what they plan to prove in the trial is the _____.

    14. _____

KEYING LEGAL TERMS

Directions: Unless otherwise instructed, use 1-inch margins and double spacing. Correct all errors. Follow one of the procedures below.

WORDS

Keyboarding Procedure

On your computer, key the following words at least two times, concentrating on the correct spelling and pronunciation.

Machine Shorthand Procedure

On your computer, key the following words once, concentrating on the correct spelling and pronunciation. Then write each word one time on your shorthand machine. Transcribe from your shorthand notes one time on your computer, or, if you are using computer-aided transcription (CAT), proofread and edit your transcript.

opening statement	testimony	witness
direct examination	cross-examination	admissible
colloquy	objection	irrelevant
motion to strike	physically expunge	sustained
overruled	mistrial	

SENTENCES

Keyboarding Procedure

Key each of the following sentences one time on your computer. Concentrate on the correct spelling and pronunciation of each underlined legal term.

Machine Shorthand Procedure

Write the following sentences one time on your shorthand machine. Transcribe from your shorthand notes one time on your computer, or, if you are using computer-aided transcription (CAT), proofread and edit your transcript.

These sentences will be used for practice dictation on the Transcription CD.

At the beginning of a trial, counsel for both sides usually presents an <u>opening statement</u> to the jury. In the opening statements, the attorneys tell the jury what they plan to prove during the trial. Each attorney will then call persons to the witness stand to give <u>testimony</u> under oath as to any facts that pertain to the case. A person who gives testimony is called a <u>witness</u>.

The first questioning of a witness in court by the attorney for the party who called the witness to testify is the <u>direct examination</u>. After the direct examination, the witness may be subjected to a <u>cross-examination</u> by the counsel for the opposing party. Evidence that is <u>admissible</u> in court is evidence that is relevant to a case. During the direct examination or the cross-examination, counsel and judge may engage in <u>colloquy</u>, or conversation relevant to the case. An <u>objection</u> to the testimony or evidence by counsel is a form of colloquy.

Counsel may object to certain evidence on the grounds that it is <u>irrelevant</u>, meaning that it is not applicable or related to the issues in the case. Counsel may make a <u>motion to strike</u> certain irrelevant testimony or evidence. The judge may rule in favor of the motion to strike and order the court reporter to <u>physically</u>

expunge the testimony or evidence from the record. To physically expunge testimony from the record means to strike it totally from the record. An objection must be either sustained or overruled by the judge. If an objection is sustained, the judge agrees with the counsel who made the objection; if the objection is overruled, the judge does not agree with the counsel who made the objection. A mistrial, or dismissal of a case, may result if a fundamental legal procedure is violated during a trial.

TRANSCRIBING FROM DICTATION

Directions: This dictation emphasizes and reinforces the legal terms and definitions you have studied. Listen carefully to the pronunciation of each of the legal terms. Unless otherwise directed, use 1-inch margins and double spacing. Correct all errors. Follow one of the procedures below.

Keyboarding Procedure
Using the Transcription CD, Lesson 7, Part B, transcribe the dictation directly at your computer.

Machine Shorthand Procedure
Using the Transcription CD, Lesson 7, Part B, take the dictation on your shorthand machine and then transcribe from your notes on your computer, or, if you are using computer-aided transcription (CAT), proofread and edit your transcript.

When you have finished transcribing Part B of the practice dictation, check your transcript with the printed copy. If you made any mistakes in the transcription, you should review and practice those words several times before going on to Lesson 8.

CHECKLIST
I have completed the following for Lesson 7:

	Part A, Date	Part B, Date	Submitted to Instructor Yes	No
Terminology and Definitions	_____	_____	_____	_____
Self-Evaluation	_____	_____	_____	_____
* Keying Legal Terms	_____	_____	_____	_____
Words	_____	_____	_____	_____
Sentences	_____	_____	_____	_____
* Transcribing from Dictation	_____	_____	_____	_____

When you have successfully completed all the exercises in this lesson and submitted to your instructor those requested, you are ready to proceed with Lesson 8.

* If you are using machine shorthand, submit to your instructor your notes along with your transcript.

CHECKLIST

Lesson
8

Litigation—Trial and Proceedings

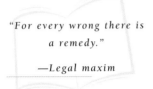

"For every wrong there is a remedy."

—*Legal maxim*

Additional legal terms relating to the proceedings that take place in the courtroom are introduced in these exercises. When you have successfully completed this lesson, you should have knowledge and a better understanding of the terminology used during the trial of a case.

Part A | TERMINOLOGY AND DEFINITIONS

Directions: Study the terms, pronunciations, and definitions until you are thoroughly familiar with them. In order to complete this lesson successfully, you must understand the meaning and usage of all the legal terms presented. If you are using a shorthand system, write each legal term one time on your shorthand machine.

Legal Term	Pronunciation	Definition
1. adduce	ə-ˈdüs	To present or introduce evidence in a case.
2. evidence	ˈev-əd-əns	Testimony, exhibits, or other matter presented in the trial of a case to prove the alleged facts.
3. opinion evidence	ə-ˈpin-yən ˈev-əd-əns	Testimony given by a witness (usually an expert) as to what that witness thinks or believes about the facts in the case.
4. expert evidence	ˈek-spərt ˈev-əd-əns	Testimony given by a person who has special qualifications to testify in regard to specific facts in the case.
5. circumstantial evidence	sər-kəm-ˈstan-chəl ˈev-əd-əns	Indirect evidence. An inference or assumption that may be made from other facts proven in the case. For example, if you have stolen property in your possession, it could be assumed that you stole it even though no one saw you do it.
6. incompetent	in-ˈkäm-pət-ənt	Not qualified legally. Pertains to evidence that is not admissible in a court case.
7. exhibit	ig-ˈzib-ət	Any document or object presented to the court as evidence in a case. Exhibits must be accepted by the court before they become a part of the evidence. An exhibit is marked for identification (usually by the court reporter) when it is introduced. (See Figure 8-1, page 111.)

8. hearsay	hir-´sā	The repeating of what one heard another say. Hearsay evidence is generally not admissible in court.
9. res gestae	rēz ´jes-tē	Latin. Things done. Things that are a part of a case. Hearsay evidence may be admitted if it can be shown that it is res gestae.
10. impeach	im-´pēch	To prove in a trial that a witness cannot or should not be believed.
11. perjury	´pərj-rē	Intentionally or knowingly giving false testimony under oath. A person who commits perjury may have criminal charges brought against him or her.
12. rebuttal	ri-´bət-l	An attempt to disprove the evidence presented by the other side.
13. hostile witness	´häs-tl ´wit-nəs	A witness who is openly prejudiced against the party who called the witness to testify in the case. A hostile witness may be cross-examined by the party who called the witness to testify.
14. averment	ə-´vər-mənt	A declaration positively stating that the facts are true.

FIGURE 8-1 An Exhibit

RECEIPT	Date _December 29_ 20 _03_	No. **5614**

Received From _Sandra Nichols_

Address _38 Meadowlark, Lansing, MI_

Three Hundred fifty and ^{00}/100   Dollars $ _350.$^{00}

For _Security Deposit on Apt. 501, Arbor_

Village Apartments

ACCOUNT			HOW PAID			
AMT OF ACCOUNT	350	00	CASH	350	00	
AMT. PAID	350	00	CHECK			By _Mark W. Adams_
BALANCE DUE	0		MONEY ORDER			

DEPOSITION EXHIBIT

_12_

PENGAD-Bayonne, N.J.

Self-Evaluation A | Terminology and Definition Recall

Directions: In the Answers column, write the legal term that is most representative of the corresponding statement. After you have completed this self-evaluation, check your answers with the key on page 495. If you have any incorrect answers, review the definitions for those terms before going on with this lesson. Then unless otherwise directed, submit this self-evaluation to your instructor.

ANSWERS

1. A witness who intentionally or knowingly gives false testimony under oath is guilty of _____.

1. _____

2. A witness who is openly prejudiced against the party who called the witness to testify in the case and who may be cross-examined by that party is a/an _____.

2. _____

3. An exception to the hearsay rule and a term meaning things done is _____.

3. _____

4. Testimony given by a witness, usually an expert, as to what the witness thinks or believes about the facts in the case is _____.

4. _____

5. The repeating of what one heard another say is _____.

5. _____

6. Indirect evidence or an inference that may be made from other facts proven in the case is _____.

6. _____

7. To prove in a trial that a witness cannot or should not be believed is to _____ the witness.

7. _____

8. Testimony, exhibits, or other matter presented in the trial of a case to prove the alleged facts are _____.

8. _____

9. A word that means not qualified legally and pertains to evidence that is not admissible in court is _____.

9. _____

10. Any document or object presented to the court as evidence in a case is a/an _____.

10. _____

11. A positive declaration or assertion as to the facts in a case is a/an _____.

11. _____

12. Testimony given by a person who has special qualifications to testify in regard to specific facts in the case is _____.

12. _____

13. A term meaning to introduce or present evidence in a case is _____.

13. _____

14. An attempt to disprove the evidence presented by the other side is a/an _____.

14. _____

KEYING LEGAL TERMS

Directions: Unless otherwise instructed, use 1-inch margins and double spacing. Correct all errors. Follow one of the procedures below.

WORDS

Keyboarding Procedure
On your computer, key the following words at least two times, concentrating on the correct spelling and pronunciation.

Machine Shorthand Procedure
On your computer, key the following words once, concentrating on the correct spelling and pronunciation. Then write each word one time on your shorthand machine. Transcribe from your shorthand notes one time on your computer, or, if you are using computer-aided transcription (CAT), proofread and edit your transcript.

adduce	evidence	opinion evidence
expert evidence	circumstantial evidence	incompetent
exhibit	hearsay	res gestae
impeach	perjury	rebuttal
hostile witness	averment	

SENTENCES

Keyboarding Procedure
Key each of the following sentences one time on your computer. Concentrate on the correct spelling and pronunciation of each underlined legal term.

Machine Shorthand Procedure
Write the following sentences one time on your shorthand machine. Transcribe from your shorthand notes one time on your computer, or, if you are using computer-aided transcription (CAT), proofread and edit your transcript.

These sentences will be used for practice dictation on the Transcription CD.

Adduce is to present or introduce evidence in a case. Evidence consists of testimony, exhibits, or other matter presented in the trial of a case to prove the alleged facts. Opinion evidence, expert evidence, and circumstantial evidence are some of the various types of evidence that may be presented in a trial. Opinion evidence is testimony given by a witness, usually an expert, as to what the witness thinks or believes about the facts in a case. Testimony given by a person who has special qualifications to testify in regard to specific facts in a case is called expert evidence.

An expert witness may be deemed incompetent to testify if his or her knowledge is lacking in the specified field. Indirect evidence, or an inference that may be made based on other facts proven in a case is referred to as circumstantial evidence. The evidence is circumstantial if the facts infer that you did something even though no one saw you do it.

An exhibit is any document or object presented to the court as evidence in a case. An exhibit that has been accepted by the court as evidence is marked for identification and made part of the case. Hearsay evidence is what the witness heard another person say. Hearsay evidence may be admitted if it can be shown that it is part of the res gestae. Res gestae means things that are a part of the case or things done.

To <u>impeach</u> a witness is to prove in a trial that the witness cannot or should not be believed. A witness who intentionally or knowingly gives false testimony under oath is guilty of perjury and may have criminal charges brought against him or her. A rebuttal is an attempt to disprove the evidence presented by the other side. A <u>hostile witness</u> is one who is openly prejudiced against the party who called the witness to testify in the case and may be cross-examined by that party. An <u>averment</u> is a positive declaration or assertion as to the facts in a case.

TRANSCRIBING FROM DICTATION

Directions: This dictation emphasizes and reinforces the legal terms and definitions you have studied. Listen carefully to the pronunciation of each of the legal terms. Unless otherwise directed, use 1-inch margins and double spacing. Correct all errors. Follow one of the procedures below.

Keyboarding Procedure
Using the Transcription CD, Lesson 8, Part A, transcribe the dictation directly at your computer.

Machine Shorthand Procedure
Using the Transcription CD, Lesson 8, Part A, take the dictation on your shorthand machine and then transcribe from your notes on your computer, or, if you are using computer-aided transcription (CAT), proofread and edit your transcript.

When you have finished transcribing Part A of the practice dictation, check your transcript with the printed copy. If you made any mistakes in the transcription, you should review and practice those words several times before going on to Part B.

Part B | TERMINOLOGY AND DEFINITIONS

Directions: Study the terms, pronunciations, and definitions until you are thoroughly familiar with them. In order to complete this lesson successfully, you must understand the meaning and usage of all the legal terms presented. If you are using a shorthand system, write each legal term one time on your shorthand machine.

Legal Term	Pronunciation	Definition
1. bailiff	ˈbā-lef	An officer of the court who is in charge of the jury. May also guard prisoners when they appear in court.
2. causal	ˈkȯ-zel	Implying a cause. Have to do with cause and effect.
3. prima facie	ˈprī-mə ˈfā-shə	Latin. At first view. Evidence that is sufficient to prove or establish a fact unless contrary evidence is presented.
4. credible evidence	ˈkred-ə-bəl ˈev-əd-əns	Evidence presented in a case that is believable.
5. alibi	ˈal-ə-bī	Latin. Elsewhere. An excuse. In a criminal case, if the defendant presents proof of being in another place at the time the crime was committed, the defendant has an alibi.
6. pendente lite	ˈpen-dən-tē ˈlī-tē	Latin. Pending litigation. The time during which the case is in court.

7. amicus curiae	ə-´mē-kəs ´kur-ē-ī	Latin. Friend of the court. A person who has no interest in a case but is called in by the judge to give advice regarding some matter of law.
8. closing arguments	´klō-ziŋ ´är-gyə-mənts	The presentations given by counsel at the end of a case summarizing the evidence presented in the trial in an effort to persuade the jury to decide the case in favor of their client.
9. burden of proof	´bərd-n əv prüf	The plaintiff in a case has the duty of proving that the defendant is guilty; therefore, the burden of proof is on the plaintiff.
10. charge to the jury	´chärj tü thə ´jur-ē	The instructions given by the judge to the jury before deliberations as to the rules of law that apply to the case.
11. deliberations	di-lib-ə-´rā- shəns	The process of the jury discussing the case in an effort to reach a verdict.
12. sequestered	si-´kwes-tərd	Latin. Secluded. The seclusion of witnesses or evidence during a case or the seclusion of the jury until a verdict is reached.
13. preponderance of evidence	pri-´pän-drəns əv ´ev-əd-əns	Greater weight of evidence. Evidence that has greater value. Does not mean the greater number of witnesses but rather the greater weight of the evidence. The jury will return a verdict in a civil case for the party that has the preponderance of evidence.

Self-Evaluation B | **Terminology and Definition Recall**

Directions: In the Answers column at the right of each statement, write the letter that represents the word or group of words that correctly completes the statement. After you have completed this self-evaluation, check your answers with the key on page 495. If you have any incorrect answers, review the definitions for those terms before going on with this lesson. Then unless otherwise directed, submit this self-evaluation to your instructor.

ANSWERS

1. The process of the jury discussing the case in an effort to reach a verdict is called (a) sequestered, (b) charge to the jury, (c) deliberations.

   1. _____

2. The duty that the plaintiff has in a case to prove the defendant guilty is the (a) preponderance of evidence, (b) burden of proof, (c) causal.

   2. _____

3. The presentations given by counsel at the end of a case in an effort to persuade the jury to decide the case in favor of their client are the (a) deliberations, (b) closing arguments, (c) prima facie.

   3. _____

4. A Latin term meaning at first view or evidence that is sufficient to prove or establish a fact unless contrary evidence is presented is (a) prima facie, (b) amicus curiae, (c) alibi.

   4. _____

5. The instructions given by the judge to the jury before deliberations as to the rules of law that apply to the case are known as the (a) burden of proof, (b) preponderance of evidence, (c) charge to the jury.

   5. _____

6. Evidence that has greater weight or greater value is referred to as the (a) preponderance of evidence, (b) credible evidence, (c) pendente lite.

   6. _____

7. If a jury is secluded from the public until a verdict is reached, the jury is said to be (a) closing arguments, (b) sequestered, (c) amicus curiae.

   7. _____

8. A Latin term meaning pending litigation or the time during which the case is in court is (a) alibi, (b) deliberations, (c) pendente lite.

   8. _____

9. In a criminal case, if the defendant presents proof of being in another place at the time the crime was committed, the defendant is said to have a/an (a) alibi, (b) credible evidence, (c) causal.

   9. _____

10. A person who has no interest in a case but is called in by the judge to give advice regarding some matter of law is a/an (a) bailiff, (b) amicus curiae, (c) pendente lite.

    10. _____

11. Evidence presented in a case that is believable is (a) preponderance of evidence, (b) prima facie, (c) credible evidence.

    11. _____

12. Implying a cause or having to do with cause and effect is (a) bailiff, (b) causal, (c) alibi.

    12. _____

13. An officer of the court who is in charge of the jury or who may also guard prisoners when they appear in court is a/an (a) bailiff, (b) causal, (c) amicus curiae.

    13. _____

KEYING LEGAL TERMS

Directions: Unless otherwise instructed, use 1-inch margins and double spacing. Correct all errors. Follow one of the procedures below.

WORDS

Keyboarding Procedure
On your computer, key the following words at least two times, concentrating on the correct spelling and pronunciation.

Machine Shorthand Procedure
On your computer, key the following words once, concentrating on the correct spelling and pronunciation. Then write each word one time on your shorthand machine. Transcribe from your shorthand notes one time on your computer, or, if you are using computer-aided transcription (CAT), proofread and edit your transcript.

bailiff	causal	prima facie
credible evidence	alibi	pendente lite
amicus curiae	closing arguments	burden of proof
charge to the jury	deliberations	sequestered
preponderance of evidence		

SENTENCES

Keyboarding Procedure
Key each of the following sentences one time on your computer. Concentrate on the correct spelling and pronunciation of each underlined legal term.

Machine Shorthand Procedure
Write the following sentences one time on your shorthand machine. Transcribe from your shorthand notes one time on your computer, or, if you are using computer-aided transcription (CAT), proofread and edit your transcript.

These sentences will be used for practice dictation on the Transcription CD.

The <u>bailiff</u> is an officer of the court who is in charge of the jury. A bailiff may also guard prisoners when they appear in court. <u>Causal</u> implies a cause or having to do with cause and effect. <u>Prima facie</u> is evidence that is sufficient to prove or establish a fact unless contrary evidence is presented. Evidence that is believable is referred to as <u>credible evidence</u>. If a defendant was somewhere else at the time a crime was committed, the defendant is said to have an <u>alibi</u>. <u>Pendente lite</u> is a Latin term meaning pending litigation or during the time the case is in court.

A person who has no interest in a case but is called in by the judge to give advice regarding some matter of law is an <u>amicus curiae</u>. An amicus curiae is also referred to as a friend of the court. After all evidence in a case is presented, counsel for each party gives speeches called <u>closing arguments</u>. In the closing arguments, counsel states his or her side of a case in an effort to persuade the jury to decide the case in favor of his or her client. The <u>burden of proof</u>, or the proving of the facts that are disputed, is usually the duty of the plaintiff. In other words, the plaintiff must prove that the defendant is in the wrong or guilty before the jury will return a verdict for the plaintiff.

The <u>charge to the jury</u> is given by the judge. When giving the charge to the jury, the judge instructs the jury as to the rules of law they must follow in their <u>deliberations</u>. The deliberations consist of the jury weighing and examining all the evidence in the case. During the course of the trial or deliberations, the jury may be <u>sequestered</u> from the public. Among the things that must be considered by the jury is which party has the greater weight of evidence, or the <u>preponderance of evidence</u>. This does not mean the greater number of witnesses but rather the evidence that carries the most weight. In a civil case, the verdict of the jury will be in favor of the party having the preponderance of evidence.

TRANSCRIBING FROM DICTATION

Directions: This dictation emphasizes and reinforces the legal terms and definitions you have studied. Listen carefully to the pronunciation of each of the legal terms. Unless otherwise directed, use 1-inch margins and double spacing. Correct all errors. Follow one of the procedures below.

Keyboarding Procedure
Using the Transcription CD, Lesson 8, Part B, transcribe the dictation directly at your computer.

Machine Shorthand Procedure
Using the Transcription CD, Lesson 8, Part B, take the dictation on your shorthand machine and then transcribe from your notes on your computer, or, if you are using computer-aided transcription (CAT), proofread and edit your transcript.

When you have finished transcribing Part B of the practice dictation, check your transcript with the printed copy. If you made any mistakes in the transcription, you should review and practice those words several times before going on to Evaluation 4.

CHECKLIST
I have completed the following for Lesson 8:

	Part A, Date	Part B, Date	Submitted to Instructor Yes	No
Terminology and Definitions	_____	_____	_____	_____
Self-Evaluation	_____	_____	_____	_____
* Keying Legal Terms	_____	_____	_____	_____
Words	_____	_____	_____	_____
Sentences	_____	_____	_____	_____
* Transcribing from Dictation	_____	_____	_____	_____

When you have successfully completed all the exercises in this lesson and submitted to your instructor those requested, you are ready to proceed with Evaluation 4.

* If you are using machine shorthand, submit to your instructor your notes along with your transcript.

Evaluation No. 4 | SECTION A

Directions: This dictation/transcription evaluation will test your spelling and transcription abilities on the legal terms that you studied in the two preceding lessons. Tab once for a paragraph indention, and use 1-inch margins and double spacing unless otherwise instructed. Correct all errors. Follow one of the procedures below.

Keyboarding Procedure

Using the Transcription CD for Evaluation 4, transcribe the dictation directly at your computer.

Machine Shorthand Procedure

Using the Transcription CD for Evaluation 4, take the dictation on your shorthand machine and then transcribe your notes on your computer, or, if you are using computer-aided transcription (CAT), proofread and edit your transcript.
Sections B and C are available from your instructor.

Lesson

9

Litigation—Verdicts and Judgments

> *"A matter which has been decided is considered true."*
> —*Legal maxim*

Verdicts by a jury and judgments by the presiding judge involve certain basic legal terminology with which all nonlawyer personnel should be familiar. The terminology in this lesson covers the most common types of verdicts and judgments. Upon successful completion of the exercises, you should be able to spell, pronounce, define, and transcribe correctly the litigation terms that are presented.

Part A | TERMINOLOGY AND DEFINITIONS

Directions: Study the terms, pronunciations, and definitions until you are thoroughly familiar with them. In order to complete this lesson successfully, you must understand the meaning and usage of all the legal terms presented. If you are using a shorthand system, write each legal term one time on your shorthand machine.

Legal Term	Pronunciation	Definition
1. opinion	ə-ˈpin-yən	A statement by a judge that gives the reasons for the decision made in a case.
2. advisement	əd-ˈvīz-mənt	The consideration and thought that a judge gives a case before a decision is made. The case is said to be under advisement.
3. dictum	ˈdik-təm	Latin. An authoritative opinion by a judge on points other than the actual issue in the case.
4. per curiam	pər ˈkur-ē-äm	Latin. By the court. Indicates an opinion by the entire court, such as the court of appeals or the supreme court.
5. res judicata	ˈrēz jüd-i-ˈkät-ə	Latin. A thing decided. Something that has been decided in a court of law.
6. judgment	ˈjəj-mənt	The decision of the court. (See Figure 9-1, page 127.)
7. judgment by default	ˈjəj-mənt bī di-ˈfȯlt	A judgment given against a party in a suit who fails to make an appearance in court. If you do not appear in court, the case will not be decided in your favor. Sometimes referred to as a default judgment.
8. verdict	ˈvər-dikt	The decision of a jury on a case submitted to it for determination.

9. polling the jury	ˈpōl-iŋ thə ˈjür-ē	After the foreman or forewoman presents the verdict of the jury to the court, each juror may be asked to state what his or her individual verdict is in the case and if he or she agrees with the verdict as presented to the court.
10. hung jury	həŋ ˈjür-ē	A jury that cannot reach a verdict.
11. exonerate	ig-ˈzän-ə-rāt	To prove or declare a person innocent of the charges made against him or her.
12. acquittal	ə-ˈkwit-l	The verdict that declares one innocent of a crime.
13. guilty	ˈgil-tē	Convicted of committing a crime. Not innocent.

FIGURE 9-1 A Judgment

Approved, SCAO		Original - Court 1st copy - Plaintiff 2nd copy - Defendant

STATE OF MICHIGAN 30th **JUDICIAL CIRCUIT**	**JUDGMENT** Civil	**CASE NO.** 92-00846

Court address
2nd Floor, City Hall, Lansing, Michigan 48933

Court telephone no.
(517) 555-0650

Plaintiff(s)
Amanda and Blake Hobbs

V.

Defendant(s)
Dorothy Benson, John and Mary Doe

Joshua C. Anderton (P 48921)
688 S. Capitol Avenue, Suite 11
Lansing, Michigan 48933
(517) 555-1664

Plaintiff/Attorney

⊠ **JUDGMENT**

For: Amanda and Blake Hobbs

Against: Dorothy Benson, John and

Mary Doe

⊠ After trial   ☐ Consent
☐ Non appearance default

In pro per

☐ **DISMISSAL**

Defendant/Attorney

☐ Without prejudice   ⊠ With prejudice

ORDER OF JUDGMENT

Damages	$ 1,087.00	Other conditions, if any:
Interest	$ 32.00	
Costs	$ 61.00	
Other (specify)	$	
	$	
Judgment	$ 1,180.00	

This judgment will earn interest at current statutory rates.

☐ A note or other written evidence of indebtedness has been filled with the clerk for cancellation.

⊠ Approved as to form, notice of entry waived.

IT IS ORDERED that this judgment is granted.

August 15, 2003
Judgment date

Joshua C. Anderton (P 48921)
XXXXXXX/Attorney

Tomas Rodriquez
XXXXXXXXJudge/XXXXXXX
Dorothy Benson
Defendant/XXXXXXX

ENTRY, NOTICE OF JUDGMENT AND CERTIFICATE OF MAILING

This judgment has been entered and will be final unless within 21 days of the judgment date a motion for a new trial or an appeal is filed. Satisfaction of the judgment may be made by payment to the clerk of the entire amount of the judgment, or by filing a satisfaction signed by either the party for whom judgment was rendered or their attorney.

I certify that copies of this judgment and notice were served upon the parties and/or their attorneys by ordinary mail.

August 18, 2003
Date of mailing

Lois McMahon
Deputy Court Clerk

DC 10 (6/86)   **JUDGMENT, CIVIL**

MCR 2.601, 2.602, 2.603

COURT

Self-Evaluation A | Terminology and Definition Recall

Directions: In the Answers column, write the letter from Column 1 that represents the word or phrase that best matches each item in Column 2. After you have completed this self-evaluation, check your answers with the key on page 495. If you have any incorrect answers, review the definitions for those terms before going on with this lesson. Then unless otherwise directed, submit this self-evaluation to your instructor.

COLUMN 1	COLUMN 2	ANSWERS
a. acquittal	1. A judgment given against a person who fails to make an appearance in court.	1. _____
b. advisement	2. The verdict that declares one innocent of a crime.	2. _____
c. dictum	3. A jury that cannot reach a verdict.	3. _____
d. exonerate	4. A Latin term that means by the court and indicates an opinion by the entire court.	4. _____
e. guilty	5. An authoritative opinion by a judge on points other than the actual issue involved in the case.	5. _____
f. hung jury	6. The consideration and thought that a judge gives case before a decision is made.	6. _____
g. judgment	7. The verdict in a case when a person is convicted of a crime.	7. _____
h. judgment by default	8. A statement by a judge that gives the reasons for the decision made in a case.	8. _____
i. opinion	9. To prove or declare a person innocent of the charges made against him or her.	9. _____
j. per curiam	10. A Latin term that means a thing decided or something that has been decided in a court of law.	10. _____
k. polling the jury	11. The decision of the jury on a case submitted to it for determination.	11. _____
l. res gestae	12. The decision of the court.	12. _____
m. res judicata	13. The asking of each individual juror what that juror's verdict is in the case.	13. _____
n. verdict		

KEYING LEGAL TERMS

Directions: Unless otherwise instructed, use 1-inch margins and double spacing. Correct all errors. Follow one of the procedures below.

WORDS

Keyboarding Procedure
On your computer, key the following words at least two times, concentrating on the correct spelling and pronunciation.

Machine Shorthand Procedure
On your computer, key the following words once, concentrating on the correct spelling and pronunciation. Then write each word one time on your shorthand machine. Transcribe from your shorthand notes one time on your computer, or, if you are using computer-aided transcription (CAT), proofread and edit your transcript.

opinion	advisement	dictum
per curiam	res judicata	judgment
judgment by default	verdict	polling the jury
hung jury	exonerate	acquittal
guilty		

SENTENCES

Keyboarding Procedure
Key each of the following sentences one time on your computer. Concentrate on the correct spelling and pronunciation of each underlined legal term.

Machine Shorthand Procedure
Write the following sentences one time on your shorthand machine. Transcribe from your shorthand notes one time on your computer, or, if you are using computer-aided transcription (CAT), proofread and edit your transcript.

These sentences will be used for practice dictation on the Transcription CD.

If a judge hears a case instead of a jury, the judge may give an <u>opinion</u> that gives the reasons for the decision made in a case. Before rendering an opinion, the court takes the case under consideration and thought, which is referred to as taking the case under <u>advisement</u>. Sometimes a judge will give an opinion on points other than the actual issue involved in the case. This authoritative opinion is called a <u>dictum</u>. When the court of appeals or the Supreme Court gives an opinion and the opinion represents the opinion of the entire court rather than just one judge, it is referred to as <u>per curiam</u>. Per curiam can also refer to an opinion written by the chief justice or presiding judge of the court.

<u>Res judicata</u> is a Latin term meaning a thing decided or something that has been decided in a court of law. The decision of the court is a <u>judgment</u>. A judgment that is rendered because one of the parties failed to appear at the time specified by the court is a <u>judgment by default</u>. If you fail to appear in court, the case will not be decided in your favor.

The <u>verdict</u> is the decision of a jury on a case submitted to them for their determination. <u>Polling the jury</u> is asking each juror if the verdict announced by the foreman or forewoman is his or her individual verdict. The attorney for the losing party will usually request that a jury be polled, anticipating that there may be one juror who will waiver on the verdict when each has to stand and announce that the verdict is his or her own verdict. A jury that cannot reach a verdict is referred to as a <u>hung jury</u>.

To <u>exonerate</u> means to prove or declare a person innocent of the charges. A verdict of <u>acquittal</u> proves or declares a person innocent of the charges. If the verdict of the jury is <u>guilty</u>, then the jury is convinced that the person so charged did commit the crime.

TRANSCRIBING FROM DICTATION

Directions: This dictation emphasizes and reinforces the legal terms and definitions you have studied. Listen carefully to the pronunciation of each of the legal terms. Unless otherwise directed, use 1-inch margins and double spacing. Correct all errors. Follow one of the procedures below.

Keyboarding Procedure
Using the Transcription CD, Lesson 9, Part A, transcribe the dictation directly at your computer.

Machine Shorthand Procedure
Using the Transcription CD, Lesson 9, Part A, take the dictation on your shorthand machine and then transcribe from your notes on your computer, or, if you are using computer-aided transcription (CAT), proofread and edit your transcript.

When you have finished transcribing Part A of the practice dictation, check your transcript with the printed copy. If you made any mistakes in the transcription, you should review and practice those words several times before going on to Part B.

Part B | TERMINOLOGY AND DEFINITIONS

Directions: Study the terms, pronunciations, and definitions until you are thoroughly familiar with them. In order to complete this lesson successfully, you must understand the meaning and usage of all the legal terms presented. If you are using a shorthand system, write each legal term one time on your shorthand machine.

Legal Term	Pronunciation	Definition
1. nonsuit	ˈnän-ˈsüt	A judgment that terminates a lawsuit because the plaintiff is unable or refuses to prove the case.
2. adjudge	ə-ˈjəj	To decide, settle, or sentence by law.
3. decision	di-ˈsizh-ən	The judgment of the court rendered in a case brought before it.
4. decree	di-ˈkrē	An official decision or order made by a court or a judge.
5. interlocutory decree	int-ər-ˈläk-yə-tor-ē di-ˈkrē	A temporary decree. Not final.
6. final decree	ˈfin-l di-ˈkrē	A final decision of the court that resolves all issues in a case.
7. decree nisi	di-ˈkrē ˈnī-sī	Latin. A decree that will take effect unless it is successfully contested.

8. order	´ord-ər	A rule of law. A command issued in writing by a court. Not a judgment. (See Figure 9-2, page 134.)
9. restraining order	ri-´strā-niŋ ´ord-ər	An order issued by the court to prevent someone from doing something until the court decides whether or not to issue an injunction.
10. dismiss	dis-´mis	To refuse to consider a case in court. Also, during the court proceedings, either counsel may make a motion to dismiss a case.
11. dismissal without prejudice	dis-´mis-əl with-´aut ´prej-əd-əs	The case is dismissed, but the plaintiff is not prevented from suing again on the same cause of action.
12. dismissal with prejudice	dis-´mis-əl with ´prej-əd-əs	The case is dismissed, and the plaintiff cannot sue again on the same cause of action.
13. stare decisis	´ster-ē di-´sī-səs	Latin. Let the decision stand. Pertains to the policy of a court to follow precedent when deciding cases.
14. sine die	´sī-ni dī	Latin. Without day. The final adjournment or dismissal of a case against a defendant.

FIGURE 9-2 An Order

Approved, SCAO			Original - Return 1st copy - Witness 2nd copy - File

STATE OF MICHIGAN XXXXXXXXXX 30th JUDICIAL CIRCUIT XXXXXXXXXXXXXX	SUBPOENA ORDER TO APPEAR	CASE NO. 92-00846

Court address
2nd Floor, City Hall, Lansing, Michigan 48933   **Court telephone no.** (517) 555-0650

Plaintiff(s)
☐ People of the State of Michigan
☒ Amanda and Blake Hobbs

v.

Defendant(s)
Dorothy Benson, John and Mary Doe

☒ CIVIL   ☐ CRIMINAL

Charge

☐ PROBATE   In the matter of

In the Name of the People of the State of Michigan. TO: Dorothy Benson
55 Sandlewood Avenue
Okemos, Michigan 48864

YOU ARE ORDERED to appear personally at the time and place stated: You may be required to appear from time to time and day to day until you are excused.

Appear at:
1. ☒ The court address above   ☐ Other:

Day 2. Friday	Date August 15, 2003	Time 9:30 a.m.

YOU ARE ALSO ORDERED to:

3. ☒ Testify at trial/examination/hearing.

4. ☐ Produce the following items: _____

_____

_____ ☐ Injunction attached

5. ☐ *Testify as to your assets, and bring with you the items listed in line 4 above.
*Affidavit on reverse side must be completed for judgment debtor examination.

6. ☐ Testify at deposition.

7. ☐ Other: _____

Person requesting subpoena 8. Joshua C. Anderton (P48921)	Telephone (517) 555-1664
Address 688 S. Capitol Avenue, Suite 11, Lansing, Michigan	City State Zip 48933

FAILURE TO APPEAR AT STATED TIME AND PLACE MAY SUBJECT YOU TO PENALTY FOR CONTEMPT OF COURT

July 25, 2003
Date _Tomas Rodriquez_ (P 48921)
Issuing Judge/XXXXXXXXXX   Bar no.

JUDGMENT DEBTOR JUDICIAL ENDORSEMENT	Court use only
Date _____ Judge _____	☐ Served ☐ Not served

MC 11 (10/85) **SUBPOENA, Order To Appear**   MCLA 600.1455, 600.1701, 600.6110; MSA 27A.1455, 27A.1701, 27A.6110, MCR 2.506

RETURN

Self-Evaluation B | Terminology and Definition Recall

Directions: In the answers column at the right of each statement, write the letter that represents the word or group of words that correctly completes the statement. After you have completed this self-evaluation, check your answers with the key on page 495. If you have any incorrect answers, review the definitions for those terms before going on with this lesson. Then unless otherwise directed, submit this self-evaluation to your instructor.

ANSWERS

1. An official decision or order made by a court or a judge is a/an (a) interlocutory decree, (b) injunction, (c) decree.   1. _____

2. A judgment that terminates a lawsuit because the plaintiff is unable or refuses to prove the case is a (a) nonsuit, (b) judgment by default, (c) dismissal with prejudice.   2. _____

3. To refuse to consider a case in court is to (a) order the case, (b) dismiss the case, (c) adjudge the case.   3. _____

4. A decree that will take effect unless it is successfully contested is a/an (a) final decree, (b) interlocutory decree, (c) decree nisi.   4. _____

5. A temporary decree is a/an (a) adjudge, (b) decree nisi, (c) interlocutory decree.   5. _____

6. To decide, settle, or sentence by law is to (a) decree, (b) adjudge, (c) dismiss.   6. _____

7. A Latin term that means let the decision stand and pertains to the policy of a court to follow precedent when deciding cases is (a) stare decisis, (b) sine die, (c) decree nisi.   7. _____

8. The judgment of the court that is rendered in a case brought before it is a/an (a) order, (b) decision, (c) stare decisis.   8. _____

9. A rule of law or command issued in writing by a court is a/an (a) order, (b) decision, (c) decree nisi.   9. _____

10. A dismissal that does not prevent the plaintiff from suing again on the same cause of action is a (a) restraining order, (b) dismissal with prejudice, (c) dismissal without prejudice.   10. _____

11. A dismissal stating that a plaintiff cannot sue again on the same cause of action is a (a) restraining order, (b) dismissal without prejudice, (c) dismissal with prejudice.   11. _____

12. The adjournment or dismissal of a case in which no future date is set to hear it is a/an (a) interlocutory decree, (b) sine die, (c) nonsuit.   12. _____

13. A final decision of the court that resolves all issues in a case is a/an (a) interlocutory decree, (b) final decree, (c) decree nisi.   13. _____

14. An order issued by the court to prevent someone from doing something until the court decides whether or not to issue an injunction is a/an (a) restraining order, (b) order, (c) final decree.   14. _____

KEYING LEGAL TERMS

Directions: Unless otherwise instructed, use 1-inch margins and double spacing. Correct all errors. Follow one of the procedures below.

WORDS

Keyboarding Procedure
On your computer, key the following words at least two times, concentrating on the correct spelling and pronunciation.

Machine Shorthand Procedure
On your computer, key the following words once, concentrating on the correct spelling and pronunciation. Then write each word one time on your shorthand machine. Transcribe from your shorthand notes one time on your computer, or, if you are using computer-aided transcription (CAT), proofread and edit your transcript.

nonsuit	adjudge	decision
decree	interlocutory decree	final decree
decree nisi	order	restraining order
dismiss	dismissal without prejudice	dismissal with prejudice
stare decisis	sine die	

SENTENCES

Keyboarding Procedure
Key each of the following sentences one time on your computer. Concentrate on the correct spelling and pronunciation of each underlined legal term.

Machine Shorthand Procedure
Write the following sentences one time on your shorthand machine. Transcribe from your shorthand notes one time on your computer, or, if you are using computer-aided transcription (CAT), proofread and edit your transcript.

These sentences will be used for practice dictation on the Transcription CD.

<u>Nonsuit</u> is a judgment that terminates a lawsuit in the defendant's favor because the plaintiff is unable or refuses to prove the case. To <u>adjudge</u> a case is to decide or settle it by law. A <u>decision</u> is a judgment of the court rendered in a case brought before it.

A <u>decree</u> is an official decision or order made by a court or judge. A decree is final and is made when the case is heard in court. The words judgment and decree are sometimes used synonymously. An <u>interlocutory decree</u> is a temporary decree that is issued prior to a <u>final decree</u>. The final decree is a final decision of the court that resolves all the issues in a case. A <u>decree nisi</u> is a temporary decree that will be made final on motion unless it is successfully contested.

An <u>order</u> is a rule of law or a command issued in writing by the court. A <u>restraining order</u> is an order issued by the court to prevent a person from doing something until the court decides whether or not to issue an injunction. If someone is harassing you, you can get a restraining order to prevent further harassment until the case is decided in court.

To <u>dismiss</u> an action or a suit is to refuse to consider a case in court. A case that has no basis in law will be dismissed. A <u>dismissal without prejudice</u> permits the plaintiff to sue again on the same cause of action, whereas a <u>dismissal with prejudice</u> prevents the plaintiff from suing again on the same cause of action.

<u>Stare decisis</u> is a Latin term meaning let the decision stand. Stare decisis pertains to the policy of a court to follow precedent when deciding cases. <u>Sine die</u> is a Latin term meaning without day. When a case is adjourned sine die, the case is dismissed and no future date is set to hear it.

TRANSCRIBING FROM DICTATION

Directions: This dictation emphasizes and reinforces the legal terms and definitions you have studied. Listen carefully to the pronunciation of each of the legal terms. Unless otherwise directed, use 1-inch margins and double spacing. Correct all errors. Follow one of the procedures below.

Keyboarding Procedure
Using the Transcription CD, Lesson 9, Part B, transcribe the dictation directly at your computer.

Machine Shorthand Procedure
Using the Transcription CD, Lesson 9, Part B, take the dictation on your shorthand machine and then transcribe from your notes on your computer, or, if you are using computer-aided transcription (CAT), proofread and edit your transcript.

When you have finished transcribing Part B of the practice dictation, check your transcript with the printed copy. If you made any mistakes in the transcription, you should review and practice those words several times before going on to Lesson 10.

CHECKLIST
I have completed the following for Lesson 9:

	Part A, Date	Part B, Date	Submitted to Instructor Yes	No
Terminology and Definitions	_____	_____	_____	_____
Self-Evaluation	_____	_____	_____	_____
* Keying Legal Terms	_____	_____	_____	_____
Words	_____	_____	_____	_____
Sentences	_____	_____	_____	_____
* Transcribing from Dictation	_____	_____	_____	_____

When you have successfully completed all the exercises in this lesson and submitted to your instructor those requested, you are ready to proceed with Lesson 10.

* If you are using machine shorthand, submit to your instructor your notes along with your transcript.

Lesson
10

Litigation—Judgments and Appeals

"Extreme justice is extreme injustice."

—Legal maxim

Litigation activities in the courtroom usually terminate in a judgment in favor of one of the parties to the action. If the party against whom judgment is rendered is not satisfied with the outcome of the case, that party may file an appeal to a higher court to have the case reviewed. The appellate court may reverse the decision of the lower court, uphold the decision, modify the decision, or order a new trial. Additional terminology dealing with judgments and terms involved in the appellate process are introduced in this lesson. Upon successful completion of the following exercises, you should be able to spell, pronounce, define, and transcribe correctly the litigation terms that are presented.

Part A | TERMINOLOGY AND DEFINITIONS

Directions: Study the terms, pronunciations, and definitions until you are thoroughly familiar with them. In order to complete this lesson successfully, you must understand the meaning and usage of all the legal terms presented. If you are using a shorthand system, write each legal term one time on your shorthand machine.

Legal Term	Pronunciation	Definition
1. nunc pro tunc	nənk prō tənk	Latin. Now for then. A decision or an order of the court that is retroactive.
2. status quo	′stāt-əs kwō	Latin. The way things are or their existing state at a given time.
3. award	ə-′wȯrd	To grant or to give. To decide or settle by law.
4. damages	′dam-ijs	An amount of money awarded by a court to one who was injured by another.
5. compensatory damages	kəm-′pen-sə-tōr-ē ′dam-ijs	Damages awarded that are equal to and no more than the amount of the actual loss. The plaintiff would be awarded damages to compensate for the plaintiff's actual loss and nothing more.
6. redress	ri-′dres	To correct a wrong. To provide satisfaction or relief for one who has been injured by another.
7. injunction	in-′jeŋ-shən	A writ issued by a court commanding a person to do or not to do some act. If someone is using your property without your permission, you could get an injunction to prevent that person from using your property.

8. enjoin	in-ˈjoin	To require a person by a writ of injunction to do or not to do a specified act. If you get an injunction against a person to prevent him or her from using your property, then that person is enjoined from using your property.
9. stay	stā	A delay or stopping of a legal proceeding by the court.
10. supersedeas	sü-pər-ˈsēd-ē-əs	Latin. A writ issued by a judge to stay a legal proceeding. It supersedes a prior writ or order.
11. suppress	sə-ˈpres	To hold back or stop something. If the evidence or the outcome of a case is suppressed, it is not made known to the public.
12. conclusion of fact	kən-ˈklü-zhən əv fakt	An assumption or a conclusion based on the facts as presented in a case.
13. conclusion of law	kən-ˈklü-zhən əv lȯ	An assumption or a conclusion arrived at by applying the law to the facts as presented in a case.

Self-Evaluation A | Terminology and Definition Recall

Directions: In the Answers column at the right of each statement, write the letter that represents the word or group of words that correctly completes the statement. After you have completed this self-evaluation, check your answers with the key on page 495. If you have any incorrect answers, review the definitions for those terms before going on with this lesson. Then unless otherwise directed, submit this self-evaluation to your instructor.

ANSWERS

1. A delay or stopping by the court of a legal proceeding is a/an (a) enjoin, (b) stay, (c) suppress.

1. _____

2. A writ issued by a judge to stay a legal proceeding is a/an (a) injunction, (b) award, (c) supersedeas.

2. _____

3. An assumption or a conclusion arrived at by applying the law to the facts as presented in a case is a (a) conclusion of law, (b) conclusion of fact, (c) nunc pro tunc.

3. _____

4. Damages that are equal to and no more than the amount of the actual loss are (a) supersedeas, (b) status quo, (c) compensatory damages.

4. _____

5. To correct a wrong or to provide satisfaction or relief for one who has been injured by another is to (a) award, (b) redress, (c) enjoin.

5. _____

6. To require or forbid an act to be or not to be done is to (a) redress, (b) stay, (c) enjoin.

6. _____

7. A decision or an order of the court that is retroactive and means now for then is (a) nunc pro tunc, (b) status quo, (c) supersedeas.

7. _____

8. The way things are or their existing state at a given time is (a) status quo, (b) supersedeas, (c) conclusion of fact.

8. _____

9. A writ issued by a judge commanding a person to do or not to do a specified act is a/an (a) stay, (b) redress, (c) injunction.

9. _____

10. An assumption or a conclusion based on the facts in a case is (a) conclusion of law, (b) redress, (c) conclusion of fact.

10. _____

11. To grant, to give, to decide or settle by law is to (a) nunc pro tunc, (b) award, (c) enjoin.

11. _____

12. An amount of money given by a court to one who was injured by another is called (a) damages, (b) award, (c) redress.

12. _____

13. To hold or stop something is to (a) stay, (b) suppress, (c) award.

13. _____

KEYING LEGAL TERMS

Directions: Unless otherwise instructed, use 1-inch margins and double spacing. Correct all errors. Follow one of the procedures below.

WORDS

Keyboarding Procedure
On your computer, key the following words at least two times, concentrating on the correct spelling and pronunciation.

Machine Shorthand Procedure
On your computer, key the following words once, concentrating on the correct spelling and pronunciation. Then write each word one time on your shorthand machine. Transcribe from your shorthand notes one time on your computer, or, if you are using computer-aided transcription (CAT), proofread and edit your transcript.

nunc pro tunc	status quo	award
damages	compensatory damages	redress
injunction	enjoin	stay
supersedeas	suppress	conclusion of fact
conclusion of law		

SENTENCES

Keyboarding Procedure
Key each of the following sentences one time on your computer. Concentrate on the correct spelling and pronunciation of each underlined legal term.

Machine Shorthand Procedure
Write the following sentences one time on your shorthand machine. Transcribe from your shorthand notes one time on your computer, or, if you are using computer-aided transcription (CAT), proofread and edit your transcript.

These sentences will be used for practice dictation on the Transcription CD.

<u>Nunc pro tunc</u> is a Latin term meaning now for then. Nunc pro tunc applies to a decision or an order of the court that is retroactive. The Latin term referring to the way things are or their existing state at a given time is <u>status quo</u>. The status quo refers to the way things were preceding a cause of action.

<u>Award</u> means to grant, to give, or to decide by law. An amount of money awarded by a court to one who was injured by another is <u>damages</u>. Damages awarded that are equal to and no more than the amount of actual loss are called <u>compensatory damages</u>. <u>Redress</u> is to correct a wrong or to provide satisfaction or relief for one who has been injured by another. The awarding of compensatory damages by a jury is redress for the plaintiff.

A <u>writ</u> issued by a court commanding a person to do or not to do some act is an <u>injunction</u>. <u>Enjoin</u> means to require or forbid an act to be or not to be done. Therefore, a writ of injunction enjoins a person to perform or not to perform some act. A <u>stay</u> is a delay or a stopping by the court of a legal proceeding. For example, a stay of execution delays the execution of a person who is sentenced to death for a crime. <u>Supersedeas</u> is the Latin name for a writ issued by a judge to stay a legal proceeding.

To <u>suppress</u> something is to hold it back or to stop it. Evidence that is suppressed by the court cannot be used in a case. Also, evidence or the outcome of a case may be suppressed from the public. A <u>conclusion of</u> <u>fact</u> is an assumption or a conclusion based on the facts in a case, whereas a <u>conclusion of law</u> is an assumption or a conclusion arrived at by applying the law to the facts as presented in a case. For example, it is a conclusion of fact to state that an accident occurred, but it is a conclusion of law to state who was at fault.

TRANSCRIBING FROM DICTATION

Directions: This dictation emphasizes and reinforces the legal terms and definitions you have studied. Listen carefully to the pronunciation of each of the legal terms. Unless otherwise directed, use 1-inch margins and double spacing. Correct all errors. Follow one of the procedures below.

Keyboarding Procedure
Using the Transcription CD, Lesson 10, Part A, transcribe the dictation directly at your computer.

Machine Shorthand Procedure
Using the Transcription CD, Lesson 10, Part A, take the dictation on your shorthand machine and then transcribe from your notes on your computer, or, if you are using computer-aided transcription (CAT), proofread and edit your transcript.

When you have finished transcribing Part A of the practice dictation, check your transcript with the printed copy. If you made any mistakes in the transcription, you should review and practice those words several times before going on to Part B.

Part B | TERMINOLOGY AND DEFINITIONS

Directions: Study the terms, pronunciations, and definitions until you are thoroughly familiar with them. In order to complete this lesson successfully, you must understand the meaning and usage of all the legal terms presented. If you are using a shorthand system, write each legal term one time on your shorthand machine.

Legal Term	Pronunciation	Definition
1. appeal	ə-ˈpēl	To request an appellate court to review a case that was tried in a lower court.
2. appellant	ə-ˈpel-ənt	One who appeals a decision or verdict.
3. respondent	ri-ˈspän-dənt	The party who must contend against an appeal. Also known as an appellee.
4. brief	brēf	A statement filed with an appellate court that gives the facts and points of law on which the appeal is based.
5. review	rē-ˈvyü	An examination by an appellate court of a case that was tried in a lower court.
6. reverse	rē-ˈvərs	To repeal or change to the opposite. The appellate court may reverse the decision of a lower court.
7. abrogate	ˈab-rə-gāt	To abolish or do away with something, such as an order issued by a lower court.

8.	remittitur	ri-ʹmit-ə-tər	Latin. The sending back of a case by the appellate court to a lower court. Also, the plaintiff returning damages awarded in a case that were in excess of what the plaintiff requested.
9.	mandamus	ʹman-ʹdā-məs	Latin. A writ issued by a higher court to a lower court commanding or mandating that a certain thing be done.
10.	rehearing	rē-ʹhir-iŋ	A retrial of a case in the court that heard it the first time in an effort to correct an error or omission.
11.	trial de novo	trīl dē ʹnō-vō	A new trial of a case conducted by an appellate court as though there had been no other trial.
12.	certiorari	sər-shə-ʹrar-ē	Latin. An order or a writ of review or inquiry used in an appellate proceeding.
13.	error coram vobis	ʹer-ər ʹkō-ram ʹvō-bis	Latin. A writ issued by an appellate court to a lower court stating that an error was made in the proceedings before you. An error coram vobis is a basis for an appellate court to reverse a decision made by a lower court.
14.	error coram nobis	ʹer-ər ʹkō-ram ʹnō-bis	Latin. A writ issued by an appellate court stating that an error was committed in the proceeding before us. This writ directs the lower court to consider issues of fact that had not been considered before.

Self-Evaluation B | Terminology and Definition Recall

Directions: In the Answers column, write the letter from Column 1 that represents the word or phrase that best match-es each item in Column 2. After you have completed this self-evaluation, check your answers with the key on page 496. If you have any incorrect answers, review the definitions for those terms before going on with this lesson. Then unless otherwise directed, submit this self-evaluation to our instructor.

COLUMN 1	COLUMN 2	ANSWERS
a. abrogate	1. To abolish or do away with something, such as an order issued by a lower court.	1. _____
b. appeal	2. To repeal or change to the opposite.	2. _____
c. appellant	3. An order or a writ of review or inquiry used in an appellate proceeding.	3. _____
d. brief	4. A writ issued by an appellate court stating that an error was committed in the proceeding before us.	4. _____
e. certiorari		
f. error coram nobis	5. A new trial of a case conducted by an appellate court as though there had been no other trial.	5. _____
g. error coram vobis	6. The party who must contend against an appeal.	6. _____
h. mandamus	7. The request for an appellate court to review a case that was tried in a lower court.	7. _____
i. rehearing		
j. remittitur	8. A writ issued by a higher court to a lower court commanding that a certain thing be done.	8. _____
k. respondent	9. One who appeals a decision or verdict.	9. _____
l. reverse	10. A retrial of a case in the court that heard it the first time in an effort to correct an error or omission.	10. _____
m. review		
n. supersedeas	11. A statement filed with an appellate court that gives the facts and points of law on which the appeal is based.	11. _____
o. trial de novo	12. The sending back of a case by the appellate court, or the plaintiff returning damages awarded in a case that were in excess of what the plaintiff requested.	12. _____
	13. A writ issued by an appellate court to a lower court that states that an error was made in the proceedings before you.	13. _____
	14. An examination by an appellate court of a case that was tried in a lower court.	14. _____

KEYING LEGAL TERMS

Directions: Unless otherwise instructed, use 1-inch margins and double spacing. Correct all errors. Follow one of the procedures below.

WORDS

Keyboarding Procedure

On your computer, key the following words at least two times, concentrating on the correct spelling and pronunciation.

Machine Shorthand Procedure

On your computer, key the following words once, concentrating on the correct spelling and pronunciation. Then write each word one time on your shorthand machine. Transcribe from your shorthand notes one time on your computer, or, if you are using computer-aided transcription (CAT), proofread and edit your transcript.

appeal	appellant	respondent
brief	review	reverse
abrogate	remittitur	mandamus
rehearing	trial de novo	certiorari
error coram vobis	error coram nobis	

SENTENCES

Keyboarding Procedure

Key each of the following sentences one time on your computer. Concentrate on the correct spelling and pronunciation of each underlined legal term.

Machine Shorthand Procedure

Write the following sentences one time on your shorthand machine. Transcribe from your notes one time on your computer, or, if you are using computer-aided transcription (CAT), proofread and edit your transcript.

These sentences will be used for practice dictation on the Transcription CD.

An <u>appeal</u> is a request to an appellate court to review a case that was tried in a lower court. The party who appeals a decision or a verdict is called the <u>appellant</u>. The <u>respondent</u> is the party who must contend against an appeal. Each party in the case must file a <u>brief</u> with the appellate court. The appellant's brief gives the facts and points of law on which the appeal is based. The respondent's brief contests the facts and points of law stated in the appellant's brief. The appellate court will <u>review</u>, or reexamine, the case based upon the information filed in the brief by the appellant's counsel.

An appeals court may <u>reverse</u> a judgment, sentence, or decree of a lower court; or the appeals court may order a new trial. The appeals court may <u>abrogate</u>, or abolish, an order by a lower court. Remittitur means a remission or surrender. <u>Remittitur</u> is involved in cases that are sent back by an appellate court to a lower court. Remittitur also refers to the plaintiff returning damages awarded that were in excess of what the plaintiff requested. This is usually done upon an order by the court.

A <u>mandamus</u> is a writ issued by a higher court to a lower court commanding that a certain thing be done, such as a <u>rehearing</u>, or retrial, of the issues. A new trial held in an appellate court is called a <u>trial de novo</u>.

Certiorari is an order or a writ of review or inquiry used in an appellate proceeding. If the appellate court needs more information on a case, a writ of certiorari or review may be issued to the lower court to obtain the required information.

An <u>error coram vobis</u> is a writ of error issued by an appellate court that an error was made in the proceedings before you. An <u>error coram nobis</u> is a writ issued by an appellate court stating that an error was committed in the proceeding before us.

TRANSCRIBING FROM DICTATION

Directions: This dictation emphasizes and reinforces the legal terms and definitions you have studied. Listen carefully to the pronunciation of each of the legal terms. Unless otherwise directed, use 1-inch margins and double spacing. Correct all errors. Follow one of the procedures below.

Keyboarding Procedure

Using the Transcription CD, Lesson 10, Part B, transcribe the dictation directly at your computer.

Machine Shorthand Procedure

Using the Transcription CD, Lesson 10, Part B, take the dictation on your shorthand machine and then transcribe from your notes on your computer, or, if you are using computer-aided transcription (CAT), proofread and edit your transcript.

When you have finished transcribing Part B of the practice dictation, check your transcript with the printed copy. If you made any mistakes in the transcription, you should review and practice those words several times before going on to Evaluation 5.

CHECKLIST

I have completed the following for Lesson 10:

	Part A, Date	Part B, Date	Submitted to Instructor Yes	No
Terminology and Definitions				
Self-Evaluation				
* Keying Legal Terms				
Words				
Sentences				
* Transcribing from Dictation				

When you have successfully completed all the exercises in this lesson and submitted to your instructor those requested, you are ready to proceed with Evaluation 5.

* If you are using machine shorthand, submit to your instructor your notes along with your transcript.

CHECKLIST

Evaluation No. 5 | **SECTION A**

Directions: This dictation/transcription evaluation will test your transcription abilities on the legal terms that you studied in the two preceding lessons. Tab once for a paragraph indention, and use 1-inch margins and double spacing unless otherwise instructed. Correct all errors. Follow one of the procedures below.

Keyboarding Procedure

Using the Transcription CD for Evaluation 5, transcribe the dictation directly at your computer.

Machine Shorthand Procedure

Using the Transcription CD for Evaluation 5, take the dictation on your shorthand machine and then transcribe from your notes on your computer, or, if you are using computer-aided transcription (CAT), proofread and edit your transcript. **Sections B and C are available from your instructor.**

Lesson
11

Civil Actions

A civil action involves a violation of an individual's legal rights. It includes all the fields of law that govern relationships between individuals, businesses, or institutions. Therefore, this lesson will cover terms that deal with civil actions in general, whereas the more specialized areas of civil actions will be presented in separate lessons. When you have successfully completed these exercises, you will be able to pronounce, define, spell, and transcribe correctly the civil law terms that are included.

Part A | TERMINOLOGY AND DEFINITIONS

Directions: Study the terms, pronunciations, and definitions until you are thoroughly familiar with them. In order to complete this lesson successfully, you must understand the meaning and usage of all the legal terms presented. If you are using a shorthand system, write each legal term on your shorthand machine.

Legal Term	Pronunciation	Definition
1. civil law	′siv-əl lȯ	Law that deals with the private rights of individuals.
2. actio civilis	′ak-shē-ō si-′vil-əs	Latin. A civil action.
3. ex delicto	eks di-′likt-ō	Latin. A cause of action based on a civil wrong or tort.
4. tort	tȯrt	A civil wrong, other than a breach of contract, for which one has the right to bring a suit for recovery in a civil court.
5. tortious activity	′tȯr-shəs ak-′tiv-ət-ē	A wrongful or devious act. Tortious describes an act that results in a tort. For example, if you break someone's window, it would be a tortious activity because you could be sued to pay for the damages.
6. willful tort	′wil-fəl tȯrt	A tort that was committed intentionally and maliciously. If you intentionally damage someone's property, you have committed a willful tort.
7. tortfeasor	′tȯrt-fē-zer	One who commits a tort or a tortious activity. The person who commits a civil wrong against another is a tortfeasor.
8. replevin	ri-′plev-ən	An action to recover personal property that another is illegally possessing.
9. actio in personam	′ak-shē-ō in pər-′sän-əm	Latin. A civil action directed against a specific person.
10. grievance	′grē-vəns	A cause or basis for a complaint.
11. allegation	al-i-′gā-shən	A statement of the facts made in a pleading that one intends to prove.
12. intent	in-′tent	The purpose that one has for doing a certain thing.

Self-Evaluation A | Terminology and Definition Recall

Directions: In the Answers column at the right of each statement, write the letter that represents the word or group of words that correctly completes the statement. After you have completed this self-evaluation, check your answers with the key on page 496. If you have any incorrect answers, review the definitions for those terms before going on with this lesson. Then unless otherwise directed, submit this self-evaluation to your instructor.

ANSWERS

1. Law that deals with the private rights of individuals is called (a) ex delicto, (b) civil law, (c) replevin.

   1. _____

2. A Latin term that means a civil action directed against a specific person is (a) replevin, (b) actio civilis, (c) actio in personam.

   2. _____

3. A civil wrong, other than a breach of contract, for which one has the right to bring a suit for recovery in a civil court is a/an (a) tort, (b) allegation, (c) actio in personam.

   3. _____

4. A cause or basis for a complaint is a/an (a) grievance, (b) actio civilis, (c) tort.

   4. _____

5. A wrongful or devious act is referred to as a/an (a) allegation, (b) tortious activity, (c) replevin activity.

   5. _____

6. The purpose that one has for doing a certain thing is referred to as (a) intent, (b) grievance, (c) tort.

   6. _____

7. A tort that was committed intentionally and maliciously is a/an (a) allegation, (b) tortious, (c) willful tort.

   7. _____

8. A statement of the facts made in a pleading that one intends to prove is a/an (a) intent, (b) tort, (c) allegation.

   8. _____

9. An action to recover personal property that another is illegally possessing is known as (a) tortfeasor, (b) replevin, (c) intent.

   9. _____

10. A cause of action based on a civil wrong or tort is expressed in Latin as (a) ex delicto, (b) replevin, (c) actio civilis.

    10. _____

11. One who commits a tortious activity is known as a/an (a) actio in personam, (b) tortfeasor, (c) ex delicto.

    11. _____

12. The Latin term for a civil action is (a) ex delicto, (b) actio in personam, (c) actio civilis.

    12. _____

KEYING LEGAL TERMS

Directions: Unless otherwise instructed, use 1-inch margins and double spacing. Correct all errors. Follow one of the procedures below.

WORDS

Keyboarding Procedure
On your computer, key the following words at least two times, concentrating on the correct spelling and pronunciation.

Machine Shorthand Procedure
On your computer, key the following words once, concentrating on the correct spelling and pronunciation. Then write each word one time on your shorthand machine. Transcribe from your shorthand notes one time on your computer, or, if you are using computer-aided transcription (CAT), proofread and edit your transcript.

civil law	actio civilis	ex delicto
tort	tortious activity	willful tort
tortfeasor	replevin	actio in personam
grievance	allegation	intent

SENTENCES

Keyboarding Procedure
Key each of the following sentences one time on your computer. Concentrate on the correct spelling and pronunciation of each underlined legal term.

Machine Shorthand Procedure
Write the following sentences one time on your shorthand machine. Transcribe from your shorthand notes one time on your computer, or, if you are using computer-aided transcription (CAT), proofread and edit your transcript.

These sentences will be used for practice dictation on the Transcription CD.

<u>Civil law</u> is the law that deals with the private rights of individuals. <u>Actio civilis</u> means a civil action. An actio civilis is every action other than a criminal action. If a mechanic does not repair your car properly, you can start an actio civilis, or a civil action, against the mechanic.

<u>Ex delicto</u> is a cause of action based on a civil wrong or tort. An action ex delicto would be an action based upon a <u>tort</u>. A tort is a civil wrong, other than a breach of contract, for which one has the right to bring a suit for recovery in a civil court. A <u>tortious activity</u> is a wrongful or devious act. A <u>willful tort</u> is committed by a tortfeasor when the tortfeasor intentionally and maliciously injures another. A person who commits a tort is a <u>tortfeasor</u>.

<u>Replevin</u> is an action to recover personal property that another is illegally possessing. A replevin may be filed against a tortfeasor who takes another's property illegally. If a mechanic refuses to return your car to you, you may file a replevin against the mechanic because your car is being held illegally.

A civil action directed against a specific person is expressed in Latin as <u>actio in personam</u>. A civil action against a mechanic would be an actio in personam because the action is directed against a specific person. A <u>grievance</u> is a cause or basis for a complaint. A grievance may become the basis for an allegation in a civil action. An <u>allegation</u> is a statement of the facts made in a pleading that one intends to prove.

<u>Intent</u> is the purpose that one has for doing a certain thing. Intent is an element in the commission of a willful tort. For example, the mechanic must intend to deprive you of your car illegally to be guilty of a tort. A person committing a tortious activity has an intent of harming another and is liable to become the defendant in an actio civilis.

TRANSCRIBING FROM DICTATION

Directions: This dictation emphasizes and reinforces the legal terms and definitions you have studied. Listen carefully to the pronunciation of each of the legal terms. Unless otherwise directed, use 1-inch margins and double spacing. Correct all errors. Follow one of the procedures below.

Keyboarding Procedure
Using the Transcription CD, Lesson 11, Part A, transcribe the dictation directly at your computer.

Machine Shorthand Procedure
Using the Transcription CD, Lesson 11, Part A, take the dictation on your shorthand machine and then transcribe from your notes on your computer, or, if you are using computer-aided transcription (CAT), proofread and edit your transcript.

When you have finished transcribing or proofreading and editing Part A of the practice dictation, check your transcript with the printed copy. If you made any mistakes in the transcription, you should review and practice those words several times before going on to Part B.

Part B | TERMINOLOGY AND DEFINITIONS

Directions: Study the terms, pronunciations, and definitions until you are thoroughly familiar with them. In order to complete this lesson successfully, you must understand the meaning and usage of all the legal terms presented. If you are using a shorthand system, write each legal term one time on your shorthand machine.

Legal Term	Pronunciation	Definition
1. in forma pauperis	in ′fȯr-mə ′pȯ-pə-rəs	Latin. Permission granted by the court to a pauper, or poor person, to bring a suit without paying the court costs.
2. right	rīt	Something to which a person is legally entitled.
3. duty	′düt-ē	An obligation that one person has to another.
4. liability	lī-ə-′bil-ət-ē	Duty, obligation, or responsibility.
5. absolute liability	′ab-sə–lüt lī-ə-′bil-ət-ē	Liability without fault. Although due care is exercised, the nature of a person's activity may constitute a risk and harm to others. In such a case, that person would be liable for any injury and damages to another person even though no negligence was involved.
6. negligence	′neg-li-jəns	The want of due care or diligence. The failure to do something or the doing of something that an ordinary, reasonable person would or would not do.

7.	contributory negligence	kən-'trib-yə-tōr-ē 'neg-li-jəns	The negligence of the plaintiff that, together with the negligence of the defendant, caused the injury. In cases of contributory negligence, the plaintiff is not permitted to recover damages from the defendant.
8.	comparative negligence	kəm-'par-ət-iv 'neg-li-jəns	A comparison of the negligence of the plaintiff and defendant. In some states, the plaintiff is permitted recovery when his or her negligence is less than that of the defendant. The amount of recovery may be decreased proportionately to the amount or degree of negligence.
9.	culpable negligence	'kəl-pə-bəl 'neg-li-jəns	Failure to act with due care. The person who commits culpable negligence is at fault or blamable for injuries or damages.
10.	imputation of negligence	im-pye-'tā-shən əv 'neg-li-jəns	A negligent act committed by one person but chargeable to another who is responsible for the other person's acts. Thus, an employer may be held responsible for the negligence of an employee.
11.	due care or diligence	dü ker ȯr 'dil-ə-jens	As much care and attention as is required by the circumstances. The care that a reasonable person would have used in the same situation.
12.	damnum absque injuria	'dam-nəm 'abs-kwē in-'jür-ē-ə	Latin. Loss without injury. A loss that cannot be recovered in a court of law.
13.	actio in rem	'ak-shē-ō in rem	Latin. An action for the recovery of a thing possessed by another rather than an action against that person.

Self-Evaluation B │ TERMINOLOGY AND DEFINITION RECALL

Directions: In the Answers column, write the legal term that is most representative of the corresponding statement. After you have completed this self-evaluation, check your answers with the key on page 496. If you have any incorrect answers, review the definitions for those terms before going on with this lesson. Then unless otherwise directed, submit this self-evaluation to your instructor.

ANSWERS

1. Permission granted by the court to a pauper, or poor person, to bring a suit without paying the the court costs is expressed in Latin as _____.

    1. _____

2. The care that a reasonable person would have used in the same situation or as much care and attention as is required by the circumstances is referred to as _____.

    2. _____

3. A duty, an obligation, or a responsibility is a/an _____.

    3. _____

4. A loss that cannot be recovered in a court of law is referred to in Latin as a/an _____.

    4. _____

5. The failure to do something or the doing of something that an ordinary, reasonable person would or would not do is _____.

    5. _____

6. An obligation that one person has to another is a/an _____.

    6. _____

7. An action for the recovery of a thing possessed by another rather than an action against that person is a/an _____.

    7. _____

8. The negligence of the plaintiff that, together with the negligence of the defendant, caused the injury is _____.

    8. _____

9. Failure to act with due care is _____.

    9. _____

10. A negligent act committed by one person but chargeable to another who is responsible for the other person's acts is _____.

    10. _____

11. A liability without fault is referred to as _____.

    11. _____

12. Something to which a person is legally entitled is a/an _____.

    12. _____

13. A comparison of the negligence of the plaintiff and defendant is _____.

    13. _____

KEYING LEGAL TERMS

Directions: Unless otherwise instructed, use 1-inch margins and double spacing. Correct all errors. Follow one of the procedures below.

WORDS

Keyboarding Procedure
On your computer, key the following words at least two times, concentrating on the correct spelling and pronunciation.

Machine Shorthand Procedure
On your computer, key the following words once, concentrating on the correct spelling and pronunciation. Then write each word one time on your shorthand machine. Transcribe from your shorthand notes one time on your computer, or, if you are using computer-aided transcription (CAT), proofread and edit your transcript.

in forma pauperis	**right**	**duty**
liability	**absolute liability**	**negligence**
contributory negligence	**comparative negligence**	**culpable negligence**
imputation of negligence	**due care or diligence**	**damnum absque injuria**
actio in rem		

SENTENCES

Keyboarding Procedure
Key each of the following sentences one time on your computer. Concentrate on the correct spelling and pronunciation of each underlined legal term.

Machine Shorthand Procedure
Write the following sentences one time on your shorthand machine. Transcribe from your shorthand notes one time on your computer, or, if you are using computer-aided transcription (CAT), proofread and edit your transcript.

These sentences will be used for practice dictation on the Transcription CD.

In forma pauperis describes permission granted by the court to a pauper, or poor person, to bring a suit without paying the court costs. A right is something to which a person is legally entitled. A duty is an obligation that one person has to another. Right and duty are reciprocal terms when used within their legal meanings. Thus, if one person has a right, then another person has a duty. Liability is a duty, an obligation, or a responsibility. Absolute liability is liability without fault. Absolute liability applies to situations where one person is doing a legal but very risky act and another is injured as a result of the act, even though there was no negligence involved.

The want of due care or diligence is negligence. If a person fails to do something or does something that an ordinary, reasonable person would or would not do, he or she may be charged with negligence. In law, negligence may be more specifically defined as contributory, comparative, and culpable. Contributory negligence means that the complaining party contributed to the cause of the injury. Comparative negligence involves negligence on the part of both parties but permits a recovery if the plaintiff's negligence is considerably less than that of the defendant. Culpable negligence is the failure to act with due care and could result in a criminal action in addition to a civil action. <u>Imputation of negligence</u> is negligence attributed to one person but actually committed by another person for whom he or she may be responsible.

 <u>Due care or diligence</u> means as much care and attention as is required by the circumstances. A loss that cannot be recovered in a court of law is expressed in Latin as <u>damnum absque injuria</u>. <u>Actio in rem</u> is an action for the recovery of something another is possessing.

TRANSCRIBING FROM DICTATION

Directions: This dictation emphasizes and reinforces the legal terms and definitions you have studied. Listen carefully to the pronunciation of each of the legal terms. Unless otherwise directed, use 1-inch margins and double spacing. Correct all errors. Follow one of the procedures below.

Keyboarding Procedure
Using the Transcription CD, Lesson 11, Part B, transcribe the dictation directly at your computer.

Machine Shorthand Procedure
Using the Transcription CD, Lesson 11, Part B, take the dictation on your shorthand machine and then transcribe from your notes on your computer, or, if you are using computer-aided transcription (CAT), proofread and edit your transcript.

When you have finished transcribing or proofreading and editing Part B of the practice dictation, check your transcript with the printed copy. If you made any mistakes in the transcription, you should review and practice those words several times before going on to Lesson 12.

CHECKLIST
I have completed the following for Lesson 11:

	Part A, Date	Part B, Date	Submitted to Instructor Yes	No
Terminology and Definitions				
Self-Evaluation				
* Keying Legal Terms				
Words				
Sentences				
* Transcribing from Dictation				

When you have successfully completed all the exercises in this lesson and submitted to your instructor those requested, you are ready to proceed with Lesson 12.

* If you are using machine shorthand, submit to your instructor your notes along with your transcript.

Lesson

12

Civil Actions

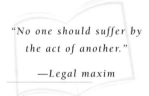

"No one should suffer by the act of another."

—*Legal maxim*

This lesson continues the study of some of the general terms involved in civil law or civil actions. A knowledge and understanding of this terminology will assist you in applying the terms to various civil actions and procedures. Upon successful completion of these exercises, you will be able to spell, pronounce, define, and transcribe correctly the legal words presented.

Part A | TERMINOLOGY AND DEFINITIONS

Directions: Study the terms, pronunciations, and definitions until you are thoroughly familiar with them. In order to complete this lesson successfully, you must understand the meaning and usage of all the legal terms presented. If you are using a shorthand system, write each legal term one time on your shorthand machine.

	Legal Term	Pronunciation	Definition
1.	misfeasance	mis-´fēz-ns	Improperly doing a legal act.
2.	nonfeasance	nän-´fēz-ns	Failure to do an act that one has a duty to perform.
3.	attractive nuisance doctrine	ə-´trak-tiv ´nüs-ns ´däk-trən	A doctrine applying to situations where something is on a person's property that will attract young children, and that person has a duty to exercise due care to prevent injury to them.
4.	trespasser	´tres-pəs-ər	One who unlawfully enters or goes upon another's property.
5.	licensee	līs-n-´sē	One who is on the premises of another for his or her own advantage and without any enticement from the owner. A salesperson would be a licensee.
6.	invitee	in-və-´tē	One who enters the premises of another by express or implied invitation of the owner and whose purpose in being there is advantageous to the owner.
7.	proximate cause	´präk-sə-mət kȯz	The actual cause of an injury. Also referred to as the efficient cause.
8.	intervening cause	int-ər-´vēn-iŋ kȯz	A cause of injury that occurs after the negligent act of another and that could not have been expected to occur. One is not liable for an injury resulting from an intervening cause.

9.	doctrine of last clear chance	'däk-trən əv last klir chans	A plaintiff who was contributorily negligent may recover for injuries if the defendant has a last clear chance to avoid the injury. For example, if a pedestrian is struck by a car while crossing a street against a red light and the car had ample time to stop and did not, the driver of the car may be held liable for the injury.
10.	tangible damages	'tan-jə-bəl 'dam-ijs	Damages that are real or actual. An essential element of torts. There must have been real or actual damages for a tort to have been committed.
11.	punitive or exemplary damages	'pyü-nət-iv ȯr ig-'zem-plə-rē 'dam-ijs	Damages that are awarded over and above the amount of the actual loss for mental anguish or the feelings of the one injured to serve as a punishment for the defendant or to set an example for others.
12.	nominal damages	'näm-ən-l 'dam-ijs	A small amount of damages awarded in cases where an injury has occurred but tangible damages cannot be determined.
13.	mental anguish	'ment-l 'aŋ-gwish	Suffering caused by emotional distress. In some states, damages may be awarded for mental anguish caused by an accident or injury.

Self-Evaluation A | Terminology and Definition Recall

Directions: In the Answers column, write the letter from Column 1 that represents the word or phrase that best matches each item in Column 2. After you have completed this self-evaluation, check your answers with the key on page 496. If you have any incorrect answers, review the definitions for those terms before going on with this lesson. Then unless otherwise directed, submit this self-evaluation to your instructor.

COLUMN 1

a. attractive nuisance doctrine

b. intervening cause

c. invitee

d. doctrine of last clear chance

e. licensee

f. malfeasance

g. mental anguish

h. misfeasance

i. nominal damages

j. nonfeasance

k. proximate cause

l. punitive or exemplary damages

m. tangible damages

n. trespasser

COLUMN 2

1. A doctrine applying to situations where something is on a person's property that will attract young children and that requires that person to exercise due care to prevent injury to the children.

2. The actual cause of an injury or the efficient cause.

3. A cause of injury that occurs after the negligent act of another and that could not have been expected to occur.

4. One who unlawfully enters or goes upon another's property.

5. One who is on the premises of another for his or her own advantage and without any enticement from the owner.

6. A rule of law stating that a plaintiff who was contributorily negligent may recover for injuries if the defendant had an opportunity to avoid the injury just before it occurred.

7. Damages that are real or actual and are an essential element of a tort.

8. Suffering that is caused by emotional distress.

9. The failure to do an act that one has a duty to perform.

10. One who is upon the premises of another by express or implied invitation of the owner and whose purpose in being there is advantageous to the owner.

11. A small amount of damages awarded in cases where an injury has occurred but tangible damages cannot be determined.

12. Improperly doing a legal act.

13. Damages that are awarded over and above the amount of the actual loss for mental anguish or the feelings of the one injured to serve as a punishment for the defendant or to set an example for others.

ANSWERS

1. _____

2. _____

3. _____

4. _____

5. _____

6. _____

7. _____

8. _____

9. _____

10. _____

11. _____

12. _____

13. _____

KEYING LEGAL TERMS

Directions: Unless otherwise instructed, use 1-inch margins and double spacing. Correct all errors. Follow one of the procedures below.

WORDS

Keyboarding Procedure
On your computer, key the following words at least two times, concentrating on the correct spelling and pronunciation.

Machine Shorthand Procedure
On your computer, key the following words once, concentrating on the correct spelling and pronunciation. Then write each word one time on your shorthand machine. Transcribe from your shorthand notes one time on your computer, or, if you are using computer-aided transcription (CAT), proofread and edit your transcript.

misfeasance	nonfeasance	attractive nuisance doctrine
trespasser	licensee	invitee
proximate cause	intervening cause	doctrine of last clear chance
tangible damages	punitive or exemplary damages	nominal damages
mental anguish		

SENTENCES

Keyboarding Procedure
Key each of the following sentences one time on your computer. Concentrate on the correct spelling and pronunciation of each underlined legal term.

Machine Shorthand Procedure
Write the following sentences one time on your shorthand machine. Transcribe from your shorthand notes one time on your computer, or, if you are using computer-aided transcription (CAT), proofread and edit your transcript.

These sentences will be used for practice dictation on the Transcription CD.

If one is accused of <u>misfeasance</u>, the person did a lawful act improperly; but if one is accused of <u>nonfeasance</u>, then the person failed to do an act that he or she had a duty to perform. If you were handling investments for another person and you did not make good decisions investing his or her money, you could be charged with misfeasance. However, if you did not invest the money and you were expected to do so, you could be charged with nonfeasance.

The <u>attractive nuisance doctrine</u> applies to situations where something is on a person's property that will attract young children, and that person has a duty to exercise due care to prevent an injury to them. <u>Trespasser</u>, <u>licensee</u>, and <u>invitee</u> are classifications of persons who enter or use another's premises. A trespasser is one who unlawfully enters or goes upon another's property; a licensee is there legally but for the licensee's own advantage; and the invitee is there for a reason that is advantageous to the owner. <u>Proximate cause</u> is the actual cause of an injury. A proximate cause is also referred to as an efficient cause. An <u>intervening cause</u> is a cause of injury that occurs after the negligent act and that could not have been expected to occur. One is not liable for an injury resulting from an intervening cause. The <u>doctrine of last clear chance</u> makes a person liable if there was a last clear chance to avoid injuring or damaging another.

Several types of damages may be awarded in a civil action. <u>Tangible damages</u> are an essential element of torts. Damages that are real or actual are tangible damages. <u>Punitive or exemplary damages</u> are damages that are awarded over and above the amount of the actual loss for mental anguish or the feelings of the one injured to serve as a punishment for the defendant or to set an example for others. <u>Nominal damages</u> are a small amount of damages awarded in cases where an injury has occurred but tangible damages cannot be determined. <u>Mental anguish</u> is suffering caused by emotional distress. In some states, damages may be awarded for mental anguish caused by an accident or injury.

TRANSCRIBING FROM DICTATION

Directions: This dictation emphasizes and reinforces the legal terms and definitions you have studied. Listen carefully to the pronunciation of each of the legal terms. Unless otherwise directed, use 1-inch margins and double spacing. Correct all errors. Follow one of the procedures below.

Keyboarding Procedure
Using the Transcription CD, Lesson 12, Part A, transcribe the dictation directly at your computer.

Machine Shorthand Procedure
Using the Transcription CD, Lesson 12, Part A, take the dictation on your shorthand machine and then transcribe from your notes on your computer, or, if you are using computer-aided transcription (CAT), proofread and edit your transcript.

When you have finished transcribing or proofreading and editing Part A of the practice dictation, check your transcript with the printed copy. If you made any mistakes in the transcription, you should review and practice those words several times before going on to Part B.

Part B | TERMINOLOGY AND DEFINITIONS

Directions: Study the terms, pronunciations, and definitions until you are thoroughly familiar with them. In order to complete this lesson successfully, you must understand the meaning and usage of all the legal terms presented. If you are using a shorthand system, write each legal term one time on your shorthand machine.

Legal Term	Pronunciation	Definition
1. act or omission	akt ȯr ō-ˈmish-ən	The doing or the failing to do something. The test is applied to determine whether a tort has been committed.
2. probable consequences	ˈpräb-ə-bəl ˈkän-sə-kwens-əs	Results that are most likely to follow a particular cause. If you drive in a reckless manner, then the probable consequence is that you will have an accident.
3. ordinary, reasonable person	ˈȯrd-n-er-ē ˈrēz-nə-bəl ˈpərs-n	A normal, average person who has good judgment in everyday affairs. The standard for measuring whether or not someone acted in a negligent manner.
4. assumption of risk	ə-ˈsəm-shən əv risk	If one voluntarily takes a chance and is injured as a result thereof, then that person is not considered to be injured in the eyes of the law.
5. foreseeability of injury	fōr-ˈsē-ə-bil-ət-ē əv ˈinj-rē	The capability of seeing and knowing that an injury may result from certain acts or omissions.

6. knowledge of the peril	ˈnäl-ij əv thə ˈper-əl	When one has knowledge of something that may cause injury to another and fails to do something about it. An element that is essential to prove negligence.
7. implied or imputed knowledge	im-ˈplīd ȯr im-ˈpyüt-əd ˈnäl-ij	Knowledge that a person should have had or is responsible for having. Usually applies to an employer-employee relationship or an agency.
8. constructive notice	kən-ˈstrək-tiv ˈnōt-əs	Knowledge that one should have when a condition has existed for such a period of time that the person would have known of the condition had due care been exercised. If you own a building that has had a broken step for a period of time and you had a reasonable amount of time to discover it, you can be held liable if an injury results even though you had not actually seen the broken step.
9. wanton, reckless, and intentional	ˈwȯnt-n ˈrek-ləs ən in-ˈtench-nəl	Willful misconduct that constitutes culpable negligence. Acts done with indifference and disregard of the consequences to others.
10. res ipsa loquitur	rēz ˈip-sə ˈlō-kwə-tər	Latin. The thing speaks for itself. A presumption that the thing that happened does not normally happen unless there is negligence involved. It is a rebuttable presumption that may be proven otherwise by the facts.
11. Good Samaritan Statute	gu̇d sə-ˈmar-ət-n ˈstach-üt	If one sees another in serious danger and tries to help the person, the one who gives assistance cannot be charged with contributory negligence. This doctrine varies from state to state.
12. sudden emergency doctrine	ˈsəd-n i-ˈmər-jən-sē ˈdäk-trən	The degree of care required of a person in an emergency situation is less than would be required if the person had time to think before acting.
13. sovereign immunity	ˈsäv-rən im-ˈyü-nət-ē	Protection from tort prosecution that is given to government units and officials in connection with the performance of their official duties.

Self-Evaluation B | Terminology and Definition Recall

Directions: In the Answers column, write the legal term that is most representative of the corresponding statement. After you have completed this self-evaluation, check your answers with the key on page 496. If you have any incorrect answers, review the definitions for those terms before going on with this lesson. Then unless otherwise directed, submit this self-evaluation to your instructor.

ANSWERS

1. A doctrine stating that if one sees another in serious danger and tries to help the person, the one giving the assistance cannot be charged with contributory negligence is the _____.

    1. _____

2. A situation in which one voluntarily takes a chance and is injured as a result thereof but is not considered to be injured in the eyes of the law is referred to as _____.

    2. _____

3. Knowledge that one should have when a condition has existed for such a period of time that the person would have known of the condition if due care had been exercised is called _____.

    3. _____

4. Protection from tort prosecution that is given to governmental units and officials in connection with the performance of their official duties is known as _____.

    4. _____

5. A result that is most likely to follow a particular cause is referred to as _____.

    5. _____

6. A normal, average person who has good judgment in everyday affairs is known as a/an _____.

    6. _____

7. When one has knowledge of something that may cause injury to another and fails to do anything about it, it is called _____.

    7. _____

8. The capability of seeing or knowing that an injury may result from certain acts or omissions is _____.

    8. _____

9. The doing or the failure to do something and the test applied to determine whether a tort has been committed is referred to as _____.

    9. _____

10. Knowledge that a person should have had or is responsible for having is _____.

    10. _____

11. A doctrine stating that the degree of care required of a person in an emergency is less than would be required if the person had time to think before acting is the _____.

    11. _____

12. Willful misconduct that constitutes culpable negligence or acts done with indifference and disregard of the consequences to others are referred to as _____.

    12. _____

13. A presumption that the thing that happened does not normally happen unless there is negligence involved is _____.

    13. _____

KEYING LEGAL TERMS

Directions: Unless otherwise instructed, use 1-inch margins and double spacing. Correct all errors. Follow one of the procedures below.

WORDS

Keyboarding Procedure
On your computer, key the following words at least two times, concentrating on the correct spelling and pronunciation.

Machine Shorthand Procedure
On your computer, key the following words once, concentrating on the correct spelling and pronunciation. Then write each word one time on your shorthand machine. Transcribe from your shorthand notes one time on your computer, or, if you are using computer-aided transcription (CAT), proofread and edit your transcript.

act or omission	probable consequences	ordinary, reasonable person
assumption of risk	knowledge of the peril	foreseeability of injury
implied or imputed knowledge	res ipsa loquitur	constructive notice
wanton, reckless, and intentional	Good Samaritan Statute	sudden emergency doctrine
sovereign immunity		

SENTENCES

Keyboarding Procedure
Key each of the following sentences one time on your computer. Concentrate on the correct spelling and pronunciation of each underlined legal term.

Machine Shorthand Procedure
Write the following sentences one time on your shorthand machine. Transcribe from your shorthand notes one time on your computer, or, if you are using computer-aided transcription (CAT), proofread and edit your transcript.

These sentences will be used for practice dictation on the Transcription CD.

The doing or the failure to do something is an <u>act or omission</u>. This is the test that is applied to determine whether or not a tort has been committed. Whenever you do something negligent, the results that are most likely to follow are called <u>probable consequences</u>.

An <u>ordinary, reasonable person</u> is one who is normal, average, and has good judgment in everyday affairs.

<u>Assumption of risk</u> means if one voluntarily takes a chance and is injured as a result thereof, then that person is not considered to be injured in the eyes of the law. <u>Knowledge of the peril</u> exists whenever one has the capability of seeing or knowing that an injury may result from certain acts or omissions. <u>Foreseeability of injury</u> is the ability to see or know in advance the probable consequences of an act or omission. <u>Implied or imputed knowledge</u> is knowledge that a person should have had or is responsible for having. Implied or imputed knowledge usually applies to an employer-employee relationship or an agency.

<u>Res ipsa loquitur</u> is a Latin phrase meaning the thing speaks for itself. Res ipsa loquitur is a presumption that something that happened would not normally happen unless there was negligence involved. If a person could have discovered a fact by exercising due care, he or she is said to have had <u>constructive notice</u>

of the fact. <u>Wanton, reckless, and intentional</u> describe an act done with indifference and disregard of the consequences to others.

The <u>Good Samaritan Statute</u> protects one from contributory negligence if assistance is given to someone who is in danger provided a certain degree of care is used. Under the <u>sudden emergency doctrine</u>, the degree of care required of a person in an emergency situation is less than that required if the person had time to think before acting. <u>Sovereign immunity</u> is protection from tort prosecution that is given to governmental units and officials in connection with the performance of their official duties.

TRANSCRIBING FROM DICTATION

Directions: This dictation emphasizes and reinforces the legal terms and definitions you have studied. Listen carefully to the pronunciation of each of the legal terms. Unless otherwise directed, use 1-inch margins and double spacing. Correct all errors. Follow one of the procedures below.

Keyboarding Procedure
Using the Transcription CD, Lesson 12, Part B, transcribe the dictation directly at your computer.

Machine Shorthand Procedure
Using the Transcription CD, Lesson 12, Part B, take the dictation on your shorthand machine and then transcribe from your notes on your computer, or, if you are using computer-aided transcription (CAT), proofread and edit your transcript.

When you have finished transcribing or proofreading and editing Part B of the practice dictation, check your transcript with the printed copy. If you made any mistakes in the transcription, you should review and practice those words several times before going on to Evaluation 6.

CHECKLIST
I have completed the following for Lesson 12:

	Part A, Date	Part B, Date	Submitted to Instructor Yes	No
Terminology and Definitions				
Self-Evaluation				
* Keying Legal Terms				
Words				
Sentences				
* Transcribing from Dictation				

When you have successfully completed all the exercises in this lesson and submitted to your instructor those requested, you are ready to proceed with Evaluation 6.

* If you are using machine shorthand, submit to your instructor your notes along with your transcript.

CHECKLIST

Evaluation No. 6 | SECTION A

Directions: This dictation/transcription evaluation will test your spelling and transcription abilities on the legal terms that you studied in the two preceding lessons. Tab once for a paragraph indention, and use 1-inch margins and double spacing unless otherwise instructed. Correct all errors. Follow one of the procedures below.

Keyboarding Procedure

Using the Transcription CD for Evaluation 6, transcribe the dictation directly at your computer.

Machine Shorthand Procedure

Using the Transcription CD for Evaluation 6, take the dictation on your shorthand machine and then transcribe from your notes on your computer, or, if you are using computer-aided transcription (CAT), proofread and edit your transcript.

Sections B and C are available from your instructor.

Lesson

13

Criminal Law

> *"An act does not make guilty unless there be a guilty intent."*
>
> *—Legal maxim*

Criminal law deals with crimes committed in violation of a law. A crime is a public wrong and is prosecuted by the state or "the people." This lesson contains some of the basic terminology involved in criminal procedures. You should be able to spell, pronounce, define, and transcribe correctly the terms presented when you have successfully completed these exercises.

Part A | TERMINOLOGY AND DEFINITIONS

Directions: Study the terms, pronunciations, and definitions until you are thoroughly familiar with them. In order to complete this lesson successfully, you must understand the meaning and usage of all the legal terms presented. If you are using a shorthand system, write each legal term one time on your shorthand machine.

Legal Term	Pronunciation	Definition
1. crime	krīm	An illegal act that is punishable in a court of law.
2. corpus delicti	′kȯr-pəs di-′lik-tī	Latin. The body of a crime. The material evidence that indicates a crime has been committed.
3. grand jury	grand ′jür-ē	A jury that makes inquiries into criminal cases and issues indictments when the evidence indicates that a crime has been committed.
4. indictment	in-′dīt-mənt	A written accusation issued by a grand jury charging that there is evidence that a crime has been committed and that the person so charged should be brought to trial.
5. information	in-fər-′mā-shən	A written accusation issued by a prosecuting attorney charging a person with a crime. (See Figure 13-1, page 181.)
6. offense	ə-′fens	A wrongdoing that is punishable by fine or imprisonment.
7. warrant	′wȯr-ənt	A written order giving the authority to arrest a person or to search or seize property. (See Figure 13-2, page 182.)
8. arrest	ə-′rest	The act of taking a person into legal custody to answer to a criminal or civil charge.
9. arraignment	ə-′rān-mənt	To bring a person before a court of law to hear the charges in the indictment or information and to enter a plea of guilty or not guilty.

10. preliminary examination	pri-ˈlim-ə-ner-ē ig-zam-ə-ˈnā-shən	A hearing conducted by a judge to determine if there is enough evidence to hold for trial a person accused of a crime. Also referred to as a preliminary hearing.
11. felony	ˈfel-ə-nē	A crime of a serious nature that is punishable by imprisonment or death.
12. misdemeanor	mis-di-ˈmē-nər	Any crime that is not a felony. Usually punishable by fine or a short jail sentence.
13. habeas corpus	ˈhā-bē-əs ˈkȯr-pəs	Latin. A writ requiring someone holding a person to bring that person into court to determine if he or she is being held justly or legally. (See Figure 13-3, page 183.)
14. extradition	ek-strə-ˈdish-ən	The delivery of a person from one state to another for trial or punishment.

FIGURE 13-1 An Information

Approved, SCAO			INFORMATION - CIRCUIT COURT ORIGINAL COMPLAINT - COURT WARRANT - COURT	RETURN - CIRCUIT COURT COMPLAINT COPY - PROSECUTOR COMPLAINT COPY - DEFENDANT/ATTORNEY

STATE OF MICHIGAN XXXXXXXXXXXX 30th **JUDICIAL CIRCUIT**	**INFORMATION** **FELONY**	CASE NO. XXXXXX **CIRCUIT CT.** 75-6482

District Court ORI: MI-   Circuit Court ORI: MI-

THE PEOPLE OF THE **STATE OF MICHIGAN** v.	Defendant name and address THORNE NATOLIE	Victim or complainant Roscoe Borg
		Complaining witness Roscoe Borg

Co-defendant(s)	Date: On or about August 13, 2003

City/Twp./Village Lansing	County in Michigan Ingham	Defendant CTN 76834	Defendant SID 10010	Defendant DOB 092239

Police agency report no. 6743	Charge Assault with intent to murder	Maximum penalty 20 years to life

Witnesses Roscoe Borg	Defendant DLN M453-789-0003

STATE OF MICHIGAN, COUNTY OF _Ingham_   .
IN THE NAME OF THE PEOPLE OF THE STATE OF MICHIGAN: The prosecuting attorney for this County appears before the court and informs the court that on the date and at the location described, the defendant:

Assaulted the complaining witness, Roscoe Borg, with a deadly weapon,
to wit: a handgun.

and against the peace and dignity of the State of Michigan.

Prosecuting Attorney

By: _Linda Soloman_ (P 78833)

August 14, 2003

Date

MCLA 764.1 et seq., MSA 28.860 et seq., MCLA 766.1 et seq., MSA 28.919 et seq., MCLA 767.1 et seq., MSA 28.941 et seq.

MC200 (3/87)   **FELONY SET, Information**

CIRCUIT COURT

FIGURE 13-2 A Warrant

		INFORMATION - CIRCUIT COURT ORIGINAL COMPLAINT - COURT WARRANT - COURT	RETURN - CIRCUIT COURT COMPLAINT COPY - PROSECUTOR COMPLAINT COPY - DEFENDANT/ATTORNEY

Approved, SCAO

STATE OF MICHIGAN XXXXXXXXXXXX 30th JUDICIAL CIRCUIT	WARRANT FELONY	XXXXXX CIRCUIT CT.	CASE NO. 75-6482

District Court ORI: MI-   Circuit Court ORI: MI-

THE PEOPLE OF THE STATE OF MICHIGAN	v.	Defendant name and address THORNE NATOLIE	Victim or complainant Roscoe Borg
			Complaining witness Roscoe Borg

Co-defendant(s)	Date: On or about August 13, 2003

City/Twp./Village Lansing	County in Michigan Ingham	Defendant CTN 76834	Defendant SID 10010	Defendant DOB 092239

Police agency report no. 6743	Charge Assault with intent to murder	Maximum penalty 20 years to life

Witnesses Roscoe Borg	Defendant DLN M453-789-0003

STATE OF MICHIGAN, COUNTY OF Ingham_____ .

To any peace officer or court officer authorized to make arrest: The complaining witness has filed a sworn complaint in this court stating that on the date and the location described, the defendant, contrary to law,

Assaulted the complaining witness, Roscoe Borg, with a deadly weapon,
to wit: a handgun.

Upon examination of the complaining witness, I find that the offense charged was committed and that there is probable cause to believe that defendant committed the offense. THEREFORE, IN THE NAME OF THE PEOPLE OF THE STATE OF MICHIGAN, I order you to arrest and bring defendant before the court immediately.

August 14, 2003
Date

By: *Standford McClain*
Judge/XXXXXXXX

RETURN	By virtue of this warrant the defendant has been taken into custody as commanded.

August 18, 2003
Date

Marcie Baker
Peace officer

MCLA 764.1 et seq., MSA 28.860 et seq., MCLA 766.1 et seq., MSA 28.919 et seq., MCLA 767.1 et seq., MSA 28.941 et seq.

MC200 (3/87)   **FELONY SET, WARRANT**

COURT COPY

FIGURE 13-3 A Writ of Habeas Corpus

ORIGINAL - COURT   3RD COPY - PROSECUTOR
1ST COPY - CUSTODIAL OFFICER   4TH COPY - RETURN
2ND COPY - TRANSPORT OFFICER

STATE OF MICHIGAN XXXXXXXXXXX 30th **JUDICIAL CIRCUIT**	**WRIT OF HABEAS CORPUS**	**CASE NO.** 75-6482

Court address
2nd Floor, City Hall, Lansing, Michigan 48933

Court telephone no.
(517) 555-0650

IN THE NAME OF THE PEOPLE OF THE STATE OF MICHIGAN:

TO   County of Cook, State of Illinois   THE AGENCY OR PERSON HAVING

CUSTODY OF   Thorne Natolie   785-643   9/22/39
          Name   I.D. no.   Date of birth

☒ To bring prisoner to court in the case of:
People of the State of Michigan
     V.
Thorne Natolie

☐ To inquire into detention/custody of:

YOU ARE ORDERED to:

1. ☐ Answer this writ, stating the authority under which you   ☐ restrain the named prisoner.
                                                         ☐ exercise custody over the minor child.
   File your answer with the   ☐ court / ☐ judge   by _____ Date

2. ☒ Deliver the person named in this writ into the custody of   Ingham County Sheriff
                                                    Name/Title/Agency
   for the following purpose: to be held pending court appearance.
                (To testify, for preliminary examination, trial, to be held pending court appearance, etc.)
   Immediately after the prisoner completes his/her appearance, the prisoner shall be returned to your custody.

3. ☐ Bring the person named in this writ before the Honorable _____

   at _____ , on _____ at _____ m.
      Location of court   Date   Time
   Bring this writ with you.

Clerk of the Court

August 18, 2003   By: _Corine Lix_____
Date

CERTIFICATE OF ALLOWANCE OF WRIT

I,   Standford McClain   , p.   48921   , certify that the above writ of habeas corpus
   Name of Judge   Bar no.

was allowed by me on   August 18, 2003   ☒ Fees are allowed in the amount of $ 300.00   .
            Date

                             _Standford McClain_____
                              Judge

MC 203 (11/85)   **WRIT OF HABEAS CORPUS**   MCLA 600.4301 et seq.; MSA 27A.4301 et seq., MCR 3.303, 3.304

COURT

Self-Evaluation A | Terminology and Definition Recall

Directions: In the Answers column at the right of each statement, write the letter that represents the word or group of words that correctly completes the statement. After you have completed this self-evaluation, check your answers with the key on page 496. If you have any incorrect answers, review the definitions for those terms before going on with this lesson. Then unless otherwise directed, submit this self-evaluation to your instructor.

ANSWERS

1. A wrongdoing that is punishable by fine or imprisonment is a/an (a) habeas corpus, (b) corpus delicti, (c) offense.

    1. c

2. A writ requiring someone holding a person to bring that person into court to determine if he or she is being held justly or legally is a writ of (a) extradition, (b) arraignment, (c) habeas corpus.

    2. c

3. The act of taking a person into legal custody to answer to a criminal charge is a/an (a) offense, (b) preliminary examination, (c) arrest.

    3. c

4. A jury that makes inquiries into criminal cases and issues indictments when the evidence indicates that a crime has been committed is a (a) grand jury, (b) corpus delicti, (c) preliminary examination.

    4. a

5. A written accusation issued by a prosecuting attorney charging a person with a crime is a/an (a) warrant, (b) information, (c) indictment.

    5. b

6. A crime of a serious nature that is punishable by imprisonment or death is a/an (a) felony, (b) misdemeanor, (c) extradition.

    6. a

7. A hearing conducted by a judge to determine if there is enough evidence to hold for trial a person accused of a crime is the (a) preliminary examination, (b) grand jury, (c) information.

    7. a

8. Any crime that is not a felony and that is usually punishable by fine or a short jail sentence is a/an (a) arrest, (b) misdemeanor, (c) warrant.

    8. b

9. A written accusation issued by a grand jury charging that there is evidence that a crime has been committed and that the person so charged should be brought to trial is a/an (a) warrant, (b) information, (c) indictment.

    9. c

10. The delivery of a person from one state to another for trial or punishment is an (a) indictment, (b) arraignment, (c) extradition.

    10. c

11. The body of a crime or the material evidence indicating that a crime has been committed is expressed in Latin as (a) habeas corpus, (b) corpus delicti, (c) arraignment.

    11. b

12. The process of bringing a person before a court of law to hear the charges in the indictment or information and to enter a plea of guilty or not guilty is the (a) indictment, (b) arraignment, (c) extradition.

    12. b

13. A written order giving the authority to arrest a person or to search or seize property is a/an (a) misdemeanor, (b) warrant, (c) offense.

    13. b

14. An illegal act that is punishable in a court of law is a/an (a) crime, (b) arrest, (c) corpus delicti.

    14. a

KEYING LEGAL TERMS

Directions: Unless otherwise instructed, use 1-inch margins and double spacing. Correct all errors. Follow one of the procedures below.

WORDS

Keyboarding Procedure
On your computer, key the following words at least two times, concentrating on the correct spelling and pronunciation.

Machine Shorthand Procedure
On your computer, key the following words once, concentrating on the correct spelling and pronunciation. Then write each word one time on your shorthand machine. Transcribe from your shorthand notes one time on your computer, or, if you are using computer-aided transcription (CAT), proofread and edit your transcript.

crime	corpus delicti	grand jury
indictment	information	offense
warrant	arrest	arraignment
preliminary examination	felony	misdemeanor
habeas corpus	extradition	

SENTENCES

Keyboarding Procedure
Key each of the following sentences one time on your computer. Concentrate on the correct spelling and pronunciation of each underlined legal term.

Machine Shorthand Procedure
Write the following sentences one time on your shorthand machine. Transcribe from your shorthand notes one time on your computer, or, if you are using computer-aided transcription (CAT), proofread and edit your transcript.

These sentences will be used for practice dictation on the Transcription CD.

A <u>crime</u> is an illegal act that is punishable in a court of law. An <u>indictment</u> issued by a grand jury is based on the <u>corpus delicti</u>. Corpus delicti means the body of a crime or the material evidence indicating that a crime has been committed.

A <u>grand jury</u> is a jury that makes inquiries into criminal cases and issues indictments when the evidence indicates that a crime has been committed. An indictment is a written accusation issued by a grand jury charging that there is evidence that a crime has been committed and that the person so charged should be brought to trial. An <u>information</u> is a written accusation issued by a prosecuting attorney charging a person with committing a criminal <u>offense</u>. When a person has been charged with the commission of a crime, a <u>warrant</u> is issued requiring the <u>arrest</u> of that person. When a person is arrested, that person is taken into custody and held to answer the charge made against him or her.

At the <u>arraignment</u>, the prisoner is brought before the court to hear the reading of the indictment or the information and to enter a plea of guilty or not guilty. A <u>preliminary examination</u> is a hearing conducted by a judge to determine if there is enough evidence to hold for trial the person accused of a crime.

A crime is classified as a <u>felony</u> or a <u>misdemeanor</u>. A felony is a crime of a serious nature that is punishable by imprisonment or death. A misdemeanor is any crime that is not a felony and is usually punishable by fine or a short jail sentence. Committing murder is a felony, but jaywalking or parking violations are only misdemeanors.

A writ of <u>habeas corpus</u> requires someone holding a person to bring that person to court. If a person charged with a crime is arrested in a state other than the one in which the crime was committed, the person may be returned to the state in which the crime was committed by the process of <u>extradition</u>.

TRANSCRIBING FROM DICTATION

Directions: This dictation emphasizes and reinforces the legal terms and definitions you have studied. Listen carefully to the pronunciation of each of the legal terms. Unless otherwise directed, use 1-inch margins and double spacing. Correct all errors. Follow one of the procedures below.

Keyboarding Procedure

Using the Transcription CD, Lesson 13, Part A, transcribe the dictation directly at your computer.

Machine Shorthand Procedure

Using the Transcription CD, Lesson 13, Part A, take the dictation on your shorthand machine and then transcribe from your notes on your computer, or, if you are using computer-aided transcription (CAT), proofread and edit your transcript.

When you have finished transcribing or proofreading and editing Part A of the practice dictation, check your transcript with the printed copy. If you made any mistakes in the transcription, you should review and practice those words several times before going on to Part B.

Part B | TERMINOLOGY AND DEFINITIONS

Directions: Study the terms, pronunciations, and definitions until you are thoroughly familiar with them. In order to complete this lesson successfully, you must understand the meaning and usage of all the legal terms presented. If you are using a shorthand system, write each legal term one time on your shorthand machine.

Legal Term	Pronunciation	Definition
1. plea	plē	An answer made by a defendant at the arraignment for a criminal offense.
2. nolo contendere	´nō-lō kən-´ten-də-rē	Latin. I do not wish to contend. The plea of a defendant in a criminal action that means the punishment will be accepted but guilt will not be admitted.
3. defense	di-´fens	The defendant's denial to an accusation. The contesting of a lawsuit.
4. confession	kən-´fesh-ən	A statement made voluntarily by a person admitting that he or she committed a crime.
5. admission	əd-´mish-ən	A statement confirming that certain facts in a case are true. It is not a confession of guilt.
6. criminal intent	´krim-ən-l in-´tent	A plan or design to commit a crime.

7. sine qua non	′sin-i kwä nän	Latin. Something that is essential. An indispensable condition or requisite without which a thing cannot be.
8. scienter	sī-′en-tər	Latin. Knowingly, intent, or knowledge.
9. insanity	in-′san-ət-ē	A state of unsound mind in which a person does not know right from wrong and is, therefore, not responsible for any acts committed.
10. non compos mentis	nän ′käm-pəs ′ment-əs	Latin. Not of sound mind. Indicates that one is mentally unable to control one's own actions or to handle one's own affairs. Insanity.
11. Durham Rule	′dər-əm rül	A rule applied in some states that does not hold a person responsible for an act if it was done as the result of mental disease or defect.
12. M'Naghten Rule	mə-′nät-ən rül	A rule applied in some states that does not hold a person criminally responsible for an act if he or she does not have the mental capacity to know right from wrong.
13. irresistible impulse	ir-i-′zis-tə-bəl ′im-pəls	An uncontrollable urge to commit a crime due to insanity or a mental defect or disease.

Self-Evaluation B | Terminology and Definition Recall

Directions: In the Answers column, write the legal term that is most representative of the corresponding statement. After you have completed this self-evaluation, check your answers with the key on page 496. If you have any incorrect answers, review the definitions for those terms before going on with this lesson. Then unless otherwise directed, submit this self-evaluation to your instructor.

ANSWERS

1. A state of unsound mind in which a person does not know right from wrong and is, therefore, not responsible for any acts committed is _____.

    1. _____

2. A statement made voluntarily by a person admitting that he or she committed a crime is a/an _____.

    2. _____

3. A statement confirming that certain facts in a case are true is a/an _____.

    3. _____

4. Something that is essential is _____.

    4. _____

5. A rule applied in some states that does not hold a person responsible for an act if it was done as the result of mental disease or defect is the _____.

    5. _____

6. The defendant's denial to an accusation or the contesting of a lawsuit is the _____.

    6. _____

7. The plan or design to commit a crime is _____.

    7. _____

8. An answer made by a defendant at the arraignment for a criminal offense is a/an _____.

    8. _____

9. A Latin term that means knowingly, intent, or knowledge is _____.

    9. _____

10. An uncontrollable urge to commit a crime due to insanity or a mental defect or disease is a/an _____.

    10. _____

11. The plea of a defendant in a criminal action that means the punishment will be accepted but guilt will not be admitted is _____.

    11. _____

12. A Latin term indicating that one is mentally unable to control one's own actions or to handle one's own affairs is _____.

    12. _____

13. A rule applied in some states that does not hold a person criminally responsible for an act if he or she does not have the mental capacity to know right from wrong is the _____.

    13. _____

KEYING LEGAL TERMS

Directions: Unless otherwise instructed, use 1-inch margins and double spacing. Correct all errors. Follow one of the procedures below.

WORDS

Keyboarding Procedure
On your computer, key the following words at least two times, concentrating on the correct spelling and pronunciation.

Machine Shorthand Procedure
On your computer, key the following words once, concentrating on the correct spelling and pronunciation. Then write each word one time on your shorthand machine. Transcribe from your shorthand notes one time on your computer, or, if you are using computer-aided transcription (CAT), proofread and edit your transcript.

plea	nolo contendere	defense
confession	admission	criminal intent
sine qua non	scienter	insanity
non compos mentis	Durham Rule	M'Naghten Rule
irresistible impulse		

SENTENCES

Keyboarding Procedure
Key each of the following sentences one time on your computer. Concentrate on the correct spelling and pronunciation of each underlined legal term.

Machine Shorthand Procedure
Write the following sentences one time on your shorthand machine. Transcribe from your shorthand notes one time on your computer, or, if you are using computer-aided transcription (CAT), proofread and edit your transcript.

These sentences will be used for practice dictation on the Transcription CD.

A <u>plea</u> is an answer made by a defendant at an arraignment. The defendant will most likely plead guilty or not guilty. However, in some cases, the defendant may not enter a plea, which is referred to as standing mute before the court, or the defendant may plead <u>nolo contendere</u>. Nolo contendere is a Latin term meaning I do not wish to contend. Nolo contendere is a plea of a defendant in a criminal action that means the punishment will be accepted but guilt will not be admitted. A <u>defense</u> is the defendant's denial to an accusation or the contesting of a lawsuit.

A <u>confession</u> is a statement made voluntarily by a person admitting that he or she committed a crime. An <u>admission</u> is a statement confirming that certain facts in a case are true, but it is not a confession of quilt.

A <u>criminal intent</u> is a plan or design to commit a crime. Criminal intent is a <u>sine qua non</u>—an essential element—for one to be guilty of a crime. <u>Scienter</u> means knowingly and when used in a pleading means that the defendant was aware of what was being done.

As a defense in criminal law, <u>insanity</u> is a state of unsound mind in which a person does not know right from wrong and is, therefore, not responsible for any acts committed. The Latin term <u>non compos mentis</u>

means not of sound mind. The <u>Durham Rule</u> and the <u>M'Naghten Rule</u> are sometimes applied to a defendant who pleads **non compos mentis**. The Durham Rule applies to persons who commit acts as a result of mental disease or defect, whereas the M'Naghten Rule applies to persons who do not have the mental capacity to know right from wrong. The Durham Rule is applied in some states as an <u>irresistible impulse</u> test. An irresistible impulse is an uncontrollable urge to commit a crime due to insanity or a mental defect or disease. The M'Naghten Rule is a right-wrong test of criminal responsibility that determines whether a person had sufficient understanding to know right from wrong.

TRANSCRIBING FROM DICTATION

Directions: This dictation emphasizes and reinforces the legal terms and definitions you have studied. Listen carefully to the pronunciation of each of the legal terms. Unless otherwise directed, use 1-inch margins and double spacing. Correct all errors. Follow one of the procedures below.

Keyboarding Procedure

Using the Transcription CD, Lesson 13, Part B, transcribe the dictation directly at your computer.

Machine Shorthand Procedure

Using the Transcription CD, Lesson 13, Part B, take the dictation on your shorthand machine and then transcribe from your notes on your computer, or, if you are using computer-aided transcription (CAT), proofread and edit your transcript.

When you have finished transcribing or proofreading and editing Part B of the practice dictation, check your transcript with the printed copy. If you made any mistakes in the transcription, you should review and practice those words several times before going on to Lesson 14.

CHECKLIST

I have completed the following for Lesson 13:

	Part A, Date	Part B, Date	Submitted to Instructor Yes	No
Terminology and Definitions	_____	_____	_____	_____
Self-Evaluation	_____	_____	_____	_____
* Keying Legal Terms	_____	_____	_____	_____
Words	_____	_____	_____	_____
Sentences	_____	_____	_____	_____
* Transcribing from Dictation	_____	_____	_____	_____

When you have successfully completed all the exercises in this lesson and submitted to your instructor those requested, you are ready to proceed with Lesson 14.

* If you are using machine shorthand, submit to your instructor your notes along with your transcript.

CHECKLIST

Lesson

Criminal Law

"One who spares the guilty threatens the innocent."

—*Legal maxim*

This lesson continues the study of some of the basic terms that are applicable to the field of criminal law. When you have successfully completed these exercises, you will be able to spell, define, pronounce, and transcribe correctly the legal terms presented that pertain to criminal law.

Part A | TERMINOLOGY AND DEFINITIONS

Directions: Study the terms, pronunciations, and definitions until you are thoroughly familiar with them. In order to complete this lesson successfully, you must understand the meaning and usage of all the legal terms presented. If you are using a shorthand system, write each legal term one time on your shorthand machine.

Legal Term	Pronunciation	Definition
1. bail	bāl	Security placed with the court in order to obtain release until the time of the trial for a person being held in jail.
2. principal	ˊprin-sə-pəl	One who actually commits a crime or who actually or constructively aids and abets in its commission.
3. accomplice	ə-käm-pləs	One who knowingly assists a principal in the commission of a crime.
4. accessory	ik-ˊses-rē	One who aids the principal in the commission of a crime but is not present when the crime is actually committed. An accessory before the fact knowingly takes steps to effect the crime, whereas an accessory after the fact knowingly assists in concealing the crime and/or the offender.
5. aid and abet	ād ən ə-ˊbet	To assist in a criminal act by giving encouragement or support to its commission.
6. reasonable doubt	ˊrēz-nə-bəl daùt	Doubt that is logical, credible, or plausible. It is not an imaginary or a fictitious doubt that one can have about anything. In a criminal case, proof must be beyond a reasonable doubt, not beyond all doubt.
7. conviction	kən-ˊvik-shən	The outcome of a criminal trial whereby a person is found guilty of the charges that were made.
8. sentence	ˊsent-ns	The punishment given by the court to one convicted of a crime.

9. imprisonment	im-ˈpriz-ən-mənt	The act of placing a person in a prison or place of confinement.
10. incarcerate	in-ˈkär-sə-rāt	To imprison in a jail or penitentiary as a result of due legal process.
11. parole	pə-ˈrōl	The release of a person from prison before the end of the sentence. A parole is conditional in that if one violates the terms of the parole, the remainder of the sentence must be served.
12. pardon	ˈpärd-n	To release a person who has committed a crime from the punishment required by law. A pardon may be absolute or conditional.
13. reprieve	ri-ˈprēv	A delay or postponement of punishment.

Self-Evaluation A | Terminology and Definition Recall

Directions: In the Answers column, write the letter from Column 1 that represents the word or phrase that best matches each item in Column 2. After you have completed this self-evaluation, check your answers with the key on page 496. If you have any incorrect answers, review the definitions for those terms before going on with this lesson. Then unless otherwise directed, submit this self-evaluation to your instructor.

COLUMN 1	COLUMN 2	ANSWERS
a. accessory	1. Doubt that is logical, credible, or plausible.	1. _____
b. accomplice	2. The act of placing a person in a prison or place of confinement.	2. _____
c. aid and abet		
d. bail	3. The outcome of a criminal trial whereby a person is found guilty of the charges that were made.	3. _____
e. conviction	4. Security placed with the court in order to obtain release for a person being held in jail until the time of the trial.	4. _____
f. imprisonment		
g. incarcerate	5. The release of a person from prison before the end of the sentence on the condition if he or she violates the terms of the release, the remainder of the sentence must be served.	5. _____
h. pardon		
i. parole		
j. principal	6. One who actually commits a crime or who actually or constructively aids and abets in its commission.	6. _____
k. reasonable doubt		
l. replevin	7. A delay or postponement of punishment.	7. _____
m. reprieve	8. To imprison in a jail or penitentiary as a result of due legal process.	8. _____
n. sentence		
	9. The punishment given by the court to one convicted of a crime.	9. _____
	10. An absolute or a conditional release from the punishment required by law of one who has committed a crime.	10. _____
	11. To assist in a criminal act by giving encouragement or support to its commission.	11. _____
	12. One who knowingly assists a principal in the commission of a crime.	12. _____
	13. One who aids the principal in the commission of a crime.	13. _____

KEYING LEGAL TERMS

Directions: Unless otherwise instructed, use 1-inch margins and double spacing. Correct all errors. Follow one of the procedures below.

WORDS

Keyboarding Procedure
On your computer, key the following words at least two times, concentrating on the correct spelling and pronunciation.

Machine Shorthand Procedure
On your computer, key the following words once, concentrating on the correct spelling and pronunciation. Then write each word one time on your shorthand machine. Transcribe from your shorthand outlines one time on your computer, or, if you are using computer-aided transcription (CAT), proofread and edit your transcript.

bail	principal	accomplice
accessory	aid and abet	reasonable doubt
conviction	sentence	imprisonment
incarcerate	parole	pardon
reprieve		

SENTENCES

Keyboarding Procedure
Key each of the following sentences one time on your computer. Concentrate on the correct spelling and pronunciation of each underlined legal term.

Machine Shorthand Procedure
Write the following sentences one time on your shorthand machine. Transcribe from your shorthand notes one time on your computer, or, if you are using computer-aided transcription (CAT), proofread and edit your transcript.

These sentences will be used for practice dictation on the Transcription CD.

A defendant may be released on <u>bail</u> prior to a trial, which means that security is placed with the court in order to obtain release for a person being held in jail until the time of the trial.

The parties to a crime may be a <u>principal</u>, an <u>accomplice</u>, and an <u>accessory</u>. One who actually commits a crime or who aids and abets in its commission is a principal. To <u>aid and abet</u> is to assist in a criminal act by giving encouragement or support to its commission. An accomplice is one who knowingly assists the principal in the commission of a crime. An accessory is one who aids the principal in the commission of a crime but is not present when the crime is actually committed. An accessory before the fact knows about the crime before it is committed and may have assisted in the planning of the crime. An accessory after the fact does not have any knowledge of the crime until after it is committed but helps conceal the known facts of the crime.

<u>Reasonable doubt</u> is a doubt that is logical, credible, or plausible. Reasonable doubt is not an imaginary or a fictitious doubt. A <u>conviction</u> is the outcome of a criminal trial whereby a person is found guilty of the charges that were made. Proof beyond a reasonable doubt is required for conviction in a criminal case.

When one is convicted of a criminal offense, the <u>sentence</u> may be <u>imprisonment</u> in a jail or penitentiary. <u>Incarcerate</u> also means to imprison.

<u>Parole</u>, <u>pardon</u>, and <u>reprieve</u> all relate to the prisoner serving a lesser sentence than that given at the end of the trial. A reprieve is a delay or postponement of punishment. A parole is a conditional release of a person from prison before the end of the sentence. A pardon releases a person who has committed a crime from the punishment required by law.

TRANSCRIBING FROM DICTATION

Directions: This dictation emphasizes and reinforces the legal terms and definitions you have studied. Listen carefully to the pronunciation of each of the legal terms. Unless otherwise directed, use 1-inch margins and double spacing. Correct all errors. Follow one of the procedures below.

Keyboarding Procedure
Using the Transcription CD, Lesson 14, Part A, transcribe the dictation directly at your computer.

Machine Shorthand Procedure
Using the Transcription CD, Lesson 14, Part A, take the dictation on your shorthand machine and then transcribe from your notes on your computer, or, if you are using computer-aided transcription (CAT), proofread and edit your transcript.

When you have finished transcribing or proofreading and editing Part A of the practice dictation, check your transcript with the printed copy. If you made any mistakes in the transcription, you should review and practice those words several times before going on to Part B.

Part B | TERMINOLOGY AND DEFINITIONS

Directions: Study the terms, pronunciations, and definitions until you are thoroughly familiar with them. In order to complete this lesson successfully, you must understand the meaning and usage of all the legal terms presented. If you are using a shorthand system, write each legal term one time on your shorthand machine.

Legal Term	Pronunciation	Definition
1. homicide	ˈhäm-ə-sīd	The killing of a human being by another, whether intentional or unintentional.
2. justifiable homicide	ˈjəs-tə-fī-ə-bəl ˈhäm-ə-sīd	The intentional killing of a human being that is done without any evil design. If a police officer kills someone to prevent the commission of a felony that could not otherwise be avoided, it would be a justifiable homicide.
3. excusable homicide	ik-ˈskyü-zə-bəl ˈhäm-ə-sīd	The killing of a human being that is the result of a person doing a legal act or of an act of self-defense.
4. felonious homicide	fə-ˈlō-nē-əs ˈhäm-ə-sīd	The wrongful killing of a human being without justification or excuse of law.
5. murder	ˈmərd-ər	The intentional killing of another human being with malice aforethought.

6. manslaughter	′man-slȯt-ər	The killing of another human being that is unlawful and done without malice aforethought. Manslaughter may be voluntary or involuntary. Voluntary manslaughter is a killing done in a heat of passion or on a provoked sudden impulse. Involuntary manslaughter is usually the result of negligence.
7. malice aforethought	′mal-əs ə-′fōr-thȯt	The deliberate planning and intention to kill or seriously injure another person. An essential element that distinguishes murder from other types of homicide.
8. assault and battery	ə-′sȯlt ən ′bat-ə-rē	Assault is an actual threat to inflict bodily harm upon another, and battery is putting the threat into effect. Usually the two terms are used together in a charge because a battery is assumed, in law, to be preceded by an assault.
9. break and enter	brāk ən ′ent-ər	Forcible and unlawful entry, such as into a building, car, or boat, with the intent to commit a crime therein. A burglary. Sometimes called a B & E.
10. constructive breaking	kən-′strək-tiv ′brāk-iŋ	A breaking and entering that is accomplished by fraud, threats, or trickery rather than a forcible physical entry, such as the breaking of a lock or a window.
11. larceny	′lärs-nē	Illegally taking and carrying away personal property belonging to another with no intention of returning the property to the owner. The value of the goods stolen determines whether it is petit larceny or grand larceny. Same as burglary.
12. robbery	′räb-rē	A felony that is committed by one person taking property from another person or in the presence of that person by the use of force or violence and with no intention of returning the property to the owner.
13. animus furandi	′an-ə-məs ′fyu̇r-an-dī	Latin. The intent to steal the property of another and permanently deprive the owner of said property. An essential element of a larceny.
14. forgery	′fōrj-rē	The alteration of anything in writing with the intention of defrauding another.
15. utter and publish	′ət-ər ən ′pəb-lish	The offering of a forged instrument with the intent to defraud. If you sign someone else's name to a check and try to cash it, you are guilty of uttering and publishing.

Self-Evaluation B | Terminology and Definition Recall

Directions: In the Answers column, write the legal term that is most representative of the corresponding statement. After you have completed this self-evaluation, check your answers with the key on page 496. If you have any incorrect answers, review the definitions for those terms before going on with this lesson. Then unless otherwise directed, submit this self-evaluation to your instructor.

ANSWERS

1. The killing of another human being resulting from self-defense or from doing a legal act is _____.

   1. _____

2. Forcible and unlawful entry, such as into a building, car, or boat, with the intent to commit a crime therein is referred to as _____.

   2. _____

3. The deliberate planning and intention to kill or seriously injure another person is _____.

   3. _____

4. The alteration of anything in writing with the intention of defrauding another is _____.

   4. _____

5. A Latin term meaning the intent to steal the property of another and permanently deprive the owner of said property is _____.

   5. _____

6. Illegally taking and carrying away personal property belonging to another with no intention of returning the property to the owner is _____.

   6. _____

7. The killing of another human being that is unlawful but done without malice aforethought is _____.

   7. _____

8. A felony that is committed by one person taking property from another person or in the presence of that person by the use of force or violence and with no intention of returning the property to the owner is _____.

   8. _____

9. The intentional killing of another human being that is done without any evil design is a/an _____.

   9. _____

10. A breaking and entering that is accomplished by fraud, threats, or trickery is a/an _____.

    10. _____

11. An actual threat to inflict bodily harm upon another and putting the threat into effect is called _____.

    11. _____

12. The offering of a forged instrument with the intent to defraud is to _____.

    12. _____

13. The wrongful killing of another human being without justification or excuse of law is _____.

    13. _____

14. The intentional killing of another human being with malice aforethought is _____.

    14. _____

15. The killing of a human being by another, whether intentional or unintentional is a/an _____.

    15. _____

KEYING LEGAL TERMS

Directions: Unless otherwise instructed, use 1-inch margins and double spacing. Correct all errors. Follow one of the procedures below.

WORDS

Keyboarding Procedure
On your computer, key the following words at least two times, concentrating on the correct spelling and pronunciation.

Machine Shorthand Procedure
On your computer, key the following words once, concentrating on the correct spelling and pronunciation. Then write each word one time on your shorthand machine. Transcribe from your shorthand notes one time on your computer, or, if you are using computer-aided transcription (CAT), proofread and edit your transcript.

homicide	justifiable homicide	excusable homicide
felonious homicide	murder	malice aforethought
manslaughter	assault and battery	break and enter
constructive breaking	larceny	robbery
animus furandi	forgery	utter and publish

SENTENCES

Keyboarding Procedure
Key each of the following sentences one time on your computer. Concentrate on the correct spelling and pronunciation of each underlined legal term.

Machine Shorthand Procedure
Write the following sentences one time on your shorthand machine. Transcribe from your shorthand notes one time on your computer, or, if you are using computer-aided transcription (CAT), proofread and edit your transcript.

These sentences will be used for practice dictation on the Transcription CD.

Homicide is the killing of a human being by another, whether intentional or unintentional. Homicide may be justifiable, excusable, or felonious. _Justifiable homicide_ is an intentional killing without any evil design, such as a situation where a police officer kills someone to prevent the commission of a felony that could not otherwise be avoided. An _excusable homicide_ is a death that results from an act of self-defense or an unintentional death resulting from someone doing a legal act. _Felonious homicide_ is the wrongful killing of a human being without justification or excuse of law. Murder and manslaughter are the two types of felonious homicide.

Homicide is a necessary ingredient of the crimes of murder and manslaughter. _Murder_ is the intentional killing of another human being with _malice aforethought_, which is the deliberate planning and intention to kill or seriously injure another person. _Manslaughter_ is the killing of another human being that is unlawful but done without malice aforethought.

Assault and battery are two terms that are often combined. Assault is a threat to inflict bodily harm upon another, whereas battery is putting the threat into effect. Forcible and unlawful entry into a building with the intent to commit a crime therein is to <u>break and enter</u>. Breaking and entering is commonly referred to as a B & E. If a burglar gains entry into a house by fraud, threats, or trickery, the entry is referred to as <u>constructive breaking</u>.

Larceny and <u>robbery</u> are both felonies that involve the taking of another's personal property unlawfully. An essential element of larceny is <u>animus furandi</u>, which is the intent to steal the property of another and permanently deprive the owner of said property.

<u>Forgery</u> is the alteration of anything in writing with the intent to defraud. For instance, one might forge a signature on a check. The offering of a forged check for payment is to <u>utter and publish</u>.

TRANSCRIBING FROM DICTATION

Directions: This dictation emphasizes and reinforces the legal terms and definitions you have studied. Listen carefully to the pronunciation of each of the legal terms. Unless otherwise directed, use 1-inch margins and double spacing. Correct all errors. Follow one of the procedures below.

Keyboarding Procedure
Using the Transcription CD, Lesson 14, Part B, transcribe the dictation directly at your computer.

Machine Shorthand Procedure
Using the Transcription CD, Lesson 14, Part B, take the dictation on your shorthand machine and then transcribe from your notes on your computer, or, if you are using computer-aided transcription (CAT), proofread and edit your transcript.

When you have finished transcribing or proofreading and editing Part B of the practice dictation, check your transcript with the printed copy. If you made any mistakes in the transcription, you should review and practice those words several times before going on to Evaluation 7.

CHECKLIST
I have completed the following for Lesson 14:

	Part A, Date	Part B, Date	Submitted to Instructor Yes	No
Terminology and Definitions	_____	_____	_____	_____
Self-Evaluation	_____	_____	_____	_____
* Keying Legal Terms	_____	_____	_____	_____
Words	_____	_____	_____	_____
Sentences	_____	_____	_____	_____
* Transcribing from Dictation	_____	_____	_____	_____

When you have successfully completed all the exercises in this lesson and submitted to your instructor those requested, you are ready to proceed with Evaluation 7.

* If you are using machine shorthand, submit to your instructor your notes along with your transcript.

Evaluation No. 7 | SECTION A

Directions: This dictation/transcription evaluation will test your spelling and transcription abilities on the legal terms that you studied in the two preceding lessons. Tab once for a paragraph indention, and use 1-inch margins and double spacing unless otherwise instructed. Correct all errors. Follow one of the procedures below.

Keyboarding Procedure

Using the Transcription CD for Evaluation 7, transcribe the dictation directly at your computer.

Machine Shorthand Procedure

Using the Transcription CD for Evaluation 7, take the dictation on your shorthand machine and then transcribe from your notes on your computer, or, if you are using computer-aided transcription (CAT), proofread and edit your transcript.

Sections B and C are available from your instructor.

Lesson
15

Probate—Wills and Estates

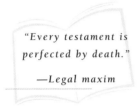

"Every testament is perfected by death."

—Legal maxim

When a person dies, his or her property must be distributed through probate procedures. State laws regarding probate procedures will vary considerably. However, the terminology and definitions in this lesson are standard in most jurisdictions. When you have satisfactorily completed the following exercises, you will be able to spell, define, pronounce, and transcribe correctly the terms that are related to probate procedures.

Part A | TERMINOLOGY AND DEFINITIONS

Directions: Study the terms, pronunciations, and definitions until you are thoroughly familiar with them. In order to complete this lesson successfully, you must understand the meaning and usage of all the legal terms presented. If you are using a shorthand system, write each legal term one time on your shorthand machine.

Legal Term	Pronunciation	Definition
1. durable power of attorney	′du̇r-ə-bəl pau̇r əv ə-′tər-nē	A written power of attorney giving someone the power to act for a person if he or she becomes disabled. To be valid, it must be signed prior to a person becoming disabled. The person appointed to act is sometimes referred to as an attorney in fact.
2. probate	′prō-bāt	The official proving of a will as being valid or genuine. In a broader sense, it refers to all matters over which a probate court has jurisdiction.
3. will	wil	A legal document that expresses how one wants property disposed of upon his or her death. Also referred to as a last will and testament or testament. (See Figure 15-1, page 211.)
4. petition for probate	pə-′tish-ən fər ′prō-bāt	A written application to a court that has jurisdiction over probate matters requesting that a will be admitted to probate.
5. attestation clause	a-tes-′tā-shən klȯz	A clause at the end of a will by which witnesses verify or certify that the will was properly executed. (See Figure 15-2, page 212.)
6. codicil	′käd-ə-səl	Something added to a will that changes or modifies it in some way. A codicil may be added to change a part of a will so that the entire will does not have to be redone. (See Figure 15-3, page 213.)

7.	nuncupative will	′nən-kyu̇-pat-iv wil	A will made in anticipation of immediate death that is stated orally before other persons and later put in written form.
8.	holographic will	hō-lə-′graf-ik wil	A will that is in the handwriting of the one making it.
9.	living will	′liv-iŋ wil	Commands an action while a person is still living. It is a means by which people can set limits on the efforts to keep them alive beyond the point they would choose themselves.
10.	testator (male); testatrix (female)	′tes-tāt-ər ′tes-tā-triks	A person who makes a will or a person who dies that has made a will.
11.	testate	′tes-tāt	A person who dies leaving a legal and valid will. If one dies leaving a will, he or she is said to die testate.
12.	intestate	in-′tes-tāt	A person who dies without a will. If one dies without a will, then he or she is said to have died intestate.
13.	animus testandi	′an-ə-məs tes-′tan-dī	Latin. The intention to make a will. Essential to a valid will.
14.	testamentary capacity	tes-tə-′ment-ə-rē kə-′pas-ət-ē	The mental ability and capacity required by law to be sufficient for one to make a valid will.

FIGURE 15-1 A Will

𝕭e it 𝕽emembered, That I, DENNIS ASHTON GRIFFIN

of 54432 Westcox Drive, Paducah, Kentucky,

being of sound mind and memory, but knowing the uncertainties of this life, do hereby make, execute and declare this to be My Last Will and Testament, in the manner of following:

First, I will and direct that all my just debts and funeral expenses be paid in full.

Second, I give, devise and bequeath unto my wife, LESLIE ANN GRIFFIN, all my tangible personalty and household effects of personal use, such as clothing, jewelry, precious stones, books, pictures, vehicles, hobby items, boats and pets of every kind and description and wherever located, and any policies of insurance on any of said property, the same to be hers absolutely. I do not intend hereby to claim an interest in any such property which may already belong to my wife, and I authorize my Executrix or Executor to honor in her or his discretion any claim of ownership with reference to any such property. If my said wife shall not survive me, I direct that the foregoing property shall become a part of my residuary estate and be distributed in the same manner as provided herein for the disposition of my residuary estate.

THIRD: All of the rest, residue and remainder of my property and estate, real, personal or mixed, now or hereafter acquired of whatever nature and wherever situate to which I may be legally or equitably entitled at the time of my death, I do give, devise and bequeath to COMMONWEALTH BANK, a Kentucky Banking corporation of Paducah, Kentucky, as Trustee, to be managed and administered and the principal thereof and income therefrom held and distributed as

FIGURE 15-2 An Attestation Clause

FOURTEENTH: Although it is my understanding that my wife is or may be executing her Last Will and Testament at or about the time of the execution of this my Last Will and Testament, it is not my nor our intention that such Wills shall be construed or deemed to be mutual, reciprocal or dependent one upon the other, and such Wills are not executed pursuant to any contract or agreement.

I hereby appoint   LESLIE ANN GRIFFIN

of   54432 Westcox Drive, Paducah, Kentucky,

execut rix   of this my Last Will and Testament.

Lastly, I do hereby revoke all former, any and every Will heretobefore made by me.

In Testimony Whereof, I have hereunto set my hand and seal, this   sixth

day of   November   in the year two thousand and   three

Dennis Ashton Griffin (SEAL)
DENNIS ASHTON GRIFFIN

On this   sixth   day of   November   in the year two thousand

and   three   ,   DENNIS ASHTON GRIFFIN

of 54432 Westcox Drive   in the County of   McCracken   and State

of   Kentucky   signed the foregoing instrument in our presence, and declared it to be   his   Last Will and Testament, and we not being interested therein, at the request of said

DENNIS ASHTON GRIFFIN   in h is   presence, and in the presence of each other, and where he could see us sign our names, did thereupon, on said above mentioned day subscribe our names hereto as witnesses thereof.

Sandra Bright   , residing at *849 Whitmore Drive*
Ralph Longshore   , residing at *1740 Marigold Lane*

Attestation Clause

FIGURE 15-3 A Codicil

CODICIL

I, DENNIS ASHTON GRIFFIN, of the City of Paducah, County of McCracken, State of Kentucky, do make, publish, and declare this to be the first codicil to my Last Will and Testament.

In the event that my wife, LESLIE ANN GRIFFIN, should predecease me or die simultaneously as defined in my Last Will and Testament, I hereby bequeath my tangible personalty and household effects of personal use as defined in my Last Will and Testament to Habitat for Humanity, Inc., of Paducah, Kentucky, the same to belong to Habitat for Humanity absolutely.

I hereby ratify, republish, and reaffirm said Last Will and Testament in all respects, except as modified by this Codicil thereto.

In witness whereof, I have hereunto set my hand and seal this third day of December, 2003.

Dennis Ashton Griffin L.S.
DENNIS ASHTON GRIFFIN

Attestation Clause

Signed, sealed, published, and declared by DENNIS ASHTON GRIFFIN the abovenamed testator, as and for a Codicil to his Last Will and Testament in the presence of us, who at his request and in his presence and in the presence of one another, have hereunto subscribed our names as witnesses, this third day of December, 2003.

Sandra Bright .... residing at *849 Whitmore Drive*

Ralph Longshore .... residing at *1740 Marigold Lane*

Self-Evaluation A | Terminology and Definition Recall

Directions: In the Answers column, write the letter from Column 1 that represents the word or phrase that best match-es each item in Column 2. After you have completed this self-evaluation, check your answers with the key on page 496. If you have any incorrect answers, review the definitions for those terms before going on with this lesson. Then unless otherwise directed, submit this self-evaluation to your instructor.

Column 1	Column 2	Answers
a. animus testandi	1. The official proving of a will as being valid or genuine.	1. _____
b. attestation clause	2. A clause at the end of a will by which witnesses verify or certify that the will was properly executed.	2. _____
c. codicil	3. Commands an action while a person is still living.	3. _____
d. durable power of attorney	4. A person who dies without a will.	4. _____
e. holographic will	5. A Latin expression meaning the intention to make a will.	5. _____
f. intestate	6. A document giving someone the power to act for a person if he or she becomes disabled.	6. _____
g. living will	7. A will made in anticipation of immediate death that is stated orally before other persons and later put in written form.	7. _____
h. nuncupative will		
i. petition for probate	8. Something added to a will that changes or modifies it in some way.	8. _____
j. power of attorney	9. A person who makes a will or a deceased person who has made a will.	9. _____
k. probate	10. A word describing a deceased person who has left a legal and valid will.	10. _____
l. testate	11. A written application to a court that has jurisdiction over probate matters requesting that a will be admitted to probate.	11. _____
m. testamentary capacity		
n. testator/testatrix	12. The mental ability and capacity required by law to be sufficient for one to make a valid will.	12. _____
o. will	13. A legal document expressing how a person wants prop-erty disposed of upon his or her death.	13. _____
	14. A will that is in the handwriting of the one making the will.	14. _____

KEYING LEGAL TERMS

Directions: Unless otherwise instructed, use 1-inch margins and double spacing. Correct all errors. Follow one of the procedures below.

WORDS

Keyboarding Procedure

On your computer, key the following words at least two times, concentrating on the correct spelling and pronunciation.

Machine Shorthand Procedure

On your computer, key the following words once, concentrating on the correct spelling and pronunciation. Then write each word one time on your shorthand machine. Transcribe from your shorthand notes one time on your computer, or, if you are using computer-aided transcription (CAT), proofread and edit your transcript.

durable power of attorney	probate	will
petition for probate	attestation clause	codicil
nuncupative will	holographic will	living will
testator	testatrix	testate
intestate	animus testandi	testamentary capacity

SENTENCES

Keyboarding Procedure

Key each of the following sentences one time on your computer. Concentrate on the correct spelling and pronunciation of each underlined legal term.

Machine Shorthand Procedure

Write the following sentences one time on your shorthand machine. Transcribe from your shorthand notes one time on your computer, or, if you are using computer-aided transcription (CAT), proofread and edit your transcript.

These sentences will be used for practice dictation on the Transcription CD.

A <u>durable power of attorney</u> gives someone the power to act for you if you become disabled. However, a durable power of attorney must be signed prior to the person becoming disabled to be valid. A power of attorney that does not contain words stating that it shall not be affected by the person's disability is not valid after the person becomes disabled.

<u>Probate</u> is the official proving of a <u>will</u> as being valid or genuine. A will is a legal document that expresses how one wants property disposed of upon his or her death. A written application to a probate court requesting that a will be admitted to probate is a <u>petition for probate</u>.

An <u>attestation clause</u> is a clause at the end of a will by which witnesses verify or certify that the will was properly executed. A will may be added to or changed by a <u>codicil</u>. A will made in anticipation of immediate death that is stated orally before other persons and later put in written form is a <u>nuncupative will</u>.

A <u>holographic will</u> is one that is in the handwriting of the person who makes it. A <u>living will</u> commands an action while a person is still living and is a means by which a person can set limits on the efforts to keep him or her alive. The intention of a living will is to assure that a patient's wishes regarding care during a terminal illness will be followed.

A <u>testator</u> or <u>testatrix</u> is a person who makes a will or one who dies who has made a will. If one dies leaving a will, then the person dies <u>testate</u>. However, if one dies without a will, he or she is said to have died <u>intestate</u>.

<u>Animus testandi</u> is essential to the making of a will. Animus testandi means the intention to make a will. Additionally, for a will to be valid, the testator or testatrix must have <u>testamentary capacity</u>. Testamentary capacity is the mental ability and capacity required by law to be sufficient for one to make a valid will. A will is also referred to as a last will and testament.

TRANSCRIBING FROM DICTATION

Directions: This dictation emphasizes and reinforces the legal terms and definitions you have studied. Listen carefully to the pronunciation of each of the legal terms. Unless otherwise directed, use 1-inch margins and double spacing. Correct all errors. Follow one of the procedures below.

Keyboarding Procedure
Using the Transcription CD, Lesson 15, Part A, transcribe the dictation directly at your computer.

Machine Shorthand Procedure
Using the Transcription CD, Lesson 15, Part A, take the dictation on your shorthand machine and then transcribe from your notes on your computer, or, if you are using computer-aided transcription (CAT), proofread and edit your transcript.

When you have finished transcribing or proofreading and editing Part A of the practice dictation, check your transcript with the printed copy. If you made any mistakes in the transcription, you should review and practice those words several times before going on to Part B.

Part B | TERMINOLOGY AND DEFINITIONS

Directions: Study the terms, pronunciations, and definitions until you are thoroughly familiar with them. In order to complete this lesson successfully, you must understand the meaning and usage of all the legal terms presented. If you are using a shorthand system, write each legal term on your shorthand machine.

Legal Term	Pronunciation	Definition
1. estate	is-ˈtāt	Property of any kind that one owns and can dispose of in a will.
2. publication	pəb-lə-ˈkā-shən	The formal declaration made by a testator or testatrix at the time a will is signed stating that it is his or her last will and testament.
3. bequest	bi-ˈkwest	Something that is given to another by a will. Usually money or personal property. A legacy.
4. bequeath	bi-ˈkwēth	The giving of something, such as personal property or money, to another by a will.
5. devise	di-ˈvīz	A bequest or to bequeath. Usually refers to real property that is given by will, but it may also refer to any property that is given by will or the giving of property by will.

6.	abatement	ə-ˈbāt-mənt	A decrease in the bequests or legacies because there is not enough money in the estate to pay the full amount. The bequests or legacies are usually decreased proportionately.
7.	residuary estate	ri-ˈzij-ə-wer-ē is-ˈtāt	The estate remaining after debts, expenses, and specific bequests have been settled.
8.	creditor's claim	ˈkred-ət-ərs klām	A written request for the payment of a bill from the estate of the deceased.
9.	hereditaments	her-ə-ˈdit-ə-mənts	Any kind of property that may be inherited.
10.	tangible property	ˈtan-jə-bəl ˈpräp-ərt-ē	Any article of personal property. Does not include real estate. Also referred to as a chattel.
11.	executor (male); executrix (female)	ig-ˈzek-ət-ər ig-ˈzek-ə-triks	A person named by a testator or testatrix to carry out the directions as stated in a will. Referred to in some states as a personal representative.
12.	administrator (male); administratrix (female)	əd-ˈmin-ə-strāt-ər əd-ˈmin-ə-ˈstrā-triks	A person who is appointed by the court to administer or take charge of an estate if the executor or executrix is unable or unwilling to serve or if a person dies intestate.
13.	letters of authority	ˈlet-ərs əv ə-ˈthär-ət-ē	A document issued by the probate court appointing a person as executor/executrix, or personal representative, of an estate. Also referred to in some states as letters testamentary. If the court document appoints a person as an administrator or administratrix, then the document is referred to as letters of administration. (See Figure 15-4, page 220.)

FIGURE 15-4 Letters of Authority

STATE OF MICHIGAN PROBATE COURT COUNTY OF Ingham	LETTERS OF AUTHORITY	FILE NO. 789345-37

Estate of HEATHER CAROL BENNETT

TRAVIS WARD BENNETT
Name
789 Prescott Avenue, Holt, Michigan 48842
Address
has been appointed Administrator

of the estate and has filed an acceptance of trust or a bond which has been approved as required by law, and by this instrument is granted full power and authority to take possession, collect, preserve, manage and dispose of all the property of the estate according to law, and to perform all acts permitted or required by statute, court rule and orders and decrees of this court, unless limited below.

RESTRICTIONS: None

July 17, 2003
Date
Natalie Lee Lamont (P 99905)
Judge of Probate   **Bar no.**

Morgan Renee Jeffery   (P 55217)
Attorney name   **Bar no.**
45 Edgewood Boulevard, Suite 17
Address
Lansing, Michigan 48910 (517) 555-7781
City, state, zip   **Telephone no.**

I certify that I have compared this copy with the original on file and that it is a correct copy of the whole of such original, and on this date, these letters are in full force and effect.

July 18, 2003
Date
Robert Lambropoulos
Deputy Probate Register

Do not write below this line - For court use only

PC 15 (1/85)   **LETTERS OF AUTHORITY**   MCL 700.533, 700.534; MSA 27.5533, 27.5534, MCR 5.705

Self-Evaluation B | Terminology and Definition Recall

Directions: In the Answers column at the right of each statement, write the letter that represents the word or group of words that correctly completes the statement. After you have completed this self-evaluation, check your answers with the key on page 497. If you have any incorrect answers, review the definitions for those terms before going on with this lesson. Then unless otherwise directed, submit this self-evaluation to your instructor.

ANSWERS

1. Any article of personal property is called (a) residuary estate, (b) tangible property, (c) devise.

1. _____

2. The formal declaration made by a testator or testatrix at the time of signing a will stating that it is his or her last will and testament is a/an (a) bequest, (b) abatement, (c) publication.

2. _____

3. _____

3. To give something, such as personal property or money, to another by a will is to (a) bequeath, (b) devise, (c) residuary estate.

4. _____

4. Property of any kind that one owns and can dispose of in a will is called (a) tangible property, (b) estate, (c) publication.

5. _____

5. A person who is appointed by the court to administer or take charge of an estate is referred to as a/an (a) executor or executrix, (b) testator or testatrix, (c) administrator or administratrix.

6. _____

6. A proportional decrease in the bequests or legacies because there is not enough money in the estate to pay the full amount is known as (a) creditor's claim, (b) bequeath, (c) abatement.

7. _____

7. The estate remaining after debts, expenses, and specific bequests have been settled is the (a) tangible property, (b) creditor's claim, (c) residuary estate.

8. _____

8. Something that is given to another by a will is a/an (a) abatement, (b) bequest, (c) publication.

9. _____

9. Any kind of property that may be inherited is called (a) hereditaments, (b) bequest, (c) estate.

10. _____

10. A bequest or to bequeath is (a) devise, (b) abatement, (c) hereditament.

11. _____

11. A document issued by a probate court appointing a person as administrator or administratrix of an estate is (a) creditor's claim, (b) publication, (c) letters of authority.

12. _____

12. A written request for the payment of a bill from the estate of the deceased is a (a) bequest, (b) creditor's claim, (c) letters of authority.

13. _____

14. _____

15. _____

13. A person named by a testator or testatrix in a will to carry out the directions as stated in the will is a/an (a) executor or executrix, (b) administrator or administratrix, (c) devise.

KEYING LEGAL TERMS

Directions: Unless otherwise instructed, use 1-inch margins and double spacing. Correct all errors. Follow one of the procedures below.

WORDS

Keyboarding Procedure
On your computer, key the following words at least two times, concentrating on the correct spelling and pronunciation.

Machine Shorthand Procedure
On your computer, key the following words once, concentrating on the correct spelling and pronunciation. Then write each word one time on your shorthand machine. Transcribe from your shorthand notes one time on your computer, or, if you are using computer-aided transcription (CAT), proofread and edit your transcript.

estate	publication	bequest
bequeath	devise	abatement
residuary estate	creditor's claim	hereditaments
tangible property	executor	executrix
administrator	administratrix	letters of authority

SENTENCES

Keyboarding Procedure
Key each of the following sentences one time on your computer. Concentrate on the correct spelling and pronunciation of each underlined legal term.

Machine Shorthand Procedure
Write the following sentences one time on your shorthand machine. Transcribe from your shorthand notes one time on your computer, or, if you are using computer-aided transcription (CAT), proofread and edit your transcript.

These sentences will be used for practice dictation on the Transcription CD.

An <u>estate</u> is property of any kind that a person owns and can dispose of in a will. <u>Publication</u> is the formal declaration made by a testator or testatrix at the time of signing a will stating that it is his or her last will and testament.

<u>Bequest</u> and <u>bequeath</u> are used in relation to personal property disposed of by a will. A bequest is money or personal property given to another by a will. Bequeath is the giving of something, such as personal property or money, to another by a will. <u>Devise</u> is a bequest, or it may also mean to bequeath. If the assets of an estate are not sufficient to pay the legacies in full, <u>abatement</u> results. Abatement is a proportional decrease of the legacies.

The <u>residuary estate</u> is what remains after all debts and expenses of a will have been settled. A written request for the payment of a bill from the estate of a deceased person is a <u>creditor's claim</u>.

Things or property that may be inherited are referred to as <u>hereditaments</u>. Hereditaments include <u>tangible property</u>, also called chattels, and real estate. Tangible property is any article of personal property but does not include real estate.

An **executor** or **executrix** is a person named by a **testator** or **testatrix** to carry out the directions as stated in a will after the testator's or testatrix's death. If a person dies intestate, the court will appoint an **administrator** or an **administratrix** to administer or take charge of the estate. If a testator or testatrix does not name an executor or executrix in a will or the persons named are incapable or unable to administer the will, the court will appoint an administrator or administratrix to handle the estate. A document issued by the probate court appointing a person as administrator or administratrix of an estate is referred to as **letters of authority**. This document gives the appointed person the authority to manage or dispose of the property in an estate.

TRANSCRIBING FROM DICTATION

Directions: This dictation emphasizes and reinforces the legal terms and definitions you have studied. Listen carefully to the pronunciation of each of the legal terms. Unless otherwise directed, use 1-inch margins and double spacing. Correct all errors. Follow one of the procedures below.

Keyboarding Procedure
Using the Transcription CD, Lesson 15, Part B, transcribe the dictation directly at your computer.

Machine Shorthand Procedure
Using the Transcription CD, Lesson 15, Part B, take the dictation on your shorthand machine and then transcribe from your notes on your computer, or, if you are using computer-aided transcription (CAT), proofread and edit your transcript.

When you have finished transcribing or proofreading and editing Part B of the practice dictation, check your transcript with the printed copy. If you made any mistakes in the transcription, you should review and practice those words several times before going on to Lesson 16.

CHECKLIST
I have completed the following for Lesson 15:

	Part A, Date	Part B, Date	Submitted to Instructor Yes	No
Terminology and Definitions	_____	_____	_____	_____
Self-Evaluation	_____	_____	_____	_____
* Keying Legal Terms	_____	_____	_____	_____
Words	_____	_____	_____	_____
Sentences	_____	_____	_____	_____
* Transcribing from Dictation	_____	_____	_____	_____

When you have successfully completed all the exercises in this lesson and submitted to your instructor those requested, you are ready to proceed with Lesson 16.

* If you are using machine shorthand, submit to your instructor your notes along with your transcript.

CHECKLIST

Lesson
16

Probate—Wills and Estates

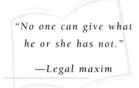

"No one can give what he or she has not."

—*Legal maxim*

This lesson continues the study of some of the basic terms that are applicable to probate procedures. When you have successfully completed the following exercises, you will be able to spell, define, pronounce, and transcribe correctly the legal terms presented.

Part A | TERMINOLOGY AND DEFINITIONS

Directions: Study the terms, pronunciations, and definitions until you are thoroughly familiar with them. In order to complete this lesson successfully, you must understand the meaning and usage of all the legal terms presented. If you are using a shorthand system, write each legal term one time on your shorthand machine.

Legal Term	Pronunciation	Definition
1. citation	sī-tā-ʹshən	A summons issued requiring a person to appear in court or risk losing a right to something. In probate matters, that right may be the right to inherit.
2. beneficiary	ben-ə-ʹfish-ē-er-ē	Anyone who is to receive benefit from a will.
3. cestui que trust	ʹses-twē kē trəst	French. A beneficiary of a trust. A person who receives benefits from a trust.
4. heir	ar	A person who has a right by law to inherit the property of another.
5. pretermitted heir	prēt-ər-ʹmit-əd ar	A legal heir who is unintentionally omitted in the will by the testator or testatrix.
6. succession	sək-ʹsesh-ən	The right to an inheritance. The taking over of property that has been inherited.
7. legacy	ʹleg-ə-sē	A bequest. Usually money or personal property given to another by a will.
8. ademption	ə-ʹdem-shən	Revoking, recalling, or voiding a legacy. This can occur when a testator or testatrix disposes of property that is included in the will prior to the testator's or testatrix's death, thus voiding that part of the will.
9. escheat	is-ʹchēt	A reversion of property to the state if there is no individual competent to inherit it.

10. cy pres doctrine	sī ′prā ′däk-trən	French. As near as possible. The court will endeavor to carry out the testator's or testatrix's general intention as near as possible.
11. per stirpes	pər ′stər-pās	Latin. A method of dividing an estate. If an estate is to be divided between two persons and one has died leaving three heirs, then one half of the estate is given to the surviving person and the other half is divided among the heirs of the deceased person.
12. precatory words	′prek-ə-tōr-ē wərds	Words in a will that express a desire on the part of the testator or testatrix that are not binding upon the court.
13. ambulatory instrument	′am-byə-lə-tōr-ē ′in-strə-mənt	A legal document that can be changed. A will is an ambulatory instrument because it can be changed during the lifetime of the testator or testatrix.

Self–Evaluation A | Terminology and Definition Recall

Directions: In the Answers column at the right of each statement, write the letter that represents the word or group of words that correctly completes the statement. After you have completed this self-evaluation, check your answers with the key on page 497. If you have any incorrect answers, review the definitions for those terms before going on with this lesson. Then unless otherwise directed, submit this self-evaluation to your instructor.

ANSWERS

1. Words in a will expressing a desire on the part of the testator or testatrix that are not binding upon the courts are called (a) precatory words, (b) ambulatory instruments, (c) cy pres doctrine.

1. _____

2. A bequest that is usually money or personal property given to another by a will is a/an (a) legacy, (b) ademption, (c) cestui que trust.

2. _____

3. A reversion of property to the state if there is no individual competent to inherit it is known as (a) beneficiary, (b) escheat, (c) cestui que trust.

3. _____

4. A summons issued requiring a person to appear in court or risk losing a right to something, which in probate matters may be the right to inherit, is a/an (a) cy pres doctrine, (b) ambulatory instrument, (c) citation.

4. _____

5. Revoking, recalling, or voiding a legacy is (a) per stirpes, (b) ademption, (c) succession.

5. _____

6. The right to an inheritance or the taking over of property that has been inherited is (a) succession, (b) escheat, (c) legacy.

6. _____

7. A person who has a right by law to inherit the property of another is known as a/an (a) heir, (b) beneficiary, (c) legacy.

7. _____

8. A legal heir who is unintentionally omitted in the will by the testator or testatrix is a/an (a) legacy, (b) pretermitted heir, (c) escheat.

8. _____

9. Anyone who is to receive benefit from a will is known as a/an (a) heir, (b) legacy, (c) beneficiary.

9. _____

10. A doctrine indicating that the court will endeavor to carry out the testator's or testatrix's general intention as near as possible is the (a) ambulatory instrument, (b) cy pres doctrine, (c) precatory words.

10. _____

11. A beneficiary of a trust or a person who receives benefits from a trust is expressed in French as (a) cestui que trust, (b) cy pres doctrine, (c) per stirpes.

11. _____

12. A method of dividing an estate is (a) ademption, (b) succession, (c) per stirpes.

12. _____

13. A legal document that can be changed, such as a will that can be changed during the lifetime of the testator or testatrix, is a/an (a) cy pres doctrine, (b) precatory words, (c) ambulatory instrument.

13. _____

KEYING LEGAL TERMS

Directions: Unless otherwise instructed, use 1-inch margins and double spacing. Correct all errors. Follow one of the procedures below.

WORDS

Keyboarding Procedure
On your computer, key the following words at least two times, concentrating on the correct spelling and pronunciation.

Machine Shorthand Procedure
On your computer, key the following words once, concentrating on the correct spelling and pronunciation. Then write each word one time on your shorthand machine. Transcribe from your shorthand notes one time on your computer, or, if you are using computer-aided transcription (CAT), proofread and edit your transcript.

citation	beneficiary	cestui que trust
heir	pretermitted heir	succession
legacy	ademption	escheat
cy pres doctrine	per stirpes	precatory words
ambulatory instrument		

SENTENCES

Keyboarding Procedure
Key each of the following sentences one time on your computer. Concentrate on the correct spelling and pronunciation of each underlined legal term.

Machine Shorthand Procedure
Write the following sentences one time on your shorthand machine. Transcribe from your shorthand notes one time on your computer, or, if you are using computer-aided transcription (CAT), proofread and edit your transcript.

These sentences will be used for practice dictation on the Transcription CD.

A <u>citation</u> issued in probate matters requires a person to appear in court or risk losing a right to inherit something. A <u>beneficiary</u> is a person who is to receive benefit from a will. The person to whom a policy of insurance is payable is also a beneficiary. The beneficiary of a trust is also known as a <u>cestui que trust</u>. An <u>heir</u> is a person who has a right by law to inherit the property of another. An heir is appointed by the court to inherit an estate if there is no will or if a person died intestate. Thus, the difference between an heir and a beneficiary is that an heir is legally entitled to an estate if there is no will, whereas a beneficiary is named in a will to inherit an intestate.

A <u>pretermitted heir</u> is a legal heir who is unintentionally omitted in a will by the testator or testatrix. <u>Succession</u> involves the transfer of property according to law to the heirs when a person dies intestate. A <u>legacy</u> is a bequest, usually money or personal property, given to another by a will.

<u>Ademption</u> involves revoking, recalling, or voiding a legacy. Ademption occurs when a testator or testatrix disposes of property named in the will prior to death. Property disposed of by ademption makes it impossible to carry out the terms of the will. <u>Escheat</u> is a reversion of property to the state if there is no individual competent to inherit it.

The <u>cy pres doctrine</u> calls for the court to endeavor to carry out the testator's or testatrix's general intention as near as possible. If an estate is divided <u>per stirpes</u>, it is divided by representation or family groups instead of by individuals. <u>Precatory words</u> in a will express a desire or a wish rather than a command. Precatory words may not be legally binding.

An <u>ambulatory instrument</u> is a legal document that can be changed. A will is an ambulatory instrument because it can be changed during the lifetime of the testator or testatrix.

TRANSCRIBING FROM DICTATION

Directions: This dictation emphasizes and reinforces the legal terms and definitions you have studied. Listen carefully to the pronunciation of each of the legal terms. Unless otherwise directed use 1-inch margins and double spacing. Correct all errors. Follow one of the procedures below.

Keyboarding Procedure
Using the Transcription CD, Lesson 16, Part A, transcribe the dictation directly at your computer.

Machine Shorthand Procedure
Using the Transcription CD, Lesson 16, Part A, take the dictation on your shorthand machine and then transcribe from your notes on your computer, or, if you are using computer-aided transcription (CAT), proofread and edit your transcript.

When you have finished transcribing or proofreading and editing Part A of the practice dictation, check your transcript with the printed copy. If you made any mistakes in the transcription, you should review and practice those words several times before going on to Part B.

Part B | TERMINOLOGY AND DEFINITIONS

Directions: Study the terms, pronunciations, and definitions until you are thoroughly familiar with them. In order to complete this lesson successfully, you must understand the meaning and usage of all the legal terms presented. If you are using a shorthand system, write each legal term one time on your shorthand machine.

Legal Term	Pronunciation	Definition
1. trust	trəst	Property that is placed in the care of one person for the benefit of another.
2. trust estate	trəst is-ʹtāt	Property that is held in trust for the benefit of another.
3. dower	daůr	The life estate to which every married woman is entitled upon her husband's death. Dower rights may vary from state to state.
4. reversion	ri-ʹvər-zhən	The future interest of the heirs of a testator or testatrix in property left to another for a specified period of time. At the end of the specified period, the property reverts back to the heirs of the testator or testatrix.
5. indefeasible	in-di-ʹfē-zə-bəl	Something that cannot be voided, annulled, or revoked. A right to an estate that cannot be defeated is said to be indefeasible.

6. revocation	rev-ə-ˈkā-shən	A voiding of a will by a testator or testatrix.
7. animus revocandi	ˈan-ə-məs rev-ə-ˈkan-dī	Latin. The intent to revoke.
8. guardian	ˈgärd-ē-ən	A person who is legally responsible for the care of a minor or an incompetent person and/or the estate of a minor or an incompetent person. The document issued by the court granting a guardian the power or authority to act on behalf of the ward is referred to as letters of guardianship.
9. guardian ad litem	ˈgärd-ē-ən ad ˈlīt-əm	Latin. A person designated by the court to conduct litigation on behalf of a minor.
10. ward	wȯrd	A person who has a legal guardian. A ward may be a minor or an incompetent person.
11. conservatorship	kən-ˈsər-vət-ər-ship	Created by law to care for the property of an incompetent person or a minor.
12. conservator	kən-ˈsər-vət-ər	One who is in charge of a conservatorship and manages the property of an incompetent person or a minor. Letters of conservatorship are issued by the court granting a conservator the power of authority to act on behalf of the conservatorship.
13. surrogate	ˈsər-ə-gāt	One appointed to act in the place of another. In some states, one who has jurisdiction over the probate of wills, guardianships, and conservatorships.

Self-Evaluation B | Terminology and Definition Recall

Directions: In the Answers column, write the legal term that is most representative of the corresponding statement. After you have completed this self-evaluation, check your answers with the key on page 497. If you have any incorrect answers, review the definitions for those terms before going on with this lesson. Then unless otherwise directed, submit this self-evaluation to your instructor.

ANSWERS

1. A person who has a legal guardian is a/an _____.   1. _____

2. A voiding of a will by a testator or testatrix is a/an _____.   2. _____

3. A person designated by the court to conduct litigation on behalf of a minor is a/an _____.   3. _____

4. A trust created by the court for the care of the property of an incompetent person or minor is a/an _____.   4. _____

5. The intent to revoke, as expressed in Latin, is _____.   5. _____

6. The life estate to which every married woman is entitled upon her husband's death is a/an _____.   6. _____

7. One who is in charge of a conservatorship and manages the property of an incompetent person or a minor is a/an _____.   7. _____

8. The future interest of the heirs in property left to another for a specified period of time after which the property reverts back to the heirs is _____.   8. _____

9. Something that cannot be voided, annulled, or revoked is said to be _____.   9. _____

10. A person who is legally responsible for the care of a minor and/or the minor's estate is a/an _____.   10. _____

11. One appointed to act in the place of another or, in some states, one who has jurisdiction over matters of probate, guardianships, and conservatorships is a/an _____.   11. _____

12. Property that is placed in the care of one person for the benefit of another is a/an _____.   12. _____

13. Property that is held in trust for the benefit of another is a/an _____.   13. _____

KEYING LEGAL TERMS

Directions: Unless otherwise instructed, use 1-inch margins and double spacing. Correct all errors. Follow one of the procedures below.

WORDS

Keyboarding Procedure
On your computer, key the following words at least two times, concentrating on the correct spelling and pronunciation.

Machine Shorthand Procedure
On your computer, key the following words once, concentrating on the correct spelling and pronunciation. Then write each word one time on your shorthand machine. Transcribe from your shorthand notes one time on your computer, or, if you are using computer-aided transcription (CAT), proofread and edit your transcript.

trust	**trust estate**	**dower**
reversion	**indefeasible**	**revocation**
animus revocandi	**guardian**	**guardian ad litem**
ward	**conservatorship**	**conservator**
surrogate		

SENTENCES

Keyboarding Procedure
Key each of the following sentences one time on your computer. Concentrate on the correct spelling and pronunciation of each underlined legal term.

Machine Shorthand Procedure
Write the following sentences one time on your shorthand machine. Transcribe from your shorthand notes one time on your computer, or, if you are using computer-aided transcription (CAT), proofread and edit your transcript.

These sentences will be used for practice dictation on the Transcription CD.

A <u>trust</u> exists when real or personal property is held by one party for the benefit and use by a beneficiary or a cestui que trust. For example, property may be held in trust for minor children until they reach a specified age. A <u>trust estate</u> is property that is held in trust for the benefit of another.

<u>Dower</u> is the life estate to which every married woman is entitled upon her husband's death. Dower rights may vary from state to state. <u>Reversion</u> is the future interest of the heirs of a testator or testatrix in property left to another for a specified period of time after which the property reverts back to the heirs of the testator or testatrix.

An estate that cannot be defeated, revoked, or made void is <u>indefeasible</u>. <u>Revocation</u> is the voiding of a will by a testator or testatrix. The intent to revoke is expressed in Latin as <u>animus revocandi</u>. Animus revocandi is an element that must be present for a will to be revoked.

A <u>guardian</u> is legally responsible for the care of a minor an/or the minor's estate. A <u>guardian ad litem</u> is a person designated by the court to conduct litigation on behalf of a minor. However, a guardian ad litem has no responsibility for the minor personally or for the property that belongs to the minor. A person or an infant who has a legal guardian is called a <u>ward</u>. If a person is incompetent and cannot care for his or her own property, a <u>conservatorship</u> may be created by law to manage the property of that person. The person who manages a conservatorship is called the <u>conservator</u>.

A <u>surrogate</u> is one appointed to act in the place of another. Thus, a surrogate parent is one who has been appointed to act in the place of a natural parent. In some states, such as New York, a surrogate is one who has jurisdiction over the probate of wills.

TRANSCRIBING FROM DICTATION

Directions: This dictation emphasizes and reinforces the legal terms and definitions you have studied. Listen carefully to the pronunciation of each of the legal terms. Unless otherwise directed, use 1-inch margins and double spacing. Correct all errors. Follow one of the procedures below.

Keyboarding Procedure

Using the Transcription CD, Lesson 16, Part B, transcribe the dictation directly at your computer.

Machine Shorthand Procedure

Using the Transcription CD, Lesson 16, Part B, take the dictation on your shorthand machine and then transcribe from your notes on your computer, or, if you are using computer-aided transcription (CAT), proofread and edit your transcript.

When you have finished transcribing or proofreading and editing Part B of the practice dictation, check your transcript with the printed copy. If you made any mistakes in the transcription, you should review and practice those words several times before going on to Evaluation 8.

CHECKLIST

I have completed the following for Lesson 16:

	Part A, Date	Part B, Date	Submitted to Instructor Yes	No
Terminology and Definitions				
Self-Evaluation				
* Keying Legal Terms				
Words				
Sentences				
* Transcribing from Dictation				

When you have successfully completed all the exercises in this lesson and submitted to your instructor those requested, you are ready to proceed with Evaluation 8.

* If you are using machine shorthand, submit to your instructor your notes along with your transcript.

Evaluation No. 8 | SECTION A

Directions: This dictation/transcription evaluation will test your spelling and transcription abilities on the legal terms that you studied in the two preceding lessons. Tab once for a paragraph indention, and use 1-inch margins and double spacing unless otherwise instructed. Correct all errors. Follow one of the procedures below.

Keyboarding Procedure

Using the Transcription CD for Evaluation 8, transcribe the dictation directly at your computer.

Machine Shorthand Procedure

Using the Transcription CD for Evaluation 8, take the dictation on your shorthand machine and then transcribe your notes on your computer, or, if you are using computer-aided transcription (CAT), proofread and edit your transcript.

Sections B and C are available from your instructor.

Lesson

17

Real Property

"One who possesses land,
possesses also that which
is above it."
—Legal maxim

The area of law dealing with property governs the ownership and transfer of lands, tenements, and hereditaments. Many of the terms dealing with hereditaments (that which can be inherited) were covered in the lessons on probate. Also, terms involving leases are included in the lessons on contracts. Therefore, this lesson will include those terms that basically apply to the ownership and transfer of real property not involved in leases or probate. Upon successful completion of these exercises, you will be able to spell, pronounce, define, and transcribe correctly the basic real estate terms presented herein.

Part A | TERMINOLOGY AND DEFINITIONS

Directions: Study the terms, pronunciations, and definitions until you are thoroughly familiar with them. In order to complete this lesson successfully, you must understand the meaning and usage of all the legal terms presented. If you are using a shorthand system, write each legal term one time on your shorthand machine.

Legal Term	Pronunciation	Definition
1. real property	rēl ′präp-ərt-ē	Land and everything that is built or growing on the land, such as buildings and trees. Also referred to as real estate.
2. realty	′rēl-tē	Real property.
3. premises	′prem-ə-sez	Generally means land that has a building on it.
4. title	′tīt-l	The ownership of real property. Also, the proof of the right to ownership in land or real property.
5. fee simple	fē ′sim-pəl	Absolute and unconditional ownership in land.
6. defeasible title	di-′fē-zə-bəl ′tīt-l	A title that can be voided or made invalid.
7. defective title	di-′fek-tiv tīt-l	A title that is deficient or incomplete in some aspect required by law.
8. freehold	′frē-hōld	A right of ownership to land for life.
9. title insurance	′tīt-l in-′shur-əns	Guarantees that a person has title to property. In case of a dispute in the title, the purchaser will be reimbursed for any loss up to the amount of the policy.
10. seisin (also seizin)	′sēz-n	Actual possession of real property with the intention of claiming title to said property.
11. deed	dēd	A document or an instrument that is used to convey a title to real property from one person to another. (See Figure 17-1, page 241.)

12. warranty deed	ˈwȯr-ənt-ē dēd	A deed guaranteeing that the person transferring real property has a good and complete title to said property.
13. quitclaim deed	ˈkwit-klām dēd	A deed that conveys only the person's interest in the property if any such interest exists. It does not warrant or guarantee the title, but it does give up any right or interest one might have in the property.
14. habendum clause	ˈha-ben-dəm klȯz	A clause in a deed that clarifies the amount of ownership in the real property being transferred. Usually begins with the words, "To have and to hold." (See Figure 17-1, page 241.)

FIGURE 17-1 A Deed

Land Description

Habendum Clause

RECORDED IN DEEDS

WARRANTY DEED -- Short **891** (Rev 1967)
(PHOTO COPY FORM)   SPACE ABOVE FOR REAL ESTATE TRANSFER STAMP

This Indenture, made September 12   ,2003
BETWEEN   KYLE RUSHING AND ABBY RUSHING, husband and wife,
as tenants by the entirety, of 34550 Circle Way, Lansing,
Michigan,
1   parties of the first part,
and JANELLE ASHLEY MOORE, a single woman,

1   party of the second part,
whose address is 7885 Riverview Boulevard, Apt. 704, Lansing, Michigan
WITNESSETH, That the said party of the first part, for and in consideration of 2 Ninety-five thousand and No/100
Dollars------($95,000.00)------- --------------------------
to him in hand paid by the said party of the second part, the receipt whereof is hereby confessed and acknowledged, does by these presents, grant,
bargain, sell, remise, release, alien and confirm unto the said party of the second part, 3 his heirs   and assigns.
FOREVER, all that certain piece or parcel of land situate and being in the City
of Lansing   County of Ingham   and State of Michigan, and described as follows, to-wit:

The South 41½ feet of the North 82½ feet of Lot 1, Block 12 of Green
Oak Addition to the City of Lansing. Also commencing 41½ feet South
of the Northeast corner of Lot 1, Block 12, said Green Oak Addition,
thence South 41½ feet, thence East 8'3", thence North 41½ feet of
Lot 1 and the East 33 feet of the North 82½ feet of Lot 2 of Block 12
of Green Oak Addition to the City of Lansing, Ingham County,
Michigan; also a strip of land described as commencing at the Northeast corner
of said Lot 1, and running thence South 41½ feet, thence East 8'3",
more or less, to East line of said Lot 1, place of beginning.

Together with all and singular the hereditaments and appurtenances thereunto belonging or in anywise appertaining: To Have and to Hold
the said premises, as herein described, with the appurtenances, unto the said party of the second part and to 3 his heirs
and assigns, FOREVER. And the said party of the first part, for himself, his heirs, executors and administrators, does covenant, grant, bargain and
agree to and with the said party of the second part, 3 his heirs   and assigns, that at the time of the delivery of these presents
he is well seized of the above granted premises in fee simple: that they are free from all encumbrances whatever, except such
liens and encumbrances as may have accrued since the 10th day of January,
2003, the date of a certain executory land contract, in pursuance of and
in fulfillment of which this conveyance is made.
and that he will, and his heirs, executors, and administrators shall Warrant and Defend the same against all lawful claims whatsoever.

When applicable, pronouns and relative words shall be read as plural, feminine or neuter.
In Witness Whereof, The said party of the first part has hereunto set his hand the day and year above written.

Signed, and Delivered in Presence of   *Kyle Rushing*
                                              * KYLE RUSHING
Bennie Andrews   *Abby Rushing*
* BENNIE ANDREWS   * ABBY RUSHING
Nina Joiner
* NINA JOINER   *

STATE OF MICHIGAN,   on September 12   , 2003
                                ss.   before me, a Notary Public, in and for said County, personally appeared
COUNTY OF   Ingham   KYLE RUSHING AND ABBY RUSHING
to me known to be the same person S   described in and who executed the within instrument, who
acknowledged the same to be their   free act and deed.
4. Prepared by: David Turner (P56780)   *Robert T. Gates*
   8546 East Michigan Avenue   * Robert T. Gates   Notary Public,
   Lansing, Michigan 48912   Ingham   County, Michigan
                                         My commission expires July 2   , 2005

SEE FOOT NOTES ON OTHER SIDE

Self-Evaluation A | Terminology and Definition Recall

Directions: In the Answers column, write the letter from Column 1 that represents the word or phrase that best match-es each item in Column 2. After you have completed this self-evaluation, check your answers with the key on page 497. If you have any incorrect answers, review the definitions for those terms before going on with this lesson. Then unless otherwise directed, submit this self-evaluation to your instructor.

COLUMN 1	COLUMN 2	ANSWERS
a. clear title	1. A title that can be voided or made invalid.	1. _____
b. deed	2. Generally means land that has a building on it.	2. _____
c. defeasible title	3. A clause in a deed that clarifies the amount of ownership in the real property being transferred.	3. _____
d. defective title	4. A document or an instrument that is used to convey a title to real property from one person to another.	4. _____
e. fee simple	5. A title that is deficient or incomplete in some aspect required by law.	5. _____
f. freehold	6. Guarantees a title to property and provides reimburse-ment for any loss incurred because of a defective title.	6. _____
g. habendum clause	7. The ownership of real property or the proof of the right of ownership in land or real property.	7. _____
h. premises	8. Land and everything that is built or growing on the land.	8. _____
i. quitclaim	9. Absolute and unconditional ownership in land.	9. _____
j. real property	10. A word meaning real property.	10. _____
k. realty	11. A deed that conveys only the person's interest in the prop-erty if any such interest exists.	11. _____
l. seisin	12. Actual possession of real property with the intention of claiming title to said property.	12. _____
m. title	13. A deed guaranteeing that the person transferring real property has a good and complete title to said property.	13. _____
n. title insurance	14. A right of ownership to land for life.	14. _____
o. warranty deed		

KEYING LEGAL TERMS

Directions: Unless otherwise instructed, use 1-inch margins and double spacing. Correct all errors. Follow one of the procedures below.

WORDS

Keyboarding Procedure
On your computer, key the following words at least two times, concentrating on the correct spelling and pronunciation.

Machine Shorthand Procedure
On your computer, key the following words once, concentrating on the correct spelling and pronunciation. Then write each word one time on your shorthand machine. Transcribe from your shorthand notes one time on your computer, or, if you are using computer-aided transcription (CAT), proofread and edit your transcript.

real property	realty	premises
title	fee simple	defeasible title
defective title	freehold	title insurance
seisin	deed	warranty deed
quitclaim deed	habendum clause	

SENTENCES

Keyboarding Procedure
Key each of the following sentences one time on your computer. Concentrate on the correct spelling and pronunciation of each underlined legal term.

Machine Shorthand Procedure
Write the following sentences one time on your shorthand machine. Transcribe from your shorthand notes one time on your computer, or, if you are using computer-aided transcription (CAT), proofread and edit your transcript.

These sentences will be used for practice dictation on the Transcription CD.

Real property consists of land and everything that is built or growing on the land, such as buildings and trees. Realty is another term for real property. Premises generally means land that has a building on it. Title is the ownership of real property. Title may also be the proof of the right to ownership in land or real property.

A fee simple is an absolute and unconditional ownership in land. A defeasible title is one that is presently valid but could be voided or made invalid. A defective title is deficient or incomplete in some aspect required by law. Freehold is a right to ownership in land for life.

Title insurance guarantees that a person has a clear title to property. In case of a defective title, the title insurance company will reimburse the purchaser for any loss up to the value of the policy. Most property transfers are now being covered by title insurance. Seisin is the actual possession of real property with the intention of claiming title to said property. A deed is a document or an instrument that is used to convey a title to real property from one person to another. A warranty deed guarantees that the person transferring real property has a good and complete title to said property. The title to most property is transferred by a warranty deed. If you sell property to someone and you hold clear title to the property, you would give the buyer a warranty deed.

A <u>quitclaim deed</u> conveys only the person's interest in the property if any such interest exists. A quitclaim deed does not warrant or guarantee the title, but it does give up any right or interest one might have in the property. Thus, if you give a quitclaim deed to property, you have given up any right you might have to that property. The <u>habendum clause</u> in a deed clarifies the amount of ownership in the real property that is being transferred.

TRANSCRIBING FROM DICTATION

Directions: This dictation emphasizes and reinforces the legal terms and definitions you have studied. Listen carefully to the pronunciation of each of the legal terms. Unless otherwise directed, use 1-inch margins and double spacing. Correct all errors. Follow one of the procedures below.

Keyboarding Procedure
Using the Transcription CD, Lesson 17, Part A, transcribe the dictation directly at your computer.

Machine Shorthand Procedure
Using the Transcription CD, Lesson 17, Part A, take the dictation on your shorthand machine and then transcribe from your notes on your computer, or, if you are using computer-aided transcription (CAT), proofread and edit your transcript.

When you have finished transcribing or proofreading and editing Part A of the practice dictation, check your transcript with the printed copy. If you made any mistakes in the transcription, you should review and practice those words several times before going on to Part B.

Part B | TERMINOLOGY AND DEFINITIONS

Directions: Study the terms, pronunciations, and definitions until you are thoroughly familiar with them. In order to complete this lesson successfully, you must understand the meaning and usage of all the legal terms presented. If you are using a shorthand system, write each legal term one time on your shorthand machine.

Legal Term	Pronunciation	Definition
1. plat	plat	A map or plot showing how a certain piece of land is divided into lots.
2. abstract	′ab-strakt	A history of the title to realty that includes previous owners and any liens or encumbrances that may affect the title to the land.
3. land description	land di-′skrip-shən	A description or an identification of a specific parcel of land that may be the subject of a conveyance. Also known as a legal description or a property description. (See Figure 17-1, page 241.)
4. metes and bounds	mēts ən baủnds	A measurement of land indicating the boundary lines, points, and angles.
5. convey	kən-′vā	To transfer the title to property from one person to another.
6. conveyance	kən-′vā-əns	The instrument by which the title to property is transferred from one person to another.

7. tenancy in common	'ten-ən-sē in 'käm-ən	Title to land held by two or more persons who own the same land or property together, with each being entitled to a distinct but undivided interest.
8. joint tenancy	joint 'ten-ən-sē	Title to land held by two or more persons who have the same interest in the land with undivided possession. In case of death of one of the owners, the other owner or owners have full ownership of the property. Also called right to survivorship.
9. tenancy by the entirety	'ten-ən-sē bī thē in-'tī-rət-ē	A husband and wife who own land together. Full ownership of the property will go to the survivor if one dies.
10. partition	pər-'tish-ən	The dividing of land held by joint tenants or tenants in common into distinct portions so that each may hold separate title to his or her portion.
11. homestead	'hōm-sted	A dwelling place and the land surrounding it that is occupied by a family and protected by law from the claims of creditors.
12. servitude	'sər-və-tüd	A right that an owner of property has in an adjoining property. For example, the owner of an adjoining property could not construct something on the property that would detract from or infringe on the neighbors' rightful use or enjoyment of their property.
13. easement	'ēz-ment	A right to use the land of another for a specified purpose. For example, a utility company may have a right to cross the property with electric wires and water or gas lines.

Self-Evaluation B | Terminology and Definition Recall

Directions: In the Answers column, write the legal term that is most representative of the corresponding statement. After you have completed this self-evaluation, check your answers with the key on page 497. If you have any incorrect answers, review the definitions for those terms before going on with this lesson. Then unless otherwise directed, submit this self-evaluation to your instructor.

ANSWERS

1. A dwelling place and the land surrounding it that is occupied by a family and protected by law from the claims of creditors is a/an _____.

    1. _____

2. Title to land held by two or more persons who have the same interest in land with undivided possession is known as a/an _____.

    2. _____

3. The dividing of land held by joint tenants or tenants in common into distinct portions so that each may hold separate title to his or her portion is known as_____.

    3. _____

4. A measurement of land indicating the boundary lines, points, and angles is _____.

    4. _____

5. A history of the title to realty that includes previous owners and any liens or encumbrances that may affect the title to the land is a/an _____.

    5. _____

6. To transfer the title to property from one person to another is to _____ the title.

    6. _____

7. The instrument by which the title to property is transferred from one person to another is a/an_____.

    7. _____

8. Title to land held by two or more persons who own the same land or property together, with each being entitled to a distinct but undivided interest, is a/an _____.

    8. _____

9. A description or an identification of a specific parcel of land that may be the subject of a conveyance is a/an _____.

    9. _____

10. A map or plot showing how a certain piece of land is divided into lots is a/an _____.

    10. _____

11. A right to use the land of another for a specified purpose is referred to as a/an _____.

    11. _____

12. A right that an owner of property has in an adjoining property is called _____.

    12. _____

13. A husband and wife who own land together with full ownership of the property going to the survivor if one dies is a/an _____.

    13. _____

KEYING LEGAL TERMS

Directions: Unless otherwise instructed, use 1-inch margins and double spacing. Correct all errors. Follow one of the procedures below.

WORDS

Keyboarding Procedure
On your computer, key the following words at least two times, concentrating on the correct spelling and pronunciation.

Machine Shorthand Procedure
On your computer, key the following words once, concentrating on the correct spelling and pronunciation. Then write each word one time on your shorthand machine. Transcribe from your shorthand notes one time on your computer, or, if you are using computer-aided transcription (CAT), proofread and edit your transcript.

plat	abstract	land description
metes and bounds	convey	conveyance
tenancy in common	joint tenancy	tenancy by the entirety
partition	homestead	servitude
easement		

SENTENCES

Keyboarding Procedure
Key each of the following sentences one time on your computer. Concentrate on the correct spelling and pronunciation of each underlined legal term.

Machine Shorthand Procedure
Write the following sentences one time on your shorthand machine. Transcribe from your shorthand notes one time on your computer, or, if you are using computer-aided transcription (CAT), proofread and edit your transcript.

These sentences will be used for practice dictation on the Transcription CD.

A map or a plot, usually drawn to a scale, showing how a certain piece of land is divided into lots is a <u>plat</u>. An <u>abstract</u> is a condensed history of the title to land consisting of a summary of all the conveyances, liens, or encumbrances that may affect the title to the land. A <u>land description</u> identifies or describes a specific parcel of land that may be the subject of a conveyance. <u>Metes and bounds</u> indicate the boundary lines, points, and angles of a parcel of land.

To <u>convey</u> the title to property is to transfer the title from one person to another. A <u>conveyance</u> is the instrument by which the title to property is transferred from one person to another.

When two or more persons own the same land or property together, with each being entitled to a distinct but undivided interest in the property, the ownership is a <u>tenancy in common</u>. <u>Joint tenancy</u> exists when two or more persons have the same interest in the land with undivided possession. <u>Tenancy by the entirety</u> refers to a husband and wife who own land together with full ownership going to the survivor if one dies. Land owned by tenancy in common or joint tenancy may be divided by <u>partition</u>. Land divided by partition gives each tenant a distinct portion that may be held separately by each tenant.

A **homestead** is a dwelling place and the land surrounding it that is occupied by a family and protected by law from the claims of creditors. **Servitude** is a right that the owner of property has in an adjoining property. For instance, something cannot be constructed on a property if it will interfere with the adjoining property. An **easement** is a right to use the land of another for a specified purpose.

TRANSCRIBING FROM DICTATION

Directions: This dictation emphasizes and reinforces the legal terms and definitions you have studied. Listen carefully to the pronunciation of each of the legal terms. Unless otherwise directed, use 1-inch margins and double spacing. Correct all errors. Follow one of the procedures below.

Keyboarding Procedure

Using the Transcription CD, Lesson 17, Part B, transcribe the dictation directly at your computer.

Machine Shorthand Procedure

Using the Transcription CD, Lesson 17, Part B, take the dictation on your shorthand machine and then transcribe from your notes on your computer, or, if you are using computer-aided transcription (CAT), proofread and edit your transcript.

When you have finished transcribing or proofreading and editing Part B of the practice dictation, check your transcript with the printed copy. If you made any mistakes in the transcription, you should review and practice those words several times before going on to Lesson 18.

CHECKLIST

I have completed the following for Lesson 17:

	Part A, Date	Part B, Date	Submitted to Instructor Yes	No
Terminology and Definitions				
Self-Evaluation				
* Keying Legal Terms				
Words				
Sentences				
* Transcribing from Dictation				

When you have successfully completed all the exercises in this lesson and submitted to your instructor those requested, you are ready to proceed with Lesson 18.

* If you are using machine shorthand, submit to your instructor your notes along with your transcript.

Lesson

18

Real Property

> *"Everything built on the soil belongs to the soil."*
> *—Legal maxim*

Additional terms that are applicable to the ownership and transfer of real property are given in this lesson. When you have successfully completed these exercises, you will be able to spell, define, pronounce, and transcribe correctly the legal terms presented herein.

Part A | TERMINOLOGY AND DEFINITIONS

Directions: Study the terms, pronunciations, and definitions until you are thoroughly familiar with them. In order to complete this lesson successfully, you must understand the meaning and usage of all the legal terms presented. If you are using a shorthand system, write each legal term one time on your shorthand machine.

Legal Term	Pronunciation	Definition
1. possession	pə-ʹzesh-ən	The control or ownership of property for one's own use.
2. domain	dō-ʹmān	The ownership of real property.
3. eminent domain	ʹem-ə-nənt dō-ʹmān	The right or power of the government to purchase private property for public use such as the purchasing of private property for the building of a road.
4. condemnation	kän-dem-ʹnā-shən	The forced sale of private property to the government for public use. The government has the right to condemn private property that is needed for public use, such as the building of a road, and force the owner to sell the property to the government.
5. public domain	ʹpəb-lik dō-ʹmān	Property that is owned by the government.
6. adverse possession	ad-ʹvərs pə-ʹzesh-ən	The possession of another's land for a certain period of time, after which time the one in possession claims title to the land.
7. prescription	pri-ʹskrip-shən	The right or title to the use of another's property.
8. prescriptive rights	pri-ʹskrip-tiv rīts	Rights acquired by prescription.
9. reversionary interest	ri-ʹvər-zhə-ner-ē ʹin-trəst	The future interest one has in property that is presently in the possession of another. For example, the owner of property that is rented to another has a reversionary interest in the property.

10. riparian owner	rə-ˈper-ē-ən ˈo-nər	One who owns property adjoining a waterway and who has the right to use the waterway. The riparian owner's rights to the waterway are referred to as riparian rights.
11. ejectment	i-ˈjek-mənt	An action for the recovery of land that was unlawfully taken away.
12. fixture	ˈfiks-chər	Chattel, or personal property, that is attached to land or a building.
13. appurtenance	ə-ˈpərt-nəns	Something that is permanently attached to land.

Self-Evaluation A | Terminology and Definition Recall

Directions: In the Answers column, write the letter from Column 1 that represents the word or phrase that best matches each item in Column 2. After you have completed this self-evaluation, check your answers with the key on page 497. If you have any incorrect answers, review the definitions for those terms before going on with this lesson. Then unless otherwise directed, submit this self-evaluation to your instructor.

COLUMN 1	COLUMN 2	ANSWERS
a. adverse possession	1. One who owns property adjoining a waterway and has a right to use the waterway.	1. _____
b. appurtenance	2. The right or power of the government to purchase private property for public use.	2. _____
c. condemnation	3. The possession of another's land for a certain period of time, after which time the one in possession claims title to the land.	3. _____
d. domain	4. Chattel, or personal property, that is attached to land or a building.	4. _____
e. ejectment	5. The future interest one has in property that is presently in the possession of another.	5. _____
f. eminent domain	6. The ownership of real property.	6. _____
g. fixture	7. Something that is permanently attached to land.	7. _____
h. possession	8. The right or title to the use of another's property.	8. _____
i. prescription	9. An action for the recovery of land that was unlawfully taken away.	9. _____
j. prescriptive rights	10. Property that is owned by the government.	10. _____
k. public domain	11. The control or ownership of property for one's own use.	11. _____
l. reversionary interest	12. Rights acquired by having the right or title to the use of another's property.	12. _____
m. riparian owner	13. The forced sale of private property to the government for public use.	13. _____
n. water rights		

KEYING LEGAL TERMS

Directions: Unless otherwise instructed, use 1-inch margins and double spacing. Correct all errors. Follow one of the procedures below.

WORDS

Keyboarding Procedure
On your computer, key the following words at least two times, concentrating on the correct spelling and pronunciation.

Machine Shorthand Procedure
On your computer, key the following words once, concentrating on the correct spelling and pronunciation. Then write each word one time on your shorthand machine. Transcribe from your shorthand notes one time on your computer, or, if you are using computer-aided transcription (CAT), proofread and edit your transcript.

possession	**domain**	**eminent domain**
condemnation	**public domain**	**adverse possession**
prescription	**prescriptive rights**	**reversionary interest**
riparian owner	**ejectment**	**fixture**
appurtenance		

SENTENCES

Keyboarding Procedure
Key each of the following sentences one time on your computer. Concentrate on the correct spelling and pronunciation of each underlined legal term.

Machine Shorthand Procedure
Write the following sentences one time on your shorthand machine. Transcribe from your shorthand notes one time on your computer, or, if you are using computer-aided transcription (CAT), proofread and edit your transcript.

These sentences will be used for practice dictation on the Transcription CD.

<u>Possession</u> is the control or ownership of property for one's own use. <u>Domain</u> is the ownership of real property. Domain also refers to real estate that is owned. <u>Eminent domain</u> is the right or power of the government to purchase private property for public use, such as for the building of a highway. If a private owner refuses to sell property for public use, the government may take the property by <u>condemnation</u>. In a condemnation proceeding, the owner is paid just compensation for the forced sale of the property. <u>Public domain</u> is property that is owned by the government.

<u>Adverse possession</u> is the possession or use of another's land for a certain period of time, after which time the one possessing or using the land claims title to the land. <u>Prescription</u> is the right or title to the use of another's property. Rights acquired by prescription are called <u>prescriptive rights</u>. A <u>reversionary interest</u> is a future interest that one has in property that is presently in the possession of another. One who owns property adjoining a waterway and has a right to use the waterway is a <u>riparian owner</u>.

Ejectment is an action for the recovery of land that was unlawfully taken away. Ejectment has been modified in many states and may include the eviction of a tenant, such as for the enforcement of a sale contract for land. A **fixture** is chattel, or personal property, that is attached to land or a building. An **appurtenance** is something that is permanently attached to land. In some cases, fixtures may be removed from realty, but an appurtenance cannot be removed.

TRANSCRIBING FROM DICTATION

Directions: This dictation emphasizes and reinforces the legal terms and definitions you have studied. Listen carefully to the pronunciation of each of the legal terms. Unless otherwise directed, use 1-inch margins and double spacing. Correct all errors. Follow one of the procedures below.

Keyboarding Procedure
Using the Transcription CD, Lesson 18, Part A, transcribe the dictation directly at your computer.

Machine Shorthand Procedure
Using the Transcription CD, Lesson 18, Part A, take the dictation on your shorthand machine and then transcribe from your notes on your computer, or, if you are using computer-aided transcription (CAT), proofread and edit your transcript.

When you have finished transcribing or proofreading and editing Part A of the practice dictation, check your transcript with the printed copy. If you made any mistakes in the transcription, you should review and practice those words several times before going on to Part B.

Part B | TERMINOLOGY AND DEFINITIONS

Directions: Study the terms, pronunciations, and definitions until you are thoroughly familiar with them. In order to complete this lesson successfully, you must understand the meaning and usage of all the legal terms presented. If you are using a shorthand system, write each legal term one time on your shorthand machine.

Legal Term	Pronunciation	Definition
1. land contract	land ′kän-trakt	A contract for the purchase of real property whereby the purchaser makes a down payment and specified payments thereafter, but the title to the property remains in the seller's name until the payments are made in full. (See Figure 18-1, pages 260-261.)
2. mortgage	′mȯr-gij	The pledging of property as security for a loan. In some states, a mortgage is a lien on the property; in others, it is a conditional conveyance of land. (See Figure 18-2, pages 262-263.)
3. lien	lēn	A legal claim on property for the payment of a debt, such as a mortgage. All liens on a property must be satisfied or released before the owner can transfer title to another party unless that party and the lienholder agree to the lien being assumed by the buyer.
4. encumbrance	in-′kəm-brəns	A lien. For example, if you mortgage property, the mortgage may be an encumbrance or a lien in some states.

5.	hypothecate	hip-ˈäth-ə-kāt	To pledge property as security for a loan or mortgage without conveying the title or possession. If property is mortgaged but the title and possession stay with the person obtaining the mortgage, then the property is hypothecated. The creditor can force the sale of the property to satisfy the loan or mortgage.
6.	collateral	kə-ˈlat-ə-rəl	Some security pledged in addition to the personal obligation of the borrower to insure repayment of a loan. When a person obtains a mortgage on real estate, the real estate is collateral for the mortgage.
7.	recording	ri-ˈkȯrd-iŋ	The filing of a lien, mortgage, title, or other documents in the public records.
8.	acceleration clause	ik-sel-ə-ˈrā-shən klȯz	A clause in a contract that requires immediate payment of the balance of the contract in the event that certain terms or conditions are not met, such as the failure to make payments when due. (See Figure 18-2, pages 262-263.)
9.	foreclosure	fōr-ˈklō-zhər	Taking away the rights a mortgagor has in property that is mortgaged. Usually occurs when payments are not made or some other condition of the mortgage is not met.
10.	release	ri-ˈlēs	The giving up of a right or claim against another person. Thus, a release of a lien means that the lien has been paid in full or satisfied.
11.	escrow	ˈes-krō	Something that is delivered to a third party to be held by that party until certain conditions are met. Thus, a mortgagee may collect money and hold it in escrow for the payment of future taxes or insurance.
12.	ad valorem	ad və -ˈlōr-əm	Latin. Taxes based upon the value of the thing being taxed. Also called a value added tax.
13.	assessment	ə-ˈses-mənt	The valuation, or appraisal, of property for the purpose of taxation.

FIGURE 18-1 A Land Contract

LAND CONTRACT —(GLEASON FORM)—INTEREST,
INSURANCE AND TAX CLAUSES.   331

This Contract, Made the ....13th.... day of ....November.... A. D., 20 03

BETWEEN COREY ALLEN JOHNSON, R.R. #1, Box 350, Clarksville, Michigan

48815, ... herein called first party,

and KIPTON LYNN D'AMATO, 87 Main Street, Portland, Michigan 48875,

.... herein called second party.

WITNESSETH, as follows:

1. Said first party, in consideration of the sum of Seventy-five Thousand and No/100
----------($75,000.00)-------------Dollars to be paid by second party to first party, and
of the covenants to be performed by second party, as hereinafter expressed, hereby agree s to sell to
second party, all that certain piece or parcel of land situate in the Township of Boston
................................., in the County of Ionia..............and State of Michigan, described as follow, viz:
Lot 136, Lot 137, and North one-half of Lot 135, Excelsior Land
Company's Addition, Township of Boston, County of Ionia, Michigan,
according to the recorded plat thereof.
_____
_____
_____
_____
_____
_____
_____
_____
_____

2. Said second party, in consideration of the covenants herein made by first party, agree s to purchase of first party, the above described premises, and to pay therefor to first party, or ...his... legal
representatives, at Clarksville, Michigan the sum of Seventy-five Thousand and
No/100-----------($75,000.00)-------------------Dollars in manner as follows, viz:
Ten Thousand and No/100 Dollars ($10,000.00) at closing and payments
of Four Hundred and No/100 Dollars ($400.00) beginning on the 13th
day of December 2003, and monthly thereafter
_____
_____
_____

together with interest on the whole sum that shall be from time to time unpaid, at the rate of 10............per
cent per annum, to be computed from November 13, 2003..... and to be paid monthly xxxxxx
Principal or interest not paid when due shall bear interest until paid at ...10............ per cent per annum.

3. Said second party shall keep all buildings now on, or that may hereafter be placed on said
premises, insured in the name of, and in manner and amount and by insurers approved by first party, and
leave the policy with first party, and in case of loss, the insurance, unless by mutual agreement used to
repair or rebuild, shall be paid to first party and be endorsed on this contract to the extent of the amount
unpaid thereon, and the balance, if any, shall belong and be paid to second party.

4. Said second party shall enter said premises for taxation in ....her...... name and shall well and
faithfully pay when due all taxes and assessments, ordinary and extraordinary, that may for any purpose
be levied or assessed on said premises, ... and shall not commit or suffer any other
person to commit any waste or damage to said premises or the appurtenances. Should second party fail
to pay any tax or assessment when due, or to keep said buildings insured, first party may pay the same
and have the buildings insured, and the amounts thus expended shall be a lien on said premises, be
added to the amount then unpaid thereon, be due at once, and bear interest until paid at ......10...........
per cent per annum.

5. Said first party further agree s that upon the full performance by second party of all covenants
and agreements by second party to be performed, and upon the payment to first party of the several
sums of money above mentioned, in time and manner and at the place mentioned, that thereupon first
party will execute and deliver to second party a good and sufficient ..warranty deed..............
deed, and thereby convey to second party the premises above described free and clear of all incumbrance
except taxes after date hereof, and claims and liens thereon due to any act or neglect of second party.

FIGURE 18-1 A Land Contract (continued)

6. All buildings and improvements now on, or that shall be placed or made on said premises, shall remain thereon as security for the performance by second party of this contract, and should default be made, and said contract be forfeited, said buildings and improvements and all payments made on said contract shall be forfeited to first party as stipulated damages for non-performance of this contract, or first party may at ......his........ option declare all sums unpaid immediately due and payable and enforce the collection thereof at law and make conveyance as aforesaid.

7. Said second party shall not assign or transfer this contract, or lease or sublet said premises, or the buildings thereon, or any part thereof, or add to or change said buildings without the previous written assent of first party thereto endorsed hereon.

8. It is further mutually agreed that second party may take possession of said premises .... and remain thereon as long as....she......... shall perform all the covenants and agreements herein mentioned on ......her... part to be performed, and no longer; and that if ....she...... shall at any time hereafter, violate or neglect to fulfill any of said covenants or agreements .....she..... shall forfeit all right or claim under this contract, and be liable to be removed from said premises in the same manner as is provided by law for the removal of a tenant that holds over premises contrary to the terms of his lease and *......... notice to quit and of forfeiture are hereby waived. And it shall be lawful for first party at any time after such default to sell and convey said premises, or any part thereof, to any other person without becoming liable to refund any part of the money received on this contract, or for any damages on account of such sale. And it is hereby expressly understood and agreed that **time** shall be deemed as of the very essence of this contract, and that unless the same shall, in all respects, be complied with by second party at the respective times, and in the manner above limited and specified, that second party shall lose and be debarred from all rights, remedies and actions, both at law and in equity, upon or under this contract.

IN WITNESS WHEREOF, The said parties have hereunto set their hands and seals the day and year first above written. (In duplicate).

Signed, Sealed and Delivered in Presence of

Nancy S. Woodford
Nancy S. Woodford
Todd M. Woodford
Todd M. Woodford
INSERT NOTICE TO QUIT AND OF FORFEITURE ARE EACH HEREBY WAIVED

Corey Allen Johnson
COREY ALLEN JOHNSON, /Seller   (L. S.)
Kipton Lynn D'Amato
KIPTON LYNN D'AMATO, Buyer   (L. S.)
   (L. S.)

FIGURE 18-2 A Mortgage

𝕶now 𝕬ll 𝕸en 𝕭y 𝕿hese 𝕻resents, That SHELLEY D. EVERT

of the   **City**   of   **East Lansing**   County of   **Ingham**

State of Michigan, part **y**   of the first part, being justly indebted unto   **SECURITY BANK AND TRUST**

of the   **City**   of   **East Lansing**   County of   **Ingham**

State of Michigan, part **y**   of the second part, in the sum of   **Five Thousand and No/100---**
--------------------($5,000.00)------------------------------ Dollars,

ha **s**   for the purpose of securing payment of said debt, and the interest thereof, granted, bargained,

sold and mortgaged, and by these presents do **es**   grant, bargain, sell and mortgage unto the said

Security Bank and Trust

the following goods, chattels and personal property, to-wit:

One Steinway Grand Piano, 7' Concert Model, Serial #2342.

which said above described goods, chattels and property, at the date hereof are the sole and absolute property of the said first part **y**   and the said goods and chattels are now in the possession of the said first part **y**   situated at **1504 Auburn Street**   in the
City   of   **East Lansing**   County of   **Ingham**
Michigan, are free and clear from all liens, conveyances, incumbrances and levies and are warranted and will be defended against all lawful claims, liens and incumbrances of all persons whomsoever, and for a valuable consideration said first part **y**   hereby warrant**s**   the above representations to be true.

    That first part y   shall not attempt to sell, encumber, assign, dispose of or transfer any interest in said property, or remove the same or any part thereof from the County of   **Ingham**
State of Michigan without the written consent of the holder hereof.

    [1]**That first part y**   shall in all respects comply with the provisions of Act No. 167 of the Public Acts of 1933 of the State Michigan as amended. (Only applicable in the event that first part **y**   at the time of execution of this instrument or any time thereafter is a tax payer as defined in said Public Acts and subject to the provisions thereof).

    And the Futher Condition of these Presents is Such, that if the said first part   **y**   shall pay or cause to be paid to the said second part **y**   the said sum of **Five Thousand and No/100--**
---------($5,000.00)-- Dollars,
being the debt aforesaid, with interest at the rate of **Ten (10)**   per cent, per annum, as follows:

Two Hundred and No/100 ($200.00) Dollars on the first day of each month commencing October 24, 2003, until said principal and interest are paid in full

according to **a promissory note**
                           bearing even date herewith, executed by said first part **y**   to said second part **y**   and to which this Mortgage is collateral security, then this Mortgage and said **promissory note**   shall be void and of no effect.
And the said first part **y**   agree **s**   to pay the same accordingly.

FIGURE 18-2 A Mortgage (continued)

Acceleration
Clause

That Upon Default in any of the terms and conditions hereof, the whole amount unpaid on the said note   shall thereupon become due and payable and the said second part **y**   **is** hereby authorized to take possession of any or all of the property above described and dispose of said property in accordance with the statue in such case made and provided.

2

In Witness Whereof, The said first part **y**   ha **s**   hereunto set   **his**   hand   and seal
the   **24th**   day of   **September**   A.D., 20 **03**   .

Shelly D. Evert
* SHELLY D. EVERT   (Name of Individual or Partnership)

By _____
*

3 _____
*   (Name of Corporation)

By _____ as its _____
*

By _____ as its _____
*

STATE OF MICHIGAN,
                                   } ss.
County of   **Ingham**   SHELLY D. EVERT   of
East Lansing, Michigan,   being duly sworn, deposes and says, that .... he is
4 **himself**   the Mortgagor .....named in the within and foregoing Chattel Mortgage, that the consideration of said Chattel Mortgage was actual and adequate, and that said Chattel Mortgage was given in good faith for the purpose therein set forth, and that this deponent has knowledge of these

Self-Evaluation B | Terminology and Definition Recall

Directions: In the Answers column at the right of each statement, write the letter that represents the word or group of words that correctly completes the statement. After you have completed this self-evaluation, check your answers with the key on page 497. If you have any incorrect answers, review the definitions for those terms before going on with this lesson. Then unless otherwise directed, submit this self-evaluation to your instructor.

ANSWERS

1. A contract for the purchase of real property whereby the purchaser makes a down payment and specified payments thereafter, but the title to the property remains in the seller's name until the property is paid for in full, is a/an (a) assessment, (b) land contract, (c) mortgage.

   1. _____

2. To pledge property as security for a loan is to (a) escrow, (b) foreclose, (c) mortgage.

   2. _____

3. The giving up of a right or claim against another is a/an (a) release, (b) lien, (c) escrow.

   3. _____

4. Something that is delivered to a third party to be held by that party until certain conditions are met is said to be in (a) assessment, (b) escrow, (c) foreclosure.

   4. _____

5. Value added taxes or taxes that are based upon the value of the thing being taxed are referred to as (a) collateral, (b) encumbrance, (c) ad valorem.

   5. _____

6. The valuation, or appraisal, of property for the purpose of taxation is a/an (a) recording, (b) assessment, (c) release.

   6. _____

7. Some security pledged in addition to the personal obligation of the borrower to insure repayment of a loan is (a) ad valorem, (b) collateral, (c) lien.

   7. _____

8. Taking away the rights a mortgagor has in property that is mortgaged is known as (a) foreclosure, (b) escrow, (c) ad valorem.

   8. _____

9. A lien is also referred to as a/an (a) acceleration clause, (b) foreclosure, (c) encumbrance.

   9. _____

10. Filing a lien, mortgage, title, or other documents in the public records is (a) accelerating, (b) hypothecating, (c) recording.

    10. _____

11. A legal claim on property for the payment of a debt, such as a mortgage, is a/an (a) lien, (b) encumbrance, (c) land contract.

    11. _____

12. To pledge property as security for a loan or mortgage without conveying the title or possession to the property is to (a) release, (b) hypothecate, (c) mortgage.

    12. _____

13. A clause in a contract that requires immediate payment of the balance of the contract in the event that certain terms or conditions are not met is a/an (a) acceleration clause, (b) foreclosure, (c) collateral.

    13. _____

KEYING LEGAL TERMS

Directions: Unless otherwise instructed, use 1-inch margins and double spacing. Correct all errors. Follow one of the procedures below.

WORDS

Keyboarding Procedure
On your computer, key the following words at least two times, concentrating on the correct spelling and pronunciation.

Machine Shorthand Procedure
On your computer, key the following words once, concentrating on the correct spelling and pronunciation. Then write each word one time on your shorthand machine. Transcribe from your shorthand notes one time on your computer, or, if you are using computer-aided transcription (CAT), proofread and edit your transcript.

land contract	mortgage	lien
encumbrance	hypothecate	collateral
recording	acceleration clause	foreclosure
release	escrow	ad valorem
assessment		

SENTENCES

Keyboarding Procedure
Key each of the following sentences one time on your computer. Concentrate on the correct spelling and pronunciation of each underlined legal term.

Machine Shorthand Procedure
Write the following sentences one time on your shorthand machine. Transcribe from your shorthand notes one time on your computer, or, if you are using computer-aided transcription (CAT), proofread and edit your transcript.

These sentences will be used for practice dictation on the Transcription CD.

If property is purchased on a <u>land contract</u>, the purchaser makes a down payment followed by specified payments thereafter, but the title of the property remains in the seller's name until the balance of the land contract is paid in full. A <u>mortgage</u> is the pledging of property as security for a loan. In some states, a mortgage is a <u>lien</u> on the property; in others, it is a conditional conveyance of land.

A lien is a legal claim, or <u>encumbrance</u>, upon property. To <u>hypothecate</u> is to pledge property as security for a loan without conveying title or possession. <u>Collateral</u> is some security pledged in addition to the personal obligation of the borrower to insure repayment of a loan. When property is pledged as security for a loan, the property is referred to as collateral.

<u>Recording</u> is the filing of a lien, mortgage, title, or other documents in the public records. An <u>acceleration clause</u> in a contract requires immediate payment of the balance of the contract in the event that certain terms or conditions are not met.

A <u>foreclosure</u> is the taking away of the rights that a mortgagor has in property that is mortgaged. A foreclosure usually occurs when payments are not made or some other condition of the mortgage is not met.

A <u>release</u> is the giving up of a right or claim against another person. A release of a lien means that it has been paid in full.

When something is delivered to a third party to be held by that party until certain conditions are met, it is in <u>escrow</u>. Thus, a mortgagee may collect money and hold it in escrow for the payment of future taxes or insurance. <u>Ad valorem</u> refers to taxes that are based upon the value of the thing being taxed. An <u>assessment</u> is the valuation, or appraisal, of property for the purpose of taxation.

TRANSCRIBING FROM DICTATION

Directions: This dictation emphasizes and reinforces the legal terms and definitions you have studied. Listen carefully to the pronunciation of each of the legal terms. Unless otherwise directed, use 1-inch margins and double spacing. Correct all errors. Follow one of the procedures below.

Keyboarding Procedure

Using the Transcription CD, Lesson 18, Part B, transcribe the dictation directly at your computer.

Machine Shorthand Procedure

Using the Transcription CD, Lesson 18, Part B, take the dictation on your shorthand machine and then transcribe from your notes on your computer, or, if you are using computer-aided transcription (CAT), proofread and edit your transcript.

When you have finished transcribing or proofreading and editing Part B of the practice dictation, check your transcript with the printed copy. If you made any mistakes in the transcription, you should review and practice those words several times before going on to Evaluation 9.

CHECKLIST

I have completed the following for Lesson 18:

	Part A, Date	Part B, Date	Submitted to Instructor Yes	No
Terminology and Definitions				
Self-Evaluation				
* Keying Legal Terms				
Words				
Sentences				
* Transcribing from Dictation				

When you have successfully completed all the exercises in this lesson and submitted to your instructor those requested, you are ready to proceed with Evaluation 9.

* If you are using machine shorthand, submit to your instructor your notes along with your transcript.

Evaluation No. 9 | Section A

Directions: This dictation/transcription evaluation will test your spelling and transcription abilities on the legal terms that you studied in the two preceding lessons. Tab once for a paragraph indention, and use 1-inch margins and double spacing unless otherwise instructed. Correct all errors. Follow one of the procedures below.

Keyboarding Procedure

Using the Transcription CD for Evaluation 9, transcribe the dictation directly at your computer.

Machine Shorthand Procedure

Using the Transcription CD for Evaluation 9, take the dictation on your shorthand machine and then transcribe your notes on your computer, or, if you are using computer-aided transcription (CAT), proofread and edit your transcript.

Sections B and C are available from your instructor.

Lesson
19

Contracts

Contract law involves agreements between persons. Contracts must consist of persons competent to contract, a proper legal subject matter, an offer, an acceptance, and sufficient and legal consideration to be legally binding. Every person has the right to make a contract, regardless of the wisdom or desirability of the provisions. The terminology presented deals with that which is involved in legally binding contracts. When you have completed this lesson successfully, you will have a knowledge of some of the broad terminology of contract law.

Part A | TERMINOLOGY AND DEFINITIONS

Directions: Study the terms, pronunciations, and definitions until you are thoroughly familiar with them. In order to complete this lesson successfully, you must understand the meaning and usage of all the legal terms presented. If you are using a shorthand system, write each legal term one time on your shorthand machine.

Legal Term	Pronunciation	Definition
1. contract law	ˈkän-trakt lȯ	Law governing agreements made between individuals.
2. contract	ˈkän-trakt	An agreement whereby two or more persons promise to do or not to do certain things. See Figure 19-1, pages (273-274.)
3. ex contractu	eks kän-ˈtrak-tü	Latin. Emerging or coming from a contract.
4. lex loci contractus	leks ˈlō-sī kän-ˈtrak-təs	Latin. The law of the place where a contract is made. For example, a contract made in Florida is subject only to the contract law for the state of Florida.
5. surety	ˈshu̇r-ət-ē	A person who agrees to be responsible for the debt of another in the event the other person fails to pay the debt.
6. bailment	ˈbāl-mənt	The delivery of personal property by the owner to another person for a specific purpose and period of time, after which time the property is to be returned to the owner. An example would be the delivery of an article for repair.
7. caveat emptor	ˈkav-ē-ät ˈem-tər	Latin. Let the buyer beware. A legal maxim meaning that a person is responsible for examining an article before purchasing it and is buying the article at his or her own risk.

8. parol evidence rule	′par-əl ′ev-əd-əns rül	Once a contract is made in writing, it cannot be changed or altered by oral, or parol, evidence unless there was a mistake or fraud involved. If you make an oral agreement that is not included in the written agreement, then the oral agreement is not enforceable.
9. offer	′öf-ər	A proposal by one person to make an agreement or a contract with another person. One of the essential elements of a contract. (See Figure 19-2, page 275.)
10. acceptance	ik-′sep-təns	An agreement to an offer received from another. An essential element of a contract. (See Figure 19-2, page 275.)
11. counteroffer	′kaunt-ər-of-ər	Changes made in an offer received from another. A counteroffer must be accepted by the person who made the original offer.
12. option	′äp-shən	An agreement whereby a person has the right to buy, sell, or lease certain property within a specified time. Thus, if a person has an option on land, he or she has the right to buy it within a certain time period. (See Figure 19-1, pages 273-274.)
13. binder	′bīn-der	Money or security given with an offer to insure the intentions of the person making the offer. May also be called earnest money or deposit money. Also refers to a temporary insurance agreement that provides coverage for property until a formal policy is issued.

FIGURE 19-1 An Option

580

This Contract,

Made the .... 29th .... day of

.... August .... A.D. 20.0.3...., by and between ...... EVA J. JACKSON ....

part...y....... of the first part, and ...... DIRK L. WATSON

part...y.......... of the second part.

WITNESSETH, That the said part.....y................ of the first part, in consideration of the sum of

...... Three Thousand and No/100 ($3,000.00) .... dollars to ...her..... in hand paid

by the said part.y..... of the second part, do.es..... hereby agree that....she....... shall and will at any time

within ...six..(6)..months.......................... from the date hereof, at the written request of the said
part ..y...... of the second part, execute and deliver to ..him.., or to any person or persons as....agents......
the said part.y....... of the second part shall direct in writing, a good and sufficient Warranty Deed of the

following described land, situated in the ...... City ...... of ... Lansing

County of........ Ingham ...., State of ...... Michigan ...., to-wit: Lot 74 of

Angels Subdivision, City of Lansing, County of Ingham, State of

Michigan,

for the sum of ...... Fifty-One Thousand and No/100 ($51,000.00) ...... Dollars
payable as follows:

In full upon closing.

And the said part.y........ of the first part do ...es.....hereby further agree that ...she......... shall and

will not within ...six..(6)..months.......................... from the date hereof, sell, convey, mortgage, or
otherwise encumber the said land, or any part thereof, or do, or permit to be done, any act or deed to
diminish or encumber the title to said land.

FIGURE 19-1 An Option (continued)

It is agreed by and between the parties hereto, that if the said part ....y...... of the second part at the expiration of the aforesaid limited time shall have declined or omitted to make application for the purchase of said land at the price aforesaid, then this instrument shall be void, and the above sum of

Three Thousand and No/100 ($3,000.00)---------------------------- Dollars

so paid as aforesaid ..on the 29th day of August, 2003,............... shall be forfeited by the

said part ...y..... of the second part, and the said part ...y... of the first part shall have the right to retain the same, as and for liquidated damages, and the said part ...y.......of the second part shall relinquish to said part ...y........ of the first part all claim to the said land, either in law or equity, and, also all claim to

the said sum of ....Three Thousand and No/100 ($3,000.00)--------------- Dollars,

so paid as aforesaid, and no claim of the said part ....y........of the second part under this Contract shall then be effectual.

In **Witness Whereof**, the said part ..ies.. ha ..ve.. hereunto

set ..their.... hand..s.. and seal..s.... the day and year first above written.

IN PRESENCE OF

Randolph Myers
Randolph Myers

Robert T. Gates
Robert T. Gates

Eva J. Jackson
EVA J. JACKSON

[SEAL]

Dirk L. Watson
DIRK L. WATSON

[SEAL]

_____ [SEAL]

State of ..Michigan............................. }
County of ....Ingham.......................... } ss.

On this ....29th.......................... day of ..August.................. A. D. 20..03..

before me, the subscriber, a ....Notary Public.................................. in and for said County

personally appeared ....Eva J. Jackson and Dirk L. Watson.................................

to me known to be the same person ..s....... described in and who executed the foregoing instrument, ~~xx~~

~~xxxxx~~.........., and acknowledged the same to be .....their........ free act and deed.

Robert T. Gates

My commission expires ...July 2............... 20..05..

FIGURE 19-2 An Offer to Purchase and Acceptance

AGREEMENT PROPOSITION ON THE SALE OF
REAL ESTATE.   118-A

Authorized Agreement through the office of .... Global Realty ....

.... Portland .... Mich., ... October 3 .... , 20 03

For a valuable consideration, I hereby agree to buy from .... Corey Allen Johnson ....
the property located and described as follows, namely:

Lot 136, Lot 137, and North one-half of Lot 135, Excelsior Land

Company's Addition, Township of Boston, County of Ionia, Michigan,

according to the recorded plat thereof.

in the ...Township... of ...Boston..., County of ...Ingham... and State
of Michigan, for the sum of $ .75,000.00...

The terms of purchase to be as follows: $ .10,000.00... on delivery of ...land contract...

and balance to be paid as follows: monthly principal and interest installments

of $400.00 or more including interest at 10 percent per annum, and

said contract shall be due and payable on or before 15 years after

closing date.
Interest to be computed at .....10..... per cent ~~XXXXX~~ to be included in said payments.
                                        PER ANNUM

An abstract showing good title written up to date, also abstract of taxes, to be furnished me clear of
expense.

Taxes assessed and unpaid to this date to be (paid) (~~assessed~~) by (seller) (~~buyer~~)

It is understood that any (~~xxxxxxxx~~)(mortgage) tax herein involved is payable by the seller.

I hereby agree to give .... seven (7) .... days to get the
owner's signature to the written acceptance of this proposition, appearing below, which, when signed,
will constitute a binding agreement between purchaser and seller, and herewith deposit $ .1,000.00...
as earnest money to apply on the purchase price. If proposition is not accepted or the title is not good,
or cannot be made good, this amount to be refunded, otherwise to be retained.

Sale to be closed on or before .... January 2 .... , 20 04 .

Possession to be given .... at closing .... , 20 ....

Witnesses: Signed:

                                                                    (Seal)

Nancy S. Woodford   *Kipton Lynn D'Amato*   (Seal)

                                                                    (Seal)

Todd M. Woodford   *Corey Allen Johnson*   (Seal)

The above proposition.

I also agree to pay .... Statewide Realty .... a commission of $ .4,200.00...
for negotiating this sale, but if not closed on account of purchaser's default the commission shall not exceed the amount of the deposit.
Witnesses: Signed:

Todd M. Woodford   *Corey Allen Johnson*   (Seal)

                                                                    (Seal)

Roberta Huggins   .... Salesman.

Self-Evaluation A | Terminology and Definition Recall

Directions: In the Answers column at the right of each statement, write the letter that represents the word or group of words that correctly completes the statement. After you have completed this self-evaluation, check your answers with the key on page 497. If you have any incorrect answers, review the definitions for those terms before going on with this lesson. Then unless otherwise directed, submit this self-evaluation to your instructor.

ANSWERS

1. Once a contract is made in writing, unless there was a mistake or fraud involved, it cannot be changed or altered by (a) bailment, (b) caveat emptor, (c) parol evidence.

1. _____

2. The delivery of personal property by the owner to another person for a specific purpose and period of time, after which time the property is to be returned to the owner, is referred to as (a) option, (b) bailment, (c) surety.

2. _____

3. An agreement whereby a person has the right to buy, sell, or lease certain property within a specified time is a/an (a) option, (b) offer, (c) contract.

3. _____

4. The law of the place where a contract is made is expressed in Latin as (a) lex loci contractus, (b) caveat emptor, (c) ex contractu.

4. _____

5. A Latin term meaning emerging or coming from a contract is (a) ex contractu, (b) lex loci contractus, (c) caveat emptor.

5. _____

6. A legal maxim meaning that a person is responsible for examining an article before purchasing it and is buying the article at his or her own risk is expressed in Latin as (a) ex contractu, (b) caveat emptor, (c) lex loci contractus.

6. _____

7. A proposal of one person to make an agreement or a contract with another person is a/an (a) offer, (b) acceptance, (c) counteroffer.

7. _____

8. An agreement whereby two or more persons promise to do or not to do certain things is a/an (a) bailment, (b) option, (c) contract.

8. _____

9. An agreement to an offer received from another is called a/an (a) counteroffer, (b) acceptance, (c) binder.

9. _____

10. When changes are made in an offer received from another, the offer is then referred to as a/an (a) contract, (b) option, (c) counteroffer.

10. _____

11. A person who agrees to be responsible for the debt of another in the event the other person fails to pay the debt is known as a (a) bailment, (b) surety, (c) binder.

11. _____

12. Money or security given with an offer to insure the intentions of the person making the offer is a/an (a) option, (b) surety, (c) binder.

12. _____

13. Law governing agreements made between individuals is (a) contract law, (b) ex contractu, (c) parol evidence rule.

13. _____

KEYING LEGAL TERMS

Directions: Unless otherwise instructed, use 1-inch margins and double spacing. Correct all errors. Follow one of the procedures below.

WORDS

Keyboarding Procedure
On your computer, key the following words at least two times, concentrating on the correct spelling and pronunciation.

Machine Shorthand Procedure
On your computer, key the following words once, concentrating on the correct spelling and pronunciation. Then write each word one time on your shorthand machine. Transcribe from your shorthand notes one time on your computer, or, if you are using computer-aided transcription (CAT), proofread and edit your transcript.

contract law	contract	ex contractu
lex loci contractus	surety	bailment
caveat emptor	parol evidence rule	offer
acceptance	counteroffer	option
binder		

SENTENCES

Keyboarding Procedure
Key each of the following sentences one time on your computer. Concentrate on the correct spelling and pronunciation of each underlined legal term.

Machine Shorthand Procedure
Write the following sentences one time on your shorthand machine. Transcribe from your shorthand notes one time on your computer, or, if you are using computer-aided transcription (CAT), proofread and edit your transcript.

These sentences will be used for practice dictation on the Transcription CD.

Contract law governs agreements made between individuals. A contract is an agreement whereby two or more persons promise to do or not to do certain things. Ex contractu means emerging or coming from a contract. Lex loci contractus is a Latin term meaning the law of the place where a contract is made.

A surety is a person who agrees to be responsible for the debt of another in the event the other person fails to pay the debt. Bailment is the delivery of personal property by the owner to another person for a specific purpose and period of time, after which time the property is to be returned to the owner. An example of a bailment would be the delivery of an article for repair.

Caveat emptor is Latin for let the buyer beware. Caveat emptor is a legal maxim meaning that a person is responsible for examining an article before purchasing it and that the purchase is made at his or her own risk. The parol evidence rule states that once a contract is made in writing, it cannot be changed by oral, or parol, evidence unless there was a mistake or fraud involved. An offer is a proposal by one person to make a contract with another person.

An <u>acceptance</u> is an agreement to an offer received by another. Offer and acceptance are two of the essential elements of a contract. If a party makes changes in an offer received from another party, it is then a <u>counteroffer</u>. An <u>option</u> is a continuing offer. If a person has an option on a property, he or she has the right to buy, sell, or lease it within a specified time. A <u>binder</u> is money or security presented with an offer to insure the intentions of the person making the offer.

TRANSCRIBING FROM DICTATION

Directions: This dictation emphasizes and reinforces the legal terms and definitions you have studied. Listen carefully to the pronunciation of each of the legal terms. Unless otherwise directed, use 1-inch margins and double spacing. Correct all errors. Follow one of the procedures below.

Keyboarding Procedure
Using the Transcription CD, Lesson 19, Part A, transcribe the dictation directly at your computer.

Machine Shorthand Procedure
Using the Transcription CD, Lesson 19, Part A, take the dictation on your shorthand machine and then transcribe from your notes on your computer, or, if you are using computer-aided transcription (CAT), proofread and edit your transcript.

When you have finished transcribing or proofreading and editing Part A of the practice dictation, check your transcript with the printed copy. If you made any mistakes in the transcription, you should review and practice those words several times before going on to Part B.

Part B | TERMINOLOGY AND DEFINITIONS

Directions: Study the terms, pronunciations, and definitions until you are thoroughly familiar with them. In order to complete this lesson successfully, you must understand the meaning and usage of all the legal terms presented. If you are using a shorthand system, write each legal term one time on your shorthand machine.

Legal Term	Pronunciation	Definition
1. consideration	kən-sid-ə-ˈrā-shən	The main reason for making a contract. An essential element of a contract. There must be consideration or benefit to both parties for a contract to be valid.
2. quid pro quo	kwid prō kwō	Latin. Something for something. The consideration in a contract.
3. mutual obligations	ˈmyüch-wəl äb-lə-ˈgā-shəns	A promise for a promise. Both parties to a legally binding contract must agree to do or not to do something.
4. competent parties	ˈkäm-pət-ənt ˈpärt-ēs	Persons who are legally qualified to make a contract. An essential element of a contract.
5. assumpsit	ə-ˈsəm-sət	Latin. A person promised. A written or oral promise made by one person to another.
6. condition	kən-ˈdish-ən	A provision in a contract pertaining to a future event that, if it occurs, would change the agreement.
7. performance	pə-ˈfȯr-məns	The fulfillment of the terms of a contract.

8. pro tanto	prō ′tan-tō	Latin. As far as it goes. One may recover on a contract that was not completely fulfilled for the value of his or her partial performance.
9. nudum pactum	′nü-dəm ′pakt-əm	Latin. An agreement made without any consideration other than a promise.
10. quantum meruit	′kwänt-əm me-′rüit	Latin. As much as one deserves. One may recover the reasonable value of his or her performance on a contract.
11. assignable	ə-′sī-nə-bəl	That which may be assigned or transferred. A contract that is assignable may be transferred to another person.
12. assignment	ə-′sīn-mənt	A transfer of the title of property from one person to another.
13. subrogation	səb-rō-gā-shən	To stand in the place of the one who made the contract. A right of recovery granted to one for whose benefit a contract was made but who was not actually a party to the contract.
14. accord and satisfaction	e-′kȯrd ən sat- əs′fak-shən	An accord is an agreement between two persons whereby one agrees to accept an amount less than the full amount in satisfaction of the debt. Accord and satisfaction is when the agreement is made and the debt has been paid.

Self-Evaluation B | Terminology and Definition Recall

Directions: In the Answers column, write the legal term that is most representative of the corresponding statement. After you have completed this self-evaluation, check your answers with the key on page 497. If you have any incorrect answers, review the definitions for those terms before going on with this lesson. Then unless otherwise directed, submit this self-evaluation to your instructor.

ANSWERS

1. That which may be assigned or transferred is said to be _____.

    1. _____

2. A promise for a promise, or when both parties to a legally binding contract must agree to do or not to do something, is called _____.

    2. _____

3. A transfer of the title of property from one person to another is a/an _____.

    3. _____

4. The fulfillment of the terms of a contract is referred to as the _____.

    4. _____

5. The main reason for making a contract is the _____.

    5. _____

6. A situation in which one may recover as much as one deserves or the reasonable value of the performance on a contract is expressed in Latin as _____.

    6. _____

7. A term meaning the agreement is made and the debt has been paid is _____.

    7. _____

8. A Latin phrase meaning as far as it goes, which applies to the recovery for the value of the partial performance on a contract that was not completely fulfilled, is _____.

    8. _____

9. A Latin term meaning something for something, or the consideration in a contract, is _____.

    9. _____

10. Persons who are legally qualified to make a contract are said to be _____.

    10. _____

11. A written or oral promise made by one person to another is _____.

    11. _____

12. A provision in a contract pertaining to a future event that, if it occurs, would change the agreement is a/an _____.

    12. _____

13. To stand in the place of the one who made the contract, or a right of recovery granted to one for whose benefit a contract was made but who was not actually a party to the contract, is referred to as _____.

    13. _____

14. An agreement made without any consideration other than a promise is expressed in Latin as a/an _____.

    14. _____

KEYING LEGAL TERMS

Directions: Unless otherwise instructed, use 1-inch margins and double spacing. Correct all errors. Follow one of the procedures below.

WORDS

Keyboarding Procedure
On your computer, key the following words at least two times, concentrating on the correct spelling and pronunciation.

Machine Shorthand Procedure
On your computer, key the following words once, concentrating on the correct spelling and pronunciation. Then write each word one time on your shorthand machine. Transcribe from your shorthand notes one time on your computer, or, if you are using computer-aided transcription (CAT), proofread and edit your transcript.

consideration	quid pro quo	mutual obligations
competent parties	assumpsit	condition
performance	pro tanto	nudum pactum
quantum meruit	assignable	assignment
subrogation	accord and satisfaction	

SENTENCES

Keyboarding Procedure
Key each of the following sentences one time on your computer. Concentrate on the correct spelling and pronunciation of each underlined legal term.

Machine Shorthand Procedure
Write the following sentences one time on your shorthand machine. Transcribe from your shorthand notes one time on your computer, or, if you are using computer-aided transcription (CAT), proofread and edit your transcript.

These sentences will be used for practice dictation on the Transcription CD.

Consideration is the main reason for making a contract. Consideration is an essential element of a contract, and there must be consideration or benefit to both parties for a contract to be valid. Quid pro quo means something for something. Quid pro quo is the consideration in a contract. Mutual obligations consist of a promise for a promise.

Competent parties are persons who are legally qualified to make a contract. Competent parties are an essential element of a contract. Assumpsit is a Latin term meaning a person promised. An assumpsit may be either a written or oral promise made by one person to another. A condition is a provision in a contract pertaining to a future event that, if it occurs, would change the agreement.

Performance refers to the fulfillment of the terms of a contract. Pro tanto means as far as it goes, or one may recover on a contract that was not completely fulfilled for the value of his or her partial performance. An agreement made without any consideration other than a promise is a nudum pactum. Quantum meruit refers to the amount one may recover for the reasonable value of his or her performance on a contract.

A contract that is <u>assignable</u> is one that may be transferred to another party. An <u>assignment</u> of a contract is the transfer or making over to another the title of any property or interest in a contract. Substituting a person in the place of the one who made the contract is called <u>subrogation</u>. When an agreement between two parties is made and the debt has been paid, the legal term is <u>accord and satisfaction</u>.

TRANSCRIBING FROM DICTATION

Directions: This dictation emphasizes and reinforces the legal terms and definitions you have studied. Listen carefully to the pronunciation of each of the legal terms. Unless otherwise directed, use 1-inch margins and double spacing. Correct all errors. Follow one of the procedures below.

Keyboarding Procedure
Using the Transcription CD, Lesson 19, Part B, transcribe the dictation directly at your computer.

Machine Shorthand Procedure
Using the Transcription CD, Lesson 19, Part B, take the dictation on your shorthand machine and then transcribe from your notes on your computer, or, if you are using computer-aided transcription (CAT), proofread and edit your transcript.

When you have finished transcribing or proofreading and editing Part B of the practice dictation, check your transcript with the printed copy. If you made any mistakes in the transcription, you should review and practice those words several times before going on to Lesson 20.

CHECKLIST
I have completed the following for Lesson 19:

	Part A, Date	Part B, Date	Submitted to Instructor Yes	No
Terminology and Definitions				
Self-Evaluation				
* Keying Legal Terms				
Words				
Sentences				
* Transcribing from Dictation				

When you have successfully completed all the exercises in this lesson and submitted to your instructor those requested, you are ready to proceed with Lesson 20.

* If you are using machine shorthand, submit to your instructor your notes along with your transcript.

Lesson
20

Contracts and Leases

Legal terms relating to contracts and leases are presented in the following exercises. Leases, which are a form of contract, involve the relationship between landlords and tenants. When you have satisfactorily completed this lesson, you should have a knowledge and understanding of the terminology involving contracts and leases.

Part A | TERMINOLOGY AND DEFINITIONS

Directions: Study the terms, pronunciations, and definitions until you are thoroughly familiar with them. In order to complete this lesson successfully, you must understand the meaning and usage of all the legal terms presented. If you are using a shorthand system, write each legal term one time on your shorthand machine.

Legal Term	Pronunciation	Definition
1. bilateral contract	bī-´lat-ə-rəl ´kän-trakt	A contract that involves mutual obligations for both sides of the contract.
2. unilateral contract	yü-ni-´lat-ə-rəl ´kän-trakt	A contract in which a promise or an obligation exists only on one side. A unilateral contract is not enforceable until the specified act has been performed.
3. express contract	ik-´spres ´kän-trakt	An actual agreement, not implied, that may be oral or written.
4. implied contract	im-´plīd ´kän-trakt	An agreement arising from the actions or legal duties of the parties rather than from an actual contract. Implied contracts may be implied in fact or implied in law.
5. implied in fact	im-´plīd in fakt	An implied contract that is created by the actions of the parties.
6. implied in law	im-´plīd in lö	An implied contract that is based on obligations created by law.
7. escalator clause	´es-kə-lāt-ər klöz	A clause in a contract stating that if costs increase or decrease, the payments may increase or decrease proportionately.
8. default	di-fölt	To fail to fulfill a legal duty.
9. breach of contract	brēch əv ´kän-trakt	Failure to fulfill the terms of a contract.

10.	privity of contract	′priv-ət-ē əv ′kän-trakt	The relationship of the parties to a contract. It is an essential element to recovery on a contract since only parties directly involved or with privity of contract have a right to sue.
11.	rescind	ri-′sind	To cancel or void a contract and to treat it as though no contract had ever been made. Also referred to as recission or revocation of a contract.
12.	vitiate	′vish-ē-āt	To destroy the legality of a contract.
13.	inchoate	in-′kō-ət	Incomplete. Relates to valid contracts or instruments that are required by law to be recorded but have not been and are, therefore, called incomplete, or inchoate, instruments.

Self-Evaluation A | Terminology and Definition Recall

Directions: In the Answers column, write the legal term that is most representative of the corresponding statement. After you have completed this self-evaluation, check your answers with the key on page 497. If you have any incorrect answers, review the definitions for those terms before going on with this lesson. Then unless otherwise directed, submit this self-evaluation to your instructor.

ANSWERS

1. Failure to fulfill a legal duty is to _____.

1. _____

2. To cancel or void a contract and to treat it as though no contract had ever been made is to _____.

2. _____

3. An implied contract that is based on obligations created by law is _____.

3. _____

4. An actual agreement, not implied, that may be oral or written is a/an _____.

4. _____

5. A contract in which a promise or obligation exists only on one side is a/an _____.

5. _____

6. An agreement arising from the actions or legal duties of the parties rather than from an actual contract is a/an _____.

6. _____

7. An implied contract that is created by the actions of the parties is _____.

7. _____

8. A contract that involves mutual obligations for both sides of the contract is a/an _____.

8. _____

9. The failure to fulfill the terms of a contract is known as _____.

9. _____

10. The relationship of the parties to a contract is known as _____.

10. _____

11. A clause in a contract stating that if costs increase or decrease, the payments may increase or decrease proportionately is called a/an _____.

11. _____

12. To destroy the legality of a contract is to _____.

12. _____

13. Instruments that are required by law to be recorded but have not been are referred to as _____.

13. _____

KEYING LEGAL TERMS

Directions: Unless otherwise instructed, use 1-inch margins and double spacing. Correct all errors. Follow one of the procedures below.

WORDS

Keyboarding Procedure

On your computer, key the following words at least two times, concentrating on the correct spelling and pronunciation.

Machine Shorthand Procedure

On your computer, key the following words once, concentrating on the correct spelling and pronunciation. Then write each word one time on your shorthand machine. Transcribe from your shorthand notes one time on your computer, or, if you are using computer-aided transcription (CAT), proofread and edit your transcript.

bilateral contract	unilateral contract	express contract
implied contract	implied in fact	implied in law
escalator clause	default	breach of contract
privity of contract	rescind	vitiate
inchoate		

SENTENCES

Keyboarding Procedure

Key each of the following sentences one time on your computer. Concentrate on the correct spelling and pronunciation of each underlined legal term.

Machine Shorthand Procedure

Write the following sentences one time on your shorthand machine. Transcribe from your shorthand notes one time on your computer, or, if you are using computer-aided transcription (CAT), proofread and edit your transcript.

These sentences will be used for practice dictation on the Transcription CD.

A <u>bilateral contract</u> involves mutual obligations for both parties of the contract. A <u>unilateral contract</u> is one in which a promise or an obligation exists only on one side. A unilateral contract is not enforceable until the specified act has been performed. An <u>express contract</u> is an actual agreement, not implied, that may be oral or written.

An <u>implied contract</u> is an agreement arising from the actions or legal duties of the parties rather than from an actual contract. Implied contracts may be <u>implied in fact</u> or <u>implied in law</u>. A contract implied in fact is created by the actions of the parties. A contract implied in law is based on obligations created by law. Thus, a legal maxim states, "Whatsoever it is certain a person ought to do, the law will suppose the person to have promised to do."

Some contracts or leases contain an <u>escalator clause</u> stating that if costs increase or decrease, the payment may increase or decrease proportionately. To fail to fulfill a legal duty is to <u>default</u>. If one defaults on a contract, he or she did not fulfill the terms of the agreement. A <u>breach of contract</u> involves the failure to fulfill the terms of a contract.

Privity of contract refers to the relationship of the parties to a contract. It is an essential element to recovery on a contract since only parties directly involved or with privity of contract have a right to sue.

To **rescind** a contract is to cancel or void it and to treat it as though no contract had ever been made. To **vitiate** a contract is to legally destroy it. Fraud will vitiate a contract. An **inchoate** contract is a valid contract or instrument that is required by law to be recorded but has not been.

TRANSCRIBING FROM DICTATION

Directions: This dictation emphasizes and reinforces the legal terms and definitions you have studied. Listen carefully to the pronunciation of each of the legal terms. Unless otherwise directed, use 1-inch margins and double spacing. Correct all errors. Follow one of the procedures below.

Keyboarding Procedure
Using the Transcription CD, Lesson 20, Part A, transcribe the dictation directly at your computer.

Machine Shorthand Procedure
Using the Transcription CD, Lesson 20, Part A, take the dictation on your shorthand machine and then transcribe from your notes on your computer, or, if you are using computer-aided transcription (CAT), proofread and edit your transcript.

When you have finished transcribing or proofreading and editing Part A of the practice dictation, check your transcript with the printed copy. If you made any mistakes in the transcription, you should review and practice those words several times before going on to Part B.

Part B | TERMINOLOGY AND DEFINITIONS

Directions: Study the terms, pronunciations, and definitions until you are thoroughly familiar with them. In order to complete this lesson successfully, you must understand the meaning and usage of all the legal terms presented. If you are using a shorthand system, write each legal term one time on your shorthand machine.

Legal Term	Pronunciation	Definition
1. inure	in-´ür	To benefit or to have effect. In a contract, inure means that if benefits accrue, they will take effect for or come to the party.
2. execute	´ek-si-kyüt	To carry out or put into effect. To execute a contract is to put it into effect by doing all the things that are necessary to make it valid and complete.
3. covenant	´kəv-nənt	An agreement between two or more persons that something will or will not be done.
4. lease	lēs	An agreement whereby a tenant or person has possession of property belonging to a landlord for a specified period of time. A landlord-tenant relationship. (See Figure 20-1, page 294.)
5. tenant	´ten-ənt	One who leases property from a landlord. A lessee. (See Figure 20-1, page 294.)
6. landlord	´lan-lȯrd	The owner of leased property. Another name for a lessor. (See Figure 20-1, page 294.)

7.	lessee	le-ˈsē	One who leases the property of another and has possession of said property. (See Figure 20-1, page 294.)
8.	lessor	ˈles-ȯr	One who owns property that is leased. (See Figure 20-1, page 294.)
9.	demise	di-ˈmīz	A lease. When used in a lease, demise means that the lessee shall have full use and enjoyment of the leased premises. (See Figure 20-1, page 294.)
10.	demised premises	di-ˈmīzd ˈprem-ə-səz	Land and buildings that are leased. (See Figure 20-1, page 294.)
11.	sublease	ˈsəb-ˈlēs	A lease whereby the lessee lets another person who is called a sublessee occupy the leased premises either for a shorter period of time than for which the premises are leased or until the lease expires.
12.	habitation	hab-ə-ˈtā-shən	The occupying of leased premises as a residence.
13.	notice to quit	ˈnōt-əs tü kwit	A written notice to the tenant from the landlord stating that the tenant is to vacate the premises by a specified time if certain conditions are not met. (See Figure 20-2, page 295.)
14.	eviction	i-ˈvik-shən	The legal removal of a tenant from leased property.
15.	writ of restitution	rit əv res-tə-ˈtü-shən	A writ issued by the court to return to the previous condition. A tenant who does not move after the court has so ordered would be served with a writ of restitution that returns the property to the landlord. The sheriff can then physically remove the tenant and his or her possessions from the premises. (See Figure 20-3, page 296.)

FIGURE 20-1 A Lease

Lessor/ Landlord

NOTICE: MICHIGAN LAW ESTABLISHES RIGHTS AND OBLIGATIONS FOR PARTIES TO RENTAL AGREEMENTS. THIS AGREEMENT IS REQUIRED TO COMPLY WITH THE TRUTH IN RENTING ACT. IF YOU HAVE A QUESTION ABOUT THE INTERPRETATION OR THE LEGALITY OF A PROVISION OF THIS AGREEMENT, YOU MAY WANT TO SEEK ASSISTANCE FROM A LAWYER OR OTHER QUALIFIED PERSON.

Lessee/ Tenant

Office of   Capitol Management Company   , Date   October 17, 2003

This is an Agreement between   Capitol Management Company   as Landlord and

Daniel and Maria Spencer   as tenant, concerning tenancy of

premises known as   Apartment 308

    4700 S. Cedar   ~~Avenue~~
                                                                          Street
in the   City   of   Lansing

Demised Premises

Said tenancy shall be on a month to month basis with monthly rent of $ 450.00   , payable in advance on the   1st   day of each month starting   November   ,20 03 upon which day said tenant shall be given possession of said premises. Both parties agree to give the other party thirty days notice in writing in case either party elects to terminate said tenancy and in such event rent shall be paid to the end of said thirty day period. Tenant agrees that said premises shall be used for residential purposes only, shall not be used for any unlawful purpose or in a manner contrary to law, and shall be occupied by not more than two (2)

adults and   -0- children whose ages are

Tenant further agrees to maintain said premises in good repair and to deliver and surrender up the same upon termination of said tenancy in the same condition as when taken except for ordinary wear and tear.

The landlord or his authorized agents shall have the right to inspect said premises and repair and maintain the same, and may at any reasonable hour show the same and any part thereof to prospective purchasers, mortgagees, tenants, or agents thereof, and may, at any time, place and maintain one "for sale" sign thereon in event said property is now or hereafter for sale.

Tenant herewith deposits the sum of $ 250.00   with Community Management Company   ~~ or his broker~~   , as renting agent of said landlord, to apply on the first month's rent in event this agreement is signed by landlord or the agent thereof within 3   days from the date hereof, otherwise to be returned to tenant. The balance of said first month's rent shall be paid prior to Oct. 15, 2003   and in any event before tenant occupies said premises or any part thereof.

Tenant further agrees to deposit one dollar to secure the return to the landlord of   two (2)   keys to said premises upon termination of said tenancy. Upon such return said sum is to be refunded to tenant.

Tenant makes the following representations of fact:

Former landlord   J & J Leasing Company

Landlord's address   6850 N. Saginaw St.   Phone   555-6700

Financial reference Federal Savings and Loan

Occupation Mail Clerk   Employer Lansing Post Office

Business address   315 West Allegan, Lansing, Michigan 48933

Name and address of nearest relative   Kenneth Spencer, 330 W. Maple,

East Lansing, Michigan 48823

Water bills are to be paid by { ~~tenant~~
                                 landlord

Tenant agrees not to make any alterations or improvements to said premises without the written consent of the landlord, and that landlord shall have sole discretion as to the necessity of any repair, decorating or other work in and about said premises and as to the quality and cost thereof.

Tenant shall have no right to and shall not assign this agreement nor sublet said premises or any part thereof, and tenant agrees to immediately inform landlord of any future change in the above facts or in the number or identity of occupants of said premises, any such assignment, subletting or change shall be cause for the immediate termination of said tenancy at the option of landlord.

TRUTH IN RENTING ACT PROVISIONS: Landlord and Tenant specifically agree that this lease shall not, is not intended, nor shall it be construed, to violate any of the provisions of the Truth in Renting Act. If, however, any provision of this lease does in fact reach any such result, then such provision shall be null and void, but the other provisions of this lease shall continue to remain in full force and effect.

The address of the landlord for purposes of notice under the Truth in Renting Act and for all other purposes is 4700 S. Cedar Street, Lansing, Michigan 48910

IN WITNESS WHEREOF, The parties have hereunto set their hands and seals the day and year first above written.

Daniel Spencer   Maria Spencer
                                                                          Tenant.

                              6850 N. Saginaw St., Apt. 605
                                                                    Present Address.

Abigail Cross
                              Landlord.

FIGURE 20-2 A Notice to Quit

| | | | | |

NOTICE TO QUIT

Termination Of Tenancy

Landlord - Tenant

To:

> Daniel and Maria Spencer
> 4700 S. Cedar Street, Apt. 308
> Lansing, Michigan 48910

1. Your landlord/~~landlady~~ __Capitol Management Company__ wants to evict you from:
   Name

Address or description of premises rented (if different from mailing address):

Same

for the reason that he/~~she~~ is terminating your tenancy.

2. You must move by___ January 17, 2004 ___ or your landlord/~~landlady~~ may take you to court to evict you.
   Date (*see note)

3. If your landlord/~~landlady~~ takes you to court to evict you, you will have the opportunity to present reasons why you believe you should not be evicted.

4. If you believe you have a good reason why you should not be evicted you may have a lawyer advise you. Call him or her soon.

December 17, 2003
Date

Abigail Cross
Signature of owner of premises, or agent
4700 S. Cedar Street
Address
Lansing, Michigan 48910   555-9920
City, state, zip   Telephone no.

*NOTE: if the lease agreement does not state otherwise, the landlord/~~landlady~~ must give notice equal in time to at least one rental period.

PROOF OF SERVICE

Abigail Cross ___ being duly sworn, says that on __Dec. 17, 2003__ ~~he~~/she served the above notice on
Name   Date

___ Daniel and Maria Spencer ___
Name

by: ☒ personal service
    ☐ substitute service
    ☐ 1st class mail

Abigail Cross
Signature

Subscribed and sworn to before me on __January 19, 2004__, __Ingham__ ___ County, Michigan.
                                        Date

My commission expires: __September 1, 2005__ Signature: *Michael Robins*
                          Date   Deputy Clerk/~~Notary Public~~

(To be copied, if necessary, to attach to the complaint)

NOTICE TO QUIT, TERMINATION OF TENANCY, Landlord-Tenant, Form No. DCH100c, Revised 2/80

COURT COPY

FIGURE 20-3 A Writ of Restitution

ORIGINAL - OFFICER RETURN
1ST COPY - COURT
2ND COPY - DEFENDANT

STATE OF MICHIGAN 54th **DISTRICT COURT**	**WRIT OF RESTITUTION** LANDLORD/TENANT—LAND CONTRACT	CASE NO. 75-8001 LT

6th Floor, City Hall, Lansing, Michigan 48933   (517) 555-3445

Court address   Court telephone no.

Plaintiff name and address
Capitol Management Company
4700 S. Cedar Street
Lansing, Michigan 48910

Defendant name (s) and address (es)
Daniel and Maria Spencer
4700 S. Cedar Street, Apt. 308
Lansing, Michigan 48910

Plaintiff's attorney, bar no., address and telephone no.
in pro per

APPLICATION

The undersigned makes application for a writ of restitution and states:

1. On __January 28, 2004__ judgment was entered against Defendant (s), and Plaintiff was awarded possession of the
   Date
   following described property: ___4700 S. Cedar Street, Apt. 308, Lansing, Michigan___

2. No payment has been made on the judgment and/or no rent has been received since the date of judgment, except the

   sum of $ _____-0-_____ received under the following conditions: _____

3. The party awarded judgment has complied with its terms.
4. The time stated in the judgment to precede the issuance of a writ of restitution has elapsed.

I declare, under penalty of contempt of court, that to the best of my knowledge, information and belief, there is good ground to support the contents of this pleading.

__February 9, 2004__
Date

Abigail Cross
Signature of Plaintiff/Attorney, Bar no.
4700 S. Cedar Street
Address
Lansing, Michigan 48910   555-9920
City, state, zip   Telephone no.

WRIT

IN THE NAME OF THE PEOPLE OF THE STATE OF MICHIGAN:
To the Court Officer: Based upon the facts set forth in the above application, you are commanded to remove the above-named Defendant (s) and other occupants from the premises described, and to restore Plaintiff to peaceful possession.

SEAL   __February 9, 2004__   _Cecil Pulaski_
              Date issued   District Judge

NOTE: This writ must be served within 60 days of the issuance date.

COURT

WRIT OF RESTITUTION, LANDLORD-TENNANT, LAND CONTRACT, Form No. DCH107, (3 part, pink) Revised 4/80

Self-Evaluation B | Terminology and Definition Recall

Directions: In the Answers column, write the letter from Column 1 that represents the word or phrase that best matches each item in Column 2. After you have completed this self-evaluation, check your answers with the key on page 498. If you have any incorrect answers, review the definitions for those terms before going on with this lesson. Then unless otherwise directed, submit this self-evaluation to your instructor.

COLUMN 1	COLUMN 2	ANSWERS
a. covenant	1. One who owns property that is leased.	1. _____
b. demise	2. Land and buildings that are leased.	2. _____
c. demised premises	3. The owner of leased property; another name for a lessor.	3. _____
d. ejectment	4. An agreement between two or more persons that something will be or will not be done.	4. _____
e. eviction		
f. execute	5. An agreement whereby a tenant or person has possession of property belonging to a landlord for a specified period of time.	5. _____
g. habitation		
h. inure	6. One who leases the property of another and has possession of said property.	6. _____
i. landlord		
j. lease	7. The occupying of leased premises as a residence.	7. _____
k. lessee	8. A word used in a contract meaning that if benefits accrue, they will take effect for or come to the party.	8. _____
l. lessor		
m. notice to quit	9. A written notice to the tenant from the landlord stating that the tenant is to vacate the premises by a specified time if certain conditions are not met.	9. _____
n. sublease		
o. tenant	10. A document issued by the court that means to return to the previous condition.	10. _____
p. writ of restitution		
	11. To put a contract into effect by doing all the things that are necessary to make it valid and complete.	11. _____
	12. A lease whereby the lessee lets another person occupy the leased premises.	12. _____
	13. The legal removal of a tenant from leased property.	13. _____
	14. Another name for a lessee.	14. _____
	15. A term used in a lease meaning that the lessee shall have full use and enjoyment of the leased premises.	15. _____

KEYING LEGAL TERMS

Directions: Unless otherwise instructed, use 1-inch margins and double spacing. Correct all errors. Follow one of the procedures below.

WORDS

Keyboarding Procedure
On your computer, key the following words at least two times, concentrating on the correct spelling and pronunciation.

Machine Shorthand Procedure
On your computer, key the following words once, concentrating on the correct spelling and pronunciation. Then write each word one time on your shorthand machine. Transcribe from your shorthand notes one time on your computer, or, if you are using computer-aided transcription (CAT), proofread and edit your transcript.

inure	execute	covenant
lease	tenant	landlord
lessee	lessor	demise
demised premises	sublease	habitation
notice to quit	eviction	writ of restitution

SENTENCES

Keyboarding Procedure
Key each of the following sentences one time on your computer. Concentrate on the correct spelling and pronunciation of each underlined legal term.

Machine Shorthand Procedure
Write the following sentences one time in on your shorthand machine. Transcribe from your shorthand notes one time on your computer, or, if you are using computer-aided transcription (CAT), proofread and edit your transcript.

These sentences will be used for practice dictation on the Transcription CD.

<u>Inure</u> means to have effect or to benefit. Inure, when used in a contract, means that if benefits accrue, they will take effect for or come to the party. To <u>execute</u> means to carry out or put into effect. To execute a contract is to put it into effect by doing all the things that are necessary to make it valid and complete. A <u>covenant</u> is an agreement between two or more persons that something will be or will not be done.

A <u>lease</u> is an agreement whereby a <u>tenant</u> or person has possession of property belonging to a <u>landlord</u> for a specified period of time. A <u>lessee</u> is the one who leases the property from another, and the <u>lessor</u> is the one who owns the property that is leased. Thus, the tenant is the lessee, and the landlord is the lessor. The use of the term <u>demise</u> in a lease means that the lessee shall have full use and enjoyment of the leased premises. <u>Demised premises</u> are land and buildings that are leased.

A <u>sublease</u> is a lease whereby the lessee lets another person occupy the leased premises. A person who occupies leased premises as a residence has the right of <u>habitation</u>.

A <u>notice to quit</u> is a written notice to the tenant from the landlord stating that the tenant is to vacate the premises by a specified time if certain conditions are not met. If a tenant does not move from the demised premises after the landlord has served the notice to quit, the tenant is subject to <u>eviction</u>. Eviction is the legal removal of a tenant from leased property.

A <u>writ of restitution</u> means to return to the previous condition. If a tenant has been evicted from the premises and fails to move by the date ordered by the court, the landlord may have a writ of restitution issued. The writ of restitution gives the sheriff authority to remove physically the tenant and his or her possessions from the premises.

TRANSCRIBING FROM DICTATION

Directions: This dictation emphasizes and reinforces the legal terms and definitions you have studied. Listen carefully to the pronunciation of each of the legal terms. Unless otherwise directed, use 1-inch margins and double spacing. Correct all errors. Follow one of the procedures below.

Keyboarding Procedure

Using the Transcription CD, Lesson 20, Part B, transcribe the dictation directly at your computer.

Machine Shorthand Procedure

Using the Transcription CD, Lesson 20, Part B, take the dictation on your shorthand machine and then transcribe from your notes on your computer, or, if you are using computer-aided transcription (CAT), proofread and edit your transcript.

When you have finished transcribing or proofreading and editing Part B of the practice dictation, check your transcript with the printed copy. If you made any mistakes in the transcription, you should review and practice those words several times before going on to Evaluation 10.

CHECKLIST

I have completed the following for Lesson 20:

	Part A, Date	Part B, Date	Submitted to Instructor	
			Yes	No
Terminology and Definitions	_____	_____	_____	_____
Self-Evaluation	_____	_____	_____	_____
* Keying Legal Terms	_____	_____	_____	_____
Words	_____	_____	_____	_____
Sentences	_____	_____	_____	_____
* Transcribing from Dictation	_____	_____	_____	_____

When you have successfully completed all the exercises in this lesson and submitted to your instructor those requested, you are ready to proceed with Evaluation 10.

* If you are using machine shorthand, submit to your instructor your notes along with your transcript.

Evaluation No. 10 | SECTION A

Directions: This dictation/transcription evaluation will test your spelling and transcription abilities on the legal terms that you studied in the two preceding lessons. Tab once for a paragraph indention, and use 1-inch margins and double spacing unless otherwise instructed. Correct all errors. Follow one of the procedures below.

Keyboarding Procedure

Using the Transcription CD for Evaluation 10, transcribe the dictation directly at your computer.

Machine Shorthand Procedure

Using the Transcription CD for Evaluation 10, take the dictation on your shorthand machine and then transcribe your notes on your computer, or, if you are using computer-aided transcription, proofread and edit your transcript.

Sections B and C are available from your instructor.

Lesson 21

Domestic Relations—Marriage, Separation, and Divorce

"Between those who are equally in the right, or equally in the wrong, the law does not interpose."
—*Legal maxim*

The area of domestic relations encompasses marriages, divorces, annulments, and separations. Most court actions in domestic relations involve divorce proceedings. Grounds and procedures for divorce actions vary widely from state to state. In this lesson, the terms presented are those that will generally be encountered, regardless of the jurisdiction. When you complete these exercises, you should have knowledge and an understanding of some of the terms used in reference to domestic relations.

Part A | TERMINOLOGY AND DEFINITIONS

Directions: Study the terms, pronunciations, and definitions until you are thoroughly familiar with them. In order to complete this lesson successfully, you must understand the meaning and usage of all the legal terms presented. If you are using a shorthand system, write each legal term one time on your shorthand machine.

Legal Term	Pronunciation	Definition
1. domestic	də-ʹmes-tik	Refers to family affairs or to a home or household.
2. civil ceremony	ʹsiv-əl ʹser-ə-mō-nē	A ceremony that creates a valid marriage and is performed by a public official who is so authorized to perform marriages.
3. religious ceremony	ri-ʹlij-əs ʹser-ə-mō-nē	A ceremony that creates a valid marriage and is performed by a duly ordained minister or a member of the clergy of any recognized religion.
4. matrimony	ʹma-trə-mō-nē	The marriage relationship between husband and wife.
5. common-law marriage	ʹkäm-ən lȯ ʹmar-ij	A marriage that is not created by the usual ceremony required by law but exists between two people who agree to live together as husband and wife. It is not recognized as a valid marriage in some states.
6. valid marriage	ʹval-əd ʹmar-ij	A marriage that is created according to the requirements of the law.
7. voidable marriage	ʹvȯid-ə-bəl ʹmar-ij	A marriage that exists for all practical purposes but contains a legal imperfection that could void the relationship in a court of law.
8. void marriage	vȯid ʹmar-ij	A marriage that is not valid and does not meet the requirements established by law for a valid marriage.
9. monogamy	mə-ʹnäg-ə-mē	A marriage relationship between only one man and one woman at a time.

10. bigamy	ˈbig-ə-mē	The state of having more than one husband or wife at any one time. A criminal offense in the United States.
11. annulment	ə-ˈnəl-mənt	The voiding of a marriage and treating it as though it never existed.
12. age of consent	āj əv kən-ˈsent	The age set by state law at which a person can marry without parental or guardian consent.
13. non-age	ˈnän-āj	Below the age of consent. In most states, non-age is a ground for obtaining an annulment.

Self-Evaluation A | Terminology and Definition Recall

Directions: In the Answers column, write the letter from Column 1 that represents the word or phrase that best matches each item in Column 2. After you have completed this self-evaluation, check your answers with the key on page 498. If you have any incorrect answers, review the definitions for those terms before going on with this lesson. Then unless otherwise directed, submit this self-evaluation to your instructor.

COLUMN 1	COLUMN 2	ANSWERS
a. age of consent	1. A marriage that is not valid and does not meet the requirements established by law for a valid marriage.	1. _m_
b. annulment	2. A marriage relationship between only one man and one woman at a time.	2. _i_
c. bigamy	3. A word meaning below the age of consent and a ground for annulment in most states.	3. _j_
d. ceremony	4. A ceremony that creates a valid marriage and is performed by a duly ordained minister or member of the clergy of any recognized religion.	4. _k_
e. civil ceremony	5. The voiding of a marriage treating it as though it never existed.	5. _b_
f. common-law marriage	6. The marriage relationship between a husband and wife.	6. _h_
g. domestic	7. A ceremony that creates a valid marriage and is performed by a public official who is authorized to perform marriages.	7. _e_
h. matrimony	8. A marriage that is not created by the usual ceremony required by law but exists between two people who live together as husband and wife.	8. _f_
i. monogamy	9. A marriage that is created according to the requirements of the law.	9. _l_
j. non-age	10. A marriage that exists for all practical purposes but contains a legal imperfection that could void the relationship in a court of law.	10. _n_
k. religious ceremony	11. The age set by state law at which a person can marry without parental or guardian consent.	11. _a_
- l. valid marriage	12. A term that refers to family affairs or to a home or household.	12. _g_
m. void marriage	13. The state of having more than one husband or wife at any one time.	13. _c_
n. voidable marriage		

KEYING LEGAL TERMS

Directions: Unless otherwise instructed, use 1-inch margins and double spacing. Correct all errors. Follow one of the procedures below.

WORDS

Keyboarding Procedure

On your computer, key the following words at least two times, concentrating on the correct spelling and pronunciation.

Machine Shorthand Procedure

On your computer, key the following words once, concentrating on the correct spelling and pronunciation. Then write each word one time on your shorthand machine. Transcribe from your shorthand notes one time on your computer, or, if you are using computer-aided transcription (CAT), proofread and edit your transcript.

domestic	civil ceremony	valid marriage
religious ceremony	matrimony	common-law marriage
voidable marriage	void marriage	monogamy
bigamy	annulment	age of consent
non-age		

SENTENCES

Keyboarding Procedure

Key each of the following sentences one time on your computer. Concentrate on the correct spelling and pronunciation of each underlined legal term.

Machine Shorthand Procedure

Write the following sentences one time on your shorthand machine. Transcribe from your shorthand notes one time on your computer, or, if you are using computer-aided transcription (CAT), proofread and edit your transcript.

These sentences will be used for practice dictation on the Transcription CD.

<u>Domestic</u> refers to family affairs or to a home or household. Domestic relations encompass the areas of marriages, divorces, annulments, and separations. A <u>civil ceremony</u> creates a <u>valid marriage</u> and is performed by a public official who is authorized to perform marriages. A marriage that is performed by a duly ordained minister or member of the clergy of any recognized religion is a <u>religious ceremony</u>. <u>Matrimony</u> is the marriage relation between a husband and wife. Matrimony does not refer to the ceremony itself.

A <u>common-law marriage</u> is one that is not created by the usual ceremony required by law but exists between two people who agree to live together as husband and wife. Common-law marriages are not recognized in many states.

A valid marriage is one that is created according to the requirements of the law. A <u>voidable marriage</u> is one that exists for all practical purposes but contains a legal imperfection that could void the relationship in a court of law. A <u>void marriage</u> is one that is not valid and does not meet the requirements established by law for a valid marriage.

Monogamy is a marriage relationship between only one man and one woman at a time. **Bigamy** is the state of having two husbands or two wives at the same time. Bigamy is a criminal offense in the United States.

An **annulment** voids a marriage and treats it as though it never existed. An annulment means in effect that there was no marriage at all. Each state sets the age at which a person may marry without parental or guardian consent. The age set by each state is referred to as the **age of consent**. **Non-age** is below the age of consent. In most states, non-age is a ground for obtaining an annulment.

TRANSCRIBING FROM DICTATION

Directions: This dictation emphasizes and reinforces the legal terms and definitions you have studied. Listen carefully to the pronunciation of each of the legal terms. Unless otherwise directed, use 1-inch margins and double spacing. Correct all errors. Follow one of the procedures below.

Keyboarding Procedure
Using the Transcription CD, Lesson 21, Part A, transcribe the dictation directly at your computer.

Machine Shorthand Procedure
Using the Transcription CD, Lesson 21, Part A, take the dictation on your shorthand machine and then transcribe from your notes on your computer, or, if you are using computer-aided transcription (CAT), proofread and edit your transcript.

When you have finished transcribing or proofreading and editing Part A of the practice dictation, check your transcript with the printed copy. If you made any mistakes in the transcription, you should review and practice those words several times before going on to Part B.

Part B | TERMINOLOGY AND DEFINITIONS

Directions: Study the terms, pronunciations, and definitions until you are thoroughly familiar with them. In order to complete this lesson successfully, you must understand the meaning and usage of all the legal terms presented. If you are using a shorthand system, write each legal term one time on your shorthand machine.

Legal Term	Pronunciation	Definition
1. premarital	prē-ˈmar-ət-l	Before the marriage.
2. antenuptial agreement	ant-i-ˈnəp-shəl ə-ˈgrē-mənt	An agreement made between two people before they are married. Sometimes called a premarital agreement.
3. cohabitation	kō-hab-ə-ˈtā-shən	The state of living together as husband and wife.
4. consanguinity	kän-san-ˈgwin-ət-ē	A blood relationship between two people.
5. affinity	ə-ˈfin-ət-ē	The relationship of one spouse to the blood relatives of the other spouse because of marriage.
6. femme sole	fem sol	French. A woman who is not married. A woman who is single, divorced, or widowed.
7. separation	sep-ə-ˈrā-shən	A partial or qualified divorce where the parties may not live together but are otherwise legally bound as husband and wife.
8. a mensa et thoro	ā ˈmen-sə et ˈthōr-ō	Latin. A legal separation.

9. separation agreement	sep-ə-'rā-shən ə-'grē-mənt	A contract between a husband and wife who are living separately that clarifies the property rights, custody, and support for each party.
10. separate maintenance	'sep-rət 'mānt-nəns	An amount granted by a court in a legal separation to one of the spouses for his or her support and for the support of the children.
11. privileged communications	'priv-lijd kə-myü-nə-'kā-shəns	A spouse is not permitted to testify as a witness against the other spouse in regard to matters revealed to each other because of the confidence that exists between them as a result of the marital relation.
12. counsel fee	'kaủn-səl fē	A fee for legal counsel. In most states, the one filing for divorce is usually required to pay the counsel fees incurred by the other spouse in the divorce action.

Self-Evaluation B | Terminology and Definition Recall

Directions: In the Answers column, write the legal term that is most representative of the corresponding statement. After you have completed this self-evaluation, check your answers with the key on page 498. If you have any incorrect answers, review the definitions for those terms before going on with this lesson. Then unless otherwise directed, submit this self-evaluation to your instructor.

ANSWERS

1. A legal term that means before the marriage is _____.

1. *premarital*

2. An amount granted by a court in a legal separation to one of the spouses for his or her support and for the support of the children is _____.

2. *maintenance*

3. The state of living together as husband and wife is referred to as _____.

3. *cohabitation*

4. The relationship between husband and wife that prohibits one from testifying against the other about matters revealed to each other because of the confidence that exists between them as a result of the marital relationship is referred to as _____.

4. *privileged communications*

5. A contract between a husband and wife who are living separately that clarifies the property rights, custody, and support for each party is a/an _____.

5. *separation agreement*

6. A French term for a woman who is not married is _____.

6. *femme sole*

7. A partial or qualified divorce where the parties may not live together but are otherwise legally bound as husband and wife is a/an _____.

7. *separation*

8. A fee for legal counsel that is usually paid by the one filing for the divorce is referred to as the _____.

8. *counsel fee*

9. The relationship of one spouse to the blood relatives of the other spouse because of the marriage is _____.

9. *affinity*

10. A blood relationship between two people is referred to as _____.

10. *consanguinity*

11. An agreement made between two people before they are married is a/an _____.

11. *antenuptial agreement*

12. A Latin term meaning a legal separation is _____.

12. *a mensa et thoro*

KEYING LEGAL TERMS

Directions: Unless otherwise instructed, use 1-inch margins and double spacing. Correct all errors. Follow one of the procedures below.

WORDS

Keyboarding Procedure

On your computer, key the following words at least two times, concentrating on the correct spelling and pronunciation.

Machine Shorthand Procedure

On your computer, key the following words once, concentrating on the correct spelling and pronunciation. Then write each word one time on your shorthand machine. Transcribe from your shorthand notes one time on your computer, or, if you are using computer-aided transcription (CAT), proofread and edit your transcript.

premarital	antenuptial agreement	cohabitation
consanguinity	affinity	femme sole
separation	a mensa et thoro	separation agreement
separate maintenance	privileged communications	counsel fee

SENTENCES

Keyboarding Procedure

Key each of the following sentences one time on your computer. Concentrate on the correct spelling and pronunciation of each underlined legal term.

Machine Shorthand Procedure

Write the following sentences one time on your shorthand machine. Transcribe from your shorthand notes one time on your computer, or, if you are using computer-aided transcription (CAT), proofread and edit your transcript.

These sentences will be used for practice dictation on the Transcription CD.

Premarital means before the marriage. An antenuptial agreement, or a premarital agreement, is an agreement made between two people before they are married. An antenuptial agreement may also be referred to as a marriage contract, and it may detail how certain things will be handled during a marriage or if a marriage ends by divorce.

Cohabitation is the state of living together as husband and wife. Consanguinity is a blood relationship between two people. In most states, persons of the opposite sex are forbidden from living together unless they are related by consanguinity or marriage. Affinity is the relationship of one spouse to the blood relatives of the other spouse because of marriage. Femme sole is a French term referring to a single woman. Femme sole also includes those women who are divorced or widowed.

A partial or qualified divorce where the parties may not live together but are otherwise legally bound as husband and wife is a separation. A separation expressed in Latin is a mensa et thoro. A mensa et thoro usually involves a separation agreement between husband and wife that clarifies the property rights, custody, and support for each party. The separation agreement may contain provisions for separate

maintenance, which is an allowance granted to one of the spouses for his or her support and for the support of the children.

Privileged communications exist between a husband and wife. Matters revealed to a spouse are privileged communications, and the spouse is not permitted to testify as a witness against the other spouse in regard to those matters. In most states, the one filing for a divorce is usually required to pay the <u>counsel fee</u> incurred by the spouse in the divorce action.

TRANSCRIBING FROM DICTATION

Directions: This dictation emphasizes and reinforces the legal terms and definitions you have studied. Listen carefully to the pronunciation of each of the legal terms. Unless otherwise directed, use 1-inch margins and double spacing. Correct all errors. Follow one of the procedures below.

Keyboarding Procedure
Using the Transcription CD, Lesson 21, Part B, transcribe the dictation directly at your computer.

Machine Shorthand Procedure
Using the Transcription CD, Lesson 21, Part B, take the dictation on your shorthand machine and then transcribe from your notes on your computer, or, if you are using computer-aided transcription (CAT), proofread and edit your transcript.

When you have finished transcribing or proofreading and editing Part B of the practice dictation, check your transcript with the printed copy. If you made any mistakes in the transcription, you should review and practice those words several times before going on to Lesson 22.

CHECKLIST
I have completed the following for Lesson 21:

	Part A, Date	Part B, Date	Submitted to Instructor Yes	No
Terminology and Definitions				
Self-Evaluation				
* Keying Legal Terms				
Words				
Sentences				
* Transcribing from Dictation				

When you have successfully completed all the exercises in this lesson and submitted to your instructor those requested, you are ready to proceed with Lesson 22.

* If you are using machine shorthand, submit to your instructor your notes along with your transcript.

Lesson
22

Domestic Relations—Marriage, Separation, and Divorce

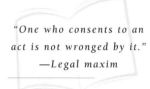

"One who consents to an act is not wronged by it."
—Legal maxim

Many of the terms relating to the dissolution of marriage are introduced in this lesson. Divorce laws are changing rapidly and vary considerably from state to state. Therefore, the terms covered are those that are generally applicable to most states. For the successful completion of these exercises, you should be able to spell, pronounce, define, and transcribe correctly each of the terms that are presented.

Part A | TERMINOLOGY AND DEFINITIONS

Directions: Study the terms, pronunciations, and definitions until you are thoroughly familiar with them. In order to complete this lesson successfully, you must understand the meaning and usage of all the legal terms presented. If you are using a shorthand system, write each legal term one time on your shorthand machine.

Legal Term	Pronunciation	Definition
1. divorce	də-ˈvōrs	The dissolving of a marriage legally by an action of the court. Also includes a legal separation. (See Figures 22-1 and 22-2, pages 317 and 318.)
2. dissolution of marriage	dis-ə-ˈlü-shən əv ˈmar-ij	The termination of a marriage by divorce.
3. no-fault divorce	ˈnō-ˈfȯlt də-ˈvōrs	The divorce laws of several states that do not require the one filing for divorce to prove the spouse at fault on any grounds previously required for a divorce to be granted. Under no-fault law, neither party has to prove the other at fault in order to obtain a divorce.
4. grounds for divorce	graůnds fər də-ˈvōrs	The foundation or basis for the granting of a divorce. The grounds for divorce will vary from state to state. In states with no-fault divorce, grounds for divorce are no longer needed.
5. conciliation procedure	kən-sil-e-ˈa-shən prə-ˈsē-jər	A procedure whereby the judge meets with the parties to a divorce and attempts to work out their differences. The judge may recommend to the parties that they attempt to reconcile the marriage possibly through marital counseling before the divorce is granted.
6. corespondent	kō-ri-ˈspän-dənt	The person charged with committing adultery with the respondent in a divorce action for which the grounds are adultery.

7. desertion	di-'zər-shən	The refusal without just cause of a husband or wife to continue a marital relationship.
8. Enoch Arden Law	'ē-nək 'ärd-n lȯ	A law in some states specifying that the unexplained absence of a spouse for a lengthy and continuous period of time constitutes grounds for divorce.
9. limited divorce	'lim-ət-əd də-'vōrs	A legal separation that does not totally dissolve the marriage.
10. absolute divorce	'ab-sə–lüt də-'vōrs	The total dissolution of a marriage.
11. a vinculo matrimonii	ā vin-'kū-lō ma-trə-'mō-nē-ī	Latin. An absolute divorce.
12. contested divorce	kən-'test-əd də-'vōrs	A divorce action in which one of the parties resists or opposes the granting of the divorce and challenges or defends the action.
13. uncontested divorce	ən-kən-'test-əd də-'vōrs	A divorce action in which the party being sued for divorce does not resist or oppose the grounds for the divorce and makes no defense thereto.

FIGURE 22-1 A Complaint for Divorce

Approved, SCAO	Original - Court 1st copy - Friend of the Court	2nd copy - Defendant 3rd copy - Plaintiff

STATE OF MICHIGAN 30th **JUDICIAL CIRCUIT** Ingham **COUNTY**	**COMPLAINT FOR DIVORCE** **Page 1 of** 1 **pages**	**CASE NO.** 88521-D

Court address 2nd Floor, City Hall, Lansing, MI 48933	Court telephone no. (517) 555-0650

Plaintiff Clara Annette Mills	☐ husband ☒ wife	v.	Defendant Scott Wendell Mills
Plaintiff's name before marriage Bolton			Defendant's name before marriage

1. Plaintiff's residence: at least   ☒ 180 days in Michigan   immediately before filing of this complaint.
       ☒ 10 days in this county

2. Defendant's residence: at least   ☒ 180 days in Michigan   immediately before filing of this complaint.
       ☒ 10 days in this county

3. Marriage: June 10, 1990   Lansing, Michigan
           Date   Place

4. There has been a breakdown of the marriage relationship to the extent that the objects of matrimony have been destroyed and there remains no reasonable likelihood that the marriage can be preserved.

5. The wife ☒ is not pregnant.   ☐ is pregnant, and the estimated date of birth is _____ .

6. Complete names and dates of birth of children under 18 of the parties or born during this marriage:
      ☒ None   Attach a Uniform Child Custody Jurisdiction Act Affidavit

7. There   ☒ is   ☐ is no   property to be divided.

                                                        Attach a verified statement.

☐ 8. I request temporary support orders for the payment of the following: Attach a motion when required.
     a. support for: ☐ child(ren)   ☐ plaintiff   ☐ defendant
     b. health care: ☐ expenses   ☐ insurance premiums   for   ☐ child(ren)   ☐ spouse
     c. residence: ☐ utilities   ☐ rent/mortgage/land contract   ☐ taxes   ☐ insurance
     d. other: Specify

☐ 9. Motion(s) are attached that request temporary restraining order(s) concerning:
     ☐ a. property
     ☐ b. domestic assault: ☐ civil   ☐ criminal
     ☐ c. other: Specify

10. I request a judgment of divorce, and:
     a. property: ☒ award to each party the property in their possession
                 ☐ divide
     ☒ b. change wife's last name to: Bolton
     ☐ c. legal custody to: ☐ plaintiff   ☐ defendant   ☐ joint/both parties
     ☐ d. physical custody to: ☐ plaintiff   ☐ defendant   ☐ joint/both parties
     ☐ e. visitation rights: ☐ reasonable   ☐ specific
     ☐ f. support money for: ☐ child(ren)   ☐ plaintiff   ☐ defendant
     ☐ g. other:Specify

January 3, 2003
Date

January 3, 2003
Date

Clara Annette Mills
Plaintiff signature

Jill F Sinclair   P 54079
Plaintiff attorney signature   Bar no.

CC 415   (11/86)   **COMPLAINT FOR DIVORCE (page 1)**   MCLA 552.6; MSA 25.86, MCR 3.204

FIGURE 22-2 A Judgment of Divorce

Original - Court 1st copy - Friend of the Court	2nd copy - Defendant 3rd copy - Plaintiff

STATE OF MICHIGAN 30th **JUDICIAL CIRCUIT** Ingham **COUNTY**	**JUDGMENT OF DIVORCE** **Page 1 of** 1 **pages**	**CASE NO.** 88521-D

Court address
2nd Floor, City Hall, Lansing, MI 48933

Court telephone no.
(517) 555-0650

Plaintiff's name, address, and social security number		Defendant's name, address, and social security number
Clara Annette Mills 6090 Sundown Avenue, Apt. 106 Lansing, MI 48933 SS# 404-39-8786	v.	Scott Wendell Mills 7110 Hickory Lane Lansing, MI 48912 SS# 783-00-3221

Plaintiff's attorney, bar no., address, and telephone no.	Defendant's attorney, bar no., address, and telephone no.
Jill F. Sinclair　　(P 70030) 700 Larch Street, Suite 17 Lansing, MI 48910 (517) 555-8890	Patrick B. Harvey　　(P 34789) 845 Wastenau Avenue, Suite 206 Lansing, MI 48906 (517) 555-5454

☐ After trial　　　☐ Default　　　☒ Consent

Date of hearing: February 17, 2003　　　　Judge: *Marsha Sanders*　　　　P 52901
Bar no.

IT IS ORDERED:

1. **DIVORCE:** The parties are divorced.

2. **PROPERTY DIVISION:**　　☐ There is no property to be divided.
   ☒ Each party is awarded the property in their possession.
   ☐ Property is divided elsewhere in this judgment.

3. **MINOR CHILDREN:**　　There　☐ are
   ☒ are not　children under 18 of the parties or born during this marriage.
   (Custody, visitation, support, and/or other required provisions are attached.)

☐ 4. **NAME CHANGE:**　　Wife's last name is changed to _____ Bolton

5. **ALIMONY:**　Alimony is　☒ not granted for　　　☒ wife.　☒ husband.
   ☐ reserved for　　　☐ wife.　☐ husband.
   ☐ granted elsewhere in this judgment for　☐ wife.　☐ husband.

6. **STATUTORY RIGHTS:** All interests of the parties in the property of the other, now owned or later acquired, arising under MCL 700.281 — 700.291, are extinguished.

7. **BENEFICIARY RIGHTS:** The rights each party has to the proceeds of policies or contracts of life insurance, endowments, or annuities upon the life of the other as a named beneficiary or by assignment during or in anticipation of marriage, are ☒ extinguished.　　　☐ provided for elsewhere in this judgment.

8. **PENSION RIGHTS:** Any rights of either party in any pension, annuity, or retirement plan benefit of the other, whether vested or unvested, accumulated or contingent, are
   ☒ extinguished.　　　☐ provided for elsewhere in this judgment.

9. **JOINT REAL ESTATE:** All real estate owned by the parties as joint tenants or as tenants by the entireties is ☒ converted to a tenancy in common.　　　☐ provided for elsewhere in this judgment.

10. **DOCUMENTATION:** Each party shall promptly and properly execute and deliver to the other appropriate documents required to carry out the terms of this judgment. A certified copy of this judgment may be recorded with the register of deeds in any county of this state where property may be located.

11. **INTERIM ORDERS:** Except as otherwise provided in this judgment, all interim orders and injunctions entered in this action are terminated.

MCLA 552.6; MSA 25.86, MCLA 552.18; MSA 25.98, MCLA 552.101; MSA 25.131
MCLA 552.102; MSA 25.132, MCLA 552.104; MSA 25.134, MCLA 552.402; MSA 25.137
MCLA 700.281 - 700.291; MSA 27.5281 - 27.5291, MCR 3.209

CC 427a (11/86)　**JUDGMENT OF DIVORCE, page 1**

Self-Evaluation A | Terminology and Definition Recall

Directions: In the Answers column, write the legal term that is most representative of the corresponding statement. After you have completed this self-evaluation, check your answers with the key on page 498. If you have any incorrect answers, review the definitions for those terms before going on with this lesson. Then unless otherwise directed, submit this self-evaluation to your instructor.

ANSWERS

1. A divorce action in which the party being sued for divorce does not resist or oppose the grounds for the divorce and makes no defense thereto is a/an _____.

1. _____

2. The dissolving of a marriage legally by an action of a court is a/an _____.

2. _____

3. A divorce action in which one of the parties resists or opposes the granting of the divorce and challenges or defends the action is a/an _____.

3. _____

4. A divorce in which the one filing for the divorce does not have to prove that the spouse is at fault on grounds previously required in most states for a divorce to be granted is a/an _____.

4. _____

5. Termination of a marriage by divorce is a/an _____.

5. _____

6. The foundation or basis for the granting of a divorce is referred to as _____.

6. _____

7. A legal separation that does not totally dissolve the marriage is a/an _____.

7. _____

8. An absolute divorce is expressed in Latin as _____.

8. _____

9. A procedure whereby the judge meets with the parties to a divorce and endeavors to reconcile them is a/an _____.

9. _____

10. A law in some states specifying that the unexplained absence of a spouse for a lengthy and continuous period of time constitutes grounds for divorce is the _____.

10. _____

11. The refusal without just cause of a husband or wife to continue a marital relationship is _____.

11. _____

12. The person charged with committing adultery with the respondent in a divorce action for which the grounds are adultery is called a/an _____.

12. _____

13. The total dissolution of a marriage is a/an _____.

13. _____

KEYING LEGAL TERMS

Directions: Unless otherwise instructed, use 1-inch margins and double spacing. Correct all errors. Follow one of the procedures below.

WORDS

Keyboarding Procedure

On your computer, key the following words at least two times, concentrating on the correct spelling and pronunciation.

Machine Shorthand Procedure

On your computer, key the following words once, concentrating on the correct spelling and pronunciation. Then write each word one time on your shorthand machine. Transcribe from your shorthand notes one time on your computer, or, if you are using computer-aided instruction (CAT), proofread and edit your transcript.

divorce	dissolution of marriage	no-fault divorce
grounds for divorce	conciliation procedure	corespondent
desertion	Enoch Arden Law	limited divorce
absolute divorce	a vinculo matrimonii	contested divorce
uncontested divorce		

SENTENCES

Keyboarding Procedure

Key each of the following sentences one time on your computer. Concentrate on the correct spelling and pronunciation of each underlined legal term.

Machine Shorthand Procedure

Write the following sentences one time on your shorthand machine. Transcribe from your shorthand notes one time on your computer, or, if you are using computer-aided transcription (CAT), proofread and edit your transcript.

These sentences will be used for practice dictation on the Transcription CD.

A <u>divorce</u> is the dissolving of a marriage legally by an action of the court. A <u>dissolution of marriage</u> is the act of terminating a marriage by divorce.

Most states have now enacted <u>no-fault divorce</u> laws. A no-fault divorce does not require the one filing for divorce to prove the spouse at fault on grounds that were previously required for a divorce action. <u>Grounds for divorce</u> are the foundation or basis for the granting of a divorce as required by state law.

If a judge feels that the marriage might possibly be reconciled, a <u>conciliation procedure</u> may be recommended. The judge may make several recommendations to the parties that they attempt to reconcile the marriage before a divorce is granted.

A <u>corespondent</u> is a person charged with committing adultery with the respondent in a divorce action for which the grounds are adultery. <u>Desertion</u> is the refusal without just cause to continue a marital relationship. The <u>Enoch Arden Law</u> in some states permits divorce on the grounds of desertion.

A divorce may be either limited or absolute. A <u>limited divorce</u> is a legal separation of husband and wife that does not totally dissolve the marriage. An <u>absolute divorce</u> is the total dissolution of the marriage. An absolute divorce expressed in Latin terms is <u>a vinculo matrimonii</u>.

A divorce action may be either contested or uncontested by the party against whom it is filed. In a <u>contested divorce</u>, the party against whom it is filed resists or opposes the granting of the divorce and challenges or defends the action. An <u>uncontested divorce</u> is one in which the party being sued for divorce does not resist or oppose the divorce and makes no defense thereto.

TRANSCRIBING FROM DICTATION

Directions: This dictation emphasizes and reinforces the legal terms and definitions you have studied. Listen carefully to the pronunciation of each of the legal terms. Unless otherwise directed, use 1-inch margins and double spacing. Correct all errors. Follow one of the procedures below.

Keyboarding Procedure
Using the Transcription CD, Lesson 22, Part A, transcribe the dictation directly at your computer.

Machine Shorthand Procedure
Using the Transcription CD, Lesson 22, Part A, take the dictation on your shorthand machine and then transcribe from your notes on your computer, or, if you are using computer-aided transcription (CAT), proofread and edit your transcript.

When you have finished transcribing or proofreading and editing Part A of the practice dictation, check your transcript with the printed copy. If you made any mistakes in the transcription, you should review and practice those words several times before going on to Part B.

Part B | TERMINOLOGY AND DEFINITIONS

Directions: Study the terms, pronunciations, and definitions until you are thoroughly familiar with them. In order to complete this lesson successfully, you must understand the meaning and usage of all the legal terms presented. If you are using a shorthand system, write each legal term one time on your shorthand machine.

	Legal Term	Pronunciation	Definition
1.	domicile	ˈdäm-ə-sīl	The legal place where a person or family resides.
2.	community property	kə-ˈmyü-nət-ē ˈpräp-ərt-ē	Any property that is acquired by husband and wife during the marriage.
3.	property settlement	ˈpräp-ərt-ē ˈset-l-ment	An agreement between the parties of a divorce action as to the division of property owned or acquired during the marriage.
4.	earning capacity	ˈər-niŋ kə-ˈpas-ət-ē	The capacity or capability of one to earn money. A consideration in the awarding of alimony in a divorce action.
5.	custody	ˈkəs-təd-ē	The care and possession of minor children of a marriage that is in a state of separation or divorce.
6.	adoption	ə-ˈdäp-shən	The taking of another person's child and giving the child all the rights and duties of one's own child.

7.	alimony	´al-ə-mō-nē	A provision for the support and maintenance of a wife by her divorced husband. In recent years, some states have ruled that a wife who is financially able has to pay alimony to the husband.
8.	permanent alimony	´pərm-nənt ´al-ə-mō-nē	Alimony that is to continue during the lifetime of the spouse.
9.	temporary alimony	´tem-pə-rer-ē ´al-ə-mō-nē	An amount paid to the wife or husband while the divorce suit is pending.
10.	alimony pendente lite	´al-ə-mō-nē pen-´den-tē ´li-tē	Latin. Temporary alimony paid while the divorce action is pending.
11.	necessaries	´nes-ə-ser-ēs	Generally means food, clothing, shelter, and medicines. Creditors who provide necessaries can file a claim for a judgment against alimony payments.
12.	support	sə-´pōrt	The payment of money in a divorce action that will provide the necessaries or maintain the lifestyle for the spouse and children.
13.	nonsupport	nän-sə-´pōrt	In some states, nonsupport is grounds for a divorce if the husband has the ability to support his wife but fails to do so. A husband's actual inability to provide for his wife is generally not sufficient grounds for divorce.

Self-Evaluation B | Terminology and Definition Recall

Directions: In the Answers column at the right of each statement, write the letter that represents the word or group of words that correctly completes the statement. After you have completed this self-evaluation, check your answers with the key on page 498. If you have any incorrect answers, review the definitions for those terms before going on with this lesson. Then unless otherwise directed, submit this self-evaluation to your instructor.

ANSWERS

1. If a husband has the ability to support his wife but fails to do so, it is grounds for divorce in some states and is referred to as (a) nonsupport, (b) earning capacity, (c) necessaries.

1. _____

2. Alimony that is to continue during the lifetime of the spouse is (a) temporary alimony, (b) support, (c) permanent alimony.

2. _____

3. The capability of an individual to earn that is considered in the awarding of alimony in a divorce action is called the (a) earning capacity, (b) nonsupport, (c) necessaries.

3. _____

4. The legal place where a person or family resides is called the (a) community property, (b) domicile, (c) property settlement.

4. _____

5. Any property that is acquired by husband and wife during the marriage is referred to as (a) pendente lite, (b) property settlement, (c) community property.

5. _____

6. The act of taking another's child into one's own family, treating the child as one's own, and giving the child all the rights and duties of one's own child is called (a) adoption, (b) custody, (c) support.

6. _____

7. Food, clothing, shelter, and medicines are generally referred to as (a) alimony pendente lite, (b) necessaries, (c) domicile.

7. _____

8. The care and possession of minor children of a marriage that is in a state of separation or divorce is (a) adoption, (b) custody, (c) domicile.

8. _____

9. Temporary alimony paid while the divorce action is pending is expressed in Latin as alimony (a) domicile, (b) custody, (c) pendente lite.

9. _____

10. An amount paid to the wife or husband while the divorce suit is pending is referred to as (a) permanent alimony, (b) alimony pendente lite, (c) temporary alimony.

10. _____

11. The payment of money in a divorce action that will provide the necessaries or maintain the lifestyle for the spouse and children is (a) support, (b) alimony, (c) property settlement.

11. _____

12. A provision for the support and maintenance of a husband or wife by the divorced spouse is (a) support, (b) alimony, (c) necessaries.

12. _____

13. An agreement between the parties of a divorce action as to the division of property owned or acquired during the marriage is the (a) property settlement, (b) earning capacity, (c) community property.

13. _____

KEYING LEGAL TERMS

Directions: Unless otherwise instructed, use 1-inch margins and double spacing. Correct all errors. Follow one of the procedures below.

WORDS

Keyboarding Procedure
On your computer, key the following words at least two times, concentrating on the correct spelling and pronunciation.

Machine Shorthand Procedure
On your computer, key the following words once, concentrating on the correct spelling and pronunciation. Then write each word one time on your shorthand machine. Transcribe from your shorthand notes one time on your computer, or, if you are using computer-aided transcription (CAT), proofread and edit your transcript.

domicile	community property	property settlement
earning capacity	custody	adoption
alimony	permanent alimony	temporary alimony
alimony pendente lite	necessaries	support
nonsupport		

SENTENCES

Keyboarding Procedure
Key each of the following sentences one time on your computer. Concentrate on the correct spelling and pronunciation of each underlined legal term.

Machine Shorthand Procedure
Write the following sentences one time on your shorthand machine. Transcribe from your shorthand notes one time on your computer, or, if you are using computer-aided transcription (CAT), proofread and edit your transcript.

These sentences will be used for practice dictation on the Transcription CD.

A <u>domicile</u> is the legal place where a person or family resides. <u>Community property</u> is acquired by husband and wife during the marriage. In community property states, the property belongs equally to both husband and wife without regard to who paid for it or whether the property is in only one party's name. The parties to a divorce must come to an agreement as to a <u>property settlement</u>. A property settlement is an agreement as to the division of property owned or acquired during the marriage.

<u>Earning capacity</u>, which affects the amount of alimony payments, is the capability or capacity of a person to earn money. Thus, the earning capacity of each spouse is taken into consideration to determine how much alimony and child support one spouse will have to pay to the other spouse.

<u>Custody</u> relates to the care and possession of minor children after a divorce. Usually the parent receiving custody of the minor children will receive support payments for their care from the other parent. The taking of another person's child and giving the child all the rights and duties of one's own child is called <u>adoption</u>.

<u>Alimony</u> is a provision for the support and maintenance of a wife by her divorced husband. In recent years, some states have ruled that a wife who is financially able has to pay alimony to her husband. Alimony may

be either permanent or temporary. <u>Permanent alimony</u> is to continue during the lifetime of the spouse. <u>Temporary alimony</u> is an amount paid while the divorce suit is pending. Temporary alimony is referred to in Latin as <u>alimony pendente lite</u>.

<u>Necessaries</u> are generally food, clothing, shelter, medicines. Creditors who provide necessaries can file a claim for a judgment against alimony payments. <u>Support</u> is the payment of money in a divorce action that will provide the necessaries or maintain the lifestyle for the spouse and children. In some states, a husband failing to provide necessaries for a wife is called <u>nonsupport</u> and is grounds for divorce.

TRANSCRIBING FROM DICTATION

Directions: This dictation emphasizes and reinforces the legal terms and definitions you have studied. Listen carefully to the pronunciation of each of the legal terms. Unless otherwise directed, use 1-inch margins and double spacing. Correct all errors. Follow one of the procedures below.

Keyboarding Procedure
Using the Transcription CD, Lesson 22, Part B, transcribe the dictation directly at your computer.

Machine Shorthand Procedure
Using the Transcription CD, Lesson 22, Part B, take the dictation on your shorthand machine and then transcribe from your notes on your computer, or, if you are using computer-aided transcription (CAT), proofread and edit your transcript.

When you have finished transcribing or proofreading and editing Part B of the practice dictation, check your transcript with the printed copy. If you made any mistakes in the transcription, you should review and practice those words several times before going on to Evaluation 11.

CHECKLIST
I have completed the following for Lesson 22:

	Part A, Date	Part B, Date	Submitted to Instructor Yes	No
Terminology and Definitions				
Self-Evaluation				
* Keying Legal Terms				
Words				
Sentences				
* Transcribing from Dictation				

When you have successfully completed all the exercises in this lesson and submitted to your instructor those requested, you are ready to proceed with Evaluation 11.

* If you are using machine shorthand, submit to your instructor your notes along with your transcript.

Evaluation No. 11 | SECTION A

Directions: This dictation/transcription evaluation will test your spelling and transcription abilities on the legal terms that you studied in the two preceding lessons. Tab once for a paragraph indention, and use 1-inch margins and double spacing unless otherwise instructed. Correct all errors. Follow one of the procedures below.

Keyboarding Procedure

Using the Transcription CD for Evaluation 11, transcribe the dictation directly at your computer.

Machine Shorthand Procedure

Using the Transcription CD for Evaluation 11, take the dictation on your shorthand machine and then transcribe your notes on your computer, or, if you are using computer-aided transcription (CAT), proofread and edit your transcript.
Sections B and C are available from your instructor.

Lesson

23

Commercial Paper

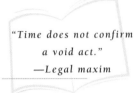

*"Time does not confirm
a void act."*
—Legal maxim

The extensive use of commercial paper in our society has resulted in uniform laws regulating commercial paper. The Uniform Commercial Code has been adopted in all states. This area of law affects the daily lives of individuals and businesses, and almost everyone has direct contact with commercial paper of some type. The terminology taught in the following exercises deals with the various trends of commercial paper. When you have satisfactorily completed the lesson, you will be able to spell, pronounce, define, and transcribe correctly each of the terms presented in the area of commercial paper.

Part A | TERMINOLOGY AND DEFINITIONS

Directions: Study the terms, pronunciations, and definitions until you are thoroughly familiar with them. In order to complete this lesson successfully, you must understand the meaning and usage of all the legal terms presented. If you are using a shorthand system, write each legal term one time on your shorthand machine.

Legal Term	Pronunciation	Definition
1. Uniform Commercial Code	′yü-nə–fȯrm kə-′mər-shəl kōd	Adopted by all states to govern and define commercial paper.
2. commercial paper	kə-′mər-shəl ′pā-per	A written promise that is capable of being transferred or assigned to another.
3. negotiable	ni-′gō-shə-bel	Capable of being transferred or assigned to another. Cash, checks, money orders, and cashier's checks are examples of negotiable instruments.
4. legal tender	′lē-gəl ′ten-dər	An accepted form of exchange that, according to law, must be accepted in the payment of a debt.
5. promissory note	′präm-ə-sȯr-ē nōt	An unconditional written commercial paper by which one promises to pay a certain amount of money to another at a definite time. (See Figure 23-1, page 333.)
6. demand note	di-′mand nōt	A promissory note that has no specific payment date but must be paid upon demand.
7. time note	tīm nōt	A promissory note that specifies the date on which it must be paid.
8. collateral note	kə-′lat-ə-rəl nōt	A note for which one has pledged security other than one's own promise to pay.
9. judgment note	′jəj-mənt nōt	A promissory note in which the maker authorizes that a judgment may be made against the maker if the note is not paid when due.

10. cognovit note	′käg-nō-vit nōt	Same as a judgment note.
11. check	chek	A commercial paper that is used to transfer money from a person's bank account to another person. (See Figure 23-2, page 333.)
12. cashier's check	ka-′shirs chek	A check issued by a bank that promises to make payment on demand. An individual can go to a bank and give the bank cash, and the bank will then draw a cashier's check on its own funds.
13. certificate of deposit	sər-′tif-i-kət əv di-′päz-ət	An instrument issued by a bank acknowledging the deposit of a specific sum of money and promising to pay the holder of the certificate that amount of money.

FIGURE 23-1 A Promissory Note

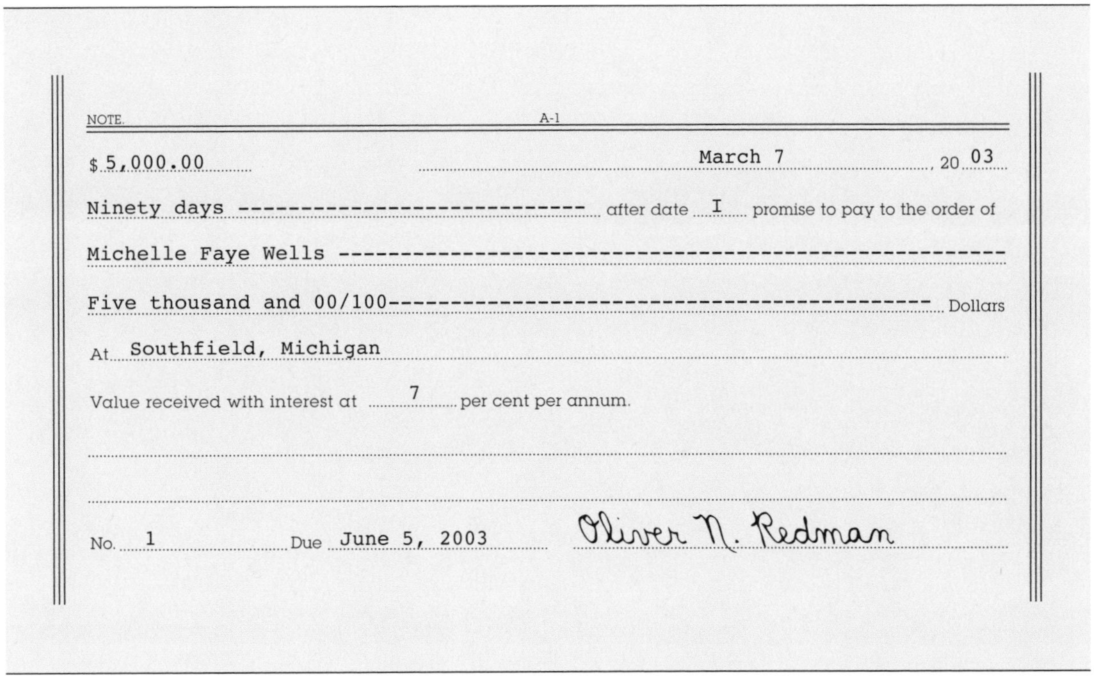

Payee

Maker/ Payer

NOTE.	A-1
$ 5,000.00	March 7 , 20 03

Ninety days -------------------------------- after date I promise to pay to the order of

Michelle Faye Wells --

Five thousand and 00/100--- Dollars

At Southfield, Michigan

Value received with interest at 7 per cent per annum.

No. 1 Due June 5, 2003   *Oliver N. Redman*

FIGURE 23-2 A Check

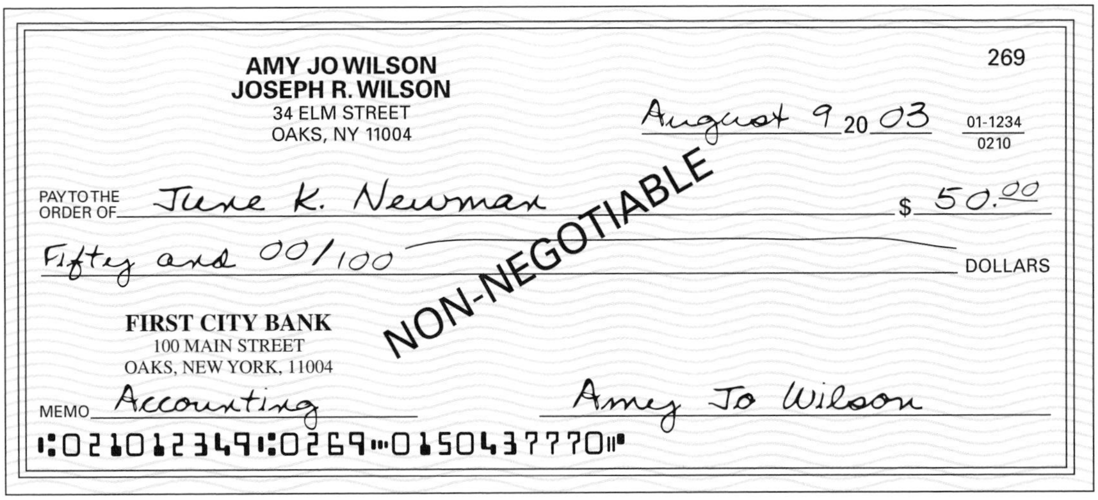

AMY JO WILSON		269
JOSEPH R. WILSON		
34 ELM STREET	*August 9* 20 *03*	01-1234
OAKS, NY 11004		0210

PAY TO THE ORDER OF *June K. Newman* $ *50.00*

Fifty and 00/100 _____ DOLLARS

FIRST CITY BANK
100 MAIN STREET
OAKS, NEW YORK, 11004

NON-NEGOTIABLE

MEMO *Accounting*   *Amy Jo Wilson*

⑆021012349⑆0269⑈01504377 70⑈

Self-Evaluation A | Terminology and Definition Recall

Directions: In the Answers column at the right of each statement, write the letter that represents the word or group of words that correctly completes the statement. After you have completed this self-evaluation, check your answers with the key on page 498. If you have any incorrect answers, review the definitions for those terms before going on with this lesson. Then unless otherwise directed, submit this self-evaluation to your instructor.

ANSWERS

1. A promissory note that has no specific payment date but must be paid upon demand is a (a) demand note, (b) judgment note, (c) cognovit note.

   1. _____

2. An accepted form of exchange that, according to law, must be accepted in the payment of a debt is a (a) check, (b) legal tender, (c) commercial paper.

   2. _____

3. Something that is capable of being transferred or assigned to another is referred to as being (a) negotiable, (b) legal tender, (c) certificate of deposit.

   3. _____

4. A written promise that is capable of being transferred or assigned to another is a (a) promissory note, (b) check, (c) commercial paper.

   4. _____

5. A note for which one pledges security other than one's promise to pay is a (a) demand note, (b) collateral note, (c) judgment note.

   5. _____

6. Another name for a judgment note is (a) cognovit note, (b) collateral note, (c) demand note.

   6. _____

7. A commercial paper that is used to transfer money from a person's bank account to another person is a (a) cashier's check, (b) commercial paper, (c) check.

   7. _____

8. A check issued by a bank that promises to make payment on demand is a (a) cashier's check, (b) collateral note, (c) demand note.

   8. _____

9. An unconditional commercial paper by which one promises to pay a certain amount of money to another at a given time is a (a) demand note, (b) time note, (c) cognovit note.

   9. _____

10. A promissory note that specifies the date on which it must be paid is a (a) cognovit note, (b) collateral note, (c) time note.

   10. _____

11. An act that has been adopted by all states to govern and define commercial paper is the (a) collateral, (b) Uniform Commercial Code, (c) certificate of deposit.

   11. _____

12. An instrument issued by a bank acknowledging the deposit of a specific sum of money and promising to pay the holder of the instrument that amount of money is a (a) promissory note, (b) cashier's check, (c) certificate of deposit.

   12. _____

13. A promissory note in which the maker authorizes that a judgment may be made against him or her if the note is not paid when due is a (a) collateral note, (b) judgment note, (c) certificate of deposit.

   13. _____

KEYING LEGAL TERMS

Directions: Unless otherwise instructed, use 1-inch margins and double spacing. Correct all errors. Follow one of the procedures below.

WORDS

Keyboarding Procedure
On your computer, key the following words at least two times, concentrating on the correct spelling and pronunciation.

Machine Shorthand Procedure
On your computer, key the following words once, concentrating on the correct spelling and pronunciation. Then write each word one time on your shorthand machine. Transcribe from your shorthand notes one time on your computer, or, if you are using computer-aided transcription (CAT), proofread and edit your transcript.

Uniform Commercial Code	**commercial paper**	**negotiable**
legal tender	**promissory note**	**demand note**
time note	**collateral note**	**judgment note**
cognovit note	**check**	**cashier's check**
certificate of deposit		

SENTENCES

Keyboarding Procedure
Key each of the following sentences one time on your computer. Concentrate on the correct spelling and pronunciation of each underlined legal term.

Machine Shorthand Procedure
Write the following sentences one time on your shorthand machine. Transcribe from your shorthand notes one time on your computer, or, if you are using computer-aided transcription (CAT), proofread and edit your transcript.

These sentences will be used for practice dictation on the Transcription CD.

The requirements of commercial paper are defined under the <u>Uniform Commercial Code</u>, which has been adopted by all states. <u>Commercial paper</u> is a written promise that is capable of being transferred or assigned to another. <u>Negotiable</u> means capable of being transferred or assigned to another. <u>Legal tender</u> is an accepted form of exchange, usually money, that, according to law, must be accepted in the payment of a debt.

A <u>promissory note</u> is a written commercial paper by which one promises to pay a certain amount of money to another at a definite time. A <u>demand note</u> is a promissory note that has no specific payment date but must be paid upon demand. A promissory note that specifies the date on which it must be paid is a <u>time note</u>. If security other than a promise to pay has been pledged, the note is referred to as a <u>collateral note</u>. A judgment note is a promissory note authorizing that a judgment may be made against the maker if the note is not paid when due. A <u>cognovit note</u> is the same as a judgment note.

A <u>check</u> is a commercial paper that is used to transfer money from a person's bank account to another person. A <u>cashier's check</u> is a check issued by a bank with a guarantee of payment on demand.

> A <u>certificate of deposit</u> is an instrument issued by a bank acknowledging the deposit of a specific sum of money and promising to pay the holder of the certificate that amount.

TRANSCRIBING FROM DICTATION

Directions: This dictation emphasizes and reinforces the legal terms and definitions you have studied. Listen carefully to the pronunciation of each of the legal terms. Unless otherwise directed, use 1-inch margins and double spacing. Correct all errors. Follow one of the procedures below.

Keyboarding Procedure
Using the Transcription CD, Lesson 23, Part A, transcribe the dictation directly at your computer.

Machine Shorthand Procedure
Using the Transcription CD, Lesson 23, Part A, take the dictation on your shorthand machine and then transcribe from your notes on your computer, or, if you are using computer-aided transcription (CAT), proofread and edit your transcript.

When you have finished transcribing or proofreading and editing Part A of the practice dictation, check your transcript with the printed copy. If you made any mistakes in the transcription, you should review and practice those words several times before going on to Part B.

Part B | TERMINOLOGY AND DEFINITIONS

Directions: Study the terms, pronunciations, and definitions until you are thoroughly familiar with them. In order to complete this lesson successfully, you must understand the meaning and usage of all the legal terms presented. If you are using a shorthand system, write each legal term one time on your shorthand machine.

Legal Term	Pronunciation	Definition
1. payee	′pā-ē	The person to whom a check, promissory note, or draft is payable. (See Figures 23-1 and 23-2, page 333.)
2. payer	′pā-ər	The one who pays a check, promissory note, or draft. (See Figures 23-1 and 23-2, page 333.)
3. maker	′mā-kər	The one who orders payment on a check or draft or who makes a promissory note. (See Figures 23-1 and 23-2, page 333.)
4. comaker	′kō-mā-kər	One who signs a commercial paper with others and is also responsible for its payment.
5. holder in due course	′hōl-dər in dü kōrs	One who has accepted a commercial paper for value on the condition that it is valid and not overdue.
6. bearer	′bar-ər	A person who is holding or in possession of a commercial paper that is made payable to bearer.
7. draft	draft	A bill of exchange. A written order drawn by one person upon another requiring that person to pay a certain amount of money to a third party on demand or at a definite time. A check is a draft.
8. bill of exchange	bil əv iks-′chānj	A draft.

9.	trade acceptance	trād ik-ˈsep-təns	A time draft drawn on the purchaser of goods by the one selling the goods and accepted by the purchaser.
10.	draft-varying acceptance	draft-ˈver-ē-iŋ ik-ˈsep-təns	A draft in which the order of the instrument varies from the acceptor's agreement.
11.	qualified acceptance	ˈkwäl-ə-fīd ik-ˈsep-təns	An acceptance that is only partial in that it varies the order of the draft in some way.
12.	accommodation paper	ə-käm-ə-ˈdā-shən ˈpā-pər	A paper, bill, or note signed by a person without consideration to accommodate another party to enable that party to obtain credit based on the paper.
13.	carte blanche	kärt blänsh	French. A blank instrument that is signed with the intention that it is to be filled in by another person without restriction.

Self-Evaluation B | Terminology and Definition Recall

Directions: In the Answers column, write the legal term that is most representative of the corresponding statement. After you have completed this self-evaluation, check your answers with the key on page 498. If you have any incorrect answers review the definitions for those terms before going on with this lesson. Then unless otherwise directed, submit this self-evaluation to your instructor.

ANSWERS

1. Another name for a draft is _____.

2. An acceptance that is only partial in that it varies the order of the draft in some way is a/an _____.

3. One who has accepted a commercial paper for value on the condition that it is valid and not overdue is a/an _____.

4. A time draft drawn on the purchaser of goods by the one selling the goods and accepted by the purchaser is a/an _____.

5. A draft, or bill of exchange, in which the order of the instrument varies from the acceptor's agreement is a/an _____.

6. A written order drawn by one person upon another requiring that person to pay a certain amount of money to a third party on demand or at a definite time is a/an _____.

7. The one who pays a check, promissory note, or draft is the _____.

8. A blank instrument that is signed with the intention that it is to be filled in by another person without restriction is a/an _____.

9. A paper, bill, or note signed by a person without consideration to accommodate another party to enable that party to obtain credit based on the paper is a/an _____.

10. The one who orders payment of a check or draft or who makes a promissory note is the _____.

11. One who signs a commercial paper with others and is also responsible for its payment is a/an _____.

12. A person who is holding or in possession of a commercial paper that is made payable to bearer is a/an _____.

13. The person to whom a check, promissory note, or draft is payable is the _____.

1. _____
2. _____
3. _____
4. _____
5. _____
6. _____
7. _____
8. _____
9. _____
10. _____
11. _____
12. _____
13. _____

KEYING LEGAL TERMS

Directions: Unless otherwise instructed, use 1-inch margins and double spacing. Correct all errors. Follow one of the procedures below.

WORDS

Keyboarding Procedure

On your computer, key the following words at least two times, concentrating on the correct spelling and pronunciation.

Machine Shorthand Procedure

On your computer, key the following words once, concentrating on the correct spelling and pronunciation. Then write each word one time on your shorthand machine. Transcribe from your shorthand notes one time on your computer, or, if you are using computer-aided transcription (CAT), proofread and edit your transcript.

payee	payer	maker
comaker	holder in due course	bearer
draft	bill of exchange	trade acceptance
draft-varying acceptance	qualified acceptance	accommodation paper
carte blanche		

SENTENCES

Keyboarding Procedure

Key each of the following sentences one time on your computer. Concentrate on the correct spelling and pronunciation of each underlined legal term.

Machine Shorthand Procedure

Write the following sentences one time on your shorthand machine. Transcribe from your shorthand notes one time on your computer, or, if you are using computer-aided transcription (CAT), proofread and edit your transcript.

These sentences will be used for practice dictation on the Transcription CD.

The person to whom a check, promissory note, or bill of exchange is payable is the <u>payee</u>. If you receive a check made out to you, you are the payee. The <u>payer</u> is the one who pays. In other words, the payer is the one who pays the amount of money for which the check is written. The one who makes or executes a promissory note is called the <u>maker</u>. If you give someone a promissory note, you are the maker. A <u>comaker</u> is one who signs a commercial paper with others and is also responsible for its payment. If another person cosigns a promissory note or other commercial paper with you, that person is the comaker and is also responsible for payment of the commercial paper.

A <u>holder in due course</u> is one who accepts a commercial paper for value on the condition that it is valid and not overdue. A <u>bearer</u> is a person who is holding or in possession of a commercial paper that is payable to bearer.

A <u>draft</u> is a written order drawn by one person upon another requiring that person to pay a certain amount of money to a third party on demand. The common term for a <u>bill of exchange</u> is draft. A <u>trade acceptance</u> is a draft, or bill of exchange, drawn on the purchaser of goods by the one selling the goods and accepted by the purchaser. If the instrument varies from the acceptor's agreement, it is called a <u>draft-varying acceptance</u>. A <u>qualified acceptance</u> is an acceptance that is only partial in that it varies the order of the draft in some way.

An <u>accommodation paper</u> is a paper, bill, or note signed by a person without consideration to accommodate another party to enable that party to obtain credit based on the paper. <u>Carte blanche</u> is a blank instrument that is signed with the intention that it is to be filled in by another person without restriction.

TRANSCRIBING FROM DICTATION

Directions: This dictation emphasizes and reinforces the legal terms and definitions you have studied. Listen carefully to the pronunciation of each of the legal terms. Unless otherwise directed, use 1-inch margins and double spacing. Correct all errors. Follow one of the procedures below.

Keyboarding Procedure
Using the Transcription CD, Lesson 23, Part B, transcribe the dictation directly at your computer.

Machine Shorthand Procedure
Using the Transcription CD, Lesson 23, Part B, take the dictation on your shorthand machine and then transcribe from your notes on your computer, or, if you are using computer-aided transcription (CAT), proofread and edit your transcript.

When you have finished transcribing or proofreading and editing Part B of the practice dictation, check your transcript with the printed copy. If you made any mistakes in the transcription, you should review and practice those words several times before going on to Lesson 24.

CHECKLIST
I have completed the following for Lesson 23:

	Part A, Date	Part B, Date	Submitted to Instructor Yes	No
Terminology and Definitions	___	___	___	___
Self-Evaluation	___	___	___	___
* Keying Legal Terms	___	___	___	___
Words	___	___	___	___
Sentences	___	___	___	___
* Transcribing from Dictation	___	___	___	___

When you have successfully completed all the exercises in this lesson and submitted to your instructor those requested, you are ready to proceed with Lesson 24.

* If you are using machine shorthand, submit to your instructor your notes along with your transcript.

Lesson

24

Commercial Paper

*"One who grants a thing
is presumed to grant also
whatever is essential
to its use."*
—*Legal maxim*

Additional terms that relate to the area of commercial paper are presented in this lesson. The Federal Reserve System requirements that govern the placement of indorsements on checks are also covered. Upon satisfactory completion of the following exercises, you will be able to spell, pronounce, define, and transcribe correctly each of the terms introduced pertaining to commercial paper.

Part A | TERMINOLOGY AND DEFINITIONS

Directions: Study the terms, pronunciations, and definitions until you are thoroughly familiar with them. In order to complete this lesson successfully, you must understand the meaning and usage of all the legal terms presented. If you are using a shorthand system, write each legal term one time on your shorthand machine.

Legal Term	Pronunciation	Definition
1. delivery	di-ˈliv-rē	The act of transferring or placing a commercial paper in the possession or control of another person.
2. maturity	mə-ˈtùr-ət-ē	The date or time on which a commercial paper comes due and is payable. (See Figure 24-1, page 347.)
3. presentment	pri-ˈzent-mənt	The presentation of a commercial paper for payment to the one who has the responsibility for making such payment.
4. dishonor	dis-ˈän-ər	To refuse to pay a commercial paper when it is due or to refuse to accept a commercial paper.
5. without recourse	with-ˈaút ˈrē-kōrs	A phrase used in an indorsement of a commercial paper meaning that the indorser cannot be held liable if the original makers of the instrument fail to make payment when due.
6. protest	ˈprō-test	A written notarized statement certifying that a commercial paper was presented for payment and refused. Also refers to the payment of a debt that one does not feel he or she owes with the intention of recovering the amount later. Such a debt is paid under protest.
7. grace period	grās ˈpir-ē-əd	An extension of time after the due date for the payment of a commercial paper without defaulting on the obligation.

Lesson 24, Part A   Terminology and Definitions   345

8. postdate	pōs-'dāt	To put a future date on a commercial paper instead of the date on which it is actually made.
9. value	'val-yü	The consideration involved in a contract. It may also be an abbreviation for valuable consideration.
10. interest	'in-trəst	An amount of money paid for the use of money belonging to another person. (See Figure 24-1, page 347.)
11. usury	'yüzh-rē	An illegal amount of interest charged for the use of money. Most states have usury laws that regulate the amount of interest that can be charged for certain types of loans.
12. accrue	ə-'krü	To be added to or to increase. Interest on a note accrues to, or is added to, the principal of the note.

FIGURE 24-1 A Promissory Note

	NOTE. _____ A-1 _____
	$ 5,000.00 _____ March 7 _____ , 20 03
	Ninety days ------------------------------ after date __I__ promise to pay to the order of
	Albert Agassi ---
	Five thousand and 00/100-- Dollars
	At. Southfield, Michigan
Interest	Value received with interest at _____7_____ per cent per annum.
Maturity	No. __1_____ Due June 5, 2003 *Mark A. Freeman*

Self-Evaluation A | Terminology and Definition Recall

Directions: In the Answers column, write the letter from Column 1 that represents the word or phrase that best match-es each item in Column 2. After you have completed this self-evaluation, check your answers with the key on page 498. If you have any incorrect answers, review the definitions for those terms before going on with this lesson. Then unless otherwise directed, submit this self-evaluation to your instructor.

COLUMN 1	COLUMN 2	ANSWERS
a. accrue	1. The presentation of a commercial paper for payment to the one who has the responsibility for making such payment.	1. _____
b. delivery		
c. dishonor	2. To put a future date on a commercial paper instead of the date on which it is actually made.	2. _____
d. grace period		
e. interest	3. To refuse to pay a commercial paper when it is due or to refuse to accept a commercial paper.	3. _____
f. maturity	4. A term that means to be added to or to increase, such as when interest on a note is added to the principal of the note.	4. _____
g. payment date		
h. postdate	5. The act of transferring or placing an instrument in the possession or control of another person.	5. _____
i. presentment		
j. protest	6. An amount of money paid for the use of money belonging to another person.	6. _____
k. usury	7. The date or time on which a commercial paper comes due and is payable.	7. _____
l. value		
m. without recourse	8. An extension of time after the due date for the payment of a commercial paper without defaulting on the obligation.	8. _____
	9. An illegal amount of interest charged for the use of money.	9. _____
	10. The consideration involved in a contract.	10. _____
	11. A phrase used in an indorsement of a commercial paper meaning that the indorser cannot be held liable if the original makers of the instrument fail to make payment when due.	11. _____
	12. A written notarized statement certifying that a commercial paper was presented for payment and refused.	12. _____

KEYING LEGAL TERMS

Directions: Unless otherwise instructed, use 1-inch margins and double spacing. Correct all errors. Follow one of the procedures below.

WORDS

Keyboarding Procedure
On your computer, key the following words at least two times, concentrating on the correct spelling and pronunciation.

Machine Shorthand Procedure
On your computer, key the following words once, concentrating on the correct spelling and pronunciation. Then write each word one time on your shorthand machine. Transcribe from your shorthand notes one time on your computer, or, if you are using computer-aided transcription (CAT), proofread and edit your transcript.

delivery	maturity	presentment
dishonor	without recourse	protest
grace period	postdate	value
interest	usury	accrue

SENTENCES

Keyboarding Procedure
Key each of the following sentences one time on your computer. Concentrate on the correct spelling and pronunciation of each underlined legal term.

Machine Shorthand Procedure
Write the following sentences one time on your shorthand machine. Transcribe from your shorthand notes one time on your computer, or, if you are using computer-aided transcription (CAT), proofread and edit your transcript..

These sentences will be used for practical dictation on the Transcription CD.

Delivery is the act of transferring or placing an instrument in the possession or control of another person. Delivery is usually a requirement for the legal transfer of a commercial paper. Maturity is the date or time on which a commercial paper comes due and is payable. On the maturity date, a commercial paper may be presented to the maker for payment. Presentment is the presentation of a commercial paper for payment to the one who has the responsibility for making such payment.

Dishonor is to refuse to pay a commercial paper when it is due or to refuse to accept a commercial paper. When an indorser writes without recourse when endorsing an instrument, the indorser cannot be held liable if the original makers of the instrument fail to make payment when due. A protest is a written notarized statement certifying that a commercial paper was presented for payment and refused. A debt paid under protest is the payment of a debt that one feels is not owed with the intention of recovering the amount later.

An extension of time after the due date of the payment of a commercial paper without defaulting on the obligation is called a grace period. To put a future date on a commercial paper instead of the date on which it is actually made is to postdate.

Value is the consideration involved in a contract. Value is also an abbreviation for valuable consideration.

Interest is an amount of money paid for the use of money belonging to another person. **Usury** is an illegal amount of interest charged for the use of money. **Accrue** means to be added to or to increase. Interest on a note accrues to, or is added to, the principal. Most states have usury laws that set a limit on the amount of interest that can be charged for different types of loans.

TRANSCRIBING FROM DICTATION

Directions: This dictation emphasizes and reinforces the legal terms and definitions you have studied. Listen carefully to the pronunciation of each of the legal terms. Unless otherwise directed, use 1-inch margins and double spacing. Correct all errors. Follow one of the procedures below.

Keyboarding Procedure
Using the Transcription CD, Lesson 24, Part A, transcribe the dictation directly at your computer.

Machine Shorthand Procedure
Using the Transcription CD, Lesson 24, Part A, take the dictation on your shorthand machine and then transcribe from your notes on your computer, or, if you are using computer-aided transcription (CAT), proofread and edit your transcript.

When you have finished transcribing or proofreading and editing Part A of the practice dictation, check your transcript with the printed copy. If you made any mistakes in the transcription, you should review and practice those words several times before going on to Part B.

Part B | TERMINOLOGY AND DEFINITIONS

Directions: Study the terms, pronunciations, and definitions until you are thoroughly familiar with them. In order to complete this lesson successfully, you must understand the meaning and usage of all the legal terms presented. If you are using a shorthand system, write each legal term one time on your shorthand machine.

Legal Term	Pronunciation	Definition
1. bona fide	´bō-nə fīd	Latin. Genuine or real. In good faith without deceit or fraud.
2. bogus	´bō-gəs	Not genuine. Counterfeit.
3. kite	kīt	To secure the temporary use of money by issuing worthless paper. Also refers to the worthless paper itself. Writing a check on an account before depositing money in the account is called kiting.
4. spoliation	spō-lē-´ā-shən	An alteration, or change, made on a commercial paper by one who is not a party to the instrument. It does not affect the validity of the instrument if the terms can be determined.
5. indorsement*	in-´dȯr-smənt	The signing of one's name on the back of a commercial paper with the purpose of transferring or assigning it to another person. Under Federal Reserve System requirements, a bank does not have to accept a check that does not have the indorsement in the proper place. (See Figure 24-2, page 354.)

*The form indorse is used in the UCC. The form endorse is commonly used in business.

6.	special or full endorsement	´spesh-əl ȯr fu̇l in-´dȯr-smənt	An indorsement that specifically names the person to whom the instrument is being transferred. (See Figure 24-3, page 355.)
7.	restrictive indorsement	ri-´strik-tiv in-´dȯr-smənt	An indorsement that contains restrictions as to any further transfer of a commercial paper. For example, if you indorse a check with "For deposit only," the check can only be deposited and cannot be transferred to another party. (See Figure 24-4, page 355.)
8.	qualified indorsement	´kwäl-ə-fīd in-´dȯr-smənt	An indorsement that qualifies, or restricts, the liability of the indorser. Includes an indorsement that contains the words "without recourse." If the maker of the commercial paper does not pay it, the indorser will not be responsible for payment. (See Figure 24-5, page 356.)
9.	blank indorsement	blaŋk ´in-´dȯr-smənt	An indorsement that consists of only the indorser's name. Anyone holding a commercial paper with a blank indorsement can receive the funds for it. (See Figure 24-6, page 356.)
10.	successive indorsement	sək-´ses-iv in-´dȯr-smənt	A series of indorsements following one after another on a commercial paper. (See Figure 24-7, page 357.)
11.	allonge	a-´lōnzh	A piece of paper attached to a commercial paper to provide space for the indorsements when there is not enough space on the instrument itself.

FIGURE 24-2 Indorsement Requirements

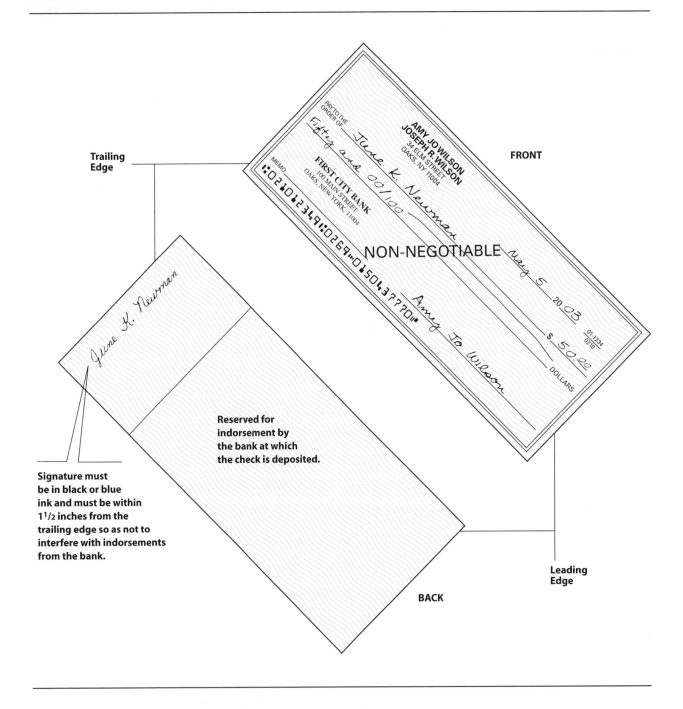

Trailing Edge

FRONT

NON-NEGOTIABLE

Signature must be in black or blue ink and must be within 1¹/₂ inches from the trailing edge so as not to interfere with indorsements from the bank.

Reserved for indorsement by the bank at which the check is deposited.

BACK

Leading Edge

FIGURE 24-3 A Special or Full Indorsement

Pay to the order of
George Matthews only
June K. Newman

FIGURE 24-4 A Restrictive Indorsement

For deposit only
June K. Newman

FIGURE 24-5 A Qualified Indorsement

Pay to the order of
George Matthews
without recourse
June K. Newman

FIGURE 24-6 A Blank Indorsement

George Matthews

FIGURE 24-7 A Successive Indorsement

June K. Newman
George Matthews
Virginia Barrett

Self-Evaluation B | Terminology and Definition Recall

Directions: In the Answers column, write the legal term that is most representative of the corresponding statement. After you have completed this self-evaluation, check your answers with the key on page 498. If you have any incorrect answers, review the definitions for those terms before going on with this lesson. Then unless otherwise directed, submit this self-evaluation to your instructor.

ANSWERS

1. A word meaning genuine or real or in good faith without deceit or fraud is _____.   1. _____

2. An alteration, or change, made on a commercial paper by one who is not a party to the instrument is called _____.   2. _____

3. A piece of paper attached to a commercial paper to provide space for the indorsements when there is not enough space on the instrument itself is a/an _____.   3. _____

4. An indorsement that specifically names the person to whom the instrument is being transferred is a/an _____.   4. _____

5. A word meaning not genuine, or counterfeit, is _____.   5. _____

6. An indorsement that contains restrictions as to any further transfer of a commercial paper is a/an _____.   6. _____

7. An indorsement that qualifies, or restricts, the liability of the indorser and includes the words "without recourse" is a/an _____.   7. _____

8. An indorsement that consists of only the indorser's name is a/an _____.   8. _____

9. Securing the temporary use of money by issuing worthless paper is to _____.   9. _____

10. A series of indorsements following one after another on a commercial paper is a/an _____.   10. _____

11. One's name signed on the back of a commercial paper with the purpose of transferring or assigning it to another person is a/an _____.   11. _____

KEYING LEGAL TERMS

Directions: Unless otherwise instructed, use 1-inch margins and double spacing. Correct all errors. Follow one of the procedures below.

WORDS

Keyboarding Procedure
On your computer, key the following words at least two times, concentrating on the correct spelling and pronunciation.

Machine Shorthand Procedure
On your computer, key the following words once, concentrating on the correct spelling and pronunciation. Then write each word one time on your shorthand machine. Transcribe from your shorthand notes one time on your computer, or, if you are using computer-aided transcription (CAT), proofread and edit your transcript.

bona fide	bogus	kite
spoliation	indorsement	special or full indorsement
restrictive indorsement	qualified indorsement	blank indorsement
successive indorsement	allonge	

SENTENCES

Keyboarding Procedure
Key each of the following sentences one time on your computer. Concentrate on the correct spelling and pronunciation of each underlined legal term.

Machine Shorthand Procedure
Write the following sentences one time on your shorthand machine. Transcribe from your shorthand notes one time on your computer, or, if you are using computer-aided transcription (CAT), proofread and edit your transcript.

These sentences will be used for practice dictation on the Transcription CD.

<u>Bona fide</u> means genuine or real or in good faith and without deceit or fraud. A commercial paper that is not genuine, or is a counterfeit, is called a <u>bogus</u> instrument. <u>Kite</u> is worthless paper used to secure the temporary use of money. Kite also refers to the worthless paper itself. Writing a check on an account before depositing money in that account is referred to as kiting.

<u>Spoliation</u> is an alteration, or change, made on a commercial paper by one who is not a party to the instrument. Spoliation does not affect the validity of the instrument if the terms can be determined.

An <u>indorsement</u> is the signing of one's name on the back of a commercial paper with the purpose of transferring or assigning it to another person. Under new Federal Reserve System requirements, a bank does not have to accept a check for deposit that does not have the indorsement in the proper place. An indorsement that specifically names the person to whom the instrument is being transferred is a <u>special or full indorsement</u>. An indorsement that contains restrictions as to any further transfer of the instrument is a <u>restrictive indorsement</u>. "For deposit only" is an example of a restrictive indorsement. If one wishes to qualify, or restrict, his or her liability for the instrument, a <u>qualified indorsement</u> would be used. A qualified indorsement contains the words "without recourse" and usually means that the indorser will not be responsible for payment of the instrument if the maker does not pay it.

A <u>blank indorsement</u> consists only of the indorser's name. A successive indorsement is a series of indorsements that follow one after the other on a commercial paper. If there is not enough space on the instrument for the indorsements, an <u>allonge</u>, or a piece of paper, may be attached to the instrument to accommodate the indorsements.

TRANSCRIBING FROM DICTATION

Directions: This dictation emphasizes and reinforces the legal terms and definitions you have studied. Listen carefully to the pronunciation of each of the legal terms. Unless otherwise directed, use 1-inch margins and double spacing. Correct all errors. Follow one of the procedures below.

Keyboarding Procedure
Using the Transcription CD, Lesson 24, Part B, transcribe the dictation directly at your computer.

Machine Shorthand Procedure
Using the Transcription CD, Lesson 24, Part B, take the dictation on your shorthand machine and then transcribe from your notes on your computer, or, if you are using computer-aided transcription (CAT), proofread and edit your transcript.

When you have finished transcribing or proofreading and editing Part B of the practice dictation, check your transcript with the printed copy. If you made any mistakes in the transcription, you should review and practice those words several times before going on to Evaluation 12.

CHECKLIST
I have completed the following for Lesson 24:

	Part A, Date	Part B, Date	Submitted to Instructor Yes	No
Terminology and Definitions				
Self-Evaluation				
* Keying Legal Terms				
Words				
Sentences				
* Transcribing from Dictation				

When you have successfully completed all the exercises in this lesson and submitted to your instructor those requested, you are ready to proceed with Evaluation 12.

* If you are using machine shorthand, submit to your instructor your notes along with your transcript.

Evaluation No. 12 | SECTION A

Directions: This dictation/transcription evaluation will test your spelling and transcription abilities on the legal terms that you studied in the two preceding lessons. Tab once for a paragraph indention, and use 1-inch margins and double spacing unless otherwise instructed. Correct all errors. Follow one of the procedures below.

Keyboarding Procedure

Using the Transcription CD for Evaluation 12, transcribe the dictation directly at your computer.

Machine Shorthand Procedure

Using the Transcription CD for Evaluation 12, take the dictation on your shorthand machine and then transcribe your notes on your computer, or, if you are using computer-aided transcription (CAT), proofread and edit your transcript.

Sections B and C are available from your instructor.

Lesson
25

Bankruptcy

"One who takes the
benefit must bear
the burden."
—Legal maxim

Due to changes in society and economic conditions, bankruptcy law is affecting more and more individuals and businesses. Bankruptcy proceedings are under the jurisdiction of the federal courts rather than the state courts. A person cannot be sent to jail for failure to pay his or her debts; however, the person's property may be taken to satisfy those debts. Bankruptcy is a branch of equity jurisprudence, but, because of its increased importance, this lesson is devoted exclusively to the terms relating to bankruptcy. When you have satisfactorily completed these exercises, you will be able to spell, pronounce, define, and transcribe correctly each of the terms presented that relate to the area of bankruptcy law.

Part A | TERMINOLOGY AND DEFINITIONS

Directions: Study the terms, pronunciations, and definitions until you are thoroughly familiar with them. In order to complete this lesson successfully, you must understand the meaning and usage of all the legal terms presented. If you are using a shorthand system, write each legal term on your shorthand machine.

Legal Term	Pronunciation	Definition
1. bankruptcy court	′baŋ-krəp-sē kōrt	Federal courts that are established to administer the bankruptcy laws.
2. petition for bankruptcy	pə-′tish-ən fər ′baŋ-krəp-sē	The document filed in a court requesting that bankruptcy proceedings be started against a certain person. May be filed by the person declaring bankruptcy or by the creditors. (See Figure 25-1, page 367.)
3. bankrupt	′baŋ-krəpt	A person who is declared by a court to be unable or unwilling to pay his or her debts.
4. bankruptcy	′baŋ-krəp-sē	The process of declaring a person bankrupt and then taking the person's assets and distributing them among the creditors.
5. creditors	′kred-ət-ərs	Person or persons to whom a debt is owed.
6. voluntary bankruptcy	′väl-ən-ter-ē ′baŋ-krəp-sē	A bankruptcy proceeding that is started by the person who is bankrupt.
7. debtor's petition	′det-ərs pə-′tish-ən	A petition filed by the debtor requesting the benefit of the bankruptcy laws. A petition for voluntary bankruptcy.
8. involuntary bankruptcy	in-′väl-ən-ter-ē ′baŋ-krəp-sē	A bankruptcy proceeding that is started by the creditors of the bankrupt person.
9. solvent	′säl-vənt	The ability or capacity of a person to pay his or her debts.
10. insolvency	in-′säl-vən-sē	The inability of a person to pay his or her debts.

11. ex parte application	eks ´pärt-ē ap-lə-´kā-shən	Latin. An application filed by one side or one party. It is made by a creditor who is not a party to the bankruptcy proceeding but who has an interest in it.
12. referee	ref-ə-´rē	An officer serving as the trial judge of a bankruptcy court who is in charge of the proceedings in that court in accordance with federal bankruptcy laws.
13. receiver	ri-´sē-vər	An impartial person appointed by the court to take charge of property involved in a bankruptcy proceeding and to follow the directions of the court in disposing of the property.
14. trustee	trəs-´tē	A person who holds the property of a bankrupt for the benefit of the creditors.

FIGURE 25-1 A Bankruptcy Petition (cover sheet)

B-103 (Rev. 5/87)	**BANKRUPTCY PETITION COVER SHEET**	CASE NUMBER (Court Use Only) 34987-VB-33

INSTRUCTIONS: This form must be completed by the debtor or the debtor's attorney and submitted to the clerk of court upon the filing of the petition.

NAME OF DEBTOR (Last, First, Middle) Findley, Anna Marie	NAME OF JOINT DEBTOR (Spouse) (Last, First, Middle) Collins, Richard Lee
ALL OTHER NAMES, INCLUDING TRADE NAMES, USED BY THE DEBTOR IN THE LAST 6 YEARS F & C Enterprises	ALL OTHER NAMES, INCLUDING TRADE NAMES, USED BY THE JOINT DEBTOR IN THE LAST 6 YEARS F & C Enterprises
SOCIAL SECURITY NO. AND/OR EMPLOYER'S TAX ID NO. 000-01-0000	SOCIAL SECURITY NO. AND/OR EMPLOYER'S TAX ID NO. 000-02-0000
ADDRESS OF DEBTOR (Street, City, State, and Zip Code) 7320 Sandstone Drive Lansing, Michigan 48906	ADDRESS OF JOINT DEBTOR (Street, City, State, and Zip Code) 7320 Sandstone Drive Lansing, Michigan 48906
NAME OF COUNTY Ingham	NAME OF COUNTY Ingham

CHECK PROPER BOXES

TYPE OF PETITION
☒ Voluntary Petition   ☐ Involuntary Petition

CHAPTER OF THE BANKRUPTCY CODE UNDER WHICH THE PETITION IS FILED (Check One Box)

☐ Chapter 7   ☐ Chapter 11 Railroad
☐ Ch. 7 Broker   ☐ Chapter 12
☐ Ch. 9   ☒ Chapter 13
☐ Chapter 11   ☐ Sec. 304

NATURE OF DEBT
☒ Business – Complete A, B, C below   ☐ Non-business/Consumer

A. FORM OF ORGANIZATION (Check One Box)
☒ Individual   ☐ Parnership
☐ Corporation Publicly Held   ☐ Corporation Closely Held

B. TYPE OF BUSINESS (Check One Box)
☐ Farmer   ☐ Transportation   ☐ Construction
☐ Professional   ☐ Manufacture/Mining   ☐ Real Estate
☒ Retail/Wholesale   ☐ Other Business

C. BRIEFLY DESCRIBE NATURE OF BUSINESS

Accounting Services

DEBTOR'S ESTIMATES

ESTIMATED NUMBER OF CREDITORS

1-15	16-49	50-99	100-999	1000-over
☒	☐	☐	☐	☐

☒ No assets will be available for distribution to creditors
☐ Assets will be available for distribution to creditors

ESTIMATED ASSETS (IN THOUSANDS OF DOLLARS)

Under 50	50-99	100-499	500-999	1000-over
☒	☐	☐	☐	☐

ESTIMATED NUMBER OF EMPLOYEES—CHAPTER 11 AND 12 ONLY

0	1-19	20-99	100-999	1000-over
☐	☐	☐	☐	☐

ESTIMATED LIABILITIES (IN THOUSANDS OF DOLLARS)

Under 50	50-99	100-499	500-999	1000-over
☐	☒	☐	☐	☐

ESTIMATED NO. OF EQUITY SECURITY HOLDERS—CH. 11 & 12 ONLY

0	1-19	20-99	100-999	1000-over
☐	☐	☐	☐	☐

ATTORNEY FOR THE DEBTOR (Firm Name, Address, Tel. No.) ☒ No Attorney	ATTORNEY FOR THE PETITIONER (IF INVOLUNTARY PETITION) (Firm Name, Address, Tel. No.)

FILING FEE (Check One Box)   ☒ Filing Fee Attached   ☐ Filing fee to be paid in installments by individuals only. Must attach signed application for the court's consideration indicating that the debtor is unable to pay fee except in installments. Rule 1006 (b).

RELATED BANKRUPTCY CASE (IF ANY)

DEBTOR		CASE NO.
DISTRICT	DIVISIONAL OFFICE	NAME OF JUDGE
DATE 12-20-03	PRINT NAME Richard Lee Collins	SIGNATURE OF ATTORNEY (OR DEBTOR) *Richard Lee Collins*

Self-Evaluation A | Terminology and Definition Recall

Directions: In the Answers column at the right of each statement, write the letter that represents the word or group of words that correctly completes the statement. After you have completed this self-evaluation, check your answers with the key on page 498. If you have any incorrect answers, review the definitions for those terms before going on with this lesson. Then unless otherwise directed, submit this self-evaluation to your instructor.

ANSWERS

1. A person who is declared by a court to be unable or unwilling to pay his or her debts is a (a) creditor, (b) referee, (c) bankrupt.   1. _____

2. An officer serving as the trial judge of a bankruptcy court who is in charge of the proceedings in that court is a (a) creditor, (b) referee, (c) trustee.   2. _____

3. One to whom a debt is owed is a (a) debtor, (b) creditor, (c) receiver.   3. _____

4. When a person has the ability or capacity to pay his or her debts, he or she is (a) solvent, (b) insolvent, (c) bankrupt.   4. _____

5. The inability of a person to pay his or her debts is referred to as (a) solvent, (b) trustee, (c) insolvency.   5. _____

6. An impartial person appointed by the court to take charge of property involved in a bankruptcy proceeding and to follow the directions of the court in disposing of the property is a (a) trustee, (b) receiver, (c) referee.   6. _____

7. A petition filed by the debtor requesting the benefit of the bankruptcy laws is a/an (a) petition for bankruptcy, (b) debtor's petition, (c) ex parte application.   7. _____

8. The process of declaring a person bankrupt and then taking the person's assets and distributing them among the creditors is (a) bankruptcy, (b) insolvency, (c) petition for bankruptcy.   8. _____

9. A bankruptcy proceeding that is started by the person who is bankrupt is referred to as (a) involuntary bankruptcy, (b) debtor's petition, (c) voluntary bankruptcy.   9. _____

10. An application filed by one side or one party that is made by a creditor who is not a party to the bankruptcy proceeding but has an interest in it is a/an (a) ex parte application, (b) petition for bankruptcy, (c) debtor's petition.   10. _____

11. A bankruptcy proceeding that is started by the creditors of the bankrupt person is called (a) voluntary bankruptcy, (b) involuntary bankruptcy, (c) petition for bankruptcy.   11. _____

12. Federal courts that are established to administer the bankruptcy laws are (a) bankruptcy courts, (b) ex parte courts, (c) receiver courts.   12. _____

13. A person who holds the property of a bankrupt for the benefit of the creditors is a (a) creditor, (b) referee, (c) trustee.   13. _____

14. The document filed in a bankruptcy court requesting that bankruptcy proceedings be started against a certain person is called a/an (a) petition for bankruptcy, (b) ex parte application, (c) debtor's petition.   14. _____

KEYING LEGAL TERMS

Directions: Unless otherwise instructed, use 1-inch margins and double spacing. Correct all errors. Follow one of the procedures below.

WORDS

Keyboarding Procedure

On your computer, key the following words at least two times, concentrating on the correct spelling and pronunciation.

Machine Shorthand Procedure

On your computer, key the following words once, concentrating on the correct spelling and pronunciation. Then write each word one time on your shorthand machine. Transcribe from your shorthand notes one time on your computer.

bankruptcy court	petition for bankruptcy	bankrupt
bankruptcy	creditors	voluntary bankruptcy
debtor's petition	involuntary bankruptcy	solvent
insolvency	ex parte application	referee
receiver	trustee	

SENTENCES

Keyboarding Procedure

Key each of the following sentences one time on your computer. Concentrate on the correct spelling and pronunciation of each underlined legal term.

Machine Shorthand Procedure

Write the following sentences one time on your shorthand machine. Transcribe from your shorthand notes one time on your computer, or, if you are using computer-aided transcription (CAT), proofread and edit your transcript.

These sentences will be used for practice dictation on the Transcription CD.

The bankruptcy laws are administered in a federal court called a <u>bankruptcy court</u>. A <u>petition for bankruptcy</u> is the document filed in a bankruptcy court requesting that bankruptcy proceedings be started against a certain person. A <u>bankrupt</u> is a person who is declared by a court to be unable or unwilling to pay his or her debts. <u>Bankruptcy</u> is the process of declaring a person bankrupt and then taking the person's assets and distributing them among the <u>creditors</u>. A creditor is a person to whom a debt is owed.

If a debtor initiates a bankruptcy proceeding, the proceeding is called <u>voluntary bankruptcy</u>. A <u>debtor's petition</u> is one filed by the debtor requesting the benefit of the bankruptcy laws. A petition for voluntary bankruptcy is a debtor's petition. However, if one is forced into bankruptcy by the petition of creditors, the proceeding is called <u>involuntary bankruptcy</u>.

If a person is <u>solvent</u>, that person has the ability or capacity to pay his or her debts. <u>Insolvency</u> is the inability of a person to pay his or her debts. Insolvency exists when one's liabilities exceed one's assets.

A petition for bankruptcy filed by a creditor for involuntary bankruptcy of a debtor is called an <u>ex parte application</u>. In bankruptcy courts, a referee is appointed by the court to assist in the bankruptcy proceedings.

A <u>referee</u> is an officer of the bankruptcy court and serves as the trial judge in charge of the proceedings in that court in accordance with federal bankruptcy laws.

A <u>receiver</u> is an impartial person appointed by the court to take charge of and dispose of the property involved in a bankruptcy proceeding under the direction of the court. A <u>trustee</u> is a person who holds the property of a bankrupt for the benefit of the creditors.

TRANSCRIBING FROM DICTATION

Directions: This dictation emphasizes and reinforces the legal terms and definitions you have studied. Listen carefully to the pronunciation of each of the legal terms. Unless otherwise directed, use 1-inch margins and double spacing. Correct all errors. Follow one of the procedures below.

Keyboarding Procedure
Using the Transcription CD, Lesson 25, Part A, transcribe the dictation directly at your computer.

Machine Shorthand Procedure
Using the Transcription CD, Lesson 25, Part A, take the dictation on your shorthand machine and then transcribe from your notes on your computer, or, if you are using computer-aided transcription (CAT), proofread and edit your transcript.

When you have finished transcribing or proofreading and editing Part A of the practice dictation, check your transcript with the printed copy. If you made any mistakes in the transcription, you should review and practice those words several times before going on to Part B.

Part B | TERMINOLOGY AND DEFINITIONS

Directions: Study the terms, pronunciations, and definitions until you are thoroughly familiar with them. In order to complete this lesson successfully, you must understand the meaning and usage of all the legal terms presented. If you are using a shorthand system, write each legal term one time on your shorthand machine.

Legal Term	Pronunciation	Definition
1. insolvent debtor	in-ˈsäl-vənt ˈdet-ər	A person who cannot pay his or her debts.
2. account stated	ə-ˈkau̇nt ˈstāt-əd	An agreement between a debtor and creditor that the amount stated as being owed to the creditor is accurate.
3. account current	ə-ˈkau̇nt ˈkər-ənt	An open or unsettled account between a debtor and creditor. The opposite of account stated.
4. summary of debts and assets	ˈsəm-ə-rē əv dets ən ˈas-ets	A listing provided to the court containing all the debt and assets of the debtor in a bankruptcy proceeding.
5. assets	ˈas-ets	The property owned by a bankrupt that may be applied to pay his or her debts.
6. liabilities	lī-ə-ˈbil-ət-ēs	Something that one owes to another and has an obligation to pay.
7. composition	käm-pə-ˈzish-ən	An agreement between a debtor and creditor in which the creditor agrees to accept less than the amount of the debt in settlement for the entire debt.
8. secured debts	si-ˈkyu̇rd dets	Debts that are guaranteed by pledged collateral, such as a mortgage.

9. balance of funds	ˈbal-əns əv fənds	The amount remaining after the secured debts are paid that is to be divided among the other creditors.
10. liquidate	ˈlik-wə-dāt	To convert assets into cash to be used to pay the amount owed to creditors.
11. deficiency decree	di-ˈfish-ən-sē di-ˈkrē	A judgment for a portion of a secured debt for which the sale of the property does not pay in full.
12. discharge	ˈdis-chärj	The release of a bankrupt from the obligation of paying his or her former debts.
13. after-acquired property	ˈaf-tər ə-ˈkwīrd ˈpräp-ərt-ē	Property acquired after a person has filed for bankruptcy. After-acquired property is not subject to the claims of bankruptcy creditors.

Self-Evaluation B | Terminology and Definition Recall

Directions: In the Answers column, write the legal term that is most representative of the corresponding statement. After you have completed this self-evaluation, check your answers with the key on page 498. If you have any incorrect answers, review the definitions for those terms before going on with this lesson. Then unless otherwise directed, submit this self-evaluation to your instructor.

ANSWERS

1. A judgment for a portion of a secured debt for which the sale of property does not pay in full is a/an _____.

    1. _____

2. Something that one owes to another and has an obligation to pay is called _____.

    2. _____

3. An agreement between a debtor and creditor in which the creditor agrees to accept less than the amount of the debt in settlement for the entire debt is referred to as _____.

    3. _____

4. The amount remaining after the secured debts are paid that is to be divided among the other creditors is the _____.

    4. _____

5. To convert assets into cash to be used to pay the amounts owed to creditors is to _____.

    5. _____

6. An open or unsettled account between a debtor and a creditor is a/an _____.

    6. _____

7. An agreement between a debtor and creditor that the amount stated as being owed to the creditor is accurate is a/an _____.

    7. _____

8. The property owned by a bankrupt that may be applied to pay his or her debts is referred to as _____.

    8. _____

9. A listing provided to the court containing all the debts and assets of the debtor in a bankruptcy proceeding is a/an _____.

    9. _____

10. The release of a bankrupt from the obligation of paying former debts is a/an _____.

    10. _____

11. Debts that are guaranteed by pledged collateral, such as a mortgage, are called _____.

    11. _____

12. A person who cannot pay his or her debts is a/an _____.

    12. _____

13. Property acquired after a person has filed for bankruptcy is called _____.

    13. _____

KEYING LEGAL TERMS

Directions: Unless otherwise instructed, use 1-inch margins and double spacing. Correct all errors. Follow one of the procedures below.

WORDS

Keyboarding Procedure
On your computer, key the following words at least two times, concentrating on the correct spelling and pronunciation.

Machine Shorthand Procedure
On your computer, key the following words once, concentrating on the correct spelling and pronunciation. Then write each word one time on your shorthand machine. Transcribe from your shorthand notes one time on your computer.

insolvent debtor	account stated	account current
summary of debts and assets	assets	liabilities
composition	secured debts	balance of funds
liquidate	deficiency decree	discharge
after-acquired property		

SENTENCES

Keyboarding Procedure
Key each of the following sentences one time on your computer. Concentrate on the correct spelling and pronunciation of each underlined legal term.

Machine Shorthand Procedure
Write the following sentences one time on your shorthand machine. Transcribe from your shorthand notes one time on your computer, or, if you are using computer-aided transcription (CAT), proofread and edit your transcript.

These sentences will be used for practice dictation on the Transcription CD.

An <u>insolvent debtor</u> is a person who cannot pay his or her debts. <u>Account stated</u> refers to an agreement between a debtor and creditor that the amount stated as being owed to the creditor is accurate. However, an open or unsettled account between a debtor and creditor is referred to as an <u>account current</u>.

When a petition for bankruptcy is filed, a <u>summary of debts and assets</u> of the debtor must be provided to the bankruptcy court. A summary of debts and assets is a list containing all that a debtor owes and owns. <u>Assets</u> are the property owned by a bankrupt that may be applied to pay his or her debts. Those debts are called <u>liabilities</u>.

If the creditors agree to accept less than the total amount owed as settlement for the entire debt, the agreement is called <u>composition</u>. Debts that are guaranteed by pledged collateral, such as a mortgage, are called <u>secured debts</u>. <u>Balance of funds</u> is the amount remaining after the secured debts are paid that is to be divided among the other creditors. To <u>liquidate</u> is to convert assets into cash to be used to pay the amounts owed to creditors.

A <u>deficiency decree</u> may be entered for the portion of a secured debt for which the sale of the property does not pay in full. A <u>discharge</u> releases a bankrupt from the obligation or liability of paying former debts.

Property that a bankrupt acquires after filing for bankruptcy is referred to as <u>after-acquired property</u> and is not subject to the claims of the bankruptcy creditors.

TRANSCRIBING FROM DICTATION

Directions: This dictation emphasizes and reinforces the legal terms and definitions you have studied. Listen carefully to the pronunciation of each of the legal terms. Unless otherwise directed, use 1-inch margins and double spacing. Correct all errors. Follow one of the procedures below.

Keyboarding Procedure

Using the Transcription CD, Lesson 25, Part B, transcribe the dictation directly at your computer.

Machine Shorthand Procedure

Using the Transcription CD, Lesson 25, Part B, take the dictation on your shorthand machine and then transcribe from your notes on your computer, or, if you are using computer-aided transcription (CAT), proofread and edit your transcript.

When you have finished transcribing or proofreading and editing Part B of the practice dictation, check your transcript with the printed copy. If you made any mistakes in the transcription, you should review and practice those words several times before going on to Lesson 26.

CHECKLIST

I have completed the following for Lesson 25:

	Part A, Date	Part B, Date	Submitted to Instructor Yes	No
Terminology and Definitions	_____	_____	_____	_____
Self-Evaluation	_____	_____	_____	_____
* Keying Legal Terms	_____	_____	_____	_____
Words	_____	_____	_____	_____
Sentences	_____	_____	_____	_____
* Transcribing from Dictation	_____	_____	_____	_____

When you have successfully completed all the exercises in this lesson and submitted to your instructor those requested, you are ready to proceed with Lesson 26.

* *If you are using machine shorthand, submit to your instructor your notes along with your transcript.*

CHECKLIST

Lesson
26

Agency

In an agency relationship, a person grants another the authority to act for him or her in the commission of certain acts. Generally an agency relationship may exist for the doing of any lawful act unless the law deems such an act as so personal that another person cannot do it, such as the making of a will. Agency relationships affect many day-to-day business transactions, including activities involving brokers, attorneys, and bankers. When you have satisfactorily completed this lesson, you should be able to pronounce, define, spell, and transcribe correctly the terms applicable to the principles of an agency.

Part A | TERMINOLOGY AND DEFINITIONS

Directions: Study the terms, pronunciations, and definitions until you are thoroughly familiar with them. In order to complete this lesson successfully, you must understand the meaning and usage of all the legal terms presented. If you are using a shorthand system, write each legal term one time on your shorthand machine.

Legal Term	Pronunciation	Definition
1. agency	′ā-jən-sē	A relationship whereby one person gives permission to another person to act for or represent him or her.
2. principal	′prin-spəl	The one who gives permission to another person to act for or represent him or her.
3. undisclosed principal	ən-dis-′klōzd ′prin-spəl	A principal who is not known to the party with whom an agent transacts business.
4. power of attorney	paůr əv ə-′tər-nē	The instrument by which the principal gives the agent the authority to represent or act for him or her. If the principal becomes incapacitated or disabled, the power of attorney is no longer valid; however, a durable power of attorney would be valid. (See Figure 26-1, page 381.)
5. agent	′ā-jənt	The one who acts for or represents a principal with the principal's permission.
6. plenipotentiary	plen-ə-pə-′tench-rē	A person who has complete authority to do a certain thing or act for another person.
7. general agent	′jen-rəl ′ā-jənt	An agent who has permission to transact any and all affairs of a particular business for a principal.
8. special agent	′spesh-əl ′ā-jənt	An agent who has permission to transact a specified act for a principal.
9. universal agent	yü-nə-′vər-səl ′ā-jənt	An agent who has the authority to transact any and all business for a principal.

10.	primary agent	′prī-mer-ē ′ā-jənt	An agent who is given direct and first authority by a principal to act as an agent.
11.	subagent	səb-′ā-jənt	An agent who is given permission by a primary agent to transact business for the principal.
12.	exclusive or irrevocable agency	iks-′klü-siv ər ir-′əv-ə-kə-bəl ′ā-jən-sē	An agency that cannot be revoked by the principal while the agency contract or agreement is in effect.
13.	implied agency	im-′plīd ′ā-jən-sē	An agency that is created by the actions of the parties in a particular situation.
14.	del credere agent	del kred-′ər-ē ′ā-jənt	Latin. An agent who guarantees or acts as a surety for the principal against the default of persons with whom the agent conducts business on behalf of the principal.

FIGURE 26-1 A Power of Attorney

POWER OF ATTORNEY.   24

Know All Men By These Presents, That   I, George S. Bartlett

have made, constituted and appointed, and By THESE PRESENTS, do make constitute and appoint

Ronald F. Bartlett------------------------------ true and lawful ATTORNEY for

me   and in my   name, place and stead,   to purchase a parcel of real

estate located in the City of Lansing, County of Ingham, State of

giving and granting unto   Ronald F. Bartlett   said Attorney, full power and
authority to do and perform all and every act and thing whatsoever requisite and necessary to be done in

and about the premises, as fully to all intents and purposes, as   I
might or could do if personally present, with full power of substitution and revocation hereby ratifying

Self-Evaluation A | Terminology and Definition Recall

Directions: In the Answers column, write the legal term that is most representative of the corresponding statement. After you have completed this self-evaluation, check your answers with the key on page 499. If you have any incorrect answers, review the definitions for those terms before going on with this lesson. Then unless otherwise directed, submit this self-evaluation to your instructor.

ANSWERS

1. The one who gives permission to another person to act for or represent him or her is a/an _____.

    1. _____

2. A principal who is not known to the party with whom an agent transacts business is a/an _____.

    2. _____

3. A person who has complete authority to do a certain thing or to act for another person is a/an _____.

    3. _____

4. An agent who has permission to transact any and all affairs of a particular business for the principal is a/an _____.

    4. _____

5. An agent who guarantees or acts as a surety for the principal against the default of persons with whom the agent conducts business on behalf of the principal is a/an _____.

    5. _____

6. A relationship whereby one person gives permission to another person to act for or represent him or her is a/an _____.

    6. _____

7. The one who is given direct and first authority by a principal to act as an agent is a/an _____.

    7. _____

8. An agent who is given permission by a primary agent to transact business for the principal is a/an _____.

    8. _____

9. An agent who has the authority to transact any or all business for a principal is a/an _____.

    9. _____

10. An agency that cannot be revoked by the principal while the agency contract or agreement is in effect is a/an _____.

    10. _____

11. The instrument by which the principal gives the agent the authority to represent or act for him or her is a/an _____.

    11. _____

12. An agent who has permission to transact a specified act for a principal is a/an _____.

    12. _____

13. An agency that is created by the actions of the parties in a particular situation is a/an _____.

    13. _____

14. The one who acts for or represents a principal with the principal's permission is a/an _____.

    14. _____

KEYING LEGAL TERMS

Directions: Unless otherwise instructed, use 1-inch margins and double spacing. Correct all errors. Follow one of the procedures below.

WORDS

Keyboarding Procedure
On your computer, key the following words at least two times, concentrating on the correct spelling and pronunciation.

Machine Shorthand Procedure
On your computer, key the following words once, concentrating on the correct spelling and pronunciation. Then write each word one time on your shorthand machine. Transcribe from your shorthand notes one time on your computer.

agency	principal	undisclosed principal
power of attorney	agent	plenipotentiary
general agent	special agent	universal agent
primary agent	subagent	exclusive or irrevocable agency
implied agency	del credere agent	

SENTENCES

Keyboarding Procedure
Key each of the following sentences one time on your computer. Concentrate on the correct spelling and pronunciation of each underlined legal term.

Machine Shorthand Procedure
Write the following sentences one time on your shorthand machine. Transcribe from your shorthand notes one time on your computer, or, if you are using computer-aided transcription (CAT), proofread and edit your transcript.

These sentences will be used for practice dictation on the Transcription CD.

An <u>agency</u> is a relationship whereby one person gives permission to another person to act for or represent him or her. A <u>principal</u> is the person who gives permission to another person to act for or represent him or her. If a third party does not know who the principal is at the time a transaction is conducted by an agent, the principal is referred to as an <u>undisclosed principal</u>.

A <u>power of attorney</u> is the instrument by which a principal gives an agent the authority to act for him or her. If the principal becomes incapacitated or disabled, the power of attorney is no longer valid. To act for a disabled principal, the agent must have a durable power of attorney.

The person who acts for or represents a principal with the principal's permission is an <u>agent</u>. A <u>plenipotentiary</u> is one who has authority to do a certain thing or to act for another person.

A <u>general agent</u> is one who has authorization to transact any or all affairs of a particular business for a principal, whereas a <u>special agent</u> is one who has permission to transact only an act specified for the principal. A <u>universal agent</u> is one who has the authority to transact any and all business for the principal. A <u>primary agent</u> is one who is given direct and first authority by a principal to act as an agent. A primary agent may give a <u>subagent</u> the authority to transact business for the primary agent's principal.

An <u>exclusive or irrevocable agency</u> is an agency that cannot be revoked by the principal while the agency contract or agreement is in effect. An <u>implied agency</u> is one that is created by the actions of the parties in the situation. A <u>del credere agent</u> is one who guarantees or acts as a surety for the principal against the default of persons with whom the agent conducts business on behalf of the principal.

TRANSCRIBING FROM DICTATION

Directions: This dictation emphasizes and reinforces the legal terms and definitions you have studied. Listen carefully to the pronunciation of each of the legal terms. Unless otherwise directed, use 1-inch margins and double spacing. Correct all errors. Follow one of the procedures below.

Keyboarding Procedure

Using the Transcription CD, Lesson 26, Part A, transcribe the dictation directly at your computer.

Machine Shorthand Procedure

Using the Transcription CD, Lesson 26, Part A, take the dictation on your shorthand machine and then transcribe from your notes on your computer, or, if you are using computer-aided transcription (CAT), proofread and edit your transcript.

When you have finished transcribing or proofreading and editing Part A of the practice dictation, check your transcript with the printed copy. If you made any mistakes in the transcription, you should review and practice those words several times before going on.

Part B | TERMINOLOGY AND DEFINITIONS

Directions: Study the terms, pronunciations, and definitions until you are thoroughly familiar with them. In order to complete this lesson successfully, you must understand the meaning and usage of all the legal terms presented. If you are using a shorthand system, write each legal term one time on your shorthand machine.

Legal Term	Pronunciation	Definition
1. delegation of authority	del-i-'gā-shən əv ə-'thär-ət-ē	One person giving or transferring his or her authority to another person.
2. mutual consent	'myüch-wəl kən-'sent	Agreement by both parties to the agent/principal relationship. An essential element of an agency.
3. third party	thord 'pärt-ē	The party with whom an agent transacts the business for a principal.
4. fiduciary relationship	fə-'dü-shē-er-ē ri-'lā-shən-ship	A relationship that exists when one person trusts and relies upon another.
5. implied ratification	im-'plīd rat-ə-fə-'kā-shən	The presumed acceptance by principal, because of the principal's actions, of the things done on his or her behalf by an agent.
6. estoppel	e-'stäp-əl	A situation that arises when a principal is forbidden by law from alleging or denying certain things done by an agent because of the principal's action or lack of action in the past.
7. ratification	rat-ə-fə-'kā-shən	The acceptance by a principal of the acts performed on the principal's behalf by an agent or another person.

8.	respondeat superior	ri-´spän-dē-at sù-´pir-ē-ər	Latin. Let the master answer. A principal is responsible for the wrongful acts that the agent does for him or her.
9.	factor	´fak-tər	An agent who is employed by a principal to sell goods for the principal. The factor usually has possession of said goods and sells them in his or her own name.
10.	nonfeasance	nän-´fēz-ns	The failure of an agent to perform the acts that the agent agreed to do for the principal.
11.	ostensible authority or apparent authority	ä-´sten-sə-bəl ə-´thär-ət-ē ər ə-´par-ənt ə-´thär-ət-ē	The authority that a principal, either intentionally or by want of due care, leads a third party to believe the agent possesses.
12.	implied authority	im-´plīd ə-´thär-ət-ē	Authority of an agent that is implied by the actions of a principal.
13.	incidental authority	in-sə-´dent-l ə-´thär-ət-ē	The authority that an agent must have in order to perform the business authorized by a principal.
14.	express authority	ik-´spres ə-´thär-ət-ē	Authority, either oral or written, that is definitely and explicitly given to an agent.

Self-Evaluation B | Terminology and Definition Recall

Directions: In the Answers column, write the letter from Column 1 that represents the word or phrase that best match-es each item in Column 2. After you have completed this self-evaluation, check your answers with the key on page 499. If you have any incorrect answers, review the definitions for those terms before going on with this lesson. Then unless otherwise directed, submit this self-evaluation to your instructor.

COLUMN 1	COLUMN 2	ANSWERS
a. delegation of authority	1. The failure of an agent to perform the acts that the agent agreed to do for the principal.	1. _____
b. estoppel	2. A relationship that exists when one person trusts and relies upon another.	2. _____
c. express authority	3. A situation that arises when a principal is forbidden by law from alleging or denying certain things done by an agent because of the principal's action or lack of action in the past.	3. _____
d. factor		
e. fiduciary relationship		
f. implied authority	4. The authority that a principal, either intentionally or by want of due care, leads a third party to believe the agent possesses.	4. _____
g. implied ratification		
h. incidental authority	5. The authority that an agent must have in order to perform the business authorized by a principal.	5. _____
i. mutual consent		
j. nonfeasance	6. The party with whom an agent transacts the business for a principal.	6. _____
k. ostensible or apparent authority	7. Authority, either oral or written, that is definitely and explicitly given to an agent.	7. _____
l. plenipotentiary	8. The giving or transferring of authority from one person to another.	8. _____
m. ratification	9. Agreement by both parties to the agent/principal relation-ship.	9. _____
n. respondeat superior	10. Authority of an agent that is implied by the actions of a principal.	10. _____
o. third party	11. A Latin phrase meaning that a principal is responsible for the wrongful acts of an agent.	11. _____
	12. An agent who is employed by a principal to sell goods for the principal.	12. _____
	13. The presumed acceptance by the principal, because of the principal's actions, of the things done on his or her behalf by an agent.	13. _____
	14. The acceptance by a principal of the acts performed on the principal's behalf by an agent or another person.	14. _____

KEYING LEGAL TERMS

Directions: Unless otherwise instructed, use 1-inch margins and double spacing. Correct all errors. Follow one of the procedures below.

WORDS

Keyboarding Procedure
On your computer, key the following words at least two times, concentrating on the correct spelling and pronunciation.

Machine Shorthand Procedure
On your computer, key the following words once, concentrating on the correct spelling and pronunciation. Then write each word one time on your shorthand machine. Transcribe from your shorthand outlines one time on your computer, or, if you are using computer-aided transcription (CAT), proofread and edit your transcript.

delegation of authority	mutual consent	third party
fiduciary relationship	implied ratification	estoppel
ratification	respondeat superior	factor
nonfeasance	ostensible authority or apparent authority	implied authority
incidental authority		express authority

SENTENCES

Keyboarding Procedure
Key each of the following sentences one time on your computer. Concentrate on the correct spelling and pronunciation of each underlined legal term.

Machine Shorthand Procedure
Write the following sentences one time on your shorthand machine. Transcribe from your shorthand notes one time on your computer, or, if you are using computer-aided transcription (CAT), proofread and edit your transcript.

These sentences will be used for practice dictation on the Transcription CD.

One person giving or transferring his or her authority to another person is <u>delegation of authority</u>. <u>Mutual consent</u> is essential in a principal/agent relationship. Mutual consent is the agreement by both parties to the agency relationship. A <u>third party</u> in an agency relationship is the one with whom an agent transacts the business for a principal.

A relationship that exists when one person trusts and relies upon another is a <u>fiduciary relationship</u>. <u>Implied ratification</u> is the presumed acceptance by the principal, because of the principal's actions, of the things done on his or her behalf by an agent.

An <u>estoppel</u> arises when a principal is forbidden by law from alleging or denying certain things that have been done because of the principal's action or lack of action in the past. The acceptance by a principal of the acts performed on the principal's behalf by an agent or another person is called <u>ratification</u>. <u>Respondeat superior</u> is a Latin phrase for let the master answer. Respondeat superior means that a principal is responsible for the wrongful acts of an agent acting for him or her.

A <u>factor</u> is an agent who is employed by a principal to sell goods for the principal. The failure of an agent to perform the acts that the agent agreed to do for the principal is called <u>nonfeasance</u>.

Ostensible authority or apparent authority is the authority that a principal, either intentionally or by want of due care, leads a third party to believe the agent possesses. **Implied authority** is the authority of an agent that is implied by the principal's actions. **Incidental authority** is the authority that an agent must have in order to perform the business authorized by a principal. **Express authority** is authority, either oral or written, that is definitely and explicitly given to an agent.

TRANSCRIBING FROM DICTATION

Directions: This dictation emphasizes and reinforces the legal terms and definitions you have studied. Listen carefully to the pronunciation of each of the legal terms. Unless otherwise directed, use 1-inch margins and double spacing. Correct all errors. Follow one of the procedures below.

Keyboarding Procedure

Using the Transcription CD, Lesson 26, Part B, transcribe the dictation directly at your computer.

Machine Shorthand Procedure

Using the Transcription CD, Lesson 26, Part B, take the dictation on your shorthand machine and then transcribe from your notes on your computer, or, if you are using computer-aided transcription (CAT), proofread and edit your transcript.

When you have finished transcribing or proofreading and editing Part B of the practice dictation, check your transcript with the printed copy. If you made any mistakes in the transcription, you should review and practice those words several times before going on to Evaluation 13.

CHECKLIST

I have completed the following for Lesson 26:

	Part A, Date	Part B, Date	Submitted to Instructor Yes	No
Terminology and Definitions				
Self-Evaluation				
* Keying Legal Terms				
Words				
Sentences				
* Transcribing from Dictation				

When you have successfully completed all the exercises in this lesson and submitted to your instructor those requested, you are ready to proceed with Evaluation 13.

* If you are using machine shorthand, submit to your instructor your notes along with your transcript.

Evaluation No. 13 | SECTION A

Directions: This dictation/transcription evaluation will test your spelling and transcription abilities on the legal terms that you studied in the two preceding lessons. Tab once for a paragraph indention, and use 1-inch margins and double spacing unless otherwise instructed. Correct all errors. Follow one of the procedures below.

Keyboarding Procedure

Using the Transcription CD for Evaluation 13, transcribe the dictation directly at your computer.

Machine Shorthand Procedure

Using the Transcription CD for Evaluation 13, take the dictation on your shorthand machine and then transcribe your notes on your computer, or, if you are using computer-aided transcription (CAT), proofread and edit your transcript.

Sections B and C are available from your instructor.

Lesson

27

Equity

Equity law is based on rules of morality rather than on judicial laws. If there is no legal remedy available, relief may be granted under equity law. Equity is flexible and may be changed to meet the needs of each individual case. Since equity is administered in the same courts as common law, many of the terms dealing with equity are presented in other lessons. This lesson introduces terms relevant to equity that have not been taught in other areas of law. When you have successfully completed these exercises, you should be able to pronounce, spell, define, and transcribe correctly the terms that are applicable to the principles of the law of equity.

Part A | TERMINOLOGY AND DEFINITIONS

Directions: Study the terms, pronunciations, and definitions until you are thoroughly familiar with them. In order to complete this lesson successfully, you must understand the meaning and usage of all the legal terms presented. If you are using a shorthand system, write each legal term one time on your shorthand machine.

Legal Term	Pronunciation	Definition
1. maxims of equity	ˈmak-səms əv ˈek-wət-ē	General rules of conduct based upon reason and justice.
2. equity	ˈek-wət-ē	A system of law that is based on good conscience, justice, honesty, and right rather than common law.
3. chancery	ˈchans-rē	Another word for equity.
4. chancery law	ˈchans-rē lȯ	The basis for equity law in the United States.
5. chancery court	ˈchans-rē kȯrt	A court of equity. Administers justice according to the rules of conscience and provides remedy for things not covered by common law.
6. preventive jurisdiction	pri-ˈvent-iv ju̇r-əs-ˈdik-shən	Jurisdiction that a court of equity has in order to prevent future wrongs from being committed, as compared to courts of law that are concerned with wrongs that have already been committed.
7. concurrent jurisdiction	kən-ˈkər-ənt ju̇r-əs-ˈdik-shən	Jurisdiction that exists when a court of law or a court of equity can try both common law cases and equity cases.
8. bill of interpleader	bil əv int-ər-ˈplēd-ər	A bill that provides that all persons who are interested in the same action will be joined together in a single lawsuit so as to prevent multiple suits for the same cause.

9. bill quia timet	bil ′kwē-ə ′tim-et	A bill filed with a court of equity that requests the court to exercise its preventive jurisdiction.
10. laches (plural, laches)	′lach-əz	An unreasonable delay on the part of a plaintiff in asserting a right. A delay that causes a disadvantage to another and for which the court will not grant relief.
11. framed questions of fact	frāmd ′kwes-chəns əv fakt	Questions that a judge gives to a jury in an equity case for their determination.
12. advisory jury	əd-′vīz-rē ′jur-ē	A jury to which framed questions of fact are presented for their determination in an equity suit. The findings of an advisory jury are not binding on the court of equity.
13. mistake of fact	mə-′stāk əv fakt	A mistake that occurs unintentionally as to what the true facts are. A court of equity will grant relief on a mistake of fact.
14. mistake of law	mə-′stāk əv lȯ	A mistake that occurs when one who knows all the facts makes an error as to their legal effect. A court of equity will not usually grant relief on a mistake of law.

Self-Evaluation A | **Terminology and Definition Recall**

Directions: In the Answers column at the right of each statement, write the letter that represents the word or group of words that correctly completes the statement. After you have completed this self-evaluation, check your answers with the key on page 499. If you have any incorrect answers, review the definitions for those terms before going on with this lesson. Then unless otherwise directed, submit this self-evaluation to your instructor.

ANSWERS

1. A mistake that occurs unintentionally as to what the true facts are is called a (a) mistake of fact, (b) mistake of law, (c) bill quia timet.

    1. _____

2. Jurisdiction that a court of equity has in order to prevent future wrongs from being committed, as compared to courts of law that are concerned with wrongs that have already been committed, is (a) advisory, (b) concurrent jurisdiction, (c) preventive jurisdiction.

    2. _____

3. General rules of conduct based upon reason and justice are (a) maxims of equity, (b) framed questions of fact, (c) bills of interpleader.

    3. _____

4. The basis for equity law in the United States is (a) maxims of equity, (b) chancery law, (c) laches.

    4. _____

5. A jury to which framed questions of fact are presented for their determination in an equity suit is a/an (a) preventive jurisdiction, (b) advisory jury, (c) concurrent jurisdiction.

    5. _____

6. A mistake that occurs when one who knows all the facts makes an error as to their legal effect is a (a) mistake of fact, (b) framed questions of fact, (c) mistake of law.

    6. _____

7. Another word for equity is (a) chancery, (b) advisory, (c) laches.

    7. _____

8. A bill that provides that all persons who are interested in the same action will be joined together in a single lawsuit so as to prevent multiple suits for the same cause is a (a) bill of interpleader, (b) bill quia timet, (c) preventive jurisdiction.

    8. _____

9. A system of law that is based on good conscience, justice, honesty, and right rather than common law is (a) interpleader, (b) equity, (c) laches.

    9. _____

10. A court of equity that administers justice according to the rules of conscience and provides remedy for things not covered by common law is a/an (a) preventive jurisdiction, (b) advisory court, (c) chancery court.

    10. _____

11. Questions that a judge gives to a jury in an equity case for their determination are (a) laches, (b) framed questions of fact, (c) maxims of equity.

    11. _____

12. A bill filed with a court of equity that requests the court to exercise its preventive jurisdiction is a (a) bill of interpleader, (b) bill quia timet, (c) framed questions of fact.

    12. _____

13. An unreasonable delay on the part of a plaintiff in asserting a right that causes a disadvantage to another and for which the court will not grant relief is referred to as (a) chancery, (b) advisory, (c) laches.

    13. _____

14. Jurisdiction that exists when a court of law or a court of equity can try both common law cases and equity cases is referred to as (a) concurrent jurisdiction, (b) preventive jurisdiction, (c) maxims of equity.

    14. _____

KEYING LEGAL TERMS

Directions: Unless otherwise instructed, use 1-inch margins and double spacing. Correct all errors. Follow one of the procedures below.

WORDS

Keyboarding Procedure
On your computer, key the following words at least two times, concentrating on the correct spelling and pronunciation.

Machine Shorthand Procedure
On your computer, key the following words once, concentrating on the correct spelling and pronunciation. Then write each word one time on your shorthand machine. Transcribe from your shorthand notes one time on your computer, or, if you are using computer-aided transcription (CAT), proofread and edit your transcript.

maxims of equity	equity	chancery
chancery law	chancery court	preventive jurisdiction
concurrent jurisdiction	bill of interpleader	bill quia timet
laches	framed questions of fact	advisory jury
mistake of fact	mistake of law	

SENTENCES

Keyboarding Procedure
Key each of the following sentences one time on your computer. Concentrate on the correct spelling and pronunciation of each underlined legal term.

Machine Shorthand Procedure
Write the following sentences one time on your shorthand machine. Transcribe from your shorthand notes one time on your computer, or, if you are using computer-aided transcription (CAT), proofread and edit your transcript.

These sentences will be used for practice dictation on the Transcription CD.

Maxims of equity are general rules of conduct that are based upon reason and justice. Equity is a system of law that is based on good conscience, justice, honesty, and rights rather than common law. Chancery is another term meaning equity. Chancery law is the basis for equity law in the United States. A chancery court administers justice according to the rules of conscience and provides a remedy for things not covered by common law.

Preventive jurisdiction is the jurisdiction that a court of equity has in order to prevent future wrongs from being committed. Concurrent jurisdiction exists when courts of law and courts of equity can try both common law cases and equity cases.

When two or more persons are interested in the same action, a bill of interpleader may be filed to join them together in one lawsuit so as to prevent multiple suits for the same cause. Bill quia timet is a bill filed with a court of equity that requests the court to exercise its preventive jurisdiction.

Laches is an unreasonable delay on the part of the plaintiff in asserting a right. Framed questions of fact are questions that a judge gives to an advisory jury in an equity case for their determination. A jury in an equity suit serves only as an advisory jury to the judge, and its findings are not binding on the court.

A <u>mistake of fact</u> is one that occurs unintentionally as to what the true facts are, and relief on a mistake of fact may be sought in a court of equity. A <u>mistake of law</u> occurs when one knows all the facts but makes an error as to their legal effect for which relief cannot be sought in a court of equity.

TRANSCRIBING FROM DICTATION

Directions: This dictation emphasizes and reinforces the legal terms and definitions you have studied. Listen carefully to the pronunciation of each of the legal terms. Unless otherwise directed, use 1-inch margins and double spacing. Correct all errors. Follow one of the procedures below.

Keyboarding Procedure
Using the Transcription CD, Lesson 27, Part A, transcribe the dictation directly at your computer.

Shorthand Procedure
Using the Transcription CD, Lesson 27, Part A, take the dictation on your shorthand machine and then transcribe from your notes on your computer, or, if you are using computer-aided transcription (CAT), proofread and edit your transcript.

When you have finished transcribing or proofreading and editing Part A of the practice dictation, check your transcript with the printed copy. If you made any mistakes in the transcription, you should review and practice those words several times before going on to Part B.

Part B | TERMINOLOGY AND DEFINITIONS

Directions: Study the terms, pronunciations, and definitions until you are thoroughly familiar with them. In order to complete this lesson successfully, you must understand the meaning and usage of all the legal terms presented. If you are using a shorthand system, write each legal term one time on your shorthand machine.

Legal Term	Pronunciation	Definition
1. consent decree	kən-ˈsent di-ˈkrē	A decree entered by consent of the parties under the sanction of the court. Both parties coming to an agreement before the case is tried is a consent decree.
2. finding of fact	ˈfin-diŋ əv fakt	A statement made by the court pertaining to the conclusions reached that are based on the evidence in an equity case.
3. declaratory judgment	di-ˈklar-ə-tōr-ē ˈjəj-mənt	A judgment that declares the existence of a right but does not provide any measure for enforcement.
4. waiver	ˈwā-vər	The intentional giving up of a right that one has.
5. reformation	ref-ər-ˈma-shən	An equity remedy that provides for the amending or correcting of a written document so that it conforms with the intentions of the parties.
6. in pari delicto	in ˈpar-ī di-ˈlikt-ō	Latin. In equal fault. Equity relief will not be granted if both parties are at fault.
7. sua sponte	suä ˈspän-tə	Latin. Of one's own will, or voluntarily.
8. de minimis non curat lex	dā ˈmin-ə-mēs nōn kü-ˈrät leks	Latin. The law is not concerned with trifles. For example, an error involving a few cents will not be considered.

9.	matter in pais	ʹmat-er in pā	French. A matter of fact that is oral and not in writing. It is an estoppel that is created by the conduct of a party.
10.	estoppel in pais	e-ʹstäp-əl in pā	French. An estoppel that arises from the conduct of a party, laches, or negligence.
11.	remedial	ri-ʹmēd-ē-əl	Providing a remedy.
12.	right and duty	rīt ən ʹdüt-ē	The foundation of equity jurisprudence.
13.	rule of morality	rül əv mə-ʹral-ət-ē	The rule of right and wrong conduct that forms the basis of the standards that people should follow in dealing with others.
14.	clean hands doctrine	klēn hands ʹdäk-trən	An equity maxim that states that one who comes into equity must come with clean hands. The one filing for equity must not be guilty of any wrongdoing.
15.	doctrine of doing complete justice	ʹdäk-trən əv ʹdü-iŋ kəm-ʹplēt ʹjəs-təs	The broad power of an equity court to dispose of all issues existing between the parties that are related to the main purpose of the suit.

Self-Evaluation B | Terminology and Definition Recall

Directions: In the Answers column, write the legal term that is most representative of the corresponding statement. After you have completed this self-evaluation, check your answers with the key on page 499. If you have any incorrect answers, review the definitions for those terms before going on with this lesson. Then unless otherwise directed, submit this self-evaluation to your instructor.

ANSWERS

1. A statement made by the court pertaining to the conclusions reached that are based on the evidence in an equity case is a/an _____.

    1. _____

2. A judgment that declares the existence of a right but does not provide any measure for enforcement is a/an _____.

    2. _____

3. The broad power of an equity court to dispose of all issues existing between the parties that are related to the main purpose of the suit is the _____.

    3. _____

4. A Latin phrase meaning the law is not concerned with trifles is _____.

    4. _____

5. The foundation of equity jurisprudence is _____.

    5. _____

6. The rule of right and wrong conduct that forms the basis of the standards that people should follow in dealing with others is the _____.

    6. _____

7. A term that means providing a remedy is _____.

    7. _____

8. A Latin phrase meaning in equal fault and for which equity will not be granted is _____.

    8. _____

9. A Latin phrase meaning of one's own will, or voluntarily, is _____.

    9. _____

10. An estoppel that arises from the conduct of a party, laches, or negligence is a/an _____.

    10. _____

11. An equity remedy that provides for the amending or correcting of a written document so that it conforms with the intentions of the parties is _____.

    11. _____

12. A matter of fact that is oral and not in writing that creates an estoppel based on the conduct of a party is a/an _____.

    12. _____

13. The intentional giving up of a right that one has is a/an _____.

    13. _____

14. A decree that is entered by agreement between the parties under the sanction of the court is a/an _____.

    14. _____

15. An equity maxim that states that one who comes into equity must not be guilty of any wrongdoing is _____.

    15. _____

KEYING LEGAL TERMS

Directions: Unless otherwise instructed, use 1-inch margins and double spacing. Correct all errors. Follow one of the procedures below.

WORDS

Keyboarding Procedure
On your computer, key the following words at least two times, concentrating on the correct spelling and pronunciation.

Machine Shorthand Procedure
On your computer, key the following words once, concentrating on the correct spelling and pronunciation. Then write each word one time on your shorthand machine. Transcribe from your shorthand notes one time on your computer, or, if you are using computer-aided transcription (CAT), proofread and edit your transcript.

consent decree	finding of fact	declaratory judgment
waiver	reformation	in pari delicto
sua sponte	de minimis non curat lex	matter in pais
estoppel in pais	remedial	right and duty
rule of morality	clean hands doctrine	doctrine of doing complete justice

SENTENCES

Keyboarding Procedure
Key each of the following sentences one time on your computer. Concentrate on the correct spelling and pronunciation of each underlined legal term.

Machine Shorthand Procedure
Write the following sentences one time on your shorthand machine. Transcribe from your shorthand notes one time on your computer, or, if you are using computer-aided transcription (CAT), proofread and edit your transcript.

These sentences will be used for practice dictation on the Transcription CD.

If the parties come to an agreement under the sanction of the court prior to trial, a <u>consent decree</u> is entered. A <u>finding of fact</u> is a statement by the court pertaining to the conclusions reached that are based on the evidence in an equity case. A <u>declaratory judgment</u> declares the existence of a right but does nothing to enforce it.

A <u>waiver</u> is the intentional giving up of a right. <u>Reformation</u> is a remedy that provides for the amending or correcting of a written document so that it conforms with the intentions of the parties.

<u>In pari delicto</u> is a Latin phrase meaning in equal fault. When both parties are in pari delicto, equity relief will not be granted. <u>Sua sponte</u> is a Latin phrase meaning of one's own will, or voluntarily. <u>De minimis non curat lex</u> is a Latin phrase meaning the law is not concerned with trifles. A <u>matter in pais</u> is a matter of fact not in writing. An <u>estoppel in pais</u> is an estoppel that arises from the conduct of a party, laches, or negligence.

<u>Remedial</u> means providing a remedy. <u>Right and duty</u> form the foundation of equity jurisprudence. Whenever a right exists, there is also a duty. The <u>rule of morality</u> is a rule of right and wrong conduct that forms the basis of the standards that people should follow in dealing with others. The <u>clean hands doctrine</u>

is an equity maxim that states that one who comes into equity must not be guilty of any wrongdoing. The <u>doctrine of doing complete justice</u> is the broad power of an equity court to dispose of all issues existing between the parties that are related to the main purpose of the suit.

TRANSCRIBING FROM DICTATION

Directions: This dictation emphasizes and reinforces the legal terms and definitions you have studied. Listen carefully to the pronunciation of each of the legal terms. Unless otherwise directed, use 1-inch margins and double spacing. Correct all errors. Follow one of the procedures below.

Keyboarding Procedure

Using the Transcription CD, Lesson 27, Part B, transcribe the dictation directly at your computer.

Machine Shorthand Procedure

Using the Transcription CD, Lesson 27, Part B, take the dictation on your shorthand machine and then transcribe from your notes on your computer, or, if you are using computer-aided transcription (CAT), proofread and edit your transcript.

When you have finished transcribing or proofreading and editing Part B of the practice dictation, check your transcript with the printed copy. If you made any mistakes in the transcription, you should review and practice those words several times before going on to Lesson 28.

CHECKLIST

I have completed the following for Lesson 27:

	Part A, Date	Part B, Date	Submitted to Instructor Yes	No
Terminology and Definitions				
Self-Evaluation				
* Keying Legal Terms				
Words				
Sentences				
* Transcribing from Dictation				

When you have successfully completed all the exercises in this lesson and submitted to your instructor those requested, you are ready to proceed with Lesson 28.

* *If you are using machine shorthand, submit to your instructor your notes along with your transcript.*

Lesson 28

Partnerships

> *"One who can and does not forbid that which is done on his or her behalf, is deemed to have bidden it."*
> —*Legal maxim*

The sole proprietorship, the partnership, and the corporation are the three most common types of business organizations. Partnerships and corporations involve more legalities than single proprietorships; thus, the terms in this lesson will deal mainly with partnerships, and the next two lessons will deal with corporations. When you complete these exercises, you should be able to spell, pronounce, define, and transcribe correctly the terms that are introduced herein.

Part A | TERMINOLOGY AND DEFINITIONS

Directions: Study the terms, pronunciations, and definitions until you are thoroughly familiar with them. In order to complete this lesson successfully, you must understand the meaning and usage of all the legal terms presented. If you are using a shorthand system, write each legal term one time on your shorthand machine.

Legal Term	Pronunciation	Definition
1. sole proprietorship	sōl prə-ˈprī-ət-ər-ship	A business owned by one person who has the legal right to the business.
2. proprietor	prə-ˈprī-ət-ər	One who is the sole owner of something, such as a business.
3. severalty	ˈsev-rəl-tē	Sole ownership of property. Owned by one person.
4. Uniform Partnership Act	ˈyü-nə-fȯrm ˈpärt-nər-ship akt	Uniform laws adopted by most states to define the legalities and requirements for the formation and operation of partnerships.
5. partnership	ˈpärt-nər-ship	A business owned by two or more persons for who share in the profits and losses for their common benefit.
6. articles of partnership	ˈärt-i-kəls əv ˈpärt-nər-ship	An agreement that contains the terms of a partnership. (See Figure 28-1, page 409).
7. Uniform Limited Partnership Act	ˈyü-nə-fȯrm ˈlim-ət-əd ˈpärt-nər-ship akt	Uniform laws that have been adopted in most states to define the legalities and requirements for the formation and operation of limited partnerships.
8. limited partnership	ˈlim-ət-əd ˈpärt-nər-ship	A partnership that consists of a general partner, who conducts the business, and one or more limited partners, who contribute capital and share in profits.
9. general partner	ˈjen-rəl ˈpärt-nər	One who conducts the business of a partnership and has unlimited liability.

10. limited partner	′lim-ət-əd ′pärt-nər	One who contributes capital and shares in the profits of a limited partnership but whose liability is limited to the amount of his or her investment.
11. senior partner	′sē-nyər ′pärt-nər	Usually one who has a greater investment, seniority, and role in the management of the business.
12. junior partner	′jün-yər ′pärt-nər	Usually one who has a lesser investment, seniority, and role in the management of the business than the senior partner.
13. silent partner	′sī-lənt ′pärt-nər	One who is not publicly known as being a partner but who shares in the profits. Sometimes called a dormant or sleeping partner.

FIGURE 28-1 Articles of Partnership

AGREEMENT (OR ARTICLES) OF CO-PARTNERSHIP.   293

Articles of Agreement, Made the 11th   day of   July

in the year two thousand and three

BETWEEN   COLLEEN J. SUMMERS and STEWART K. ROSS

Witnesseth as follows:

1. The said parties above named have agreed to become co-partners in business, and by these presents do agree to become co-partners together under the firm and partnership name of

SUMMERS AND ROSS

in the business of   retail sales of office supplies

the said partnership to commence on the 1st   day of August   2003

and to continue for five (5) years   thereafter.

2. To that end and purpose the said   Colleen J. Summers

has contributed in cash the sum of Twenty-five thousand and 00/100 dollars ($25,000.00)

and the said   Stewart K. Ross has contributed in cash the sum of Twenty-five thousand and 00/100 dollars ($25,000.00) to

the capital stock so formed to be used and employed in common between them, for the support and management of the said business, to their mutual benefit and advantage.

3. **It is Agreed** by and between the parties hereto that at all times during the continuance of their co-partnership, they and each of them shall and will give their personal attention to the said business, and will to the utmost of their skill and power exert themselves for their joint interest, profit, benefit and advantage, in the said business.

Self-Evaluation A | Terminology and Definition Recall

Directions: In the Answers column, write the legal term that is most representative of the corresponding statement. After you have completed this self-evaluation, check your answers with the key on page 499. If you have any incorrect answers, review the definitions for those terms before going on with this lesson. Then unless otherwise directed, submit this self-evaluation to your instructor.

ANSWERS

1. Sole ownership of property is referred to as _____.
   1. _____

2. One who conducts the business of a partnership and has unlimited liability is a/an _____.
   2. _____

3. An agreement that contains the terms of a partnership is a/an _____.
   3. _____

4. A business owned by one person who has the legal right to the business is a/an _____.
   4. _____

5. A partnership that consists of a general partner, who conducts the business, and one or more limited partners, who contribute capital and share in profits, is a/an _____.
   5. _____

6. A business owned by two or more persons who share in the profits and losses for their common benefit is called a/an _____.
   6. _____

7. Usually one who has a lesser investment, seniority, and role in the management of the business than the senior partner is a/an _____.
   7. _____

8. One who is the sole owner of something, such as a business, is a/an _____.
   8. _____

9. Usually one who has a greater investment, seniority, and role in the management of the business is a/an _____.
   9. _____

10. Uniform laws adopted by most states to define the legalities and requirements for the formation and operation of limited partnerships are referred to as the _____.
    10. _____

11. One who is not publicly known as being a partner but who shares in the profits is a/an _____.
    11. _____

12. Uniform laws adopted by most states to define the legalities and requirements for the formation and operation of partnerships are referred to as _____.
    12. _____

13. One who contributes capital and shares in the profits of a limited partnership but whose liability is limited to the amount of his or her investment is a/an _____.
    13. _____

KEYING LEGAL TERMS

Directions: Unless otherwise instructed, use 1-inch margins and double spacing. Correct all errors. Follow one of the procedures below.

WORDS

Keyboarding Procedure

On your computer, key the following words at least two times, concentrating on the correct spelling and pronunciation.

Machine Shorthand Procedure

On your computer, key the following words once, concentrating on the correct spelling and pronunciation. Then write each word one time on your shorthand machine. Transcribe from your shorthand notes one time on your computer, or, if you are using computer-aided transcription (CAT), proofread and edit your transcript.

sole proprietorship	**proprietor**	**severalty**
Uniform Partnership Act	**partnership**	**articles of partnership**
Uniform Limited Partnership Act	**limited partnership**	**general partner**
limited partner	**senior partner**	**junior partner**
silent partner		

SENTENCES

Keyboarding Procedure

Key each of the following sentences one time on your computer. Concentrate on the correct spelling and pronunciation of each underlined legal term.

Machine Shorthand Procedure

Write the following sentences one time on your shorthand machine. Transcribe from your shorthand notes one time on your computer, or, if you are using computer-aided transcription (CAT), proofread and edit your transcript.

These sentences will be used for practice dictation on the Transcription CD.

A <u>sole proprietorship</u> is a business owned by one person who has the legal right to the business. A <u>proprietor</u> is one who is the sole owner of something. Sole ownership of property is also called <u>severalty</u>.

The <u>Uniform Partnership Act</u> consists of uniform laws that have been adopted by most states to define the legalities and requirements for the formation and operation of partnerships. A <u>partnership</u> is a business owned by two or more persons for their common benefit and who share in the profits and losses. When parties enter into a partnership, the written agreement stating the terms and conditions is called the <u>articles of partnership</u>.

Most states have adopted the <u>Uniform Limited Partnership Act</u> to define the legalities and requirements for the formation and operation of limited partnerships. A <u>limited partnership</u> is a partnership that consists of a general partner, who conducts the business, and one or more limited partners, who contribute capital and share in profits.

A <u>general partner</u> is one who conducts the business of a partnership and has unlimited liability, whereas a limited partner is one who contributes capital and shares in the profits but whose liability is limited to the amount of his or her investment. The <u>senior partner</u> has a greater investment, seniority, and role in the management of the business than the <u>junior partner</u>. A <u>silent partner</u> is one whose name is not publicly known as being a partner but who shares in the profits.

TRANSCRIBING FROM DICTATION

Directions: This dictation emphasizes and reinforces the legal terms and definitions you have studied. Listen carefully to the pronunciation of each of the legal terms. Unless otherwise directed, use 1-inch margins and double spacing. Correct all errors. Follow one of the procedures below.

Keyboarding Procedure
Using the Transcription CD, Lesson 28, Part A, transcribe the dictation directly at your computer.

Machine Shorthand Procedure
Using the Transcription CD, Lesson 28, Part A, take the dictation on your shorthand machine and then transcribe from your notes on your computer, or, if you are using computer-aided transcription (CAT), proofread and edit your transcript.

When you have finished transcribing or proofreading and editing Part A of the practice dictation, check your transcript with the printed copy. If you made any mistakes in the transcription, you should review and practice those words several times before going on to Part B.

Part B | TERMINOLOGY AND DEFINITIONS

Directions: Study the terms, pronunciations, and definitions until you are thoroughly familiar with them. In order to complete this lesson successfully, you must understand the meaning and usage of all the legal terms presented. If you are using a shorthand system, write each legal term one time on your shorthand machine.

Legal Term	Pronunciation	Definition
1. secret partner	′sē-krət ′pärt-nər	A dormant or silent partner.
2. nominal partner	′näm-ən-l ′pärt-nər	One who permits his or her name to be used as though the person were a partner but who really has no financial interest in the business.
3. joint venture	jȯint ′ven-chər	Two or more persons joined together in a business venture without forming an actual partnership or corporation.
4. assumed name	ə-′sümd nām	A name other than one's own under which business is transacted. The law usually requires the name to be filed so that the persons operating under the assumed name are known. (See Figure 28-2, page 416.)
5. D/B/A	′dü-iŋ ′biz-nəs əz	Abbreviation for doing business as. Used when identifying a person who is doing business under an assumed name.
6. Securities and Exchange Commission	si-′kyu̇r-ət-ēs ən iks-′chānj kə-′mish-ən	A commission formed to regulate the exchange of securities. Stocks, securities, and shares in limited partnerships must comply with SEC requirements.
7. syndicate	′sin-di-kət	A joint venture composed of individuals who have the purpose of conducting a specific business transaction.

8. underwriting syndicate	′ən-də-rīt-iŋ ′sin-di-kət	A joint venture that consists of investment banking companies and whose purpose is to sell large issues of stocks and bonds.
9. capital	′kap-ət-l	The assets of a company or corporation. The money that partners are required to invest in a business venture.
10. commingle	kə-′miŋ-gəl	To put two different persons' money together into one account.
11. prospectus	prə-′spek-təs	A printed document issued by a company or corporation that describes a proposed business venture, such as a limited partnership.
12. subscription	səb-′skrip-shən	A written contract by which one agrees to purchase shares, debentures, or other securities issued by a company or corporation. (See Figure 28-3, page 417.)

FIGURE 28-2 An Assumed Name Certificate

CERTIFICATE OF PERSONS CONDUCTING BUSINESS
UNDER ASSUMED NAME—Act No. 151, P.A. 1949.   **M310 (REVISED 1978)**

Certificate of Persons Conducting Business Under Assumed Name

STATE OF MICHIGAN.⎱ ss.

COUNTY OF __Ingham__   FILING FEE $10.00

The undersigned hereby certifies that __they__ (it) now own __(or) intend __ to own, conduct or transact

business at __7320 Sandstone Drive__
(Street and No.)

in the __City of Lansing__ of __Ingham__
(City, Village or Township)

------------------------------ County, Michigan, under the assumed name, designation and style of

__F & C Enterprises__

The undersigned further certifies that the true or real full name and address of the person [1] owning,
conducting or transacting said business is:

PRINT OR TYPE NAMES AND ADDRESS

NAME	STREET ADDRESS	CITY OR TOWN
Anna Marie Findley	7320 Sandstone Drive	Lansing, Michigan
Richard Lee Collins	7320 Sandstone Drive	Lansing, Michigan

In Witness Whereof, I/We have this __3rd__ day of __January__ __2003__,
made and signed this certificate.

SIGNATURES OF PERSONS CONDUCTING BUSINESS UNDER ASSUMED NAME

Anna Marie Findley

Richard Lee Collins

STATE OF MICHIGAN.⎱ ss.

COUNTY OF __Ingham__   On __3rd__, 20 __03__, before
me, a Notary Public, personally appeared the above named person or persons, whose signatures appear above,
and who executed the foregoing instrument, and __they__ acknowledged to me that __they__ executed the
same, and that they are all of the persons now owning, conducting and transacting or who intend to own,
conduct and transact the business under the above name, style and designation.

FIGURE 28-3 A Subscription

ZENITH OIL AND GAS CORP.
1997 DRILLING PROGRAM
SUBCRIPTION

The undersigned prospective Limited Partner ("Subscriber") hereby offers to purchase a Limited Parnership interest in the Zenith Oil and Gas Corp. 1997 Drilling Program Limited Partnership No. __2__ and encloses herewith the entire purchase price of _Five thousand and 00/100_ Dollars ($5,000.00   ) for _1_ Limited partnership Unit(s) at $5,000 each.

The Subscriber acknowledges receipt of the Prospectus containing the Limited Partnership Agreement relating to this offering and agrees to be bound and governed by the provisions of the Limited Partnership Agreement of which this Subscription shall become a part upon its execution. The Subscriber states that he has relied solely upon the Prospectus in making his investment decision. The Subscriber understands the speculative nature of this Program and the risks involved in said offering, including the possible loss of his entire investment; the lack of liquidity of the Units offered and the restrictions on their transferability; the tax consequences of his investment; and the background and qualifications of Zenith Oil and Gas Corp. as sponsor of this offering. The Subscriber hereby represents that the prospective purchase is for his own account and that he is not subscribing with the present intention of reselling such securities. The Subscribers agrees that this offer shall remain irrevocable for a period of six (6) months.

The Subscriber hereby represents that: (a) he has a net worth of not less than $200,000 (exclusive of home, furnishings and automobiles); or (b) he has a net worth of not less than $50,000 (exclusive of home, furnishings and automobiles) and some portion of his taxable income for the previous year was, or some portion of his estimated taxable income for the current year will be, subject to Federal income tax at a rate of less than 50%; and (c) he is a citizen of the United States of America.

Zenith Oil and Gas Corp., upon the acceptance of this Subscription will forward to the Subscriber a notice of acceptance in the Zenith Oil and Gas Corp. 1997 Drilling Program Limited Partnership No. __2__.

California: The issuance of any Limited Partnership interests resulting from any offer and/or sale in the State of California of the Limited Partnership interests is subject to the following legend condition restricting transfer.

CALIFORNIA: IT IS UNLAWFUL TO CONSUMMATE A SALE OR TRANSFER OF THIS SECURITY OR ANY INTEREST THEREIN, OR TO RECEIVE ANY CONSIDERATION THEREFOR, WITHOUT THE PRIOR WRITTEN CONSENT OF THE COMMISSIONER OF CORPORATIONS OF THE STATE OF CALIFORNIA, EXCEPT AS PERMITTED IN THE COMMISSIONER'S RULES.

Dated this __17th__ day of __October__, 2003

Social Security No. or __000-00-0001__
Federal Identification No.

Marion O. Klotz
Signature

Mailing Address: __2660 Columbia St.__
__Holt, Michigan__

Signature
Marion O. Klotz
Please Print Name(s)

Occupation: __Investor__

Dealer Name: __Hartman, Inc.__

Dealer Branch Office: __Lansing, MI__

Representative: __Manuel Hartman__

Representative Number: __00910__

☐ Tenants in common (each person must sign)
☐ Joint tenants with right of survivorship, and not as tenants in common
☐ Tenants by the entirety
☐ _____, as Custodian for
_____ under the _____
Uniform Gifts to Minors Act   (State)

MAIL THE ORIGINAL EXECUTED SUBSCRIPTION AND ONE COPY WITH CHECK PAYABLE TO "ZENITH OIL AND GAS CORP., GENERAL PARTNER" TO ZENITH PROGRAMS, INC., P.O. BOX 1000, BLOOMFIELD HILLS, MICHIGAN 48013. THE SUBSCRIBER AND THE SELLING BROKER-DEALER EACH RETAIN ONE COPY.

Self-Evaluation B | Terminology and Definition Recall

Directions: In the Answers column, write the letter from Column 1 that represents the word or phrase that best matches each item in Column 2. After you have completed this self-evaluation, check your answers with the key on page 499. If you have any incorrect answers, review the definitions for those terms before going on with this lesson. Then unless otherwise directed, submit this self-evaluation to your instructor.

COLUMN 1	COLUMN 2	ANSWERS
a. assumed name	1. One who permits his or her name to be used as though the person were a partner but who really has no financial interest in the business.	1. _____
b. capital	2. A name other than one's own under which business is transacted.	2. _____
c. commingle	3. A dormant or silent partner.	3. _____
d. D/B/A	4. A joint venture that consists of investment banking companies and whose purpose is to sell large issues of stocks and bonds.	4. _____
e. joint venture	5. Two or more persons joined together in a business venture without forming an actual partnership or corporation.	5. _____
f. nominal partner	6. A written contract by which one agrees to purchase shares, debentures, or other securities issued by a company or corporation.	6. _____
g. prospectus	7. A printed document issued by a company or corporation that describes a proposed business venture, such as a limited partnership.	7. _____
h. secret partner	8. A commission formed to regulate the exchange of securities.	8. _____
i. Securities and Exchange Commission	9. To put two different persons' money together into one account.	9. _____
j. silent partner	10. An abbreviation used when identifying a person who is doing business under an assumed name.	10. _____
k. subscription	11. A joint venture composed of individuals who have the purpose of conducting a specific business transaction.	11. _____
l. syndicate	12. The assets of a company or corporation or the money that partners are required to invest in a business venture.	12. _____
m. underwriting syndicate		

KEYING LEGAL TERMS

Directions: Unless otherwise instructed, use 1-inch margins and double spacing. Correct all errors. Follow one of the procedures below.

WORDS

Keyboarding Procedure
On your computer, key the following words at least two times, concentrating on the correct spelling and pronunciation.

Machine Shorthand Procedure
On your computer, key the following words once, concentrating on the correct spelling and pronunciation. Then write each word one time on your shorthand machine. Transcribe from your shorthand notes one time on your computer, or, if you are using computer-aided transcription (CAT), proofread and edit your transcript.

secret partner	nominal partner	joint venture
assumed name	D/B/A	Securities and Exchange Commission
syndicate	underwriting syndicate	prospectus
capital	commingle	
subscription		

SENTENCES

Keyboarding Procedure
Key each of the following sentences one time on your computer. Concentrate on the correct spelling and pronunciation of each underlined legal term.

Machine Shorthand Procedure
Write the following sentences one time on your shorthand machine. Transcribe from your shorthand notes one time on your computer, or, if you are using computer-aided transcription (CAT), proofread and edit your transcript.

These sentences will be used for practice dictation on the Transcription CD.

A <u>secret partner</u> is a dormant or silent partner. A <u>nominal partner</u> permits one's name to be used as though he or she were a partner but who really has no financial interest in the business.

A <u>joint venture</u> is where two or more persons join together in a business venture without forming an actual partnership or corporation.

An <u>assumed name</u> is a name other than one's own under which business is transacted. The abbreviation for doing business as is <u>D/B/A</u> and is used to identify a person who is doing business under an assumed name; for example, Sally and Jerry Bates D/B/A Bates Enterprises.

The <u>Securities and Exchange Commission</u> regulates the exchange of securities. Stocks, securities, and shares in limited partnerships must comply with SEC requirements.

A <u>syndicate</u> is a joint venture composed of individuals who have the purpose of conducting a specific business transaction. An <u>underwriting syndicate</u> is a group of investment banking companies who enter into a joint venture for the purpose of selling large issues of stocks and bonds.

The assets of a corporation or company are referred to as <u>capital</u>. Capital is also the money required of partners when entering into a business arrangement. To <u>commingle</u> is to put two different persons' money into one account.

A company or corporation that invites the public to subscribe to shares, debentures, or other securities publishes a <u>prospectus</u>. The prospectus describes the proposed business venture. A <u>subscription</u> is a written contract by which one agrees to purchase shares, debentures, or other securities issued by a company or corporation.

TRANSCRIBING FROM DICTATION

Directions: This dictation emphasizes and reinforces the legal terms and definitions you have studied. Listen carefully to the pronunciation of each of the legal terms. Unless otherwise directed, use 1-inch margins and double spacing. Correct all errors. Follow one of the procedures below.

Keyboarding Procedure

Using the Transcription CD, Lesson 28, Part B, transcribe the dictation directly at your computer.

Machine Shorthand Procedure

Using the Transcription CD, Lesson 28, Part B, take the dictation on your shorthand machine and then transcribe from your notes on your computer, or, if you are using computer-aided transcription (CAT), proofread and edit your transcript.

When you have finished transcribing or proofreading and editing Part B of the practice dictation, check your transcript with the printed copy. If you made any mistakes in the transcription, you should review and practice those words several times before going on to Evaluation 14.

CHECKLIST

I have completed the following for Lesson 28:

	Part A, Date	Part B, Date	Submitted to Instructor Yes	No
Terminology and Definitions				
Self-Evaluation				
* Keying Legal Terms				
Words				
Sentences				
* Transcribing from Dictation				

When you have successfully completed all the exercises in this lesson and submitted to your instructor those requested, you are ready to proceed with Evaluation 14.

* If you are using machine shorthand, submit to your instructor your notes along with your transcript.

Evaluation No. 14 | SECTION A

Directions: This dictation/transcription evaluation will test your spelling and transcription abilities on the legal terms that you studied in the two preceding lessons. Tab once for a paragraph indention, and use 1-inch margins and double spacing unless otherwise instructed, Correct all errors. Follow one of the procedures below.

Keyboarding Procedure

Using the Transcription CD for Evaluation 14, transcribe the dictation directly at your computer.

Machine Shorthand Procedure

Using the Transcription CD for Evaluation 14, take the dictation on your shorthand machine and then transcribe your notes on your computer, or, if you are using computer-aided transcription (CAT), proofread and edit your transcript.

Sections B and C are available from your instructor.

Lesson
29

Corporations

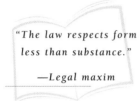

"The law respects form less than substance."

—*Legal maxim*

Of the three types of businesses, corporations are the most legally complex. Corporate law is a specialty for some law firms and involves many different legal activities. Even though corporate law varies from state to state, most of the terminology presented is used in most states. When you have satisfactorily completed the following exercises, you will be able to spell, pronounce, define, and transcribe correctly the terms that are introduced relating to the field of corporate law.

Part A | TERMINOLOGY AND DEFINITIONS

Directions: Study the terms, pronunciations, and definitions until you are thoroughly familiar with them. In order to complete this lesson successfully, you must understand the meaning and usage of all the legal terms presented. If you are using a shorthand system, write each legal term one time on your shorthand machine.

Legal Term	Pronunciation	Definition
1. legal entity	´lē-gəl ´en-ət-ē	Legal being or existence.
2. corporation	kȯr-pə-´rā-shən	An artificial being created by law.
3. articles of incorporation	´ärt-i-kəls əv in-kȯr-pə-´rā-shən	The instrument that provides for the organization of a corporation. (See Figure 29-1, pages 427-428.)
4. charter	´chärt-ər	The authority granted by a legislature that gives a corporation the right to exist. (See Figure 29-2, page 429.)
5. franchise	´fran-chīz	A special privilege that does not belong to the general public but is granted by the government to an individual or a corporation. A corporation is a franchise.
6. domestic corporation	də-´mes-tik kȯr-pə-´rā-shən	A corporation created by or organized under the laws of the state in which it is transacting business.
7. foreign corporation	´fȯr-ən kȯr-pə-´rā-shən	A corporation created by or under the laws of another state, government, or country other than the one in which it is transacting business.
8. de jure corporation	dē ´jùr-ē kȯr-pə-´rā-shən	A corporation that is created in total compliance with the laws of the state in which it is organized.
9. de facto corporation	di ´fak-tō kȯr-pə-´rā-shən	A corporation existing in fact and that, in good faith, has made an effort to comply with state law but has failed to meet one or more of the requirements of the law.

10. eleemosynary corporation	el-i-'mäs-ən-er-ē kȯr-pə-'rā-shən	A corporation organized for a charitable or benevolent purpose. In many states, an eleemosynary corporation is now referred to as a charitable or nonprofit or not-for-profit corporation.
11. subsidiary corporation	səb-'sid-ē-er-ē kȯr-pə-'rā-shən	A corporation that is under the control of another corporation that owns a majority of the shares.
12. board of directors	bōrd əv də-'rek-tərs	The group of persons who is responsible for governing a corporation.
13. chairperson	'cher-pərs-n	The presiding officer of the board of directors of a corporation.
14. president	'prez-əd-ənt	The chief officer of a corporation who implements the policies established by the board of directors.

FIGURE 29-1 Articles of Incorporation

MICHIGAN DEPARTMENT OF COMMERCE — CORPORATION AND SECURITIES BUREAU	
(FOR BUREAU USE ONLY)	**Date Received**
EFFECTIVE DATE	
CORPORATION IDENTIFICATION NUMBER	

ARTICLES OF INCORPORATION
For use by Domestic Profit Corporations
(Please read instructions and Paperwork Reduction Act notice on last page)

Pursuant to the provisions of Act 284, Public Acts of 1972, as amended, the undersigned corporation executes the following Articles:

Article I

The name of the corporations is:

COLLIER PLASTICS CORPORATION

Article II

The purpose or purposes for which the corporation is organized is to engage in any activity within the purposes for which corporations may be organized under the Business Corporation Act of Michigan.

Manufacturing of plastic products.

Article III

The total authorized capital stock is:

1. Common Shares _____ 100 _____ Par Value Per Share $ 1.00 _____

   Preferred Shares _____ -0- _____ Par Value Per Share $ _____

and/or shares without par value as follows:

2. Common Shares _____ Stated Value Per Share $ _____

   Preferred Shares _____ Stated Value Per Share $ _____

3. A statement of all or any of the relative rights, preferences and limitations of the shares of each class is as follows:
        None

FIGURE 29-1 Articles of Incorporation (continued)

Article IV

1. The address of the registered office is:

   9001 Okemos Road, Okemos
   (Street Address)   (City) , Michigan   48864 (ZIP Code)

2. The mailing address of the registered office if different than above:

   Same
   (P.O. Box)   (City) , Michigan   (ZIP Code)

3. The name of the resident agent at the registered office is:

Article V

The name(s) and address(es) of the incorporator(s) is (are) as follows:

Name	Residence or Business Address
John D. Mazzo	9001 Okemos Road, Okemos, MI 48864
Silvia P. Hatcher	9001 Okemos Road, Okemos, MI 48864
Alfred J. Jennings	9001 Okemos Road, Okemos, MI 48864
Teresa L. Canton	9001 Okemos Road, Okemos, MI 48864

Article VI   **(Optional. Delete if not applicable)**

When a compromise or arrangement or a plan of reorganization of this corporation is proposed between this corporation and it creditors or any class of them or between this corporation and it shareholders or any class of them, a court of equity jurisdiction within the state, on application of this corporation or of a creditor or shareholder thereof, or on application of a receiver appointed for the corporation, may order a meeting of the creditors or class of creditors or of the shareholders or class of shareholders to be affected by the proposed compromise or arrangement or reorganization, to be summoned in such manner as the court directs. If a majority in number representing 3/4 in value of the creditors or class of creditors, or of the shareholders or class of shareholders to be affected by the proposed compromise or arrangement or a reorganization, agree to a compromise or arrangement or a reorganization of this corporation as a consequence of the compromise or

FIGURE 29-2 A Charter

UNITED STATES OF AMERICA

The State of Michigan

Michigan Department of Commerce

Lansing Michigan

This is to Certify That Articles of Incorporation of

COLLIER PLASTICS CORPORATION

were duly filed in this office on the 19TH day of MARCH , 20 03 , in conformity with Act 284, Public Acts of 1972, as amended.

In testimony whereof, I have hereunto set my hand and affixed the Seal of the Department, in the City of Lansing, this 19TH day, of MARCH , 2003

Edith M. Craig Director

C & S—175

Self-Evaluation A | Terminology and Definition Recall

Directions: In the Answers column at the right of each statement, write the letter that represents the word or group of words that correctly completes the statement. After you have completed this self-evaluation, check your answers with the key on page 499. If you have any incorrect answers, review the definitions for those terms before going on with this lesson. Then unless otherwise directed, submit this self-evaluation to your instructor.

ANSWERS

1. A corporation created by or under the laws of a state, government, or country other than the one in which it is transacting business is a/an (a) eleemosynary corporation, (b) foreign corporation, (c) subsidiary corporation.

   1. _____

2. A corporation that is under the control of another corporation that owns a majority of the shares is a (a) foreign corporation, (b) domestic corporation, (c) subsidiary corporation.

   2. _____

3. A corporation organized for a charitable or benevolent purpose is a/an (a) subsidiary corporation, (b) de jure corporation, (c) eleemosynary corporation.

   3. _____

4. The group of persons who is responsible for governing a corporation is the (a) chairperson, (b) board of directors, (c) president.

   4. _____

5. The authority granted by a legislature that gives a corporation the right to exist is a/an (a) franchise, (b) charter, (c) articles of incorporation.

   5. _____

6. A corporation created by or organized under the laws of the state in which it is transacting business is a (a) de facto corporation, (b) de jure corporation, (c) domestic corporation.

   6. _____

7. A corporation that is organized in total compliance with the laws of the state in which it is organized is a/an (a) de facto corporation, (b) eleemosynary corporation, (c) de jure corporation.

   7. _____

8. The presiding officer of the board of directors of a corporation is the (a) president, (b) chairperson, (c) franchise.

   8. _____

9. A special privilege that does not belong to the general public but is granted by the government to an individual or a corporation is a (a) franchise, (b) charter, (c) legal entity.

   9. _____

10. An artificial being created by law is a (a) corporation, (b) legal entity, (c) franchise.

    10. _____

11. A legal being or existence is referred to as a (a) franchise, (b) charter, (c) legal entity.

    11. _____

12. A corporation that exists in fact and that has made an effort to comply with state law but has failed to meet one or more of the requirements of the law is a (a) de jure corporation, (b) de facto corporation, (c) foreign corporation.

    12. _____

13. The instrument that provides for the organization of a corporation is referred to as the (a) articles of incorporation, (b) franchise, (c) charter.

    13. _____

14. The chief officer of a corporation who implements the policies established by the board of directors is the (a) president, (b) chairperson, (c) legal entity.

    14. _____

KEYING LEGAL TERMS

Directions: Unless otherwise instructed, use 1-inch margins and double spacing. Correct all errors. Follow one of the procedures below.

WORDS

Keyboarding Procedure
On your computer, key the following words at least two times, concentrating on the correct spelling and pronunciation.

Machine Shorthand Procedure
On your computer, key the following words once, concentrating on the correct spelling and pronunciation. Then write each word one time on your shorthand machine. Transcribe from your shorthand notes one time on your computer, or, if you are using computer-aided transcription (CAT), proofread and edit your transcript.

legal entity	corporation	articles of incorporation
charter	franchise	domestic corporation
foreign corporation	de jure corporation	de facto corporation
eleemosynary corporation	subsidiary corporation	board of directors
chairperson	president	

SENTENCES

Keyboarding Procedure
Key each of the following sentences one time on your computer. Concentrate on the correct spelling and pronunciation of each underlined legal term.

Machine Shorthand Procedure
Write the following sentences one time on your shorthand machine. Transcribe from your shorthand notes one time on your computer, or, if you are using computer-aided transcription (CAT), proofread and edit your transcript.

These sentences will be used for practice dictation on the Transcription CD.

A <u>legal entity</u> refers to a legal being or existence. A <u>corporation</u> is an artificial being created by law. The instrument that provides for the organization of a corporation is called <u>articles of incorporation</u>. A <u>charter</u> is the authority granted by a legislature that gives a corporation the right to exist.

A special privilege that does not belong to the general public but is granted by the government to an individual or a corporation is a <u>franchise</u>. A corporation is a franchise.

A <u>domestic corporation</u> is a corporation created by the laws of the state in which it is transacting business; whereas a <u>foreign corporation</u> is a corporation created by the laws of another state, government, or country other than the one in which it is transacting business.

A corporation that is in total compliance with the laws of the state in which it is organized is a <u>de jure corporation</u>. A corporation that exists in fact and has made a good faith effort to comply with the state laws but has failed to meet one or more of the requirements of the law is called a <u>de facto corporation</u>. An <u>eleemosynary corporation</u> is a corporation that organized for a charitable or benevolent purpose. In many states, an eleemosynary corporation is now referred to as a charitable or nonprofit corporation. A <u>subsidiary corporation</u> is one that is under the control of another corporation that owns a majority of the shares.

A private corporation is governed by a <u>board of directors</u>. The presiding officer of the board of directors of a corporation is the <u>chairperson</u>. The <u>president</u> is the chief officer of a corporation who implements the policies established by the board of directors.

TRANSCRIBING FROM DICTATION

Directions: This dictation emphasizes and reinforces the legal terms and definitions you have studied. Listen carefully to the pronunciation of each of the legal terms. Unless otherwise directed, use 1-inch margins and double spacing. Correct all errors. Follow one of the procedures below.

Keyboarding Procedure
Using the Transcription CD, Lesson 29, Part A, transcribe the dictation directly at your computer.

Machine Shorthand Procedure
Using the Transcription CD, Lesson 29, Part A, take the dictation on your shorthand machine and then transcribe your notes on your computer, or, if you are using computer-aided transcription (CAT), proofread and edit your transcript.

When you have finished transcribing or proofreading and editing Part A of the practice dictation, check your transcript with the printed copy. If you made any mistakes in the transcription, you should review and practice those words several times before going on to Part B.

Part B | TERMINOLOGY AND DEFINITIONS

Directions: Study the terms, pronunciations, and definitions until you are thoroughly familiar with them. In order to complete this lesson successfully, you must understand the meaning and usage of all the legal terms presented. If you are using a shorthand system, write each legal term one time on your shorthand machine.

Legal Term	Pronunciation	Definition
1. share	sher	A specific part or portion of the capital of a company or corporation. (See Figure 29-3, page 436.)
2. stock	stäk	Shares of ownership in a corporation.
3. common stock	′käm-ən stäk	The ordinary stock of a corporation that has no preference or special rights.
4. preferred stock	pri-′ferd stäk	Stock that has priority as to dividends over the common stock of the corporation.
5. par value	pär ′val-yü	Face value of all shares of stock in a particular class.
6. book value	bůk ′val-yü	The net worth of a share of stock.
7. shareholder (stockholder)	′sher-hōl-dər ′stäk-hōl-dər	A person who owns shares of stock in a corporation. (See Figure 29-3, page 436.)
8. stock certificate	stäk sər-′tif-i-kət	A written document stating that the named person owns a certain number of shares of stock in a corporation. (See Figure 29-3, page 436.)
9. promoters	prə-′mōt-ərs	The persons who organize a corporation.
10. transfer agent	′trans-fər ′ā-jənt	A bank or other institution that handles the transfer of stock for a corporation.

11. treasury stock	′trezh-rē stäk	Stock that belongs to a corporation.
12. watered stock	′wȯt-ərd stäk	Stock that is issued as paid-up stock, but is not, and that is issued below par value.

FIGURE 29-3 A Stock Certificate

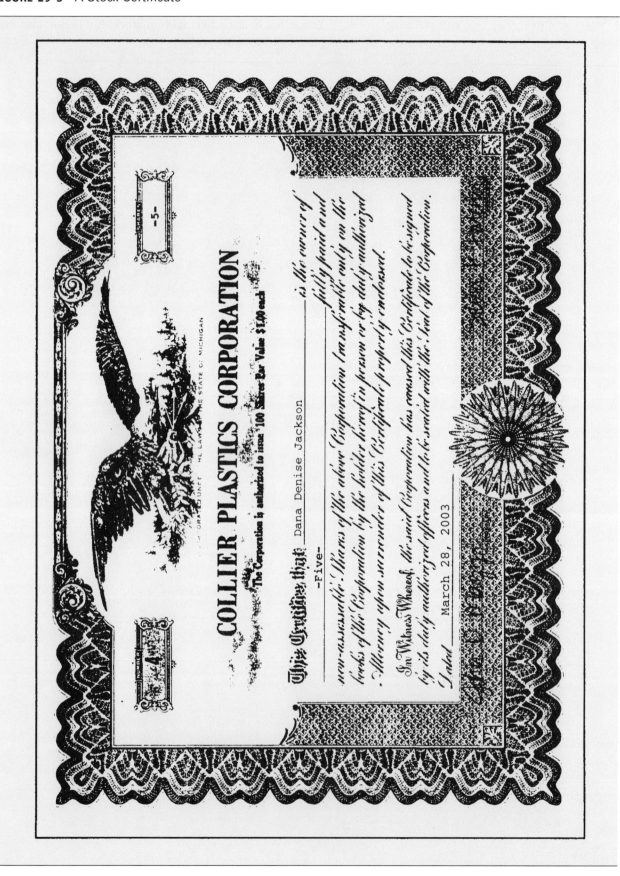

Self-Evaluation B | **Terminology and Definition Recall**

Directions: In the Answers column, write the legal term that is most representative of the corresponding statement. After you have completed this self-evaluation, check your answers with the key on page 499. If you have any incorrect answers, review the definitions for those terms before going on with this lesson. Then unless otherwise directed, submit this self-evaluation to your instructor.

ANSWERS

1. The face value of all shares of stock in a particular class is the _____.   1. _____

2. The ordinary stock of a corporation that has no preference or special rights is _____.   2. _____

3. A specific part or portion of the capital of a company or corporation is called a/an _____.   3. _____

4. Stock that belongs to a corporation is _____.   4. _____

5. The persons who organize a corporation are known as the _____.   5. _____

6. Shares of ownership in a corporation are referred to as _____.   6. _____

7. Stock that has priority as to dividends over other stock of the corporation is _____.   7. _____

8. A written document stating or acknowledging that the named person is owner of a designated number of shares of stock in a corporation is a/an _____.   8. _____

9. A bank or other institution that handles the transfer of stock for a corporation is a/an _____.   9. _____

10. The net worth of a share of stock is the _____.   10. _____

11. A person who owns shares of stock in a corporation is a/an _____.   11. _____

12. Stock that is issued as paid-up stock, but is not, and that is issued below par value is _____.   12. _____

KEYING LEGAL TERMS

Directions: Unless otherwise instructed, use 1-inch margins and double spacing. Correct all errors. Follow one of the procedures below.

WORDS

Keyboarding Procedure
On your computer, key the following words at least two times, concentrating on the correct spelling and pronunciation.

Machine Shorthand Procedure
On your computer, key the following words once, concentrating on the correct spelling and pronunciation. Then write each word one time on your shorthand machine. Transcribe your shorthand notes one time on your computer, or, if you are using computer-aided transcription (CAT), proofread and edit your transcript.

share	**stock**	**common stock**
preferred stock	**par value**	**book value**
shareholder (stockholder)	**stock certificate**	**promoters**
transfer agent	**treasury stock**	**watered stock**

SENTENCES

Keyboarding Procedure
Key each of the following sentences one time on your computer. Concentrate on the correct spelling and pronunciation of each underlined legal term.

Machine Shorthand Procedure
Write the following sentences one time on your shorthand machine. Transcribe from your shorthand notes one time on your computer, or, if you are using computer-aided transcription (CAT), proofread and edit your transcript.

These sentences will be used for practice dictation on the Transcription CD.

A <u>share</u> is a specific part or portion of the capital of a company or corporation. Shares of ownership in a corporation are called <u>stock</u>.

The ordinary stock of a corporation that has no preference or special rights is known as <u>common stock</u>. <u>Preferred stock</u> is a stock that has priority as to dividends over the common stock of the corporation.

<u>Par value</u> is the face value of all shares of stock in a particular class. Par value is the value of the stock listed on the stock certificate regardless of the amount actually paid for the stock. The net worth of a share of stock is the <u>book value</u>. The book value is determined by deducting the liabilities from the assets.

One who owns shares of stock in a corporation is called a <u>shareholder</u>, or <u>stockholder</u>. A <u>stock certificate</u> is a written document stating that the named person owns a certain number of shares of stock in a corporation.

<u>Promoters</u> are persons who organize a corporation. A <u>transfer agent</u> is a bank or other institution that handles the transfer of stock for a corporation.

Stock that is owned by a corporation is referred to as <u>treasury stock</u>. Stock that is issued by a corporation as fully paid-up stock when in fact it is not and is sold below par value is called <u>watered stock</u>.

TRANSCRIBING FROM DICTATION

Directions: This dictation emphasizes and reinforces the legal terms and definitions you have studied. Listen carefully to the pronunciation of each of the legal terms. Unless otherwise directed, use 1-inch margins and double spacing. Correct all errors. Follow one of the procedures below.

Keyboarding Procedure

Using the Transcription CD, Lesson 29, Part B, transcribe the dictation directly at your computer.

Machine Shorthand Procedure

Using the Transcription CD, Lesson 29, Part B, take the dictation on your shorthand machine and then transcribe your notes on your computer, or, if you are using computer-aided transcription (CAT), proofread and edit your transcript.

When you have finished transcribing or proofreading and editing Part B of the practice dictation, check your transcript with the printed copy. If you made any mistakes in the transcription, you should review and practice those words several times before going on to Lesson 30.

CHECKLIST

I have completed the following for Lesson 29:

	Part A, Date	Part B, Date	Submitted to Instructor Yes	No
Terminology and Definitions	_____	_____	_____	_____
Self-Evaluation	_____	_____	_____	_____
* Keying Legal Terms	_____	_____	_____	_____
Words	_____	_____	_____	_____
Sentences	_____	_____	_____	_____
* Transcribing from Dictation	_____	_____	_____	_____

When you have successfully completed all the exercises in this lesson and submitted to your instructor those requested, you are ready to proceed with Lesson 30.

* *If you are using machine shorthand, submit to your instructor your notes along with your transcript.*

Lesson
30

Corporations

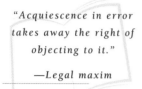

"Acquiescence in error takes away the right of objecting to it."

—Legal maxim

This lesson continues the study of some of the terms relating to corporate law. A knowledge of these terms will assist your understanding of corporations and the laws that govern them. You will be able to spell, define, pronounce, and transcribe correctly the legal terms presented in the following exercises when you have satisfactorily completed the lesson.

Part A | TERMINOLOGY AND DEFINITIONS

Directions: Study the terms, pronunciations, and definitions until you are thoroughly familiar with them. In order to complete this lesson successfully, you must understand the meaning and usage of all the legal terms presented. If you are using a shorthand system, write each legal term one time on your shorthand machine.

Legal Term	Pronunciation	Definition
1. ultra vires	ˈəl-trə ˈvī-rēz	Latin. Acts that are not within the powers of a corporation as defined in its charter.
2. blue-sky laws	ˈblü-ˈskī lȯs	Laws to protect persons from investing in fraudulent companies.
3. antitrust acts	ant-i-ˈtrəst akts	Laws to prevent monopolies. A corporation cannot own or control so much of a market as to eliminate competition.
4. merger	ˈmər-jər	The joining of one corporation with another that continues in existence as one corporation.
5. bylaws	ˈbī-lȯs	The rules or regulations by which a corporation is managed. (See Figure 30-1, pages 443-444.)
6. minutes	ˈmin-əts	A written record of the proceedings that took place at a board of directors' or shareholders' meeting.
7. quorum	ˈkwȯr-əm	A majority. The number of members required to be present at a meeting for business to be transacted.
8. proxy	ˈpräk-sē	A person who is designated to represent or act for another in a meeting. Also refers to the instrument that gives the authority.
9. annual report	ˈan-yəl ri-ˈpȯrt	A report to the shareholders of a corporation at the end of a fiscal year that presents financial statements and operational information for the corporation for the preceding year.

10. goodwill	´gu̇d-´wil	The favorable reputation of an established business with its customers.
11. dissolution	dis-ə-´lü-shən	The termination of the legal existence of a corporation.
12. liquidation	lik-wə-´dā-shən	The distribution of the assets of a business to settle accounts with creditors.

FIGURE 30-1 Bylaws

BYLAWS OF

COLLIER PLASTICS CORPORATION

Incorporated under the Laws of the State of Michigan

Registered office address: 9001 Okemos Road, Okemos, MI 48864

Annual meeting time: Month December Day 2nd Monday Hour 10:00 a.m.

Fiscal year begins: Month November Day 1st

ARTICLE I - OFFICES

The address of the registered office of the corporation in Michigan is stated at the beginning of these bylaws. The corporation may have other offices or branches as determined by the board of directors.

ARTICLE II - FISCAL YEAR

The date on which the fiscal year of the corporation begins each year is stated at the beginning of these bylaws.

ARTICLE III - MEETINGS OF SHAREHOLDERS

1. PLACE

Shareholders' meetings shall be held at the registered office of the corporation or at another location determined by the board of directors and stated in the notice of the meeting.

2. TIME

The time of the annual meeting of shareholders is stated at the beginning of these bylaws. If this date falls on a legal holiday then the annual meeting shall be held on the next business day.

3. PURPOSE

The purpose of the annual meeting shall be to elect a board of directors and transact other business as may come before the meeting.

4. SPECIAL MEETINGS

Special meetings of the shareholders may be called by the president, two directors or by the holders of at least 10% of the shares entitled to vote at a meeting. A special meeting may be called anytime for any business purpose, unless otherwise prohibited by statute and shall be held at the registered office of the corporation.

5. NOTICE

Written notice stating the place, day and time of the meeting and, in case of a special meeting, the purpose or purposes for which the meeting is called shall be delivered not less than 10 nor more than 60 days before the date of the meeting. If mailed, such notice shall be considered to be delivered when deposited in the United States Postal Service, addressed to the shareholder at his/her address as it appears on the share transfer books of the corporation, with the correct amount of postage on it.

6. FIXING RECORD DATE

For the purpose of determining the shareholders entitled to notice of or to vote at any meeting of shareholders or for any purpose of any other action, the board of directors shall fix in advance a date as a record date. The date shall not be more than 60 nor less than 10 days before the meeting, nor more than 60 days prior to any other action.

FIGURE 30-1 Bylaws (continued)

7.   QUORUM

    At any meeting of shareholders a majority of the outstanding shares of the corporation entitled to vote, represented in person or by proxy, shall constitute a quorum. The shareholders present in person or by proxy at such meeting may continue to do business until adjournment even if this means the withdrawal of enough shareholders to leave less than a quorum. If a quorum is not present, the shareholders present in person or by proxy may adjourn to a date they agree upon.

8.   PROXIES

    At all meetings of shareholders, a shareholder may vote by proxy executed in writing by the shareholder or his/her duly authorized attorney in fact. A proxy is not valid after the expiration of 3 years from its date unless otherwise provided in the proxy. A proxy is not invalidated by the death or incompetency of the shareholder, unless, before the authority is exercised, written notice of such an adjudication is received by the corporate office responsible for maintaining the list of shareholders.

9.   VOTING

    Each outstanding share is entitled to 1 vote on each matter submitted to a vote. A vote may be cast either orally or in writing in

Self-Evaluation A | Terminology and Definition Recall

Directions: In the Answers column, write the letter from Column 1 that represents the word or phrase that best match-es each item in Column 2. After you have completed this self-evaluation, check your answers with the key on page 499. If you have any incorrect answers, review the definitions for those terms before going on with this lesson. Then unless otherwise directed, submit this self-evaluation to your instructor.

COLUMN 1	COLUMN 2	ANSWERS
a. annual report	1. A written record of the proceedings that took place at a board of directors' or shareholders' meeting.	1. _____
b. antitrust acts		
c. blue-sky laws	2. A person who is designated to represent or act for anoth-er in a meeting or the instrument that gives a person authority to act for another in a meeting.	2. _____
d. bylaws		
e. charter	3. The termination of the legal existence of a corporation.	3. _____
f. dissolution	4. A report to the shareholders of a corporation at the end of a fiscal year that presents financial statements and opera-tional information for the corporation for the preceding year.	4. _____
g. goodwill		
h. liquidation		
i. merger	5. The joining of one corporation with another that contin-ues in existence as one corporation.	5. _____
j. minutes	6. The favorable reputation of an established business with its customers.	6. _____
k. proxy		
l. quorum	7. The rules or regulations by which a corporation is managed.	7. _____
m. ultra vires	8. The Latin term for acts that are not within the powers of a corporation as defined in its charter.	8. _____
	9. Laws that are for the purpose of preventing monopolies.	9. _____
	10. The distribution of the assets of a business to settle accounts with creditors.	10. _____
	11. A majority or the number of members required to be pres-ent at a meeting for business to be transacted.	11. _____
	12. Laws that are designed to protect persons from investing in fraudulent companies.	12. _____

KEYING LEGAL TERMS

Directions: Unless otherwise instructed, use 1-inch margins and double spacing. Correct all errors. Follow one of the procedures below.

WORDS

Keyboarding Procedure
On your computer, key the following words at least two times, concentrating on the correct spelling and pronunciation.

Machine Shorthand Procedure
On your computer, key the following words once, concentrating on the correct spelling and pronunciation. Then write each word one time on your shorthand machine. Transcribe from your shorthand notes one time on your computer, or, if you are using computer-aided transcription (CAT), proofread and edit your transcript.

ultra vires	blue-sky laws	antitrust acts
merger	bylaws	minutes
quorum	proxy	annual report
goodwill	dissolution	liquidation

SENTENCES

Keyboarding Procedure
Key each of the following sentences one time on your computer. Concentrate on the correct spelling and pronunciation of each underlined legal term.

Machine Shorthand Procedure
Write the following sentences one time on your shorthand machine. Transcribe from your shorthand notes one time on your computer, or, if you are using computer-aided transcription (CAT), proofread and edit your transcript.

These sentences will be used for practice dictation on the Transcription CD.

Ultra vires is a Latin term referring to acts that are not within the powers of a corporation as defined in its charter. Blue-sky laws are designed to protect persons from investing in fraudulent companies. Antitrust acts are laws to prevent monopolies. The antitrust acts prevent a corporation from controlling so much of a market as to eliminate competition. The joining of two or more corporations into one corporation is a merger.

The rules and regulations that govern the operations of a corporation are the bylaws. The written record of the proceedings that took place at a board of directors' or shareholders' meeting is the minutes. A quorum is a majority or the number of members required to be present at a meeting for business to be transacted. A proxy is a person who is designated to represent or act for another in a meeting. A proxy is also the instrument that gives such authority.

A corporation makes an annual report to its shareholders at the end of a fiscal year that presents financial statements and operational information for the corporation for the preceding year.

Goodwill refers to the favorable reputation of an established business with its customers. The dissolution of a corporation is the termination of its legal existence. Liquidation is the distribution of the assets of a business to settle accounts with creditors.

TRANSCRIBING FROM DICTATION

Directions: This dictation emphasizes and reinforces the legal terms and definitions you have studied. Listen carefully to the pronunciation of each of the legal terms. Unless otherwise directed, use 1-inch margins and double spacing. Correct all errors. Follow one of the procedures below.

Keyboarding Procedure

Using the Transcription CD, Lesson 30, Part A, transcribe the dictation directly at your computer.

Machine Shorthand Procedure

Using the Transcription CD, Lesson 30, Part A, take the dictation on your shorthand machine and then transcribe your notes on your computer, or, if you are using computer-aided transcription (CAT), proofread and edit your transcript.

When you have finished transcribing or proofreading and editing Part A of the practice dictation, check your transcript with the printed copy. If you made any mistakes in the transcription, you should review and practice those words several times before going on to Part B.

Part B | TERMINOLOGY AND DEFINITIONS

Directions: Study the terms, pronunciations, and definitions until you are thoroughly familiar with them. In order to complete this lesson successfully, you must understand the meaning and usage of all the legal terms presented. If you are using a shorthand system, write each legal term one time on your shorthand machine.

Legal Term	Pronunciation	Definition
1. dividend	′div-ə-dend	A portion of the profits of a corporation that is to be divided among the shareholders.
2. earnings per share	′ər-niŋz pər sher	The average earnings based on the number of shares of stock issued by the corporation.
3. working capital	wərk-iŋ ′kap-ət-l	Cash or other assets that are readily available for the use of a corporation.
4. sinking fund	′siŋk-iŋ fənd	A sum of money set aside by a corporation to pay off a debt.
5. financial reports	fə-′nan-chəl ri-′pōrts	Statements of the financial condition of a company or corporation that include the balance sheet, the income statement, the statement of retained earnings, and other statements relating to the financial condition of a corporation. (See Figures 30-2, 30-3, and 30-4, pages 450 and 451.)
6. balance sheet	′bal-ens shēt	A statement that summarizes the net worth of a business at the end of a fiscal period and shows the assets and liabilities of the company. (See Figure 30-2, page 450.)
7. income statement	′in-kəm ′stāt-mənt	A statement showing the income of the business, the cost of goods sold, the expenses, and the net income that resulted from the operation of the business for a specified fiscal period.
8. retained earnings	ri-′tānd ′ər-niŋz	That portion of the earnings that a company keeps for operations or additional capital investments.
9. net worth	net wərth	The worth of a business after deducting the liabilities from the assets.

10. auditor	′öd-ət-ər	A person who examines the financial accounts and statements of a corporation or company and verifies their accuracy.
11. liability	lī-ə-′bil-ət-ē	A debt or an obligation of a business or company. That which is owed.
12. debenture	di-′ben-chər	An instrument that acknowledges a debt of a corporation.

FIGURE 30-2 Financial Reports (Balance Sheet)

FINANCIAL REPORTS
CONSOLIDATED BALANCE SHEET
December 31, 2002 and 2003

ASSETS

	2002	2003
	(In thousands of dollars)	
Current assets:		
Cash and cash equivalents	$ 7,984	$ 6,767
Receivables—		
Joint operations, net of allowance for doubtful accounts of $1,009,000 and $567,000............................	9,188	9,449
Oil and gas sales....................................	12,782	9,085
Notes	891	1,741
Windfall profit tax refund	3,771	—
Equity in net current assets of, and advances to, managed partnerships	1,318	—
Tubular inventories, at lower of cost or market	838	1,324
Prepaid expenses and other	1,153	507
Total current assets	37,925	28,873

FIGURE 30-3 Financial Reports (Statement of Changes in Financial Position)

FINANCIAL REPORTS
CONSOLIDATED STATEMENT OF CHANGES IN FINANCIAL POSITION
For the years ended December 31, 2003, 2002, 2001
(In thousands of dollars)

	2003	2002	2001
Source of funds:			
Net income	$ 4,218	$ 5,165	$ 9,653
Items not affecting working capital in the current year:			
Depreciation, depletion and amortization	20,309	16,341	20,581
Deferred income taxes	2,802	3,599	9,547
Litigation settlement	1,537	—	—
Other..	546	1,847	526
Funds provided by operations	29,412	26,952	40,307
Proceeds from sales of oil and gas properties	3,011	8,156	5,825
Benefit from utilization of tax loss of acquired entity	1,649	—	—
Long-term borrowings, including capital lease of geothermal equipment....................................	19,682	3,018	11,000
Common stock issued in merger with Integrated Energy Inc., net of direct acquisition costs......................	13,006	—	—
Other, net	150	1,207	1,461
Total source of funds	66,910	39,333	58,593

FIGURE 30-4 Financial Reports (Statement of Operations)

FINANCIAL REPORTS
CONSOLIDATED STATEMENT OF OPERATIONS
For the years ended December 31, 2003, 2002, 2001
(In thousands of dollars, except per share amounts)

	2003	2002	2001
Revenues:			
Oil and gas	$56,811	$60,374	$77,377
Other, primarily interest income	3,619	699	2,665
	60,430	61,073	80,042
Costs and expenses:			
Oil and gas production	16,546	17,999	19,099
Windfall profit tax refund	(5,517)	—	—
General and administrative	13,778	12,112	13,710
Depreciation, depletion and amortization	20,309	16,341	20,581
Interest and other	6,197	5,627	7,252
	51,313	52,079	60,642
Income before income taxes	9,117	8,994	19,400
Provision for income taxes	4,899	3,829	9,747
Net income	4,218	5,165	9,653

Self-Evaluation B | Terminology and Definition Recall

Directions: In the Answers column, write the legal term that is most representative of the corresponding statement. After you have completed this self-evaluation, check your answers with the key on page 499. If you have any incorrect answers, review the definitions for those terms before going on with this lesson. Then unless otherwise directed, submit this self-evaluation to your instructor.

ANSWERS

1. A person who examines the financial accounts and statements of a corporation or company and verifies their accuracy is a/an _____.

   1. _____

2. Cash or other assets that are readily available for the use of a corporation are referred to as _____.

   2. _____

3. The worth of a business after deducting the liabilities from the assets is the _____.

   3. _____

4. A debt or an obligation of a business or company or that which is owed is a/an _____.

   4. _____

5. A portion of the profits of a corporation that is to be divided among the shareholders is referred to as a/an _____.

   5. _____

6. A sum of money set aside by a corporation to pay off a debt is a/an _____.

   6. _____

7. A statement that summarizes the net worth of a business at the end of a fiscal period and shows the assets and liabilities of the company is a/an _____.

   7. _____

8. An instrument that acknowledges a debt of a corporation is a/an _____.

   8. _____

9. A statement showing the income of the business, the cost of goods sold, the expenses, and the net income that resulted from the operation of the business for a specified fiscal period is a/an _____.

   9. _____

10. Statements of the financial condition of a company or corporation are referred to as _____.

    10. _____

11. That portion of the earnings that a company keeps for operations or additional capital investments is _____.

    11. _____

12. The average earnings of a corporation based on the number of shares of stock issued by the corporation are _____.

    12. _____

KEYING LEGAL TERMS

Directions: Unless otherwise instructed, use 1-inch margins and double spacing. Correct all errors. Follow one of the procedures below.

WORDS

Keyboarding Procedure
On your computer, key the following words at least two times, concentrating on the correct spelling and pronunciation.

Machine Shorthand Procedure
On your computer, key the following words once, concentrating on the correct spelling and pronunciation. Then write each word one time on your shorthand machine. Transcribe from your shorthand notes one time on your computer, or, if you are using computer-aided transcription (CAT), proofread and edit your transcript.

dividend	earnings per share	working capital
sinking fund	financial reports	balance sheet
income statement	retained earnings	net worth
auditor	liability	debenture

SENTENCES

Keyboarding Procedure
Key each of the following sentences one time on your computer. Concentrate on the correct spelling and pronunciation of each underlined legal term.

Machine Shorthand Procedure
Write the following sentences one time on your shorthand machine. Transcribe from your shorthand notes one time on your computer, or, if you are using computer-aided transcription (CAT), proofread and edit your transcript.

These sentences will be used for practice dictation on the Transcription CD.

A <u>dividend</u> is a portion of the profits of a corporation that is to be divided among the shareholders. The average earnings of a corporation based on the number of shares of stock issued by the corporation are referred to as <u>earnings per share</u>. <u>Working capital</u> is cash and other assets that a corporation has readily available for use. A <u>sinking fund</u> is a sum of money set aside by a corporation to pay off a debt.

<u>Financial reports</u> consist of statements of the financial condition of a company or corporation. Financial reports include the <u>balance sheet</u>, the <u>income statement</u>, the statement of <u>retained earnings</u>, and other statements relating to the financial condition of a corporation. A balance sheet summarizes the <u>net worth</u> of a business at the end of a fiscal period and shows the assets and liabilities of the company. Net worth is the worth of a business after deducting the liabilities from the assets. An income statement shows the income of the business, the cost of goods sold, the expenses, and the net income that resulted from the operation of the business for a specified period of time. Retained earnings is that portion of the earnings that the company keeps for operations or additional capital investments.

A person who examines the financial accounts and financial statements of a corporation or company and verifies their accuracy is an <u>auditor</u>. A <u>liability</u> is a debt or an obligation of a business or company. A <u>debenture</u> is an instrument that acknowledges a debt of a corporation.

TRANSCRIBING FROM DICTATION

Directions: This dictation emphasizes and reinforces the legal terms and definitions you have studied. Listen carefully to the pronunciation of each of the legal terms. Unless otherwise directed, use 1-inch margins and double spacing. Correct all errors. Follow one of the procedures below.

Keyboarding Procedure

Using the Transcription CD, Lesson 30, Part B, transcribe the dictation directly at your computer.

Machine Shorthand Procedure

Using the Transcription CD, Lesson 30, Part B, take the dictation on your shorthand machine and then transcribe from your notes on your computer, or, if you are using computer-aided transcription (CAT), proofread and edit your transcript.

When you have finished transcribing or proofreading and editing Part B of the practice dictation, check your transcript with the printed copy. If you made any mistakes in the transcription, you should review and practice those words several times before going on to Evaluation 15.

CHECKLIST
I have completed the following for Lesson 30:

	Part A, Date	Part B, Date	Submitted to Instructor	
			Yes	No
Terminology and Definitions	_____	_____	_____	_____
Self-Evaluation	_____	_____	_____	_____
* Keying Legal Terms	_____	_____	_____	_____
Words	_____	_____	_____	_____
Sentences	_____	_____	_____	_____
* Transcribing from Dictation	_____	_____	_____	_____

When you have successfully completed all the exercises in this lesson and submitted to your instructor those requested, you are ready to proceed with Evaluation 15.

* If you are using machine shorthand, submit to your instructor your notes along with your transcript.

Evaluation No. 15 | SECTION A

Directions: This dictation/transcription evaluation will test your spelling and transcription abilities on the legal terms that you studied in the two preceding lessons. Tab once for a paragraph indention, and use 1-inch margins and double spacing unless otherwise instructed. Correct all errors. Follow one of the procedures below.

Keyboarding Procedure

Using the Transcription CD for Evaluation 15, transcribe the dictation directly at your computer.

Machine Shorthand Procedure

Using the Transcription CD for Evaluation 15, take the dictation on your shorthand machine and then transcribe your notes on your computer, or, if you are using computer-aided transcription (CAT), proofread and edit your transcript. **Sections B and C are available from your instructor.**

Lesson
31

Additional Legal Terms—General and Real Property

"Extreme law is the greatest injury; strict law is great punishment."

—Legal maxim

This lesson consists of additional general legal terms and terms relating to real property that were not presented in earlier lessons. When you complete these exercises, you should have knowledge and an understanding of more general legal terms and terms that are used in reference to real property.

Part A | TERMINOLOGY AND DEFINITIONS

Directions: Study the terms, pronunciations, and definitions until you are thoroughly familiar with them. In order to complete this lesson successfully, you must understand the meaning and usage of all the legal terms presented. If you are using a shorthand system, write each legal term one time on your shorthand machine.

Legal Term	Pronunciation	Definition
1. clerk of the court	klərk əv thə kōrt	An officer of the court whose duties include issuing the process or docket of the court, filing of court documents, issuing summonses, and keeping the seal of the court and records of court proceedings.
2. docket	′däk-ət	The schedule of cases to be tried by a court. When a case is filed, the clerk of the court assigns a number to the case which is called the docket, file, or case number.
3. joinder	′join-dər	The joining or uniting with others in a litigation. For example, a new party may be brought in to join with the plaintiff or the defendant in a lawsuit. Two or more matters may also be combined in the same suit.
4. cross-complaint	krȯs kəm-′plānt	A complaint brought by a defendant against a co-defendant. For example, if you and your roommate are sued by your landlord for damages and you feel that your roommate was responsible, then you may file a cross-complaint against your roommate.
5. certificate of service	sər-′tif-i-kət əv ′sər-vəs	A statement that avers that the opposing party has been given a copy of a designated document. Also referred to as proof of service. (See Figure 31-1, page 461.)
6. alias summons	′ā-lē-əs ′səm-ənz	When the first summons is returned because it could not be served due to a defect or manner of service, a second summons is issued with the defect, such as an incorrect address, corrected.

7.	pluries summons	ˈplu̇r-ēz ˈsəm-ənz	A third and subsequent summonses issued when the first two summonses have not been effective.
8.	disclosure statement	dis-ˈklō-zhər ˈstāt-mənt	A statement that makes known or reveals information. For example, a party who owes money to another party may be forced to reveal to the court the location of all of his or her assets. In real estate law, a seller may be required to provide a statement to the buyer which reveals the condition of the property. Also, the Truth in Lending Act requires a mortgagee to issue a disclosure statement to the mortgagor that states the annual percentage rate of the mortgage (APR).
9.	certificate of readiness	sər-ˈtif-i-kat əv ˈred-ē-nəs	A document filed with the court in some states that specifies that all the parties are ready for trial.
10.	discovery	dis-ˈkəv-rē	The gathering of information about a case prior to trial. Interrogatories and depositions are part of the discovery process. Also, attorneys may be required to provide any relevant items to the opposing party.
11.	proffer	ˈpräf-ər	To offer or propose. An avowal or offer of proof that is usually made out of the presence of the jury which may have an effect on an appeal.
12.	sidebar	ˈsīd-bär	A conference held in the courtroom between the judge and counsel out of the hearing of the jury.
13.	realtime	ˈrēl-tīm	A computer-aided transcript produced instantaneously as the court reporter records the proceedings. A realtime transcript is not edited or certified but is used by the judge and attorneys as reference notes for the proceedings.
14.	undue influence	ən-ˈdü ˈin-flü-əns	Improperly putting pressure on a person so as to affect that person's free will, acts, or decisions.
15.	chose in possession	ˈshōz in pə-ˈzesh-ən	Personal property of which one has possession.
16.	perfect	pər-ˈfekt	To make complete, without defect, or enforceable. For example, when a document such as a deed is recorded, it is said to become enforceable or perfect.

FIGURE 31-1 A Certificate of Service

<u>CERTIFICATE OF SERVICE</u>

I HEREBY CERTIFY that a true and correct copy of the
foregoing Motion for Judgment and all supporting Affidavits were
duly furnished to Randall Corbett as the Guardian Ad Litem,
Administrator Ad Litem and Attorney Ad Litem of Defendants Craig
R. Stevens and Conrad S. Albany, at the Corbett Building, Suite
1105, Pensacola, Florida 32501 by hand delivery and to Defendant
James R. Scott, a/k/a Jim R. Scott, a/k/a Jimmy Scott at 6871
Admiral Road, Pensacola, Florida 32506, by U.S. Mail on this
25th day of November, 2003.

Evan M. Fitzgerald
EVAN M. FITZGERALD of
FITZGERALD & ASSOCIATES
Second Floor, Vlahakis Tower
Post Office Box 7003
Pensacola, Florida 32598-5321
(904) 555-5555
Attorneys for Plaintiffs
Florida Bar No.: 9984106

Self–Evaluation A | Terminology and Definition Recall

Directions: In the Answers column, write the legal term that is most representative of the corresponding statement. After you have completed this self-evaluation, check your answers with the key on page 500. If you have any incorrect answers, review the definitions for those terms before going on with this lesson. Then unless otherwise directed, submit this self-evaluation to your instructor.

ANSWERS

1. An officer of the court whose duties include issuing the process or docket of the court, filing of court documents, issuing summonses, and keeping the seal of the court and records of court proceedings is the _____.

1. _____

2. A schedule of cases to be tried by a court is a/an _____.

2. _____

3. The joining or uniting with others in a litigation is referred to as _____.

3. _____

4. A third and subsequent summonses that are issued when the first two have not been effective is called a/an _____.

4. _____

5. A statement that makes known or reveals information is a/an _____.

5. _____

6. A conference held in the courtroom between the judge and counsel out of the hearing of the jury is referred to as a/an _____.

6. _____

7. A complaint brought by a defendant against a co-defendant is a/an _____.

7. _____

8. A statement that avers that the opposing party has been given a copy of a designated document is a/an _____.

8. _____

9. The second summons that is issued when the first summons cannot be delivered is called a/an _____.

9. _____

10. To offer or propose is called _____.

10. _____

11. A computer-aided transcript produced instantaneously as the court reporter records the proceedings is referred to as _____.

11. _____

12. The gathering of information about a case prior to trial is called _____.

12. _____

13. To make complete, without defect, or enforceable is referred to as to _____.

13. _____

14. Improperly putting pressure on a person so as to affect that person's free will, acts, or decisions is called _____.

14. _____

15. Personal property of which one has possession is referred to as _____.

15. _____

16. A document filed with the court in some states that specifies that all the parties are ready for trial is a/an _____.

16. _____

KEYING LEGAL TERMS

Directions: Unless otherwise instructed, use 1-inch margins and double spacing. Correct all errors. Follow one of the procedures below.

WORDS

Keyboarding Procedure
On your computer, key the following words at least two times, concentrating on the correct spelling and pronunciation.

Machine Shorthand Procedure
On your computer, key the following words once, concentrating on the correct spelling and pronunciation. Then write each word one time on your shorthand machine. Transcribe from your shorthand notes one time on your computer, or, if you are using computer-aided transcription (CAT), proofread and edit your transcript.

clerk of the court	docket	joinder
cross-complaint	certificate of service	alias summons
pluries summons	disclosure statement	certificate of readiness
discovery	proffer	sidebar
realtime	undue influence	chose in possession
perfect		

SENTENCES

Keyboarding Procedure
Key each of the following sentences one time on your computer. Concentrate on the correct spelling and pronunciation of each underlined legal term.

Machine Shorthand Procedure
Write the following sentences one time on your shorthand machine. Transcribe from your shorthand notes one time on your computer, or, if you are using computer-aided transcription (CAT), proofread and edit your transcript.

These sentences will be used for practice dictation on the Transcription CD.

The <u>clerk of the court</u> is a court officer who is responsible for issuing the process or docket of the court, filing of court documents, issuing summonses, and keeping the seal of the court and records of court proceedings. The schedule of cases to be tried by a court is called the <u>docket</u>. When a case is filed, the clerk of the court assigns a number to the case which is called the docket, file, or case number.

When a new party is brought in to join with the plaintiff or the defendant in a lawsuit or two or more matters are combined in the same suit, it is called <u>joinder</u>. Joinder means joining or uniting with others in a litigation. If a defendant brings a complaint against a co-defendant, it is called a <u>cross-complaint</u>. If you and your roommate are sued by your landlord for damages and you feel that your roommate was responsible, then you may file a cross-complaint against your roommate.

A <u>certificate of service</u> is a statement that avers that the opposing party has been given a copy of a designated document. A certificate of service may also be called a proof of service. An <u>alias summons</u> is issued when the first summons is returned because it could not be served due to a defect or manner of service. If a third and subsequent summonses have to be issued because the first two are not effective, they are called a <u>pluries summons</u>.

A **disclosure statement** makes known or reveals information. A party who owes money to another party may be required to come into court and reveal the location of his or her assets in a disclosure statement. A seller of real property may be required to give the buyer a disclosure statement which reveals the condition of the property. Also, the Truth in Lending Act requires a mortgagee to issue a disclosure statement which states the annual percentage rate of the mortgage.

In some states when both parties to a lawsuit are ready to proceed to trial, a **certificate of readiness** is filed with the court. A certificate of readiness is filed when **discovery** or the gathering of information about a case prior to trial is completed. To offer or propose is referred to as **proffer**. A proffer is usually made out of the presence of the jury and may have an effect on an appeal. During the trial, the judge and the attorneys may have a conference out of the hearing of the jury which is called a **sidebar**. When the court reporter produces a transcript instantaneously as the proceedings are recorded, it is referred to as **realtime**.

Undue influence is improperly putting pressure on a person so as to affect that person's free will, acts, or decisions. Personal property which one has in their possession is called **chose in possession**. To make complete, without defect, or enforceable is to **perfect**. When a document such as a deed is recorded, it is said to be perfected or enforceable.

TRANSCRIBING FROM DICTATION

Directions: This dictation emphasizes and reinforces the legal terms and definitions you have studied. Listen carefully to the pronunciation of each of the legal terms. Unless otherwise directed, use 1-inch margins and double spacing. Correct all errors. Follow one of the procedures below.

Keyboarding Procedure
Using the Transcription CD, Lesson 31, Part A, transcribe the dictation directly at your computer.

Machine Shorthand Procedure
Using the Transcription CD, Lesson 31, Part A, take the dictation on your shorthand machine and then transcribe from your notes on your computer, or, if you are using computer-aided transcription (CAT), proofread and edit your transcript.

When you have finished transcribing or proofreading and editing Part A of the practice dictation, check your transcript with the printed copy. If you made any mistakes in the transcription, you should review and practice those words several times before going on to Part B.

| Part B | TERMINOLOGY AND DEFINITIONS

Directions: Study the terms, pronunciations, and definitions until you are thoroughly familiar with them. In order to complete this lesson successfully, you must understand the meaning and usage of all the legal terms presented. If you are using a shorthand system, write each legal term one time on your shorthand machine.

Legal Term	Pronunciation	Definition
1. grantor	′grant-ər	The person who transfers the title to real property.
2. grantee	grant-′ē	The person to whom the title to real property is transferred.

3. purchase-money mortgage	ˈpər-chəs-ˈmən-ē ˈmȯr-gij	A realty property mortgage that is held by the seller of the real property. Differs from a land contract in that the title passes at the time of the sale and the purchase-money mortgage is a lien on the property.
4. mortgagor	mȯr-gi-ˈjȯr	One who pledges his or her property as security for a debt. For example, if you borrow money from a bank and pledge your ownership in your home as collateral or security for the loan, you are a mortgagor.
5. mortgagee	mȯr-gi-ˈjē	One who takes or receives a mortgage as security or collateral for a loan. For example, if you borrow money from a bank and the bank holds your home as collateral or security for the loan, the bank is the mortgagee.
6. sales or purchase agreement	sālz ər ˈpər-chəs ə-ˈgrē-mənt	An agreement between two parties whereby the seller is obligated to sell and the buyer is obligated to purchase specified real property under the terms specified in the agreement.
7. deed of trust	dēd əv trəst	Differs from a mortgage in that the title to real property is placed in the name of a third party or trustee who holds title until the mortgage is paid or other specified conditions are met.
8. derivation clause	der-ə-ˈvä-shən klȯz	A clause in a deed of trust that names the parties from whom the current owner purchased the real property. It also provides information regarding the recording of that transfer.
9. affidavit of value	af-ə-ˈdā-vət əv ˈval-yü	Some states require an affidavit as to the sale price or value of the real property, whichever is greater, to be included in the deed. Other states require that a separate affidavit of value be filed with the tax assessor's office.
10. amortization	am-ərt-ə-ˈzā-shən	The paying of an obligation by installments. For example, if you mortgage your home, each month you will be required to pay a specified amount for principal and interest for a definite number of years after which the mortgage will be paid in full.
11. Mechanic's Lien	mi-ˈkan-iks lēn	A claim that a worker or contractor has against real property for work performed or materials used on the property.
12. waiver of lien	ˈwā-vər əv lēn	A release of any and all claims relating to Mechanic's Liens that a worker or contractor has against real property. (See Figure 31-2, page 468.)
13. tax sale	taks sāl	A sale of land for unpaid taxes. If real property taxes are not paid by a date determined by state law, the property is sold, usually at auction, for the amount of the unpaid taxes.
14. tax certificate	taks sər-ˈtif-i-kat	At a tax sale, some states sell only a tax certificate, which gives the purchaser the right to receive a deed (title) for the property if the owner does not redeem the certificate by paying the taxes within a specified period of time.
15. tax deed	taks dēd	A deed that conveys title to the purchaser for real property sold at a tax sale.

FIGURE 31-2 A Waiver of Lien

WAIVER OF LIEN—MATERIAL OR LABOR

𝔖𝔱𝔞𝔱𝔢 𝔬𝔣 Illinois

PARTIAL ☐
COMPLETE ☒

𝕮𝖔𝖚𝖓𝖙𝖞 𝖔𝖋 DuPage ⎬ ss.

July 18 20 03

TO ALL WHOM IT MAY CONCERN:

Whereas __I__ the undersigned Sarkis Tajari

ha __ve__ been employed by Gates Construction Company

to furnish materials and labor

for the Building known as 7849 Marissa Avenue

City of Wheaton

Lot No. __64__   Section __768__   Township Monroe   Range 41

County of DuPage   State of Illinois

NOW, THEREFORE, KNOW YE, That Sarkis Tajari   the undersigned

for and in consideration of the sum of One and 00/100   Dollars

and other good and valuable considerations, the receipt whereof is hereby acknowledged, do hereby waive and release any and all lien, or

claim or right to lien on said above described building and premises under the Statutes of the State of Illinois

relating to Mechanics' Liens, on account of labor or materials, or both, furnished or which may be furnished, by the undersigned to or on

account of the said Gates Construction Company

                               for said building or premises.

Given under __my__ hand ____ and seal ____ this 18th   Day of July   A.D., 20 03

Witness: *Terri F. Thurmond*   _____ *Sarkis Tajari* _____ (SEAL)

_____   _____ (SEAL)

Self-Evaluation B | Terminology and Definition Recall

Directions: In the Answers column, write the letter from Column 1 that represents the word or phrase that best matches each item in Column 2. After you have completed this self-evaluation, check your answers with the key on page 500. If you have any incorrect answers, review the definitions for those terms before going on with this lesson. Then unless otherwise directed, submit this self-evaluation to your instructor.

COLUMN 1	COLUMN 2	ANSWERS
a. affidavit of value	1. The person who transfers title to real property.	1. _____
b. amortization	2. The person to whom the title to real property is transferred.	2. _____
c. deed of trust	3. Conveys title to the purchaser for real property that is sold at a tax sale.	3. _____
d. derivation clause	4. A realty property mortgage that is held by the seller of the property.	4. _____
e. grantee	5. One who pledges his or her real property as security for a debt.	5. _____
f. grantor	6. A claim that a worker or contractor has against real property for work performed or materials used on the property.	6. _____
g. Mechanic's Lien	7. One who takes or receives a mortgage as security or collateral for a loan.	7. _____
h. Mortgage	8. A document that places the title to real property in the name of a third party or trustee who holds title until the mortgage is paid or other specific conditions are met.	8. _____
i. Mortgagee	9. A sale of land for unpaid taxes.	9. _____
j. Mortgagor	10. An agreement between two parties whereby the seller is obligated to sell and the buyer is obligated to purchase specified real property under the terms of the agreement.	10. _____
k. purchase-money mortgage	11. A statement that verifies the value or sales price of real property.	11. _____
l. sales or purchase agreement	12. A document that gives the purchaser the right to receive title to property if the owner does not pay the taxes within a specified period of time.	12. _____
m. tax certificate	13. A portion of a deed of trust that names the parties from whom the current owner purchased the real property.	13. _____
n. tax deed	14. The paying of an obligation by installments.	14. _____
o. tax sale	15. A release of any and all claims relating to Mechanic's Liens that a worker or contractor may have against a real property.	15. _____
p. waiver of lien		

KEYING LEGAL TERMS

Directions: Unless otherwise instructed, use 1-inch margins and double spacing. Correct all errors. Follow one of the procedures below.

WORDS

Keyboarding Procedure

On your computer, key the following words at least two times, concentrating on the correct spelling and pronunciation.

Machine Shorthand Procedure

On your computer, key the following words once, concentrating on the correct spelling and pronunciation. Then write each word one time on your shorthand machine. Transcribe from your shorthand notes one time on your computer, or, if you are using computer-aided transcription (CAT), proofread and edit your transcript.

grantor	grantee	purchase-money mortgage
mortgagor	mortgagee	sales or purchase agreement
deed of trust	derivation clause	affidavit of value
amortization	Mechanic's Lien	waiver of lien
tax sale	tax certificate	tax deed

SENTENCES

Keyboarding Procedure

Key each of the following sentences one time on your computer. Concentrate on the correct spelling and pronunciation of each underlined legal term.

Machine Shorthand Procedure

Write the following sentences one time on your shorthand machine. Transcribe from your shorthand notes one time on your computer, or, if you are using computer-aided transcription (CAT), proofread and edit your transcript.

These sentences will be used for practice dictation on the Transcription CD.

A <u>grantor</u> is the person who transfers the title to real property. A <u>grantee</u> is the person to whom the title to real property is transferred. A realty property mortgage that is held by the seller of the real property is called a <u>purchase-money mortgage</u>. A purchase-money mortgage differs from a land contract in that the title passes at the time of the sale and the mortgage is a lien on the property.

A person who pledges his or her property as security for a debt is referred to as a <u>mortgagor</u>. A <u>mortgagee</u> is the one who takes or receives a mortgage as security or collateral for a loan. Therefore, if you borrow money from a bank and pledge your ownership in your home as collateral or security for the loan, you are the mortgagor and the bank is the mortgagee.

An agreement between two parties whereby the seller is obligated to sell and the buyer is obligated to purchase specified real property under the terms specified in the agreement is a <u>sales or purchase agreement</u>. When a <u>deed of trust</u> is used in a real estate transaction, the title to real property is placed in the name of a third party who holds title until the mortgage is paid or other specified conditions are met. The <u>derivation clause</u> in a deed of trust names the parties from whom the current owner purchased the real property and also provides information regarding the recording of that transfer. An <u>affidavit of value</u> stating the price or value of the real property may also be included in the deed or filed with the tax assessor's office. <u>Amortization</u> refers to the paying of an obligation by installments. A <u>Mechanic's Lien</u> is a claim that a worker or contractor has against real property for work performed or materials used on the property. A <u>waiver of lien</u> is used to release any and all claims that a worker or contractor has against real property.

If real property taxes are not paid by a date determined by state law, the property is sold at a <u>tax sale</u>, usually at auction, for the amount of the unpaid taxes. At a tax sale, some states sell only a <u>tax certificate</u>, which gives the purchaser the right to receive a <u>tax deed</u> or title for the property if the owner does not redeem the tax certificate within a specified period of time.

TRANSCRIBING FROM DICTATION

Directions: This dictation emphasizes and reinforces the legal terms and definitions you have studied. Listen carefully to the pronunciation of each of the legal terms. Unless otherwise directed, use 1-inch margins and double spacing. Correct all errors. Follow one of the procedures below.

Keyboarding Procedure

Using the Transcription CD, Lesson 31, Part B, transcribe the dictation directly at your computer.

Machine Shorthand Procedure

Using the Transcription CD, Lesson 31, Part B, take the dictation on your shorthand machine and then transcribe from your notes on your computer, or, if you are using computer-aided transcription (CAT), proofread and edit your transcript.

When you have finished transcribing or proofreading and editing Part B of the practice dictation, check your transcript with the printed copy. If you made any mistakes in the transcription, you should review and practice those words several times before going on to Lesson 32.

CHECKLIST

I have completed the following for Lesson 31:

	Part A, Date	Part B, Date	Submitted to Instructor Yes	No
Terminology and Definitions	_____	_____	_____	_____
Self-Evaluation	_____	_____	_____	_____
* Keying Legal Terms	_____	_____	_____	_____
Words	_____	_____	_____	_____
Sentences	_____	_____	_____	_____
* Transcribing from Dictation	_____	_____	_____	_____

When you have successfully completed all the exercises in this lesson and submitted to your instructor those requested, you are ready to proceed with Lesson 32.

* If you are using machine shorthand, submit to your instructor your notes along with your transcript.

Lesson
32

Additional Legal Terms—Domestic Relations, Corporations, Probate, Bankruptcy, and Contracts and Leases

> *"Suppression of the truth is equivalent to the expression of what is false."*
>
> —*Legal maxim*

This lesson consists of additional legal terms relating to domestic relations, corporations, probate, bankruptcy, and contracts and leases that were not presented in earlier lessons. When you complete these exercises, you should have knowledge and understanding of more terms that are used in reference to these areas of law.

Part A | TERMINOLOGY AND DEFINITIONS

Directions: Study the terms, pronunciations, and definitions until you are thoroughly familiar with them. In order to complete this lesson successfully, you must understand the meaning and usage of all the legal terms presented. If you are using a shorthand system, write each legal term one time on your shorthand machine.

Legal Term	Pronunciation	Definition
		Domestic Relations:
1. irreconcilable differences	ir-ek-ən-ˈsī-lə-bəl ˈdif-ərn-səz	Unspecified differences which cannot be reconciled that parties to a divorce action have. A ground for divorce in states that have no-fault divorce laws.
2. stalking laws	ˈstȯ-kiŋ lȯz	Laws in some states that prevent a person from following or harassing another person.
3. alleged father	ə-ˈlejd ˈfäth-ər	One who is assumed to be the natural father of a child.
4. paternity test	pə-ˈtər-nət-ē test	A comparison of genetic traits called blood groups that is used to determine if a given man could be the biological father of a given child.
5. adoptee	ə-däp-ˈtē	One who is adopted.
6. issue of marriage	ˈish-ü əv ˈmar-ij	Children who are born to the parties of a marriage. Generally, the term is used to apply only to legitimate children.
7. sole custody	sōl ˈkəs-təd-ē	Custody in which the total care and responsibility for the care of a minor child of a marriage that is in a state of separation or divorce is placed with one parent.
8. joint custody	jȯint ˈkəs-təd-ē	Custody in which the care and responsibility for the care of a minor child of a marriage that is in a state of separation or divorce is placed equally with both parents.

9.	split custody	split ′kəs-təd-ē	Custody in which the child spends part of the time with one parent and part of the time with the other parent. One parent is designated as the custodial parent who makes the decisions regarding the care of the child.
10.	noncustodial parent	nän-kəs-′tōd-ē-əl ′par-ənt	The parent who is not responsible for the care of a minor child of a marriage that is in a state of separation or divorce. A noncustodial parent may have visitation rights.

Corporations:

11.	corporate resolution	′kȯr-prət rez-ə-′lü-shən	A motion or intention adopted by a corporate board of directors directing that a certain thing be done. For example, a corporate resolution may be passed giving the officers the authority to open a bank account in the corporation's name. (See Figure 32-1, page 475.)
12.	corporate seal	′kȯr-prət sēl	An official seal used by a corporation to imprint the corporation's legal documents.
13.	subscription right	səb-′skrip-shən rīt	A right of shareholders to purchase additional shares of stock when new stock is issued by the corporation.
14.	public corporation	′pəb-lik kȯr-pə′-rā-shən	One that is created by the state to act as an agency in administrating civil government such as a county, city, town, or school district.
15.	professional corporation	prə-′fesh-nəl kȯr-pə-′rā-shən	One that is formed by one or more licensed professionals such as doctors, lawyers, or accountants.

FIGURE 32-1 A Corporate Resolution

ACTION BY WRITTEN CONSENT OF

THE BOARD OF DIRECTORS

OF

LAMBDA OMEGA CORPORATION, INC.

The undersigned, being a Director of Lambda Omega Corporation, Inc., (hereinafter referred to as the "Corporation"), a Michigan non-profit corporation, hereby authorizes the following action by written consent, pursuant to the Michigan Business Corporation Act, as amended:

1. PURCHASE OF REAL PROPERTY: The Directors hereby resolve that the Corporation purchase by Land Contract certain real property commonly known as 1600 Perry Street, East Lansing, Michigan.

2. DESIGNATION OF AGENTS: The Directors hereby resolve that Benjamin Klotz be authorized to execute, on behalf of the Corporation, a Promissory Note in connection with the aforesaid purchase in a principal amount not to exceed Five Thousand and 00/100 Dollars ($5,000.00). The Directors further authorize Casey Ginovelli, the Corporation's attorney, to execute all necessary or reasonably desirable documents of conveyance in connection with the aforesaid acquisition.

DATED: December 30, 2003   BY: *Cyrus Schevenko*
                                 Cyrus Schevenko

Self-Evaluation A | Terminology and Definition Recall

Directions: In the Answers column at the right of each statement, write the letter that represents the word or group of words that correctly completes the statement. After you have completed this self-evaluation, check your answers with the key on page 500. If you have any incorrect answers, review the definitions for those terms before going on with this lesson. Then unless otherwise directed, submit this self-evaluation to your instructor.

ANSWERS

1. A corporation that is created by the state to act as an agency in administrating civil government such as a county, city, town, or school district is a (a) public corporation, (b) professional corporation, (c) corporate seal.

1. _____

2. A right of shareholders to purchase additional shares of stock when new stock is issued by a corporation is (a) corporate seal, (b) corporate resolution, (c) subscription right.

2. _____

3. When the parties to a divorce action have unspecified differences that cannot be reconciled, it is referred to as (a) issue of marriage, (b) irreconcilable differences, (c) split custody.

3. _____

4. A comparison of genetic traits called blood groups that is used to determine if a given man could be the biological father of a given child is a (a) paternity test, (b) subscription right, (c) stalking law.

4. _____

5. The parent who is not responsible for the care of a minor child of a marriage that is in a state of separation or divorce is a/an (a) adoptee, (b) alleged father, (c) noncustodial parent.

5. _____

6. One who is assumed to be the natural father of a child is a/an (a) noncustodial parent, (b) alleged father, (c) adoptee.

6. _____

7. Children who are born to the parties of a marriage are referred to as (a) issue of marriage, (b) adoptee, (c) paternity test.

7. _____

8. An official seal used by a corporation to imprint the corporation's legal documents is a (a) corporate resolution, (b) corporate seal, (c) subscription right.

8. _____

9. A corporation that is formed by one or more licensed professionals, such as doctors, lawyers, or accountants, is a (a) public corporation, (b) professional corporation, (c) joint custody.

9. _____

10. Custody in which the child spends part of the time with one parent and part of the time with the other parent, but one parent is designated as the custodial parent who makes the decisions regarding the care of the child, is (a) split custody, (b) joint custody, (c) sole custody.

10. _____

11. A motion or intention adopted by a corporate board of directors directing that a certain thing be done is a (a) corporate seal, (b) subscription right, (c) corporate resolution.

11. _____

12. Laws in some states that prevent a person from following or harassing another person are (a) stalking laws, (b) paternity test, (c) subscription rights.

12. _____

13. Custody in which the care and responsibility for the care of a minor child of a marriage that is in a state of separation or divorce is placed with both parents is (a) sole custody, (b) split custody, (c) joint custody.

13. _____

14. One who is adopted is an (a) issue of marriage, (b) alleged father, (c) adoptee.

14. _____

15. Custody in which the total care and responsibility for the care of a minor child of a marriage that is in a state of separation or divorce is placed with one parent is (a) sole custody, (b) joint custody, (c) split custody.

15. _____

KEYING LEGAL TERMS

Directions: Unless otherwise instructed, use 1-inch margins and double spacing. Correct all errors. Follow one of the procedures below.

WORDS

Keyboarding Procedure
On your computer, key the following words at least two times, concentrating on the correct spelling and pronunciation.

Machine Shorthand Procedure
On your computer, key the following words once, concentrating on the correct spelling and pronunciation. Then write each word one time on your shorthand machine. Transcribe from your shorthand notes one time on your computer, or, if you are using computer-aided transcription (CAT), proofread and edit your transcript.

irreconcilable differences	**stalking laws**	**alleged father**
paternity test	**adoptee**	**issue of marriage**
sole custody	**joint custody**	**split custody**
noncustodial parent	**corporate resolution**	**corporate seal**
subscription right	**public corporation**	**professional corporation**

SENTENCES

Keyboarding Procedure
Key each of the following sentences one time on your computer. Concentrate on the correct spelling and pronunciation of each underlined legal term.

Machine Shorthand Procedure
Write the following sentences one time on your shorthand machine. Transcribe from your shorthand notes one time on your computer, or, if you are using computer-aided transcription (CAT), proofread and edit your transcript.

These sentences will be used for practice dictation on the Transcription CD.

Parties to a divorce action may have <u>irreconcilable differences</u>, which are unspecified differences that cannot be reconciled. Irreconcilable differences are a ground for divorce in states that have no-fault divorce laws. Some states have passed <u>stalking laws</u> that prevent a person from following or harassing another person.

An <u>alleged father</u> is one who is assumed to be the natural father of a child. A <u>paternity test</u>, a comparison of genetic traits called blood groups, may be used to determine if a given man could be the biological father of a given child. A child who is adopted is referred to as an <u>adoptee</u>, but children who are born to the parties of a marriage are referred to as <u>issue of marriage</u>. Generally, issue of marriage applies only to legitimate children.

Custody in which the total care and responsibility for the care of a minor child of a marriage that is in a state of separation or divorce is placed with one parent is <u>sole custody</u>. <u>Joint custody</u> is custody in which the care and responsibility for the care of a minor child of a marriage that is in a state of separation or divorce is placed equally with both parents. If the child spends part of the time with one parent and part of the time with the other parent, and one parent is designated as the custodial parent who makes the decisions regarding the care of the child, it is called <u>split custody</u>. The parent who is not responsible for the care of a minor child of a marriage that is in a state of separation or divorce is a <u>noncustodial parent</u>.

A motion or intention adopted by a corporate board of directors directing that a certain thing be done is a <u>corporate resolution</u>. A <u>corporate seal</u> is an official seal used by a corporation to imprint the corporation's legal documents. A <u>subscription right</u> is a right of shareholders to purchase additional shares of stock when new stock is issued by the corporation. A <u>public corporation</u> is one that is created by the state to act as an agency in administrating civil government such as a county, city, town, or school district. If one or more licensed professionals such as doctors, lawyers, or accountants form a corporation, it is called a <u>professional corporation</u>.

TRANSCRIBING FROM DICTATION

Directions: This dictation emphasizes and reinforces the legal terms and definitions you have studied. Listen carefully to the pronunciation of each of the legal terms. Unless otherwise directed, use 1-inch margins and double spacing. Correct all errors. Follow one of the procedures below.

Keyboarding Procedure
Using the Transcription CD, Lesson 32, Part A, transcribe the dictation directly at your computer.

Machine Shorthand Procedure
Using the Transcription CD, Lesson 32, Part A, take the dictation on your shorthand machine and then transcribe your notes on your computer, or, if you are using computer-aided transcription (CAT), proofread and edit your transcript.

When you have finished transcribing or proofreading and editing Part A of the practice dictation, check your transcript with the printed copy. If you made any mistakes in the transcription, you should review and practice those words several times before going on to Part B.

Part B | TERMINOLOGY AND DEFINITIONS

Directions: Study the terms, pronunciations, and definitions until you are thoroughly familiar with them. In order to complete this lesson successfully, you must understand the meaning and usage of all the legal terms presented. If you are using a shorthand system, write each legal term one time on your shorthand machine.

Legal Term	Pronunciation	Definition
		Probate:
1. legatee	leg-ə´tē	The person to whom a legacy is given.
2. declarant	di-´klar-ənt	In probate, a declarant is a person who signs a living will. In general, a declarant is a person who makes an unsworn statement of facts in a case.
3. decedent	di-´sēd-nt	Refers to a deceased person whether he or she died testate or intestate.
4. devise	dev-ə-´zē	The person to whom real property is given by will.
5. testamentary instrument	tes-tə-´ment-ə-rē ´in-strə-mənt	A written document that is in the nature of a will although it is not formally a will. Upon court approval, a testam entary instrument will have the same effect as a will.
6. testamentary trust	tes-tə-´ment-ə-rē trəst	A trust that is set up by the terms of a will and that does not come into being until the death of the person making the will.

7. life estate	līf is-ˈtāt	One's right to the lifetime use and enjoyment of property that is owned by another. For example, a person may pass ownership of his or her home to children or other heirs but retain the right to live there until his or her death.
8. succession	sək-ˈsesh-ən	That which is established by law as to the rights of heirs to inherit property of a person who dies intestate. For example, if a person dies without a will, the laws of succession determine how the property is to be divided and who is the heir at law.
9. distribute	dis-ˈtrib-yət	If a person dies intestate, the estate is divided equally among the legal heirs. Also referred to as per capita, which is the opposite of per stirpes.
10. exception	ik-ˈsep-shən	The excluding or intentionally leaving someone out of a will. Also may refer to a document filed with the court that disputes the claim of a creditor against an estate.
11. age of majority	āj əv mə-ˈjör-ət-ē	The age established by law at which a person is entitled to manage his or her own affairs. Eighteen is the age of majority in most states.

Bankruptcy:

12. statutory lien	ˈstach-ə-tōr-ē lēn	An encumbrance imposed on property by law. For example, if you do not pay your property taxes, they become a lien on your property as specified by law.
13. secured claim	si-ˈkyürd klām	An indebtedness for which property was pledged as security. If the debt is not paid, the property can be sold to satisfy the claim. A mortgage on real property is an example of a secured claim.
14. exempt property	ig-ˈzemt ˈpräp-ərt-ē	Property as defined by federal or state statutes that is exempt from bankruptcy proceedings and that can, therefore, be retained by the person filing for bankruptcy.

Contracts and Leases:

15. lawful purpose	ˈlȯ-fəl ˈpər-pəs	An essential element of a legal contract. For example, a contract cannot be enforced if it involves committing a crime, harming someone, or committing fraud.
16. security deposit	si-ˈkyür-ət-ē di-ˈpäz-ət	Money paid by a tenant to a landlord as security for the tenant's performance in fulfilling the terms of the lease. State laws vary as to the amount of deposit that can be collected and under what conditions it can be retained by the landlord.

Self-Evaluation B | Terminology and Definition Recall

Directions: In the Answers column, write the legal term that is most representative of the corresponding statement. After you have completed this self-evaluation, check your answers with the key on page 500. If you have any incorrect answers, review the definitions for those terms before going on with this lesson. Then unless otherwise directed, submit this self-evaluation to your instructor.

ANSWERS

1. A trust that is set up by the terms of a will and which does not come into being until the death of the person making the will is a/an _____.   1. _____

2. The term _____ refers to the equal division of an estate among the legal heirs of a person who dies intestate.   2. _____

3. The person to whom real property is given by will is a/an _____.   3. _____

4. The excluding or intentionally leaving someone out of a will is called _____.   4. _____

5. Money paid by a tenant to a landlord as security for the tenant's performance in fulfilling the terms of the lease is a/an _____.   5. _____

6. One's right to the lifetime use and enjoyment of property that is owned by another is a/an _____.   6. _____

7. The person to whom a legacy is given is a/an _____.   7. _____

8. An indebtedness for which property was pledged as security is referred to as a/an _____.   8. _____

9. In probate, a person who signs a living will is a/an _____.   9. _____

10. An essential element of a legal contract that means that a contract cannot be enforced if it involves committing a crime is _____.   10. _____

11. Property that is defined by federal or state statutes that is exempt from bankruptcy proceedings and that can, therefore, be retained by the person filing for bankruptcy is known as _____.   11. _____

12. An encumbrance imposed on property by law is a/an _____.   12. _____

13. The age established by law at which a person is entitled to manage his or her own affairs is the _____.   13. _____

14. The term _____ refers to a deceased person whether he or she died testate or intestate.   14. _____

15. A written document that is in the nature of a will although it is not formally a will is called a/an _____.   15. _____

16. That which is established by law as the rights of heirs to inherit property of a person who dies intestate is referred to as _____.   16. _____

KEYING LEGAL TERMS

Directions: Unless otherwise instructed, use 1-inch margins and double spacing. Correct all errors. Follow one of the procedures below.

WORDS

Keyboarding Procedure
On your computer, key the following words at least two times, concentrating on the correct spelling and pronunciation.

Machine Shorthand Procedure
On your computer, key the following words once, concentrating on the correct spelling and pronunciation. Then write each word one time on your shorthand machine. Transcribe your shorthand notes one time on your computer, or, if you are using computer-aided transcription (CAT), proofread and edit your transcript.

legatee	declarant	decedent
devise	testamentary instrument	testamentary trust
life estate	succession	distribute
exception	age of majority	statutory lien
secured claim	exempt property	lawful purpose
security deposit		

SENTENCES

Keyboarding Procedure
Key each of the following sentences one time on your computer. Concentrate on the correct spelling and pronunciation of each underlined legal term.

Machine Shorthand Procedure
Write the following sentences one time on your shorthand machine. Transcribe from your shorthand notes one time on your computer, or, if you are using computer-aided transcription (CAT), proofread and edit your transcript.

These sentences will be used for practice dictation on the Transcription CD.

A <u>legatee</u> is a person to whom a legacy is given. In probate, a <u>declarant</u> is a person who signs a living will. In general, a declarant is a person who makes an unsworn statement of facts in a case. <u>Decedent</u> refers to a deceased person whether they died testate or intestate. The person to whom real property is given by will is a <u>devise</u>.

A written document that is in the nature of a will although it is not formally a will is a <u>testamentary instrument</u>. A <u>testamentary trust</u> is set up by the terms of a will and does not come into being until the death of the person who makes the will. Upon court approval, a testamentary instrument will have the same effect as a will. A <u>life estate</u> is one's right to the lifetime use and enjoyment of property that is owned by another. For example, a person may pass ownership of his or her home to children or other heirs but retain the right to live there until his or her death.

<u>Succession</u> is that which is established by law as to the rights of heirs to inherit property of a person who dies intestate. If a person dies without a will, the laws of succession determine how the property is to be divided and who is the heir at law. <u>Distribute</u> refers to a situation where a person dies intestate and the estate is divided equally among the legal heirs. Distribute is also referred to as per capita, which is the

opposite of per stirpes. <u>Exception</u> is the excluding or intentionally leaving someone out of a will. Exception also may refer to a document filed with the court which disputes the claim of a creditor against an estate.

The age established by law at which a person is entitled to manage his or her own affairs is the <u>age of majority</u>. Eighteen is the age of majority in most states.

A <u>statutory lien</u> is an encumbrance imposed on property by law. An indebtedness for which property was pledged as security is known as a <u>secured claim</u>. <u>Exempt property</u> is property as defined by federal or state statutes that is exempt from bankruptcy proceedings and that can, therefore, be retained by the person filing for bankruptcy.

<u>Lawful purpose</u> is an essential element of a legal contract and means that a contract cannot be enforced if it involves committing a crime, harming someone, or committing fraud. A <u>security deposit</u> is money paid by a tenant to a landlord as security for the tenant's performance in fulfilling the terms of the lease. State laws vary as to the amount of deposit that can be collected and under what conditions it can be retained by the landlord.

TRANSCRIBING FROM DICTATION

Directions: This dictation emphasizes and reinforces the legal terms and definitions you have studied. Listen carefully to the pronunciation of each of the legal terms. Unless otherwise directed, use 1-inch margins and double spacing. Correct all errors. Follow one of the procedures below.

Keyboarding Procedure
Using the Transcription CD, Lesson 32, Part B, transcribe the dictation directly at your computer.

Machine Shorthand Procedure
Using the Transcription CD, Lesson 32, Part B, take the dictation on your shorthand machine and then transcribe your notes on your computer, or, if you are using computer-aided transcription (CAT), proofread and edit your transcript.

When you have finished transcribing or proofreading and editing Part B of the practice dictation, check your transcript with the printed copy. If you made any mistakes in the transcription, you should review and practice those words several times before going on to Evaluation 16.

CHECKLIST
I have completed the following for Lesson 32:

	Part A, Date	Part B, Date	Submitted to Instructor Yes	No
Terminology and Definitions				
Self-Evaluation				
* Keying Legal Terms				
Words				
Sentences				
* Transcribing from Dictation				

When you have successfully completed all the exercises in this lesson and submitted to your instructor those requested, you are ready to proceed with Evaluation 16.

* If you are using machine shorthand, submit to your instructor your notes along with your transcript.

Evaluation No. 16 | SECTION A

Directions: This dictation/transcription evaluation will test your spelling and transcription abilities on the legal terms that you studied in the two preceding lessons. Tab once for a paragraph indention, and use 1-inch margins and double spacing unless otherwise instructed. Correct all errors. Follow one of the procedures below.

Keyboarding Procedure

Using the Transcription CD for Evaluation 16, transcribe the dictation directly at your computer, or, if you are using computer-aided transcription (CAT), proofread and edit your transcript.

Machine Shorthand Procedure

Using the Transcription CD for Evaluation 16, take the dictation on your shorthand machine and then transcribe your notes on your computer, or, if you are using computer-aided transcription (CAT), proofread and edit your transcript.

Sections B and C are available from your instructor.

Latin Words and Phrases

This section contains some additional Latin words and phrases that will expand your knowledge and understanding of Latin as it is used in the legal field. Even though the direction of the legal field has been to simplify the language and to use less Latin, many are still in common use today. Therefore, it would be to your benefit if you are working in the legal field to be acquainted with as many of the Latin terms as possible.

Latin Word	Pronunciation	Definition
a fortiori	ə fōr-ˈshə-ə-rē	With greater force or with greater reason.
a priori	ə ˈprī-ə-rē	From what has previously transpired; from the cause to the effect.
ab initio	əb in-ˈish-ə-ō	From the beginning; entirely.
ad curiam	ad ˈkyür-ē-əm	At a court; before the court; to the court.
ad infinitum	ad in-fə-ˈnī-tum	Without end; to any extent; indefinitely.
consortium	kən-ˈsȯrt-ē-əm	The legal right each spouse has to the company, affection, and service of the other.
contra	ˈkän-trə	In opposition or contrast to; against; confronting; on the other hand.
duces tecum	ˈdü-cēz ˈtek-kəm	Bring with you.
ex officio	eks ə-ˈfis-ē-ō	From office or by virtue of the office.
fiat	ˈfē-ət	Let it be done.
in camera	in ˈkam-rə	In chambers; in private.
in loco	in ˈlō-kō	In the natural place; in lieu; instead.
in personam	in pər-ˈsän-əm	Against the person.
in toto	in ˈtō-tō	In the whole; completely; altogether.
indicia	in-ˈdish-ē-a	Signs; indications.
infra	ˈin-frə	Below, beneath, or under.
inter alia	in-ˈtər ˈā-lē-ə	Among other things.
inter vivos	in-ˈtər ˈvi-vōs	Between living persons; from one living person to another.
intra	ˈin-trə	Within; in the space of.
locus delicti	ˈlō-kəs di-ˈlik-tī	The place of the crime or tort. The place where the crime was committed.
mala in se	ˈmal-ə in sā	Wrong in themselves. Acts that are morally wrong.
mala prohibita	ˈmal-ə prō-ˈhib-ə-tə	Acts that are prohibited by human laws but are not necessarily wrong in themselves.
non sequitur	nän si-ˈkwe- tər	It does not follow.
non sui juris	nän ˈsü-ī ˈjür-əs	Not his own master; not in its own right; not of full legal capacity.
nota bene	ˈnōt-ə ˈbē-nē	Note well; take notice; used to call attention to something important.
onus probandi	ˈō-nəs ˈprō-band-ē	The burden of proof; burden of proving.
pro forma	prō ˈfȯr-mə	As a matter of form; tentatively.
pro tempore	prō ˈtem-pə-rē	For the time being; temporarily. Abbreviated to pro tem.
supra	ˈsü-prə	Above; upon; in addition to.
vis a vis	ˈvis ə vē	Force against force; face to face; in relation to each other.

Proofreading Guidelines

Even though most word processing software programs have a feature to check spelling, you must still be able to proofread your work for errors that cannot be detected by the software program. A software spell check program will only pick up misspelled words that do not make another word. For example, if you key "on" for "in," the program will not detect the error. Therefore, you cannot rely on your computer program to eliminate the need to proofread.

Following are some tips and guidelines to help you become a better proofreader.

1. Run your software program spell check.
2. Read the document word for word for context. Say each word to yourself as you are reading so you can determine if there are any incorrect, omitted, or additional words.
3. If you keyed from rough draft copy, cross-check the keyed copy with the rough draft. This will help you find any omissions or additions.
4. Check for format, i.e., spacing, paragraph indentions, and punctuation.
5. Carefully double-check all numbers, land descriptions, citations, names, and addresses. When proofing land descriptions or other material with numbers, it is helpful to have someone read them to you as you proof the copy.
6. If you are proofreading hard copy, or if someone else will be making the corrections, use the proofreader's marks listed below. Additionally, it is helpful to put a mark in the margin beside any line that has a correction or use a contrasting ink color. This will help assure that you will see and make all the noted corrections.

Proofreader's Marks

Mark	Meaning	Mark	Meaning
∧	Insert	ss	Single space
⁀	Close up	ds	Double space
	Transpose	ts	Triple space
ℓ	Take out or delete	¶	New Paragraph
stet	Let it stand or leave as it was	no ¶	No Paragraph
	Move as indicated	∧,	Insert comma
[	Move to the left	⊙	Insert period
]	Move to the right	(:)	Insert colon
___	Underscore	(;)	Insert semicolon
#	Insert space	(?)	Insert question mark
≡ or cap	Capitalize	◯	Spell out or do not abbreviate
/ or lc	Lowercase—no caps		

Enough emphasis cannot be placed on careful proofreading, and it is important that you take the necessary time to carefully proofread all your work. Remember: It is easier and less time-consuming to correct an error that could cause a problem than to correct a problem that was caused by an error.

Words Often Confused

There are many words that sound alike or are very close in spelling that are often confused. Following is a list of some of those words that often appear in legal documents or transcripts. Knowledge of these words and their definitions will help you make the correct choice when proofreading. If you are unsure about a word, check a dictionary for the definition to be sure that it fits the context of the sentence.

Word	Definition
accede	To become a party to; give in.
exceed	To extend outside of; to be greater than; to be superior.
accept	To take; to receive.
except	To exclude; to object.
access	Right to use; approach.
excess	Extra; surplus.
adapt	Conform; change to suit.
adept	Highly skilled; proficient.
adopt	Take as one's own; choose.
adduce	To offer as example, proof, or reason.
educe	To elicit or bring out.
adjoin	To be next to or in contact with.
adjourn	To postpone or suspend.
advice	Recommendation. (noun)
advise	To give counsel. (verb)
affect	To influence or alter. (verb)
effect	Consequence or result. (noun)
affiance	To pledge; to solemnly promise.
affiants	Persons who swear to an affidavit.
err	To make a mistake or be wrong.
heir	One who inherits.
arraign	To call before a court; to accuse of a wrong.
arrange	To put in order or classify.
bail	Security to guarantee a court appearance.
bale	A bundle.
casual	Subject to, resulting from, or occurring by chance.
causal	Relating to or constituting the cause.
cede	To grant; give up.
seed	Source or origin.
collaborate	To assist; to cooperate.
corroborate	To support.
command	To order or lead.
commend	To entrust; praise.
complement	Something that fills up, completes, or makes perfect.
compliment	An expression of esteem; a flattering remark.
consul	A government official in a foreign country.
council	An assembly.
counsel	Advice; lawyer.

corpse	A dead body.
corpus	A collection or body of knowledge or evidence.
correspondence	Communication by letters.
correspondents	Persons who communicate by letter.
corespondents	Persons named as guilty of adultery with the defendant in a divorce action.
credible	Believable.
creditable	Deserving of praise.
decedent	A person who has died.
dissident	One who does not agree.
decent	Respectable.
descent	Lineage; a step downward.
dissent	Difference of opinion.
demur	To object or delay.
demure	Serious or modest.
elicit	To draw forth or bring out.
illicit	Illegal, unlawful, or prohibited.
farther	In space or distance.
further	To promote.
formally	According to established form.
formerly	Previously.
gilt	Something resembling gold.
guilt	Having committed a crime or offense.
grievance	Reason for complaint.
grievous	Severe pain, suffering, or sorrow.
hearsay	Rumor. Based on what someone else said.
heresy	An opinion, doctrine, or practice contrary to the truth.
incite	Stir up or arouse.
insight	Knowledge or understanding.
indict	To accuse one of a crime.
indite	To compose and write.
interstate	Between or among states.
intestate	Without a will.
intrastate	Within a state.
laches	Undue delay in asserting a legal right.
latches	Fasteners.
lean	To incline.
lien	An encumbrance.
liable	Responsible or answerable.
libel	Defamation of character.
mandatary	One to whom a mandate is given.
mandatory	Required.
marital	Of marriage.
martial	Of war or military.

meat	Flesh of animals; meaning; gist.
meet	To confront; to assemble.
mete	To give out; to allot.
militant	Aggressive; warlike.
militate	To influence.
mitigate	To lessen or make less severe.
ordinance	Law; a municipal regulation.
ordnance	Arms or ammunitions.
parol	Oral.
parole	Conditional freedom from incarceration.
peremptory	Putting an end to or precluding a right of action.
preemptory	Take precedence over.
perpetrate	To commit; to be guilty of.
perpetuate	To make lasting.
persecute	To torment.
prosecute	To sue.
plaintiff	The one who files a suit.
plaintive	Mournful.
precedence	Priority.
precedents	Things prior in time.
reality	That which is real.
realty	Real property or real estate.
residents	The ones who live there.
residence	The place where one lives.
statue	Figurine or sculpture.
stature	Natural height; achievement.
statute	A law.
steal	To unlawfully take another's possession.
steel	Metal; processed iron.
tort	A civil wrong.
torte	A rich cake.
tortious	Involving a tort or civil wrong.
tortuous	Crooked or winding.
torturous	Involving torture.
trustee	One who holds something in trust for another.
trusty	Dependable. A convicted person who is considered trustworthy.
undo	Untie or destroy.
undue	Unwarranted or improper.
waive	To forego or give up.
wave	Signal with hands.
waiver	The legal instrument by which one gives up a right.
waver	To fluctuate in opinion, allegiance, or direction.

Legal Transcription Basics

Since the format for legal instruments varies from state to state and there are so many variations in the computer software programs, the information presented in this section will serve only as a general guideline for the preparation of legal documents.

Margins:

(1) Left margin: Plain paper—1 1/2 inches; Legal cap—At least one space inside the vertical line.

(2) Right margin: Plain paper—1/2 inch; Legal cap—At least one space inside the vertical line.

(3) Top margin: Unbound—1 inch; Bound—2 inches

(4) Bottom margin: 1 inch

Spacing:

(1) Body—double spaced

(2) Land descriptions—single spaced

Paragraph Indentions: 5 or 10 spaces

Capitalization:

Type the following in all caps:

(1) Title of document.

(2) The first word or phrase of a paragraph (especially if it is the first or last paragraph of the document).

(3) Names of documents.

(4) Names of individuals.

(5) Names of firms.

Numbers:

(1) Dates may be written in figures or spelled out.

(2) Amounts of money are first spelled out and then written in figures in parentheses.

(3) Measurements are usually written the same as amounts of money.

(4) Numbers in land descriptions may be spelled out or written in figures.

(5) Symbols for feet, degrees, etc., may be used with numbers that are written in figures.

Signature Lines:

(1) Leave 3 or 4 blank lines between the last line of the document and the signature line.

(2) The witness signature lines start at the left margin and are approximately 3 inches long.

(3) The party signature lines start at the center and are approximately 3 inches long.

(4) Leave 2 or 3 blank lines between signature lines.

For more specific details for the preparation of legal instruments, you should check the guidelines for the state in which you will be working. Also, many legal offices have examples of their formats available for the use of new employees.

Key

Lesson 1
Self-Evaluation A

1. c
2. a
3. c
4. b
5. a
6. a
7. b
8. b
9. a
10. c
11. c
12. b
13. b
14. a
15. c

Lesson 1
Self-Evaluation B

1. a
2. d
3. m
4. n
5. j
6. g
7. i
8. e
9. l
10. b
11. f
12. k
13. h

Lesson 2
Self-Evaluation A

1. jurisprudence
2. lexicon
3. prosecuting attorney
4. lex
5. bar
6. judge
7. jurist
8. a. in propria persona
   b. in pro per
9. statute
10. Corpus Juris Secundum
11. a. esquire
    b. Esq.
12. defense attorney
13. code books
14. bench

Lesson 2
Self-Evaluation B

1. d
2. l
3. e
4. o
5. m
6. b
7. a
8. c
9. g
10. n
11. j
12. k
13. i
14. h

Lesson 3
Self-Evaluation A

1. writ
2. plea
3. tribunal
4. petition
5. narratio
6. declaration or complaint
7. pleadings
8. gravamen
9. retainer
10. contest
11. complaint or declaration
12. champerty
13. adjudicate
14. count

Lesson 3
Self-Evaluation B

1. b
2. c
3. b
4. a
5. c
6. b
7. c
8. c
9. a
10. a
11. a
12. a
13. c

Lesson 4
Self-Evaluation A

1. ipso facto
2. acknowledgement
3. testimonium clause
4. scilicet
5. sui generis
6. cause of action
7. locus sigilli
8. legal back
9. notary public
10. endorsement
11. seal
12. to wit
13. interpolate
14. ancillary

Lesson 4
Self-Evaluation B

1. f
2. e
3. a
4. g
5. m
6. k
7. l
8. d
9. h
10. j
11. b
12. n
13. c

Lesson 5
Self-Evaluation A

1. c
2. c
3. a
4. a
5. c
6. b
7. b
8. a
9. c
10. a
11. a
12. c
13. b
14. c

Lesson 5
Self-Evaluation B

1. f
2. b
3. m
4. a
5. l
6. h
7. i
8. n
9. e
10. g
11. c
12. j
13. o
14. k

Lesson 6
Self-Evaluation A

1. verbatim
2. concealment
3. subpoena duces tecum
4. transcript
5. subpoena
6. disclosure
7. interrogatories
8. deposition
9. bench warrant
10. fishing expedition
11. contempt of court
12. court reporter
13. pretrial stipulations

Lesson 6
Self-Evaluation B

1. c
2. a
3. b
4. b
5. c
6. a
7. b
8. b
9. c
10. c
11. c
12. a
13. a

Lesson 7
Self-Evaluation A

1. m
2. a
3. h
4. l

5. e
6. i
7. j
8. k
9. d
10. c
11. f
12. b
13. n

Lesson 7
Self-Evaluation B

1. objection
2. admissible
3. testimony
4. sustained
5. witness
6. direct examination
7. overruled
8. motion to strike
9. cross-examination
10. mistrial
11. irrelevant
12. colloquy
13. physically expunge
14. opening statement

Lesson 8
Self-Evaluation A

1. perjury
2. hostile witness
3. res gestae
4. opinion evidence
5. hearsay
6. circumstantial evidence
7. impeach
8. evidence
9. incompetent
10. exhibit
11. averment
12. expert evidence
13. adduce
14. rebuttal

Lesson 8
Self-Evaluation B

1. c
2. b
3. b
4. a
5. c
6. a
7. b
8. c
9. a

10. b
11. c
12. b
13. a

Lesson 9
Self-Evaluation A

1. h
2. a
3. f
4. j
5. c
6. b
7. e
8. l
9. d
10. m
11. n
12. g
13. k

Lesson 9
Self-Evaluation B

1. c
2. a
3. b
4. c
5. c
6. b
7. a
8. b
9. a
10. c
11. c
12. b
13. b
14. a

Lesson 10
Self-Evaluation A

1. b
2. c
3. a
4. c
5. b
6. c
7. a
8. a
9. c
10. c
11. b
12. a
13. b

Lesson 10
Self-Evaluation B
1. a
2. l
3. e
4. f
5. o
6. k
7. b
8. h
9. c
10. i
11. d
12. j
13. g
14. m

Lesson 11
Self-Evaluation A
1. b
2. c
3. a
4. a
5. b
6. a
7. c
8. c
9. b
10. a
11. b
12. c

Lesson 11
Self-Evaluation B
1. in forma pauperis
2. due care and diligence
3. liability
4. damnum absque injuria
5. negligence
6. duty
7. actio in rem
8. contributory negligence
9. culpable negligence
10. imputation of negligence
11. absolute liability
12. right
13. comparative negligence

Lesson 12
Self-Evaluation A
1. a
2. k
3. b
4. n
5. e
6. d
7. m
8. g
9. j
10. c
11. i
12. h
13. l

Lesson 12
Self-Evaluation B
1. Good Samaritan Statute
2. assumption of risk
3. constructive notice
4. sovereign immunity
5. probable consequences
6. ordinary, reasonable person
7. knowledge of the peril
8. foreseeability of injury
9. act or omission
10. implied or imputed knowledge
11. sudden emergency doctrine
12. wanton, reckless, and intentional
13. res ipsa loquitur

Lesson 13
Self-Evaluation A
1. c
2. c
3. c
4. a
5. b
6. a
7. a
8. b
9. c
10. c
11. b
12. b
13. b
14. a

Lesson 13
Self-Evaluation B
1. insanity
2. confession
3. admission
4. sine qua non
5. Durham Rule
6. defense
7. criminal intent
8. plea
9. scienter
10. irresistible impulse
11. nolo contendere
12. non compos mentis
13. M'Naghten Rule

Lesson 14
Self-Evaluation A
1. k
2. f
3. e
4. d
5. l
6. j
7. m
8. g
9. n
10. h
11. c
12. b
13. a

Lesson 14
Self-Evaluation B
1. excusable homicide
2. break and enter
3. malice aforethought
4. forgery
5. animus furandi
6. larceny
7. manslaughter
8. robbery
9. justifiable homicide
10. constructive breaking
11. assault and battery
12. utter and publish
13. felonious homicide
14. murder
15. homicide

Lesson 15
Self-Evaluation A
1. k
2. b
3. g
4. f
5. a
6. d
7. h
8. c
9. n
10. l
11. i
12. m
13. o
14. e

Lesson 15
Self-Evaluation B

1. b
2. c
3. a
4. b
5. c
6. c
7. c
8. b
9. a
10. a
11. c
12. b
13. a

Lesson 16
Self-Evaluation A

1. a
2. a
3. b
4. c
5. b
6. a
7. a
8. b
9. c
10. b
11. a
12. c
13. c

Lesson 16
Self-Evaluation B

1. ward
2. revocation
3. guardian ad litem
4. conservatorship
5. animus revocandi
6. dower
7. conservator
8. reversion
9. indefeasible
10. guardian
11. surrogate
12. trust
13. trust estate

Lesson 17
Self-Evaluation A

1. c
2. h
3. g
4. b
5. d
6. n
7. m
8. j
9. e
10. k
11. i
12. l
13. o
14. f

Lesson 17
Self-Evaluation B

1. homestead
2. joint tenancy
3. partition
4. metes and bounds
5. abstract
6. convey
7. conveyance
8. tenancy in common
9. land description
10. plat
11. easement
12. servitude
13. tenancy by the entirety

Lesson 18
Self-Evaluation A

1. m
2. f
3. a
4. g
5. l
6. d
7. b
8. i
9. e
10. k
11. h
12. j
13. c

Lesson 18
Self-Evaluation B

1. b
2. c
3. a
4. b
5. c
6. b
7. b
8. a
9. c
10. c
11. a
12. b
13. a

Lesson 19
Self-Evaluation A

1. c
2. b
3. a
4. a
5. a
6. b
7. a
8. c
9. b
10. c
11. b
12. c
13. a

Lesson 19
Self-Evaluation B

1. assignable
2. mutual obligations
3. assignment
4. performance
5. consideration
6. quantum meruit
7. accord and satisfaction
8. pro tanto
9. quid pro quo
10. competent parties
11. assumpsit
12. condition
13. subrogation
14. nudum pactum

Lesson 20
Self-Evaluation A

1. default
2. rescind
3. implied in law
4. express contract
5. unilateral contract
6. implied contract
7. implied in fact
8. bilateral contract
9. inchoate contract
10. privity of contract
11. escalator clause
12. vitiate
13. inchoate

Lesson 20
Self-Evaluation B

1. l
2. c
3. i
4. a
5. j
6. k
7. g
8. h
9. m
10. p
11. f
12. n
13. e
14. o
15. b

Lesson 21
Self-Evaluation A

1. m
2. i
3. j
4. k
5. b
6. h
7. e
8. f
9. l
10. n
11. a
12. g
13. c

Lesson 21
Self-Evaluation B

1. premartial
2. separate maintenance
3. cobahitation
4. privileged communications
5. separation agreement
6. femme sole
7. separation
8. counsel fee
9. affinity
10. consanguinity
11. antenuptial agreement
12. a mensa et thoro

Lesson 22
Self-Evaluation A

1. uncontested divorce
2. divorce
3. contested divorce
4. no-fault divorce
5. dissolution of marriage
6. grounds for divorce
7. limited divorce
8. a vinculo matrimonii
9. conciliation procedure
10. Enoch Arden Law
11. desertion
12. corespondent
13. absolute divorce

Lesson 22
Self-Evaluation B

1. a
2. c
3. a
4. b
5. c
6. a
7. b
8. b
9. c
10. c
11. a
12. b
13. a

Lesson 23
Self-Evaluation A

1. a
2. b
3. a
4. c
5. b
6. a
7. c
8. a
9. b
10. c
11. b
12. c
13. b

Lesson 23
Self-Evaluation B

1. bill of exchange
2. qualified acceptance
3. holder in due course
4. trade acceptance
5. draft-varying acceptance
6. draft
7. payer
8. carte blanche
9. accommodation paper
10. maker
11. comaker
12. bearer
13. payee

Lesson 24
Self-Evaluation A

1. i
2. h
3. c
4. a
5. b
6. e
7. f
8. d
9. k
10. l
11. m
12. j

Lesson 24
Self-Evaluation B

1. bona fide
2. spoliation
3. allonge
4. special or full indorsement
5. bogus
6. restrictive indorsement
7. qualified indorsement
8. blank indorsement
9. kite
10. successive indorsement
11. indorsement

Lesson 25
Self-Evaluation A

1. c
2. b
3. b
4. a
5. c
6. b
7. b
8. a
9. c
10. a
11. b
12. a
13. c
14. a

Lesson 25
Self-Evaluation B

1. deficiency decree
2. liabilities
3. composition
4. balance of funds

5. liquidate
6. account current
7. account stated
8. assets
9. summary of debts and assets
10. discharge
11. secured debts
12. insolvent debtor
13. after-acquired property

Lesson 26
Self-Evaluation A

1. principal
2. undisclosed principal
3. plenipotentiary
4. general agent
5. del credere agent
6. agency
7. primary agent
8. subagent
9. universal agent
10. exclusive or irrevocable agency
11. power of attorney
12. special agent
13. implied agency
14. agent

Lesson 26
Self-Evaluation B

1. j
2. e
3. b
4. k
5. h
6. o
7. c
8. a
9. i
10. f
11. n
12. d
13. g
14. m

Lesson 27
Self-Evaluation A

1. a
2. c
3. a
4. b
5. b
6. c
7. a
8. a
9. b
10. c
11. b
12. b
13. c
14. a

Lesson 27
Self-Evaluation B

1. finding of fact
2. declaratory judgment
3. doctrine of doing complete justice
4. de minimis non curat lex
5. right and duty
6. rule of morality
7. remedial
8. in pari delicto
9. sua sponte
10. estoppel in pais
11. reformation
12. matter in pais
13. waiver
14. consent decree
15. clean hands doctrine

Lesson 28
Self-Evaluation A

1. severalty
2. general partner
3. articles of partnership
4. sole partnership
5. limited partnership
6. partnership
7. junior partner
8. proprietor
9. senior partner
10. Uniform Limited Partnership Act
11. silent partner
12. Uniform Partnership Act
13. limited partner

Lesson 28
Self-Evaluation B

1. f
2. a
3. h
4. m
5. e
6. k
7. g
8. i
9. c

10. d
11. l
12. b

Lesson 29
Self-Evaluation A

1. b
2. c
3. c
4. b
5. b
6. c
7. c
8. b
9. a
10. a
11. c
12. b
13. a
14. a

Lesson 29
Self-Evaluation B

1. par value
2. common stock
3. share
4. treasury stock
5. promoters
6. stock
7. preferred stock
8. stock certificate
9. transfer agent
10. book value
11. shareholder
12. watered stock

Lesson 30
Self-Evaluation A

1. j
2. k
3. f
4. a
5. i
6. g
7. d
8. m
9. b
10. h
11. l
12. c

Lesson 30
Self-Evaluation B

1. auditor
2. working capital

3. net worth
4. liability
5. dividend
6. sinking fund
7. balance sheet
8. debenture
9. income statement
10. financial reports
11. retained earnings
12. earnings per share

6. b
7. a
8. b
9. b
10. a
11. c
12. a
13. c
14. c
15. a

Lesson 31
Self-Evaluation A

1. clerk of the court
2. docket
3. joinder
4. pluries summons
5. disclosure statement
6. sidebar
7. cross-complaint
8. certificate of service
9. alias summons
10. proffer
11. realtime
12. discovery
13. perfect
14. undue influence
15. chose in possession
16. certificate of readiness

Lesson 31
Self-Evaluation B

1. e
2. j
3. c
4. a
5. b
6. p
7. m
8. k
9. f
10. i
11. l
12. d
13. o
14. g
15. n

Lesson 32
Self-Evaluation A

1. a
2. c
3. b
4. a
5. c

Lesson 32
Self-Evaluation B

1. testamentary trust
2. distribute
3. devise
4. exception
5. security deposit
6. life estate
7. legatee
8. secured claim
9. declarant
10. lawful purpose
11. exempt property
12. statutory lien
13. age of majority
14. decedant
15. testamentary instrument
16. succession

Index

interpolate, 45
interrogatories, 77
intervening cause, 165
intervenor, 69
intestate, 210
inure, 292
invitee, 165
involuntary bankruptcy, 365
ipso facto, 45
irreconcilable differences, 473
irrelevant, 101
irresistible impulse, 189
irrevocable, 52
irrevocable agency, 380
issue of marriage, 473

J

joinder, 459
joint custody, 473
joint tenancy, 247
joint venture, 414
jointly and severally, 38
judge, 15
judgment, 125
judgment by default, 125
judgment note, 331
junior partner, 408
jurat, 69
jurisdiction, 61
jurisprudence, 15
jurist, 15
juror, 95
jury, 95
justice, 21
justifiable homicide, 200

K

kite, 352
knowledge of the peril, 171

L

laches, 396
land contract, 258
land description, 246
landlord, 292
larceny, 201
lawful purpose, 481
lease, 292
legacy, 225
legal back, 46
legal entity, 425
legal procedure, 20
legal tender, 331
legatee, 480
lessee, 293
lessor, 293
letters of authority, 219
lex, 15
lex loci contractus, 271
lexicon, 15
liabilities, 372
liability, 158, 449
licensee, 165
lien, 258
life estate, 481
limited divorce, 316
limited partner, 408
limited partnership, 407
liquidate, 373
liquidation, 442
litigant, 21
litigation, 20
living will, 210
local and municipal ordinances, 9
locus sigilli, 46
lower court, 2

M

M'Naghten Rule, 189
maker, 338
malfeasance, 39
malice, 53
malice aforethought, 201
malicious prosecution, 38
mandamus, 145
manslaughter, 201
matrimony, 303
matter in pais, 401
maturity, 345
maxims of equity, 395
Mechanic's Lien, 467
mens rea, 53
mental anguish, 166
merger, 441
metes and bounds, 246
minor, 39
minutes, 441
misdemeanor, 180
misfeasance, 165
mistake of fact, 396
mistake of law, 396
mistrial, 101
monogamy, 303
moot, 85
mortgage, 258
mortgagee, 467
mortgagor, 467
motion, 68
motion to strike, 101
murder, 200
mutual consent, 386
mutual obligations, 280

N

Napoleonic Code, 9
narratio, 29
necessaries, 323
negligence, 158
negotiable, 331
net worth, 448
no-fault divorce, 315
nolo contendere, 188
nominal damages, 166
nominal partner, 414
non compos mentis, 189
non-age, 304
noncustodial parent, 474
nonfeasance, 165, 387
nonsuit, 132
nonsupport, 323
notary public, 46
notice of lis pendens, 84
notice to quit, 293
nudum pactum, 281
nunc pro tunc, 139
nuncupative will, 210

O

oath, 96
objection, 101
offense, 179
offer, 272
omnibus clause, 68
opening statement, 100
opinion, 125
opinion evidence, 109
option, 272
order, 133
ordinary reasonable person, 170
ostensible authority, 387
overruled, 101

P

par value, 434
pardon, 196
parol evidence rule, 272
parole, 196
partition, 247
partnership, 407
party, 21
paternity test, 473
payee, 338
payer, 338
penal, 52
pendente lite, 116
per curiam, 125
per se, 39
per stirpes, 226
peremptory challenge, 96
perfect, 460
performance, 280
perjury, 110
permanent alimony, 323
petition, 30
petition for bankruptcy, 365
petition for probate, 209
physically expunge, 101
plaintiff, 21
plat, 246
plea, 29, 188
pleadings, 29
plenipotentiary, 379
pluries summons, 460
polling the jury, 126
possession, 253
postdate, 346
power of attorney, 379
prayer for relief, 61
precatory words, 226
precedent, 84
preferred stock, 434
preliminary examination, 180
premarital, 308
premises, 239
preponderance of evidence, 117
prescription, 253
prescriptive rights, 253
presentment, 345
president, 426
pretermitted heir, 225
pretrial conference, 84
pretrial stipulations, 78
preventive jurisdiction, 395
prima facie, 116
primary agent, 380
principal, 195, 379
private law, 9
privileged communications, 309
privity of contract, 288
pro tanto, 281
probable consequences, 170
probate, 209
probate court, 2
procedural law, 9
proceeding, 20
professional corporation, 474
proffer, 460
promissory note, 331
promoters, 434
property settlement, 322
proprietor, 407
prosecuting attorney, 16
prospectus, 415
protest, 345
proximate cause, 165
proxy, 441
public corporation, 474
public domain, 253
public law, 9
publication, 218
punitive damages, 166
purchase-money mortgage, 467

KEYING LEGAL TERMS

Directions: Unless otherwise instructed, use 1-inch margins and double spacing. Correct all errors. Follow one of the procedures below.

WORDS

Keyboarding Procedure
On your computer, key the following words at least two times, concentrating on the correct spelling and pronunciation.

Machine Shorthand Procedure
On your computer, key the following words once, concentrating on the correct spelling and pronunciation. Then write each word one time on your shorthand machine. Transcribe from your shorthand notes one time on your computer, or, if you are using computer-aided transcription (CAT), proofread and edit your transcript.

public law	private law	constitutional law
administrative law	statutory law	case law
Napoleonic Code	common law	substantive law
procedural law	federal law	state law
local and municipal ordinances		

SENTENCES

Keyboarding Procedure
Key each of the following sentences one time on your computer. Concentrate on the correct spelling and pronunciation of each underlined legal term.

Machine Shorthand Procedure
Write the following sentences one time on your shorthand machine. Transcribe from your shorthand notes one time on your computer, or, if you are using computer-aided transcription (CAT), proofread and edit your transcript.

These sentences will be used for practice dictation on the Transcription CD.

The sources of law in the United States are the federal and state constitutions, statutes enacted by the U.S. Congress and the state legislatures, common or case law principles, and the Napoleonic or Civil Code. Law that is classified on the basis of the parties involved is known as <u>public law</u> or <u>private law</u>. Public law is that body of law to which the general public is subject. It includes <u>constitutional law</u>, <u>administrative law</u>, and criminal law. Constitutional law is based on the federal and state constitutions and may be amended by the U.S. Supreme Court or the highest state courts. For example, the right to vote is a constitutional law. Administrative law governs the various agencies created by the government and defines the scope of their authority. The licensing of builders or pharmacists is an example of administrative law. Private law deals with relationships between private individuals, such as contracts, civil injuries, domestic relations, and partnerships.

The form of law is another basis for classifying law. <u>Statutory law</u>, common or <u>case law</u>, and the <u>Napoleonic Code</u> are based on the form of law. Statutory law, sometimes called written law, is created by statute or legislation passed by the U.S. Congress or the state legislatures. The laws giving individuals the right to work are statutory laws. <u>Common law</u>, or case law, originated in England and is the basis for the law in most of our states. Under common law, the rights of the individual are emphasized over the rights of the government. It is based on cases used as precedents rather than on statutes, and the rights of the individual are emphasized over the rights of the government. The Napoleonic Code originated in France and is used in the state of Louisiana. It is also referred to as Code Civil, Civil law, or Code Napoleon. The Napoleonic Code emphasizes the rights of the state over the rights of the individual. Under this system of law, you are presumed to be guilty until you prove you are innocent.

<u>Substantive law</u> and <u>procedural law</u> are two classifications based on the nature of law. Substantive law creates and defines our rights and duties; whereas procedural law, which is also known as adjective law, establishes the procedures to be followed for remedial action in court when one's rights have been violated. Other types of law are <u>federal law</u>, <u>state law</u>, and <u>local and municipal ordinances</u>. Federal law is created by the federal government and applies to all states. State law and local and municipal ordinances are created by states, counties, cities, or townships and are effective only in the state or governmental unit that created them.

TRANSCRIBING FROM DICTATION

Directions: This dictation emphasizes and reinforces the legal terms and definitions you have studied. Listen carefully to the pronunciation of each of the legal terms. Unless otherwise directed, use 1-inch margins and double spacing. Correct all errors. Follow one of the procedures below.

Keyboarding Procedure
Using the Transcription CD, Lesson 1, Part B, transcribe the dictation directly at your computer.

Machine Shorthand Procedure
Using the Transcription CD, Lesson 1, Part B, take the dictation on your shorthand machine and then transcribe from your notes on your computer, or, if you are using computer-aided transcription (CAT), proofread and edit your transcript.

When you have finished transcribing or proofreading and editing Part B of the practice dictation, check your transcript with the printed copy. If you made any mistakes in the transcription, you should review and practice those words several times before going on to Lesson 2.

CHECKLIST
I have completed the following for Lesson 1:

	Part A, Date	Part B, Date	Submitted to Instructor Yes	No
Terminology and Definitions	_____	_____	_____	_____
Self-Evaluation	_____	_____	_____	_____
* Keying Legal Terms	_____	_____	_____	_____
Words	_____	_____	_____	_____
Sentences	_____	_____	_____	_____
* Transcribing from Dictation	_____	_____	_____	_____

When you have successfully completed all the exercises in this lesson and submitted to your instructor those requested, you are ready to proceed with Lesson 2.

* If you are using machine shorthand, submit to your instructor your notes along with your transcript.